DATE DUE	
JUL 16 2003	

UPI 261-2505 G · PRINTED IN U.S.A.

WORLD FUTURES AND THE UNITED NATIONS

An Annotated Guide
to 250 Recent Books and Reports

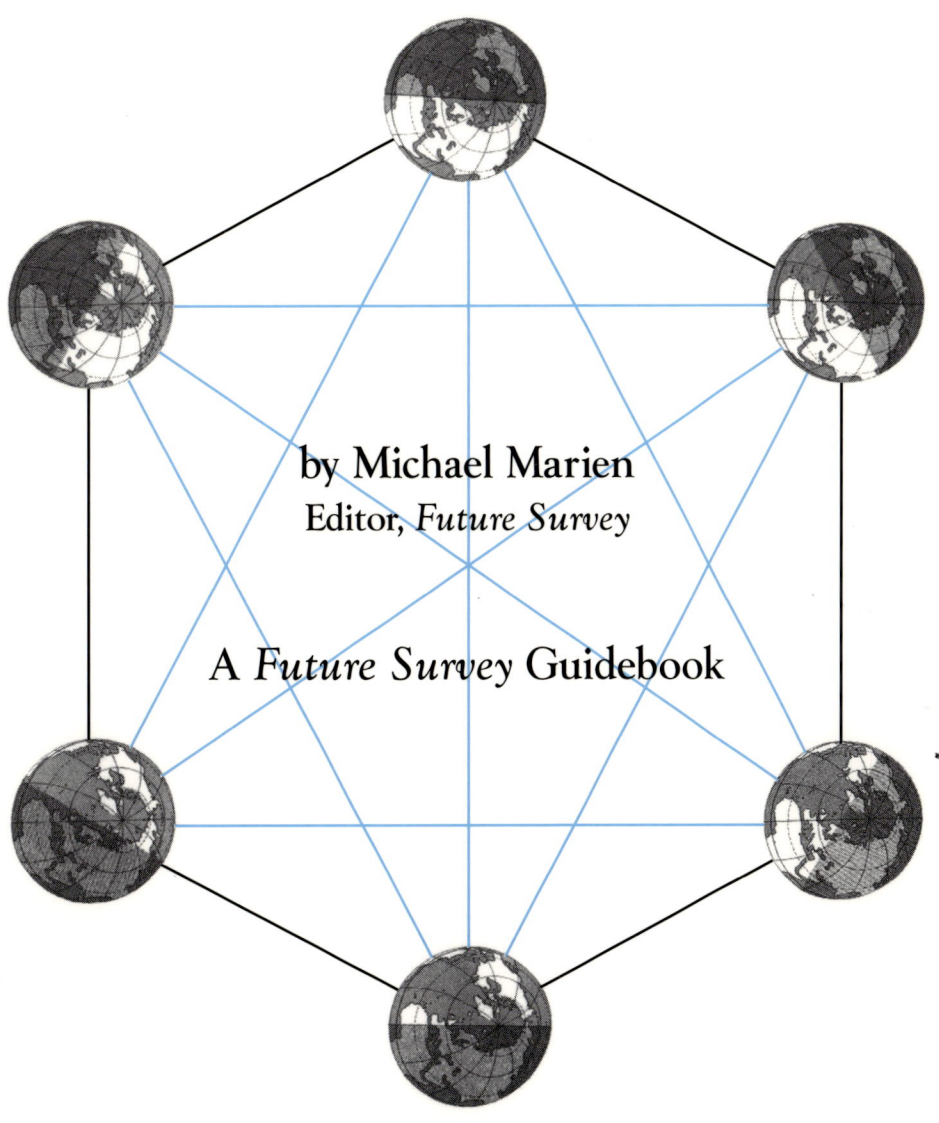

by Michael Marien
Editor, Future Survey

A *Future Survey* Guidebook

World Future Society
Bethesda, Maryland U.S.A.
1995

WORLD FUTURES AND THE UNITED NATIONS

An Annotated Guide
to 250 Recent Books and Reports

by Michael Marien
Editor, *Future Survey*

A *Future Survey* Guidebook

World Future Society
Bethesda, Maryland U.S.A.
1995

Published by:
The World Future Society
7910 Woodmont Avenue, Suite 450
Bethesda, Maryland 20814
U.S.A.
Phone: 301/656-8274
Fax: 301/951-0394

The World Future Society is a non-profit educational and scientific association founded in 1966 for the study of alternative futures. It acts as an impartial clearinghouse for a variety of different views and does not take positions on what will or should happen in the future.

Copyright © 1995 by World Future Society

All rights reserved. Except as permitted under the United States Copyright Act of 1976, no part of this publication may be reproduced or distributed in any form or by any means, or stored in a data base or retrieval system, without the prior written consent of the publisher.

Library of Congress Cataloging-in-Publication Data:

Marien, Michael.
    World futures and the United Nations : an annotated guide to 250
    recent books and reports / by Michael Marien
        p. cm. — (Future Survey guidebooks ; 1)
    Includes bibliographical references and indexes.
    ISBN 0-930242-49-1
    1. Twenty-first century—Forecasts—Abstracts.
    2. Twenty-first century—Forecasts—Bibliography.
    3. Civilization, Modern—1950- —Abstracts.
    4. Civilization, Modern—1950- —Bibliography.
    5. Policy sciences—Abstracts.
    6. Policy sciences—Bibliography.
    I. Title. II. Series.
    CB161.M375 1995   95-13952
    303.49'09'05—dc20   CIP

WORLD FUTURES AND THE UNITED NATIONS

CONTENTS

- **Foreword** by Harlan Cleveland v
- **Challenge** by Rashmi Mayur vii
- **Preface** by Yehezkel Dror ix
- **Introduction** by Michael Marien xi

Part I. Bibliographic Essay

A. Overviews 1
B. Eight Key Elements 2
C. Improving Governance and Learning 7
D. Conclusion: Six Proposals 9
E. 250 References 10

Part II. 250 Abstracts from *Future Survey*

A. OVERVIEWS

1. Recent Trends and Near-Term Futures 21
2. Evolution and Long-Term Futures 29

B. EIGHT KEY ELEMENTS

1. Politics in the Post-Cold War Era 38
2. Democratization and Peacemaking 45
3. Globalizing Information 54
4. The Globalizing Economy 59
5. Population Growth and Health Threats 66
6. Global Environmental Problems 71
7. A New Path for Development 82
8. Women and Children 87

C. IMPROVING GOVERNANCE AND LEARNING

1. Globally Shared Values 91
2. Expanding and Reshaping the U.N. Role 94
3. Culture Lag and UNESCO's Potential Role 100

- **Publisher/Title Index** 107
- **Subject Index** 111
- **Author Index** 114

FOREWORD
by Harlan Cleveland

When I was growing up, a hundred-or-so wars ago, I was taught that the key to stuffing my head with useful insights was *access* to the information I would need. But my first visit to a great library—it happened to be the Library of Congress, as a teenage tourist—cured me of that illusion.

Confronting those serried ranks of dusty "literature," I quickly figured out that my problem would never be access, but *selection*. I later learned, after a good deal of trial and error, that this always requires me first to decide what most interests me and why, before reaching for a reading.

Modern information technology doesn't solve *this* problem. Just before writing this Foreword, I was using my computer to browse on the Internet. But I hadn't decided what I wanted to know; so that worldwide miracle of computerized access turned out to be, this evening, a trackless information desert.

* * *

The information flow to which we are all exposed today—in newspapers, office memos, journals, magazines, or in the mail, voice-mail, or electronic mail—is almost as overwhelming as the world's greatest Library seemed to a thirteen-year-old many years ago. Today's puzzle is even more obviously not access, but selection.

Now, after half a century of reflective practice, teaching, and writing, I know what I am interested in: the future. Not my personal future; I can work that out as I go along. But in order to make judgments about my local, national, and global communities—for each of which I am in some degree responsible—I try to focus, with a wide-angle lens, on the futures of everything and everybody.

That's a "mission impossible:" to keep up to date on the futures of politics and diplomacy, of prosperity and poverty, of science and technology, of work and leisure, of markets and morality, of business and governance, of war and peace—and especially, just now, on the future of the United Nations, fifty years after it was invented "to save succeeding generations from the scourge of war."

Michael Marien has devoted himself for 16 years to the task of scanning "the literature" that probes the future. Many libraries and retrieval systems could provide "access" to what he uniquely summarizes and comments on every month in *Future Survey*—the world's best scan of what's being written about probable, possible, and preferable futures.

The U. N.'s intellectual arm, UNESCO, recently asked Dr. Marien to produce a guide to the main recent English-language contributions to "the literature" on **World Futures and the United Nations**. His essay for UNESCO contained 250 references to books and articles. This volume combines the same integrative essay with abstracts of *each* book and article, as originally prepared for *Future Survey*.

The resulting compendium is an ideal guide to much of the best recent thinking (published in English) about "world futures and the United Nations role." It provides a comprehensive guide to what's been written on the subject in the last half dozen years. It tells us what we need to know about the essence of the writer's way of thinking. And it gives us the clues we need to find the full texts of those writings we need to read in full.

If you have already read everything you need to know on the subject, and still found time to eat, sleep, and brush your teeth, you may not need this volume. But for the rest of us, who are curious about the world's future but not omniscient, Michael Marien has performed an indispensable service, and we are all profoundly grateful.

— Minneapolis, November, 1994

Harlan Cleveland, President of the World Academy of Art and Science and former Dean, Hubert H. Humphrey Institute of Public Affairs, University of Minnesota, has woven together multiple careers as public executive, diplomat, editor, educator, and author on executive leadership and international affairs.

CHALLENGE

by Rashmi Mayur

How do we govern our anarchic world?

Fifty years ago, at the end of the Second World War, the United Nations was set up to bring an end to the scourge of war and establish a new world order based on peace and security. Since then, a profound transformation, unparalleled in human history, has taken place. In countless ways, the world is globalized—more than a trillion dollars circle the earth every day; the population has more than doubled to 5.7 billion people; vast quantities of information are transmitted instantly and ceaselessly around the world; international trade encompasses every nation; membership in the United Nations has more than tripled; and over one hundred wars and conflicts rage in the world.

As we celebrate the 50th anniversary of the UN, the fundamental questions in the minds of thinkers, political leaders, diplomats, scholars and scientists are: What kind of global governance do we need beyond 1995? How do we restructure the United Nations? What is the future of the nation-state? How do we prepare for a peaceful, just, equitable, and sustainable governance system for the twenty-first century?

The Commission on Global Governance headed by Ingvar Carlsson, Prime Minister of Sweden, and Shridath Ramphal, President of IUCN—The World Conservation Union, has just released its report. The Commission members included 26 eminent leaders from around the world. One would have expected dramatic recommendations not only concerning the restructuring of the United Nations, but also with regard to the management of the global economy, environment, sovereignty, and social development.

Unfortunately, the proposals offered in the Commission's report, **Our Global Neighborhood** (Oxford University Press, Feb 1995, 300p/$39.95;$14.95pb), will not redeem us from the anarchic world we live in. The Security Council would be preserved (minus the member veto); a new Economic Council is suggested; and an International Criminal Court is to be set up. But far more is needed.

The seasoned and knowledgeable Commission members well know that the world is not so simple—nor would their prescriptions bring any rational order that the world so desperately needs. Leading experts in international affairs would like to know: What is the future of national sovereignty? Who will domesticate transnational corporations? How do we bring about total disarmament? What enforceable mechanisms can we set up to resolve international conflicts? How do we govern governments? And what is the role of civil society in global governance?

Innumerable organizations, including the UN, NGOs, and groups of scholars and experts are all searching for answers to these complex issues. History cannot teach us much, since never before have we faced environmental disasters like ozone depletion and the prospect of dramatic climate change, or economic crises which go far beyond the boundaries of nations, continents, ideologies, and military might.

Both realists and visionaries must face the discomforting fact that we live in one of the most chaotic and uncertain eras humankind has ever experienced. It is as if environmental dynamics and human affairs have developed their own momentum beyond the puny abilities and powers of finite individuals and their institutions, including all international organizations.

We have only five years left before the dawn of the new millennium; and, in any case, we ought to be in a hurry. The rules that governed our simple societies in the past fill history's wastepaper basket, and the present is becoming more irrelevant with every quantum leap towards tomorrow. The earth is littered with the ruins, deaths, miseries, and collapse of all the institutions which for so long governed our lives. Now our task is to create or discover simple but larger-than-human-size institutions, which can bring logic to global affairs, to our activities around the world, to our relations with each other and to the earth, to our security, to our survival, and to our own and our children's dreams of a secure, peaceful, just, equitable, and sustainable world order. There are stupendous opportunities, but do we have the will to scale this Everest to its peak?

Those who are searching for a means to celebrate the 50th anniversary of the United Nations will find this guidebook to be a most insightful survey and analysis of world governance and possible U.N. futures. This unique publication is a beginning toward sorting out our problems and possibilities—what we should look at, and who we should listen to. The challenge is to listen to many voices, to learn, and to become wiser if we can.

— Bombay, January 1995

Rashmi Mayur is President of the Global Futures Network, Bombay India, and a frequent consultant to various United Nations agencies.

PREFACE
by Yehezkel Dror

All actions are future oriented, with the exception of behavior determined by motives disregarding consequences, by aesthetic taste, by what is regarded as categoric imperatives, or by emotion-discharging catharses. The majority of individual and collective choice is based, in large part, on tacit or implicit assumptions concerning the future, on hidden or explicit goals in the future, and on expected consequences of present acts for future realities. This is true for individuals in their daily life. All the more so, action by decision-makers explicitly in charge of influencing the future is and should be largely conditioned by images of what is changing and the impacts of alternative courses of action on what is to come.

Therefore, a minimally rational individual would, among other considerations, ponder the future in most cases when facing a choice between alternative acts. And, surely, minimally responsible public or corporate decision-makers must carefully explore alternative futures, including unknowable and inconceivable ones, whenever they confront significant choices.

Evaluated in terms of such minimum quality criteria, most of us individuals are dumb; and most of our decision-makers are reckless. Very few individuals make serious efforts to consider salient futures when making critical choices directed at having impacts on the future. Instead, they rely on vague rumors and mass-media fantasies. Worse yet, though surrounded by advisors, top decision-makers too often neglect serious consideration of futures in favor of shallow impressions. And their advisors too, though inundated with intelligence papers, have little or no time to engage in serious study of choice-relevant futures. Even many intelligence paper producers are very superficial, neglecting longer-range perspectives in their hurry to respond to current tactical pressures.

These rather damning conclusions are justified by nearly all studies of decision-making behavior, starting with individuals who do not trouble themselves to read consumer reports before making major investments in hardware, up to Presidents and Prime Ministers and their staffs, who are quite blind to relevant contingencies when making critical choices. My own investigations into the decision patterns and equipment of high level policy makers have led to the same dismal findings: a lack of serious thinking on the future is the rule in most decision making, with some distinguished exceptions.

More complex proof of this statement is provided by comparing the faculties needed for serious consideration of the future with available ones, even in relatively highly developed "central minds of governments." To mention just one illustration: uncertainty sophistication is a must for thoughtful consideration of the future, as are numeracy on the one hand and thinking-in-history on the other. But such capacities are scarce in policy elites. This lack also incapacitates them from utilizing knowledgeable advisors, who are rarely found in the corridors of power. And almost no schools or universities provide the youth entrusted to them with even a modicum of uncertainty sophistication.

But much simpler proof of my claim that actual behavior is ignorant of relevant futures is easily available. Clearly, the easiest and most cost-effective way to explore salient futures is to study the relevant literature. However, anyone starting to read the proliferating publications on trends, possible and probable futures, and long-range policy proposals will either despair rapidly or—even worse—will be captivated by those publications that excel at presentation, quite regardless of their substantive merits or defects. Hence the need for a helping hand which can guide us in seeking the best futures studies relevant to the problems we have to face.

Such a guide is available, in the form of *Future Survey* edited by Michael Marien. Under-utilization of this guide, in my view, is a nearly conclusive proof of the lack of serious coping with the future in contemporary action. However, to provide a critical test of my proposition, this monthly guide and its annual cumulations must be made available in more convenient, compact, and handy format. This is what the present volume does, by presenting a well-structured, selective and reader-friendly guide to literature dealing with world futures.

The test is on: If this guide is widely used and stimulates others to supply comparable aids to future-knowledge-thirsty decision-makers—then my evaluation of actual action choice behavior may be hasty and extreme. However, if this guide is also largely ignored then, I am afraid, Dante must supply another level of Hell for all of us who neglect the help Marien offers by grounding action to better explore the future. There is also a third possibility, namely that the calibre of this guide will encourage selective reading of futures literature and thus better grounding of action on consideration of multiple trends and alternative futures, thus having an impact on the future!

In any case, the publication of this overview of recent literature on global futures and the U. N. role ought to make a significant contribution. If it is utilized, it will demonstrate that human beings as decision-makers are not so ridiculous as policy scientists such as Dror make them out to be. If it is largely ignored and universally under-utilized, as is the case with the monthly *Future Survey*, this overview will at least provide some evidence of *homo sapiens*' insistence to rush blindfolded into the future, even when supplied with tools to remove the blinders and glance ahead into the fog, at least a little. In that case, more radical changes in decision-making patterns may be required as a precondition for fully benefitting from this labor of Marien.

These are the challenges and tests that this publication poses to us, the readers. Dr. Marien deserves plenty of appreciation. Let us see how we respond.

— Jerusalem, November 1994

Yehezkel Dror is Professor of Political Science at the Hebrew University of Jerusalem, and author of many books and articles on policy-making, futures-thinking, and public administration, notably *The Capacity to Govern: Report to the Club of Rome* (1995). He recently served as President of the Policy Studies Organization.

INTRODUCTION
by Michael Marien

It has become a commonplace to hear of "radical" or "profound" changes in the post-Cold War era. Or of the global economy, global networks, global culture, and globalization in general. Or of "turbulence" and "transformation" in many countries and industries. Or of the emerging Postmodern or Third Wave Era. Or of the imperative to create sustainable societies and a sustainable world.

Although each of these statements about global change is frequently made with ample supporting arguments, it is seldom that one finds several of these statements brought together. When they are, it is quite obvious that we live in an "era of multiple transformations." Moreover, when differing views of each of these transformations are considered, it also becomes obvious that multiple perspectives should be acknowledged.

This guidebook is an initial attempt to link together many of the multiple perspectives on our multiple global transformations. To reflect emerging complexities, the reality of many worthy commentators, both as individuals and as groups, should be given greater consideration than the views of any single writer. Yet we are still prone to consider worldviews one-at-a-time, and to favor the thinking of individuals over that of collectivities such as commissions and UN agencies. This is not to suggest that the thinking of a large group is necessarily superior to that of an individual, but only to plead for more equal consideration—judgment of thinking on its merits, rather than whether the author is an individual or a group, similar to the way that we should judge individual thinking regardless of the race, gender, or nationality of the author.

Much of the thinking in this guidebook can be considered as futures thinking, whether or not it is explicitly labeled as such. Similar to the above-mentioned prejudice against group thinking, there is also a thoughtless prejudice against thinking about the future, both by academics and journalists, who too often assume that futures thinking is confined to naive visions of "futuristic" technology, popular tracts by well-known self-styled futurists, and/or flamboyant "predictions" about what will happen.

This guidebook should amply demonstrate that futures thinking is much broader and far deeper than the popular prejudices suggest. Although a few odd or ill-considered views are included here in the interests of diversity (e.g., #061, #233), this guide focuses largely on the best thinking about the most important global problems of our time.

"World Futures" encompasses alternative views of recent global changes, forecasts of what is probable or possible, and prescriptions of desirable futures and how to attain them. The United Nations is emphasized in the title because of its increasingly important role in shaping the human condition on planet Earth, and the widely-acknowledged need to reflect on this role as the UN observes its 50th anniversary in 1995.

World Futures can be seen as a major component of futures studies, an ill-defined and underdeveloped "field" that considers probable, possible, and preferable futures at all levels of organization (world, nation, state, community) and in all sectors (health, education, economy, government, justice, etc.). World Futures can also be seen as a broadening of the international relations field (the traditional realm in which "world affairs" is considered), as well as the often parochial fields of international economics, international communications, demographics, environmental studies, development studies, peace studies, and women's studies.

This guide is the first in a proposed series that re-arranges abstracts first appearing in *Future Survey*. A second guide is planned on environment and sustainability, and subsequent guides will focus on such topics as methodology and social change, and information technology and communications.

Part I of this guide, the bibliographic essay, was commissioned by the UNESCO Bureau of Studies and Programming in Paris, for publication in its *FUTURESCO* bibliographical bulletin of future-oriented literature. The biblioessay on ***World Futures and the United Nations*** cites 250 items, mostly books, in three sections:

- Section A brings together near-term futures and long-term futures, as well as single-theme and multi-theme overviews of the global condition. Many of the contributions in this section are by general futurists.
- Section B highlights somewhat more specialized thinking in eight key areas: post-Cold War era politics, democratization and peacemaking, globalizing information, the global economy, population growth and health threats, global environmental problems, development issues, and gender perspectives. Most of the contributions in this section are by scholars in international relations and other fields (see listing above), although some of the contributors might be seen as general or specialized futurists.
- Section C considers globally shared values as an antidote to tribalism (one might add that this guide seeks to be an antidote to intellectual tribalism), the need for some degree of global governance through a reformed United Nations, and the learning that will be necessary to appreciate shared values and support some form of global governance.
- Section D offers six proposals arising from considering the literature surveyed here: 1) establish 50 graduate programs in world futures by 2010; 2) set up multi-perspective courses on world problems at every school and college worldwide by 2010; 3) create a comprehensive information-gathering capability; 4) promote selected UN publications as other major publishers do; 5) overcome the intellectual tribalism among UN agencies; and 6) encourage serious research on World Futures.
- Section E provides concise bibliographic references for the publications mentioned in the essay.

Part II of the guide consists of 250 abstracts first prepared for *Future Survey*, arranged in the order in which they were cited in the biblioessay.

The literature cited here is confined to the English language, and most is by American authors. There are surely many other visions of World Futures, expressed in many other languages by the 95% of humanity that does not reside in the US. It is hoped that in the near future, perhaps by the year 2000, a forum can be developed so that all worthy perspectives can be seriously heard. This guide is an initial step.

— LaFayette NY, January 1995

Michael Marien is founder and editor of *Future Survey*, published monthly since 1979 by the World Future Society (see back page for subscription information). The support of UNESCO for the initial part of this guide is gratefully acknowledged. Views expressed in this publication are not necessarily those of UNESCO, or WFS.

WORLD FUTURES AND THE UNITED NATIONS: A BIBLIOGRAPHIC ESSAY

by Michael Marien

Much has been written on globalization, turbulence, multiple transformations, and various threats to the future of humanity. In sifting through the literature, three questions are paramount: 1) Who has best articulated the major global trends and possibilities? 2) What normative futures deserve our efforts? and 3) Which directions should the United Nations pursue to improve its capacity to facilitate a positive future for all?

This bibliographic essay surveys a broad range of recent English-language literature, first appearing as abstracts in *Future Survey*, a monthly publication of the World Future Society in Bethesda, Maryland, USA. In doing do, it offers a framework to improve thinking about world futures, illustrating the vast but untapped potential for integrative scholarship.

In all, a total of 250 books, reports, and articles are cited, nearly all of them published in the early 1990s. Although many of the authors are Americans, the views of Canadians, Europeans, and a few non-Western thinkers are also noted here, in addition to many UN reports. As this survey makes abundantly clear, the UN and its far-flung agencies has become a major actor in serious thinking about world futures, although there is a lag in perceiving this emerging role.

A. OVERVIEWS

1. Recent Trends and Near-Term Futures

An excellent starting point for this essay is *Global Outlook 2000*, published for the UN General Assembly in 1990 and bringing together research and projections prepared by many parts of the UN system (1). Topics include environmental deterioration, regional diversity in expected economic growth, widening technology gaps, the AIDS epidemic, energy, food self-sufficiency, growing literacy rates, etc.—prefiguring many of the topics in this essay. The *Report on the World Social Situation 1993*, published by the UN Department of Economic and Social Development, also provides a valuable overview of population projections, hunger, health, education, housing, unemployment and underemployment, poverty, social services, quality of life, ethnic conflicts, financial crises, social consequences of technology, and trends in use of drugs, tobacco, and alcohol (2). Essays from the UNDP's 1990 Round Table on Global Development Challenges (3), as well as from the 1992 Round Table Conference on Global Change (4), touch on an equally broad range of topics, but are of limited value because of their generality.

More adventuresome single-theme overviews of the present world transition are provided by several futurists. Alexander King and Bertrand Schneider of the Club of Rome point to the formation of a new type of world society—what amounts to "a major revolution on a worldwide scale" (5). In a brief version of this argument, Alexander King argues that this fundamental transition to a new society is as different from the world of recent decades as the industrial revolution was from the agrarian world (6). Walter Truett Anderson describes this transformation as the emerging postmodern era giving birth to a global culture (7). William Van Dusen Wishard views the death throes of the Modern Age, as we move to a new global future of greater equality, interdependence, and disappearing boundaries (8).

Several other futurists offer multiple-theme overviews of the present and near future. Ernest Sternberg observes that eight new ages are occurring at once: the new information economy, the worldwide economy of proliferating images, a globalized economy, the new mercantilism, the age of spreading corporate power, the age of flexible specialization, the age of new social movements, and the age of new fundamentalisms (9). William Halal lists key driving forces or supertrends, such as population growth, growing industrial output, the IT revolution, global integration, more diversity and complexity, and movement toward universal standards of freedom and human rights (10). Joseph F. Coates makes 83 assumptions about the year 2025, including substantial movement toward a global managed environment, emergence of a worldwide middle class, effective UN peacemaking and peacekeeping, regulation of migration, and an electronic global village with a global currency (11).

Unlike the more balanced trio of overviews mentioned above, several other multiple-theme overviews are largely or entirely optimistic (an exuberance characteristic of some North American writers). McKinley Conway unabashedly arrays technology developments in the next 30 years such as efficient use of solar energy in desalinizing seawater, automatic language translation for almost everyone everywhere, and domed cities and bubble farms (12). Marvin Cetron and Owen Davies view the world as more peaceful and prosperous in the 1990s than in recent decades, although "lands without hope" will persist in their poverty (13). Writing in *The Futurist*, Cetron and Davies describe a world of new medical technologies, biotechnology bringing new protein to the world, cheaper desalinization, falling oil prices, new and larger multinational companies, and growing importance of the

UN (14). Richard Carlson and Bruce Goldman view a "technotopia" of total access to information by 2020, and nation-states coalescing into mega-states (15). Canadian Frank Feather confidently lists 35 global "G-Forces" such as globalizing values, reduced work weeks, global information sharing boosting the creation of wealth, industrializing the Third World, a shrinking rich-poor gap, and better UN management based on a Mission Statement for planet Earth (16). And John Naisbitt and Patricia Aburdene's new set of "megatrends" for the 1990s include a global economic boom, free-market socialism worldwide, and global lifestyles offset by cultural nationalism (17).

In contrast to these trends and probable futures over the next few decades, John D. Rockfellow suggests several multinational "wild cards" such as collapse of the Japanese real estate market, mass migration from poorer countries by 2000, a major nuclear accident with global consequences, and global agreement on a no-carbon economy by 2050 (18). These "wild cards" are not necessarily as improbable as the authors suggest by their definition of less than 10% chance of occurrence. The list could be substantially extended to include such possibilities as a major earthquake in Japan or California, a major war or terrorist attack, very rapid global warming, a major viral epidemic far worse than AIDS, widespread life extension technology, or discovery of extraterrestrial intelligence. These possible futures, many of them arguably "not-so-wild" (e.g., 20-30% probability), are a sober reminder that too much attention confined to probable world futures, especially pleasant developments, can leave one open to rude shocks. Wild cards can be pleasant (e.g., the fall of communism), but they generally tend to be unpleasant.

2. Evolution and Long-Term Futures

The world futures overviews cited above are broad in space, but generally lack a broad sense of time. Evolutionary thinking offers a long time-frame that complements the shorter-term thinking of merely a few decades. Ervin Laszlo is one of the leading thinkers about evolution; his "preliminary sketch" of the main elements of a grand synthesis, uniting physical, biological, and social evolution, serves as a useful introduction (19). Laszlo is also founder of the General Evolution Research Group, which has been thinking about a new evolutionary paradigm (20). In a recent popularized account of his thinking, Laszlo points to the urgent need for "evolutionary literacy" (21). In a similar tone, Walter Truett Anderson advocates governance of evolution and restoration of Earth as a global learning project (22), and Robert Wesson argues that, as evolution advances, it derives less from chance and more from choice (23). The late John Platt views the world as passing through "its greatest evolutionary jump in human history" creating something like an "integrated global organism" (24). Duane Elgin ambitiously offers a co-evolutionary view of humanity in the midst of eight stages of consciousness as it moves toward the maturity of planetary civilization (25).

"The universe story" provided by Brian Swimme and Thomas Berry describes transition from the Cenozoic era of the last 67 million years to the Ecozoic era where the well-being of the planet is foremost (26). Other recent views of evolution include transition from our adolescent Epoch II to our adult Epoch III (27), the four-dimensional evolution of culture (28), our postmodern condition when evolution becomes fully self-aware (29), "the revelation" of Barbara Marx Hubbard that the next phase of evolution is a Planetary Birth Experience (30), transition to the Life Era and planetary ethics (31), and creation of "Metaman" as a global superorganism embracing humanity and its creations (32). Frank White argues that space exploration is creating an "overview effect" that enhances evolution (33) and that the search for extra-terrestrial intelligence is changing our view of the universe (34).

Views of evolution are not always positive, especially among non-American thinkers. Anthropologist Konrad Lorenz warns of the long-term waning of humaneness and "retrograde evolution" (35). The late Jacques Ellul sees the key to our posthistoric period as the social environment being replaced by a technological environment that develops with ever-increasing speed (36). And Rajni Kothari bleakly surveys the present situation as moving toward the "unipolar/corporate/technocratic globalizing model" that leaves little scope for alternatives (37). Francis Fukuyama, in a notably shallow but much-cited work (cited not for its brilliance but to criticize its many blindspots) views this same condition of "liberal democracy" as the end point of mankind's ideological evolution (38). Futurist/historian W. Warren Wagar takes a longer view of the emerging "megacorporate global economy" leading to a socialist world commonwealth in the mid-21st century, followed by a decentralized order of autonomous societies in the 22nd century (39). This ambitious futures history was made somewhat obsolete by the wild card surprises of 1989, leading to a new edition in 1992 (40). Wagar also published a 1991 non-fictional version of the same "three futures" thesis (41).

B. EIGHT KEY ELEMENTS

The broad overviews mentioned so far, both short-term and long-term, are immensely valuable for providing an introduction to world futures. But, although necessary for a sophisticated understanding, they are still not sufficient.

More specialized views of world futures provide further illumination of prospects and problems. Although sometimes cross-disciplinary in nature,

1. Politics in the Post-Cold War Era

A variety of observers writing in a variety of styles (ranging from densely academic to lightly popular) all point in the same direction of a disorderly era in world politics. Some emphasize the new opportunities for cooperation, while others point to rising fragmentation and new axes of conflict. Ironically, all of the writers are intellectually isolated from each other, seemingly reinforcing the growing fragmentation and tribalism worldwide.

Harlan Cleveland points to a "new world disorder" with nobody in charge, while applauding the emergence of a flexible "club of democracies" (42). This theme of coalition politics in an unruly world is repeated in a briefer essay by Cleveland (43). Joshua Goldstein and David Rapkin also point to growing great power cooperation under lingering US leadership as the most plausible of four scenarios (44). James Rosenau and Ernst-Otto Czempiel emphasize the proliferation of "governance without government, of access points in a polyarchal world" (45), characterizing what Rosenau earlier called "postinternational politics" (46). Australian political scientists Joseph Camilleri and Jim Falk focus on increasing diversity, complexity, and proliferation of state structures, grounded in "a multiplicity of overlapping allegiances and jurisdictions" (47). In describing an emerging but highly decentralized "international society," Evan Luard of Oxford University notes more diffuse and tenuous links between individuals, and no sense of community (48).

Similar to Harlan Cleveland, Peter F. Drucker also describes a "new world disorder" in an age of the post-sovereign state, where transnationalism and regionalism challenge the nation-state from the outside, while tribalism undermines it from within (49). Drucker writes that "the more transnational the world becomes, the more tribal it will also be." This parallels the economic "global paradox" identified by John Naisbitt, who states that as the global economy gets larger, the component parts get smaller—to the point where we are moving toward a world of 1,000 countries, perhaps by the mid-21st century (50). In a bombastic torrent of verbiage, Alvin Toffler also points to the disintegrating structure of world power (51). Zbigniew Brzezinski, the former foreign policy advisor to President Jimmy Carter, views discontinuity as the central reality of our time, and worries that world politics in the post-utopian age "could simply spiral out of control," due to the acceleration of history, our increased capacities to shape the world, our rapidly expanding material desires, and our moral ambiguity (52).

U.S. Senator Daniel Patrick Moynihan argues that ethnicity has been and will be an elemental force in world politics (53). Similar to John Naisbitt, he anticipates new states to be created from ethnic conflict (less dramatically, he suggests only 50-150 new states in the next 50 years). In a widely-noted essay on "The Coming Anarchy," *Atlantic Monthly* editor Robert Kaplan points to West Africa as a model of the way the political earth will be a few decades hence, where the grid of nation-states is "replaced by a jagged-glass pattern of city-states, shanty-states, and nebulous and anarchic regionalism" (54). Ted Robert Gurr has quantified the sharp growth of ethnopolitical conflict, and wonders whether there can be some constructive coexistence of ethnic groups and plural states (55). Gidon Gottlieb supplies a positive answer in a "states plus nations" approach to avoiding global fragmentation that extends the present system of states to make room for a system of nations (56). Michael Walzer makes a similar suggestion of protected spaces of many different sorts to accommodate the "new tribalism" (57).

Paradoxically, the problems of tribes and ethnic groups might be overshadowed by the problems of civilization itself, viewed by anthropologist Jack Weatherford as producing a savagery far worse than that once imputed to primitive tribes (58). But is there a single "civilization", or 7 or 8 major civilizations which, according to Harvard's Samuel Huntington (59), will provide the fundamental source of future global conflict? Or will the critical axis of conflict result from religious nationalism confronting the secular state? The possibilities of this "new Cold War," compellingly argued by Mark Juergensmeyer (60), are not to be lightly dismissed. Consider, for example, a recent best-selling polemic by Pat Robertson (Republican candidate for US President and Chairman of the Christian Broadcasting Network), on the "epic struggle" between "people of faith and people of the humanistic-occultic sphere" (61). Religious organizations aside, the growth of the nonprofit sector in national and international affairs is an important development (62), and could be creating an international public (63). Both secular and religious NGOs are a growing element of the new "governance without government" (45).

2. Democratization and Peacemaking

The second key element of world futures is the hopeful but fragile global trend toward democracy, which has a positive correlation with peacefulness.

As pointed out by Samuel Huntington, we are in the midst of a third wave of democratization over the past two decades, although this may be followed by a reverse wave, and then a fourth wave sometime in the 21st century (64). Bruce Russett argues that this has great consequences for policy, presenting an opening for positive change more fundamental even than at the end of other big wars (65). Max Singer and the late Aaron Wildavsky point to democratic "zones of peace" as an important new development in world affairs (66). Others more cautiously point to continuing threats to democracy (67), the large majority of current transitions as restricted and frail (68), and "low intensity democracy" that preserves ossified political and economic structures (69).

Even with a deeper and more robust transition to democracy, there are many reasons to worry about peacefulness because of the transformation of war. As noted by Martin van Creveld, future war will not be waged by national armies, but by groups of terrorists and guerrillas, with blurring distinctions between soldiers and civilians and use of cheap weapons such as gas (70). Alvin and Heidi Toffler forecast a radical diversification in the kinds of future wars (71). In a Special Report, *Newsweek* magazine points to emergence of a "global Mafia" as a major threat (72). The new warfare may also increasingly involve the international community intervening in internal conflicts (73), and it could be chillingly transformed by mass production of cheap and effective anti-eye laser weapons (74).

Planning for the postmodern military is increasingly difficult because of constricted budgets, many possible tasks, and the lack of a clear focal enemy and consensus on what is important (75). World military expenditures are declining from their peak year of 1987, but have produced a relatively minor "peace dividend" (76). Nuclear arsenals are being reduced, but the wild card of a nuclear winter still remains for the foreseeable future (77). Fears are growing about nuclear proliferation, not only to new nations (78,79) but to terrorist groups (78,80), and arguments are made for a new international nonproliferation regime (79,80). Concern has also been expressed about a biological arms race (81,82) and the possibility that as many as 100 countries already have the means of making their own biological weapons (82). These concerns are aggravated by the proliferation of ballistic missiles (83).

To cope with the threats, there have been recent suggestions for integrating the various weapons control regimes (84). New post-Cold War security principles could emphasize conflict prevention and resolution, nonprovocative policies, multilateral approaches, and promoting democratic practices (85). Other proposals include non-offensive defense (86), cooperative security (87), collective security (88), multilateral peacekeeping with a permanent UN land force (89,90), and a UN Maritime Agency for naval peacekeeping (91).

The growing interest in UN peacekeeping is to be welcomed. But there is a problem of financing this mission. Michael Renner proposes taxes on the international arms trade and giving the Secretary-General authority to borrow on commercial markets or issue bonds (92). Saul Mendlovitz proposes a global tax scheme to support an alternative security system and maintain a basic needs regime (93), and Mark Sommer points out that a 1% tax imposed on every traceable purchase of military weapons and materials could finance all current peacekeeping operations and contribute substantially to the UN's general operating budget (94). But even with a peacekeeping regime in place, which seems quite likely in the next decade, Paul Diehl (90) cautions that it will not be a panacea for all threats.

3. Globalizing Information

Proliferation of information technology and globalization of communications is widely viewed as a major driving force in transnationalization of the world economy and in democratizing values (95,96). In contrast to the threats of new and proliferating weapons in the hands of unruly new national and sub-national groups, the third key element in world futures is generally characterized by exuberant visions. British consultant Michael Conners sees further shrinking of the world, a culturally richer international society, most households and offices connected to an integrated public network of some kind by 2005, and positive impacts in the developing world far more noticeable than in the developed world (97). Canadian economist Maurice Estabrooks sees an emerging age of programmed capitalism in a computer-mediated global society integrating all national markets into one (98). A group of Canadian thinkers, considering issues of governing in an information society, point to the new patterns of interconnection within and across national borders (99). Japanese thinker Yoneji Masuda extols the spirit of the information society as the spirit of globalism, and envisions a future global information utility with cheap information for all (100). This is similar to other glowing and acritical visions of a global hypernetwork society (101), the emerging global brain (102), the emerging worldwide electronic university (103), telecomputing enriching and strengthening democracy and capitalism around the world (104), and the computer enhancing the sense of human possibility (105).

For better and/or worse, the information technology revolution will surely continue to unfold (105,106). There are, of course, a few dissenting voices. For example, Herbert Schiller questions the global commercialization of broadcasting due to the central force of transnational corporate culture (107). Cees Hamelink cautions that our massive investment in information technology is a gamble (108). And the late Jacques Ellul excoriates the widespread proliferation of techniques in general, creating higher costs, a flood of incoherent and useless data, and "enormous global disorder" (109).

4. The Globalizing Economy

The world economy is obviously becoming more global and more dominated by information technology (110,111). Peter Drucker notes that formal and informal alliances are becoming the dominating form of economic integration in the world economy, and that "for developed economies, the distinction between the domestic and international economy has ceased to be a reality" (112). As international corporate alliances emerge, they make national economies more interdependent (113). Arguably, a network of 25 "meganational" corporations now "rule the world" (114). Even if somewhat overstated, transnational corporations are a major force at local, national, and international levels, and a potential if not actual source of global leadership (115).

Outlooks for the world economy vary widely. A European group sketched a variety of scenarios to 2000, with the black and grey scenarios (0.5% and 1.5% GNP growth) more probable than the others, and the expectation of new oil shocks up to 2005 (116). In 1990, a group associated with the American Assembly offered four year 2000 scenarios of the global economy, with world growth averaging 2.5-3.0% a year and regional self-interest as most probable (117). The OECD estimates average annual world growth to 2000 in the 3% range, with growth in the Asia-Pacific region at well over 5.5% (118). The UN's timid *World Economic Survey 1993* does not offer a forecast or scenarios, but views the recovery of the early 1990s as "delicately poised," with considerable risks and uncertainties (119). James Dale Davidson and Lord William Rees-Mogg are far more blunt in forthrightly predicting a world depression in the 1990s (120)—a major development not even considered as a wild card by the others mentioned here. Joel Kurtzman does not explicitly discuss such a calamity, but he does worry that the new electric economy based on megabyte money is "much more volatile" than the monetary system it replaced over the past two decades (121).

Other elements of the emerging world economy include the globalization of services (122) and the agro-food industry (123), the effect of economic globalization on the development of cities (124), travel and tourism as the world's largest industry and still growing at 4-5% in the 1990s (125,126), Jacques Attali's image of "rich nomads" and "poor nomads" roaming the planet (127), the emerging global labor market (128) in the midst of a global job crisis (129), the world-system perspective of core and periphery states (130,131), the developing countries' declining share in the increasingly important activity of foreign direct investment (132), and the need for a new supranational form of credit-money as a logical step in the evolution of capitalism (133).

5. Population Growth and Health Threats.

Population growth, the fifth key element of world futures, is surely a—if not *the*—major fact of the future. Yet it is seldom mentioned in any discussion of world politics, security issues, globalized information, or the global economy. Despite a declining *rate* of growth, today's 5.6 billion people will continue to expand rapidly in the decades ahead, reaching 8.96 billion in 2025 in the IIASA central scenario (134), or merely 8.34 billion in 2025, according to the 1994 Population Reference Bureau projection (135). Despite growing use of birth control worldwide, 22 countries still have virtually no access to birth control information or services, and many others have less than optimal access (136). Many family planning programs exclude youth, the unmarried, and even men from information and services (137). Population policies may well be due for reconsideration: proposed directions include broadly investing in health and women's empowerment (137), moving toward a directed cultural evolution that fully addresses the population crisis (138), and governments learning to integrate population factors into development planning (139).

Large numbers of people not only strain carrying capacity where they reside, but are especially troublesome when they move. Norman Myers forecasts 150 million environmental refugees in a world of 10 billion people in 2050 (140), which is not that unlikely if one considers the rapid growth of refugees from 2.8 million in 1976 to nearly 18 million at the end of 1992 (141), and the various environmental threats such as rising sea levels that are expected in future decades. In addition to forcibly displaced people outside of their countries, about 25 million people worldwide are presently reported as displaced within their countries (142). Millions more migrate to cities, such that the world's urban population is projected to grow from 34% in 1960 and 40% in 1980 to 48% in 2000 and 62% in 2025 (143). Both legal and illegal immigration is emerging as a major concern of the "Trilateral" receiving countries (144), as well as humanitarian assistance (145).

Large numbers of unhealthy people are an additional problem. Environmental degradation in general leads to a variety of adverse health effects (146). The global HIV/AIDS pandemic is volatile and dynamic, and its major impacts are yet to come (147). Even more worrisome in an era of easy global travel is the threat of other deadly viruses spreading much faster than HIV (148). Designating this threat as a mere "wild card" could vastly underestimate the likelihood of its realization.

6. Global Environmental Threats

Global environmental issues, as well as world population growth, are a major element that ought to be considered by those who write about world politics, security issues, the information society, and the global economy. Far too many scholars and writers on world futures and related matters still omit consideration of population and environment issues with no explanation, or cite a few easily-dismissed sources as a way to downplay the issues (e.g., a ploy used by Francis Fukuyama, #38).

The massive and authoritative overview of world environmental issues over the past two decades, edited by Mostafa Tolba and Osama El-Kholy, should convince any fair-minded person that the state of the world environment is worsening (149). The bi-annual series on *World Resources*, sponsored by the World Resources Institute in collaboration with UNEP and UNDP, also provides an authoritative assessment of a wide range of global problems such as population, urbanization, food and agriculture, forests, energy, freshwater, oceans and coasts, and the atmosphere (150). For those who distrust large collective projects, Oxford geographer Andrew Goudie provides a good one-man survey of the human impact on the natural environment (151). Other books on single topics focus on destruction of marine species and ecosystems (152), the need for a comprehensive ocean governance regime (153), the international crisis of freshwater (154), global deforestation (155), and threats to the world's mountain areas (156). All serve to reinforce the theme of environmental deterioration worldwide despite rising green consciousness and many efforts to face the problems.

Fueled by this concern, there are numerous proposals for a sustainable world future. The best-known is *Agenda 21*, prepared for the 1992 UN Conference on Environment and Development (157, 158). As background to UNCED, Shridath Ramphal (President of IUCN—The World Conservation Union) provided a scenario of enlightened change that forges a partnership for survival (159). The IUCN, along with UNEP and the World Wildlife Fund, has promulgated a "Strategy for Sustainable Living" as follow-up to its 1980 *World Conservation Strategy* (160). Before becoming Vice President of the United States, Al Gore proposed a "Global Marshall Plan" to stabilize world population, share appropriate technology, rethink economics and taxation, and educate the world's citizens (161). In the 1992 update to *The Limits to Growth*, Donella Meadows and colleagues warn that the human world is already beyond its limits and offer a scenario for sustainability by the early 21st century (162). In his 1993 update to *The Global 2000 Report to the President*, Gerald Barney outlines elements of a new world order such as new participatory mechanisms in the UN, replacing the outmoded UN System of National Accounts, accelerating transfer of beneficial technology, and a continuing forum for global discussions of the whole human mega-problem (163). And a statement by 1,575 scientists from 69 countries, coordinated by the Union of Concerned Scientists, urges a great change in our stewardship of the earth (164).

In *Saving the Planet*, Mostafa Tolba of UNEP offers an excellent list of priorities for the next two decades, having to do with regulation, assessment, management, and estimating the costs of failing to deal with various problems (165). In another book with the same title, Lester Brown and his Worldwatch Institute colleagues describe the shape of a sustainable global economy (166). The Worldwatch Institute also publishes an annual analysis of selected key indicators (167) and its widely-distributed *State of the World* reports in the cause of a sustainable future (168,169). A report from the Trilateral Commission urges meshing of the world's economy and earth's ecology, broadening the concept of national security, and creating global bargains and new structures such as a World Environment and Development Forum (170). Harlan Cleveland proposes a Global Commons Trusteeship Commission (171), Norman Myers urges a green redefinition of national security (172), Ernst von Weizsäcker points to the emerging "Century of the Environment" (173), Vaclav Smil urges planetary management from above (174), and others urge "ecology from below" (175).

These voices for a sustainable world future are merely a sampling of the more prominent arguments. There is much more literature on environmental problems and sustainable futures (176). But there is a serious question whether any of it has breached the disciplinary walls of political scientists and economists who continue to view world futures in their traditional ways. In the vaunted information society, the vitally important message about population and environment is still not being communicated to those who ought to receive it and/or too many have a trained incapacity to hear it.

7. A New Path for Development

The gap between rich and poor nations continues to widen, and it is generally conceded that development efforts over the past few decades have largely failed.

A recent report by Boutros Boutros-Ghali seeks to make "a first contribution to the search for a revitalized vision of development," pointing to five major and interlinked dimensions: peace, economic growth, environmental sustainability, justice, and democracy (177). The UN Development Programme's annual *Human Development Report*, initiated in 1990, provides a broad range of data, analysis, and intelligent advocacy. The 1994 Report proposes a New World Social Charter and a Global Human Security Fund (178). The 1993 Report describes five "pillars of a people-centered world order": new concepts of human security, new models of sustainable human development, new partnerships between state and market, new patterns of national and global governance, and new forms of international cooperation (179). The 1992 Report calls for a post-Cold War global compact on human development and a social safety net for poor nations and poor people (180). James Gustave Speth, former president of the World Resources Institute and now the head of UNDP, issued a 1992 call for a "Post-Rio

Compact" (181) and was part of the New World Dialogue on Environment and Development in the Western Hemisphere, which called for a "compact for a new world" in 1991 (182).

Other recent thinking on development concerns such matters as an international development tax (183), debt relief as a necessary condition for Third World cooperation (184), more attention to the environmental debt of the North (185), more attention to development's castaways as the Fourth World of marginalized people (186), grassroots movements for global change (187), marginalization of the "Third World" as the term becomes even less meaningful (188), and growing concern for the cultures of the world's 250 million indigenous people (189,190).

8. Women and Children

A final key element in world futures is the growing attention to the status and rights of women and children. In 1991, the United Nations provided an excellent global overview of trends related to the world's women, pointing to major gaps in policy, investment, and earnings that "prevent women from performing to their full potential" (191). The UNU Household, Gender, and Age project found that decision-makers are frequently not aware of women's needs and that patriarchy still persists in many national settings (192). In recent years the UN has been a major actor in making women matter (193). The women's movement has also been a major actor in changing the way development issues are defined (194), and in articulating strategies for empowerment (195). When viewed through a gender-sensitive lens, world politics can be seen quite differently (196), as well as social science and the desirable future in general (197).

Global advocacy for child health and children's rights, notably in UNICEF's valuable *State of the World's Children* reports, increasingly overlaps with women's health and rights. The 1994 Report points to the need for primary education for all children but especially for girls as a key to overcoming the poverty/population/environment problem (198). The 1992 report eloquently states that "a new world order should oppose the apartheid of gender as vigorously as the apartheid of race" (199).

C. IMPROVING GOVERNANCE AND THINKING

Reflecting "the new world disorder," a wide melange of trends, forecasts, and proposals have been briefly discussed here, all related to world futures in general and eight key elements of world futures. A common theme is new and improved governance—not only in the sense of a sovereign authority, but as a constructive influence in an era of "governance without government" (45). In his preliminary thoughts on a forthcoming Club of Rome report on governance in the 21st century, Yehezkel Dror asserts that governance must play a pivotal role, but it lags behind a rapidly changing world (200). Seyom Brown also notes the failure to develop systems of governance to keep pace with the expanding power of humans in the world (201), and advocates a theory of the world polity, starting with assumptions about world interests that we might share.

1. Globally Shared Values

New and improved institutions of global governance are essential. But before discussing the various proposals that have been recently made, a discussion of shared values is warranted. Perhaps as a reaction to growing fragmentation of interests and ethnic conflicts, a recent wavelet of concern about shared values can be detected. Seyom Brown suggests survival of the human species, reduction in killing and brutality, enabling basic subsistence of the world's peoples, protecting individual rights, preserving cultural diversity, and protecting the environment (201). Vaclav Havel points to the creation of a new model of co-existence as the central political task of the 1990s, perhaps anchored in a broad "anthropic cosmological principle" (202). Relatedly, two advocates of "spiritual politics" propose a unitive spirit to heal the Earth, based on the Ageless Wisdom that connects the major religious traditions (203). Theologian Hans Kung advocates a "world ethic" based on "planetary responsibility" (204). Ruth Nanda Anshen proposes a Cultural Magna Carta so we can see ourselves as members of a single world society based on a single moral system (205).

From interviews with leading thinkers, Rushworth Kidder distilled four basic global goals for the 21st century (206), as well as eight universal values for humanity: love, truthfulness, fairness, freedom, unity, tolerance, responsibility, and respect for life (207). To overcome our "serious case of culture lag," Ervin Laszlo underscores the "truly universal values" of brotherhood, love for one's neighbor, and treating others as we wish to be treated (208). Katsuhiko Yazaki, Tae-Chang Kim, and others propose a uniting focus on caring for future generations (209). And Harlan Cleveland encourages the Global Commons (the atmosphere, outer space, the oceans, Antarctica) as a new policy frontier (210), and agreement on common norms as a key to world peace (211).

Shared values can serve as a general source of governance. Equally important, shared values provide the precondition for new and improved institutions of global governance. Conversely, sole emphasis or over-emphasis on the clash of civilizations and cultures (59) can greatly inhibit development of needed institutions. Regrettably, the authors who advocate shared values fail to suggest how to promote them in an era of fragmentation and infoglut. It would seem, however, that UNESCO should have a major role in this task, which has much to do with both education and culture.

2. Expanding the U.N. Role

Many of the authors mentioned here advocate a reformed and/or expanded UN role in peacekeeping, environmental affairs, assisting development, and enhancing understanding of global issues. No author proposes that the UN remain the same, or that its role should be reduced. Many other authors ignore the UN role in world affairs (which may implicitly suggest disapproval, or simply indicate mediocre scholarship that fails to acknowledge the UN as an increasingly important world actor).

There is no dispute that the United Nations needs reform. But there are many competing (and complimentary) ideas of what must be done and how to finance it. Even the Secretary General, Boutros Boutros-Ghali, acknowledges the need for many UN changes, especially in peacekeeping services (212).

Many others have valuable ideas to consider. James Rosenau proposes a permanent UN mission in the capital of every UN member, a global Peace Corps, a people's assembly to the UN, and five new Deputy Secretary-Generals to enlarge the bully pulpit (213). Erskine Childers and Brian Urquhart also suggest new Deputy Secretary-Generals, as well as bringing the headquarters of the scattered UN agencies together, a single UN Development Authority, and a comprehensive program and budget for the UN system (214). The UN Management and Decision-Making Project also urges a single Development Assistance Board, as well as a capacity to monitor data on global watch issues and multilateral arms reduction inspection teams (215). Harold Stassen, who worked on the original UN Charter in 1945, proposes a UN Legion as a police and peace force, a super peacemaking corps, and expanding the Security Council (216). Harlan Cleveland and Lincoln Bloomfield recommend bringing NGOs into the planning and decision-making process, developing a body of norms for the global commons, and taxing transnational transactions (217). Similarly, Christopher Stone proposes a Global Commons Trust Fund with revenues from ocean use and a tax on carbon emissions (218). US Congressman Lee Hamilton advocates a "peace endowment" created by public and private donations and taxes on airline travel and arms sales (219). An important book-length study of international public finance, by Ruben Mendez of UNDP, discusses various forms of international taxes, charges for use of the global commons, and measures such as a UN lottery (220).

The Iowa-based Stanley Foundation holds periodic meetings on UN issues, with reports advocating a sharp reduction in the General Assembly agenda (221), including NGOs in UN decision-making processes (222), a viable security system to address the roots of insecurity (223), keeping pace with changing concepts of sovereignty (224), and enhancing the UN ability to intervene in conflicts (225). Bertram Gross and Vladimir Kartashkin propose a UN High Commissioner for Human Rights, creating an International Criminal Court, completing an initial draft of a Global Bill of Rights and Duties in 1998 (marking the 50th anniversary of the Universal Declaration of Human Rights), and proclaiming the first decade of the new millennium as "The Human Rights Decade" (226). Gerald Helman and Steven Ratner suggest expanding UN effort to save failed nations through various models of guardianship (227). Other proposals suggest global watch capabilities (228,229) and applying world order values (230).

A few observers, thinking that needed UN reform will be too little or too late, propose idealistic schemes such as a Constitution for the Federation of the Earth (231), a Federal Union of Democratic Nations (232), or a Federation of Nations (233). And Ha-Sang Yoo, finding major shortcomings in the present UN location, proposes an idealized UN city headquartered in a neutral nation (234).

The proposals for UN expansion and reform that are identified here are doubtlessly only a small fraction of those that have been recently made. A widely accessible clearinghouse for UN reform proposals would be of considerable value. Or, more ambitiously, a clearinghouse for all visions of desirable world futures, including governance schemes, could give every idea a fair hearing and offer easy access to those who are interested in such matters—presumably, an increasing number of global citizens and leaders.

3. UNESCO's Potential Role

Clearly, in an emerging global era with many global problems, the United Nations and other transnational institutions will have an important role in shaping a better future. Yet, remarkably, in all of the proposals for UN reform identified here, no author mentions UNESCO, with the exception of Ervin Laszlo (24), who merely calls for its strengthening. Yet it is the broad realm of education, science, and culture than may well be the key to any viable world future. The 1990 "Vancouver Declaration," arising from the UNESCO Symposium on Science and Culture for the 21st Century, suggests the necessary direction: an integration of science and culture that leads to a sense of purpose, to overcome the fragmentation that has led to a breakdown in cultural communication (235). But this idea is overly generalized, and does not appear to have led to any specific suggestions, let alone significant action.

Some other ideas point the way for UNESCO's potential role. Willis Harman identifies a "global mind change" underway (236), albeit with no suggestions on how to speed up the transformation. Stephen Toulmin also discusses broad changes of mind to insure that intellectual and social procedures are more adaptive in the transition to post-modernity (237). Robert Ornstein and Paul Ehrlich propose creating a new evolutionary process based on some different kind of education and training to help us understand long-term threats—a "curriculum about humanity" (238). Clark Kerr, a major figure in American higher education for several decades, advocates a modern version of Jose Ortega y Gasset's emphasis on "general culture"—the system of ideas about the world which belongs to our time, enabling students to think horizontally (239). Yale historian Paul Kennedy, in his outstanding survey of the preparedness of the world's regions and nations for the 21st century, concludes that his analysis call for "the reeducation of humankind" (240). And Alexander King of the Club of Rome urges an "Introduction to Great World Problems" as a compulsory course for all students (5).

A much different kind of science is also needed. Harvard biologist Edward Wilson argues that a redirection of much of science and technology will be required in the upcoming Century of the Environment (241). Silvio Funtowicz and Jerome Ravetz call for a post-normal science that is systemic, synthetic, and humanistic (242). Howard Newby points to a broad "interactive model" of science that takes into account the relationship between science, technology, and society (243). And David Orr points to a broader science and more inclusive rationality, and the need for widespread ecological education (244).

This essay, and the underlying literature, should itself make the key point. Is "World Futures," more or less as presented here, an important area of multidisciplinary study? If so, then consider the startling fact that there is not a single program of graduate study in the world where a student could earn a Ph.D. by studying World Futures or what the Club of Rome has called the "global problematique." There are scattered courses here and there, as suggested by the Peace and World Security Studies curriculum guide (245). There are textbooks on global issues that pursue a particular theme: global humanist values (246), an International Futures computer simulation model (247), global order (248), and world political trends (249). But there are no serious programs (i.e., those with a modest concentration of first-rate scholars) to study World Futures at the graduate level, and very little opportunity to take courses on general culture, problems of humanity, or alternative world futures at the undergraduate level. In an age of complex global issues and an emerging global citizenry, there is no corresponding professional education or general civic education.

The potential role of UNESCO should be to give top priority to promoting a better understanding of World Futures, so as to develop the political will for constructive reform. UNESCO should not merely promote education, but a broad-based general culture/world problems/alternative futures curriculum in every school and college worldwide. It should not merely promote science, but a broadly integrative science that links up the many fragmented pieces of knowledge produced by industrial era science. It should not merely promote culture, but should emphasize formation of globally shared values and a culture for survival, in addition to advocating cultural diversity.

D. SIX PROPOSALS

In conclusion, this initial survey of World Futures literature prompts six broad proposals for action.

1) Establish a goal of 50 Ph.D.-producing graduate programs in World Futures (or equivalent labeling) in leading universities worldwide by 2010, and immediately begin monitoring progress toward that end. These programs will serve to reconfigure the plethora of knowledge that is presently being produced and not used well, and serve as a "horizontal" integrative core to universities that are grossly imbalanced toward "vertical" and specialized inquiry. A 1990 report by Ernest Boyer, President of the Carnegie Foundation for the Advancement of Teaching, provides a compelling argument for this "new vision of scholarship" (250).

2) Establish a goal of at least one broad-based course on world problems at every school and college worldwide by 2010 and immediately begin monitoring progress toward that end. Supporting a mere handful of futures studies courses, however, will do little or nothing to achieve this goal.

3) Create a comprehensive information-gathering capacity so that critical information on World Futures generated anywhere in the world can be quickly identified and easily disseminated in a variety of formats for a variety of users. (The FUTURESCO system is a mere hint of what ought to be done to cope with growing information overload.)

4) In that the United Nations system is increasingly a major actor in producing literature that is relevant to World Futures, a major effort should be made to integrate selected UN publications into a general catalog issued in the spring and fall of each year, and widely distributed to thought leaders, as are catalogs of other publishers. (The present catalog of UN publications is issued every two years, and lacks an appealing format.) Additional efforts should be made to insure that major UN publications are reviewed in the mass media and considered by relevant scholars. Many social scientists, who are still trained to engage in individual inquiry, tend to be prejudiced against collectively-produced documents. As in the physical sciences, however, collective inquiry and advocacy is increasingly important.

5) Efforts should be made by each UN agency to refer to other relevant UN publications. The parochial tribalism that is widely practiced in academia, where disciplines and professions ignore each other at the expense of a broader understanding of the world, should be discouraged in UN agencies. The UN should be leading universities away from their tendency to be "trivia factories" and toward a broader understanding of world problems, rather than acting itself like a fragmented university.

6) Serious research on world futures should be encouraged in a variety of ways by bringing together those with short-term and long-term general perspectives, as well as those who specialize in the eight key elements of world futures identified here. Discussions and debates are especially needed among scholars who are locked into narrow and out moded disciplinary or ideological perspectives. The Tokyo-based United Nations University claims to sponsor multidisciplinary, "holistic" research, but much of its work is not any broader or more important than work done elsewhere, and simply adds to the global flood of undigested information. A new and much broader meaning should be given to "holistic" inquiry and futures studies, as suggested by this brief survey.

Michael Marien is founder and editor of *Future Survey*, published monthly since 1979 by the World Future Society in Bethesda, Maryland. The views expressed in this essay are not necessarily those of UNESCO or the World Future Society.

E. 250 REFERENCES

[All items in this guide are noteworthy; however, 32 of them (indicated by an asterisk), are especially recommended starting points. Full abstracts for each item follow in Part II of this literature guide.]

OVERVIEWS

Recent Trends and Near-Term Futures

*1. United Nations, **Global Outlook 2000: An Economic, Social, and Environmental Perspective** (New York: United Nations Publications, May 1990).

2. United Nations Department of Economic and Social Development, **Report on the World Social Situation 1993** (New York: United Nations Publications, Aug 1993).

3. Üner Kirdar (editor), **Change: Threat or Opportunity for Human Progress?** (New York: United Nations Publications, Feb 1992/ 1209 pages in five volumes).

4. Üner Kirdar and Leonard Silk (editors), **A World Fit for People: Thinkers from Many Countries Address the Political, Economic, and Social Problems of Our Time** (New York: New York University Press, Nov 1993).

*5. Alexander King and Bertrand Schneider, **The First Global Revolution: A Report by the Council of The Club of Rome** (New York: Pantheon Books, Sept 1991).

6. Alexander King, **The Great Transition Restated**, *Science and Public Policy*, 18(1), Feb 1991, pages 15-22.

*7. Walter Truett Anderson, **Reality Isn't What It Used to Be: Theatrical Politics, Ready-to-Wear Religion..., and Other Wonders of the Postmodern World** (San Francisco: Harper & Row, Aug 1990).

8. William Van Dusen Wishard, **Reinventing the Condition of a Civilized Life: The Spiritual Search**, *Vital Speeches of the Day*, 60(3), 15 Nov 1993, pages 84-88.

9. Ernest Sternberg, **Transformations: The Eight New Ages of Capitalism**, *Futures*, 25 (10), Dec 1993, pages 1019-1040.

10. William Halal, **WORLD 2000: An International Planning Dialogue to Help Shape the New Global System**, *Futures*, 25(1), Jan-Feb 1993, pages 5-21.

*11. Joseph F. Coates, **The Highly Probable Future: 83 Assumptions...**, *The Futurist*, 28(4), July-Aug 1994/7-page insert.

12. McKinley Conway, **A Glimpse of the Future: Technology Forecasts for Global Strategists** (Norcross GA: Conway Data Inc, Nov 1992).

13. Marvin Cetron and Owen Davies, **Crystal Globe: The Haves and Have-Nots of the New World Order** (New York: St. Martin's Press, Oct 1991).

14. Marvin Cetron and Owen Davies, **50 Trends Shaping the World**, *The Futurist*, 25(5), Sept-Oct 1991, pages 11-21.

15. Richard Carlson and Bruce Goldman, **Fast Forward: Where Technology, Demographics, and History Will Take America and the World in the Next Thirty Years** (New York: HarperBusiness, April 1994).

16. Frank Feather, **G-Forces: Reinventing the World. The 35 Global Forces Restructuring Our Future** (Toronto: Summerhill Press, Nov 1989; New York: William Morrow, Aug 1990).

17. John Naisbitt and Patricia Aburdene, **Megatrends 2000...** (New York: William Morrow, Jan 1990).

18. John D. Rockfellow, *Wild Cards: Preparing for "The Big One"*, The Futurist, 28(1), Jan-Feb 1994, pages 14-19.

Evolution and Long-Term Futures

19. Ervin Laszlo, **Evolution: The Grand Synthesis** (Boston: New Science Library/Shambhala, 1987). Preface by Alexander King. Foreword by Jonas Salk.

20. Ervin Laszlo (editor), **The New Evolutionary Paradigm** (New York: Gordon and Breach, 1991). Foreword by Ilya Prigogine.

*21. Ervin Laszlo, **The Choice: Evolution or Extinction? A Thinking Person's Guide to Global Issues** (New York: Jeremy P. Tarcher/Putnam, Aug 1994). Afterword by Federico Mayor.

22. Walter Truett Anderson, **To Govern Evolution: Further Adventures of the Political Animal** (Boston and San Diego: Harcourt Brace Jovanovitch, 1987).

23. Robert Wesson, **Beyond Natural Selection** (Cambridge MA: MIT Press, 1991).

24. John Platt, *Invariances and Determinism in Global Forecasting*, Futures Research Quarterly, 9(2), Summer 1993, pages 23-32.

25. Duane Elgin, **Awakening Earth: Exploring the Evolution of Human Culture and Consciousness** (New York: William Morrow, Oct 1993).

26. Brian Swimme and Thomas Berry, **The Universe Story: From the Primordial Flaring Forth to the Ecozoic Era—A Celebration of the Unfolding of the Cosmos** (San Francisco: HarperSanFrancisco, Dec 1992).

27. Robert Keck, **Sacred Eyes** (Indianapolis IN: Knowledge Systems Inc, Dec 1992).

28. Charles M. Johnston, **The Creative Imperative: A Four-Dimensional Theory of Human Growth & Planetary Evolution** (Berkeley CA: Celestial Arts, 1986).

29. Frederick Turner, **Tempest, Flute, and Oz: Essays on the Future** (New York: Persea Books, 1991).

30. Barbara Marx Hubbard, **The Revelation: Our Crisis Is a Birth** (Sonoma CA: The Foundation for Conscious Evolution, May 1993).

31. Eric Chaisson, **The Life Era: Cosmic Selection and Conscious Evolution** (New York: Atlantic Monthly Press, 1987).

32. Gregory Stock, **Metaman: The Merging of Humans and Machines into a Global Superorganism** (New York: Simon & Schuster, Sept 1993).

33. Frank White, **The Overview Effect: Space Exploration and Human Evolution** (Boston: Houghton Mifflin, 1987).

34. Frank White, **The SETI Factor...the Search for Extraterrestrial Intelligence....** (New York: Walker and Co., 1990).

35. Konrad Lorenz, **The Waning of Humaneness** (Boston: Little Brown, 1987). First published in Munich in 1983.

36. Jacques Ellul, **What I Believe** (Grand Rapids MI: William B. Eerdmans Publishing Co, 1989). First published in France in 1987.

37. Rajni Kothari, *The Yawning Vacuum: A World Without Alternatives*, Alternatives: Social Transformation and Humane Governance, 18(2), Spring 1993, pages 119-139.

38. Francis Fukuyama, **The End of History and the Last Man** (New York: The Free Press, Jan 1992).

39. W. Warren Wagar, **A Short History of the Future** (Chicago: University of Chicago Press, Nov 1989). Afterword by Immanuel Wallerstein.

40. W. Warren Wagar, **A Short History of the Future**, Second edition (Chicago: University of Chicago Press, Aug 1992).

41. W. Warren Wagar, **The Next Three Futures** (Westport CT: Greenwood Press, Oct 1991).

Eight Key Elements

Politics in the Post-Cold War Era

*42. Harlan Cleveland, **Birth of a New World: An Open Moment for International Leadership** (San Francisco: Jossey-Bass Publishers, April 1993). Foreword by Robert McNamara.

43. Harlan Cleveland, *Rethinking International Governance: Coalition Politics in an Unruly World*, The Futurist, 25(3), May-June 1991, pages 20-27.

44. Joshua S. Goldstein and David P. Rapkin, *After Insularity: Hegemony and the Future World Order*, Futures, 23(9), Nov 1991, pages 935-959.

*45. James N. Rosenau and Ernst-Otto Czempiel (editors), **Governance Without Government: Order and Change in World Politics** (Cambridge UK and New York: Cambridge University Press, 1992).

46. James N. Rosenau, **Turbulence in World Politics: A Theory of Change and Continuity** (Princeton NJ: Princeton University Press, 1990).

*47. Joseph A. Camilleri and Jim Falk, **The End of Sovereignty? The Politics of a Shrinking and Fragmenting World** (Aldershot UK: Edward Elgar, 1992).

48. Evan Luard, **International Society** (New York: New Amsterdam Books, 1990).

49. Peter F. Drucker, **Post-Capitalist Society** (New York: HarperBusiness, April 1993).

50. John Naisbitt, **Global Paradox: The Bigger the World Economy, the More Powerful Its Smallest Players** (New York: William Morrow, Jan 1994).

51. Alvin Toffler, **Powershift: Knowledge, Wealth, and Violence at the Edge of the 21st Century** (New York: Bantam Books, 1990).

*52. Zbigniew Brzezinski, **Out of Control: Global Turmoil on the Eve of the 21st Century** (New York: Charles Scribner's Sons, April 1993).

53. Daniel Patrick Moynihan, **Pandaemonium: Ethnicity in International Politics** (New York: Oxford U. Press, Feb 1993).

54. Robert D. Kaplan, *The Coming Anarchy*, *The Atlantic Monthly*, 273(2), Feb 1994, pages 44-76.

55. Ted Robert Gurr, **Minorities at Risk: A Global View of Ethnopolitical Conflicts** (Washington: U.S. Institute of Peace Press, July 1993).

56. Gidon Gottlieb, **Nation Against State: A New Approach to Ethnic Conflicts and the Decline of Sovereignty** (New York: Council on Foreign Relations Press, Dec 1993).

57. Michael Walzer, *The New Tribalism: Notes on a Difficult Problem*, Dissent, Spring 1992, pages 164-171.

58. Jack Weatherford, **Savages and Civilization: Who Will Survive?** (New York: Crown Publishers, Jan 1994).

59. Samuel P. Huntington, *The Coming Clash of Civilizations: Or, the West Against the Rest*, The New York Times Op-Ed, Sunday, 6 June 1993, page 19. Adapted from *The Clash of Civilizations*, Foreign Affairs, 72(3), Summer 1993, pages 22-49.

*60. Mark Juergensmeyer, **The New Cold War? Religious Nationalism Confronts the Secular State** (Berkeley: University of California Press, May 1993).

61. Pat Robertson, **The New World Order** (Dallas TX: Word Publishing, 1991).

62. Lester M. Salamon, *The Rise of the Nonprofit Sector*, Foreign Affairs, 73(4), July-Aug 1994, pages 109-122.

63. Kathleen D. McCarthy, Virginia A. Hodgkinson, and Russy D. Sumariwalla, **The Nonprofit Sector in the Global Community** (San Francisco: Jossey-Bass Publishers, 1992).

Democratization and Peacekeeping

64. Samuel P. Huntington, **The Third Wave: Democratization in the Late Twentieth Century** (Norman OK: University of Oklahoma Press, 1991).

65. Bruce Russett, **Grasping the Democratic Peace: Principles for a Post-Cold War World** (Princeton NJ: Princeton University Press, Sept 1993).

66. Max Singer and Aaron Wildavsky, **The Real World Order: Zones of Peace/Zones of Turmoil** (Chatham NJ: Chatham House Publishers, Fall 1993).

67. Larry Diamond and Marc F. Plattner (editors), **The Global Resurgence of Democracy** (Baltimore MD: Johns Hopkins University Press, March 1993).

68. Georg Sorensen, **Democracy and Democratization: Processes and Prospects in a Changing World** (Boulder CO: Westview Press, June 1993).

69. Barry Gills, Joel Rocamora, and Richard Wilson (editors), **Low Intensity Democracy: Political Power in the New World Order** (London and Boulder CO: Pluto Press, Dec 1993).

*70. Martin van Creveld, **The Transformation of War** (New York: The Free Press, 1991).

71. Alvin and Heidi Toffler, **War and Anti-War: Survival at the Dawn of the 21st Century** (Boston: Little, Brown and Co, Oct 1993).

72. Michael Elliott, ***Global Mafia: Crime Goes International*** (Special Report), Newsweek, 13 Dec 1993, pages 22-31.

73. Lori Fisler Damrosch (editor), **Enforcing Restraint: Collective Intervention in Internal Conflicts** (New York: Council on Foreign Relations Press, Oct 1993).

74. Bengt Anderberg and Myron L. Wolbarsht, **Laser Weapons: The Dawn of a New Military Age** (New York: Plenum Press, 1992).

75. James Burk (editor), **The Military in New Times: Adapting Armed Forces in a Turbulent World** (Boulder CO: Westview Press, Feb 1994).

76. Ruth Leger Sivard, **World Military and Social Expenditures 1993** (Washington: World Priorities Inc, Nov 1993).

77. Carl Sagan and Richard P. Turco, *Nuclear Winter in the Post-Cold War Era*, Journal of Peace Research, 30(4), Nov 1993, pages 369-373.

78. Kathleen C. Bailey, **Strengthening Nuclear Nonproliferation** (Boulder CO: Westview Press, Dec 1993).

79. George Perkovich, *The Plutonium Genie*, Foreign Affairs, 72(3), Summer 1993, pages 153-165.

*80. Frank Barnaby, **How Nuclear Weapons Spread: Nuclear-Weapon Proliferation in the 1990s** (London and New York: Routledge, Dec 1993).

81. Susan Wright (editor), **Preventing a Biological Arms Race** (Cambridge MA: MIT Press, 1990).

82. Brad Roberts (editor), **Biological Weapons: Weapons of the Future?** (Boulder CO: Westview Press, 1993).

83. William C. Potter and Harlan W. Jencks, **The International Missile Bazaar: The New Suppliers' Network** (Boulder CO: Westview Press, Jan 1994).

84. Leonard S. Spector and Virginia Foran, **Preventing Weapons Proliferation: Should the Regimes Be Combined?** (Muscatine IA: The Stanley Foundation, Feb 1993).

85. Michael H. Shuman and Hal Harvey, **Security Without War: A Post-Cold War Foreign Policy** (Boulder CO: Westview, Nov 1993).

86. Bjørn Møller and Hakan Wiberg (editors), **Non-Offensive Defence for the Twenty-First Century** (Boulder CO: Westview Press, March 1994).

87. Janne E. Nolan (editor), **Global Engagement: Cooperation and Security in the 21st Century** (Washington: The Brookings Institution, April 1994).

88. Thomas G. Weiss (editor), **Collective Security in a Changing World** (Boulder CO: Lynne Rienner Publishers, March 1993).

89. John Roper et al, **Keeping the Peace in the Post-Cold War Era: Strengthening Multilateral Peacekeeping** (New York, Paris, and Tokyo: The Trilateral Commission, Dec 1993).

90. Paul F. Diehl, **International Peacekeeping** (Baltimore: Johns Hopkins University Press, Aug 1993).

91. Robert Stephens Staley II, **The Wave of the Future: The United Nations and Naval Peacekeeping** (Boulder CO: Lynne Rienner Publishers, Nov 1992).

92. Michael Renner, **Critical Juncture: The Future of Peacekeeping** (Washington: Worldwatch Institute, Worldwatch Paper 114, May 1993).

93. Saul H. Mendlovitz, *Struggles for a Just World Peace: A Transition Strategy*, Alternatives: Social Transformation and Humane Governance, 14(3), July 1989, pages 363-369.

94. Mark Sommer, *Who Will Pay for Peace?* The Christian Science Monitor, 19 Feb 1992, page 18.

Globalizing Information

95. Howard H. Frederick, **Global Communications & International Relations** (Belmont CA: Wadsworth Publishing Co, March 1993).

96. Majid Tehranian, *Information Technology and World Development*, InterMedia, 16(3), May 1988, pages 30-38.

97. Michael Connors, **The Race to the Intelligent State: Towards the Global Information Economy of 2005** (Oxford UK & Cambridge MA: Blackwell Business, July 1993).

98. Maurice Estabrooks, **Programmed Capitalism: A Computer-Mediated Global Society** (Armonk NY: M.E. Sharpe, 1988).

*99. Steven A. Rosell et al., **Governing in an Information Society** (Montreal: Institute for Research on Public Policy, 1992).

100. Yoneji Masuda, **Managing in the Information Society** (Oxford UK & Cambridge MA: Basil Blackwell, 1990).

101. Linda M. Harasim (editor), **Global Networks: Computers and International Communication** (Cambridge MA: MIT Press, Aug 1993/).

102. Joseph N. Pelton, *Telepower: The Emerging Global Brain*, The Futurist, 23(5), Sept-Oct 1989, pages 9-14.

103. Parker Rossman, **The Emerging Worldwide Electronic University: Information Age Global Higher Education** (Westport CT: Greenwood Press, Sept 1992).

104. George Gilder, **Life After Television** (New York: W.W. Norton, June 1992).

105. Derek Leebaert (editor), **Technology 2001: The Future of Computing and Communications** (Cambridge MA: MIT Press, 1991).

106. William E. Halal, **The Information Technology Revolution: Computer Hardware, Software, and Services into the 21st Century**, Technological Forecasting and Social Change, 44(1), Aug 1993, pages 69-86.

107. Herbert I. Schiller, **Mass Communications and American Empire**, Second edition (Boulder CO: Westview Press, Oct 1992).

108. Cees J. Hamelink, **The Technology Gamble. Informatics and Public Policy: A Study of Technology Choice** (Norwood NJ: Ablex Publishing Corp, 1988).

*109. Jacques Ellul, **The Technological Bluff** (Grand Rapids MI: William B. Eerdmans Publishing Co, 1990).

The Globalizing Economy

110. Martin Carnoy et al., **The New Global Economy in the Information Age: Reflections on Our Changing World** (University Park PA: Penn State Univ. Press, July 1993).

111. Peter Dicken, **Global Shift: The Internationalization of Economic Activity**, Second edition (New York: The Guilford Press, Feb 1992).

112. Peter F. Drucker, **Trade Lessons from the World Economy**, Foreign Affairs, 73(1), Jan-Feb 1994, pages 99-108.

113. Peter F. Cowhey and Jonathan D. Aronson (editors), **Managing the World Economy: The Consequences of Corporate Alliances** (New York: Council on Foreign Relations Press, March 1993).

114. Janet Lowe, **The Secret Empire: How 25 Multinationals Rule the World** (Homewood IL: Business One Irwin, 1992).

115. Jack N. Behrman and Robert E. Grosse, **International Business and Governments: Issues and Institutions** (Columbia SC: University of South Carolina Press, 1990).

116. Michel Godet et al., **Global Scenarios: Geopolitical and Economic Context to the Year 2000**, Futures, 26(3), April 1994, pages 275-288.

117. William Brock and Robert D. Hormats (editors), **The Global Economy: America's Role in the Decade Ahead** (New York: W.W. Norton, 1990). Published for The American Assembly.

118. Organisation for Economic Co-operation and Development, **Long-Term Prospects for the World Economy** (Paris: OECD, 1992).

119. UN Department of Economic and Social Information and Policy Analysis, **World Economic Survey 1993: Current Trends and Policies in the World Economy** (New York: United Nations, Aug 1993).

120. James Dale Davidson and Lord William Rees-Mogg, **The Great Reckoning: Protect Yourself in the Coming Depression**, Revised edition (New York: Touchstone, Dec 1993).

*121. Joel Kurtzman, **The Death of Money: How the Electric Economy Has Destabilized the World's Markets and Created Financial Chaos** (New York: Simon & Schuster, April 1993/256 pages; Boston: Little Brown Back Bay Books, April 1994 paperback).

122. P.W. Daniels, **Service Industries in the World Economy** (Oxford UK & Cambridge MA: Blackwell Publishers, Aug 1993).

123. Philip McMichael (editor), **The Global Restructuring of Agro-Food Systems** (Ithaca NY: Cornell University Press, July 1994).

124. J.N. Behrman, *Globalization and the Future of Cities*, Futures Research Quarterly, 8(1), Spring 1992, pages 41-74.

125. Donald E. Hawkins and J.R. Brent Ritchie (editors), **World Travel and Tourism Review: Indicators, Trends and Forecasts.** Volume 1, 1991 (Wallingford, Oxon UK: C.A.B. International, 1991). Distributed in US by University of Arizona Press.

126. Stephen F. Witt et al., **The Management of International Tourism** (London & Boston: Unwin Hyman, 1991).

127. Jacques Attali, **Millennium: Winners and Losers in the Coming World Order** (New York: Times Books, 1991). Foreword by Alvin Toffler. First published in France in 1990.

128. William B. Johnston, *Global Work Force: The New World Labor Market*, Harvard Business Review, 69(2), March-April 1991, pages 115-127.

129. Richard J. Barnet, *The End of Jobs*, Harper's Magazine, Sept 1993, pages 47-52.

130. Thomas Richard Shannon, **An Introduction to the World-System Perspective** (Boulder CO: Westview Press, 1989).

131. Christopher Chase-Dunn, **Global Formation: Structures of the World Economy** (Cambridge MA: Basil Blackwell, 1989).

132. United Nations Centre on Transnational Corporations, **World Investment Report 1991: The Triad in Foreign Direct Investment** (New York: United Nations Publications, 1991).

133. Robert Guttman, **How Credit-Money Shapes the Economy: The United States in a Global System** (Armonk NY: Sharpe, June 1994).

Population Growth and Health Threats

*134. Wolfgang Lutz, *The Future of World Population*, *Population Bulletin* (PRB), 49(1), June 1994/47 pages.

135. Carl Haub and Machiko Yanagishita, **1994 World Population Data Sheet** (Washington: Population Reference Bureau, May 1994 (20x28 wall chart).

136. Sharon L. Camp (editor), **World Access to Birth Control** (Washington: Population Crisis Committee, Oct 1992 (25x22 wall chart).

137. Gita Sen *et al.* (editors), **Population Policies Reconsidered: Health, Empowerment, and Rights** (Cambridge MA: Harvard Center for Population and Development Studies, July 1994).

138. Paul R. Ehrlich and Anne H. Ehrlich, **The Population Explosion** (New York: Simon & Schuster, 1990).

139. Norman Myers, **Population, Resources and the Environment: The Critical Challenges** (New York: United Nations Population Fund, 1991).

140. Norman Myers, *Environmental Refugees in a Globally Warmed World*, *BioScience*, 43(11), Dec 1993, pages 752-761.

141. Gil Loescher, **Beyond Charity: International Cooperation and the Global Refugee Crisis** (New York: Oxford University Press, Dec 1993).

142. Francis M. Deng, **Protecting the Dispossessed: A Challenge for the International Community** (Washington: The Brookings Institution, Sept 1993).

143. *Cities in the 21st Century: The Urban Half*, *Work in Progress* (United Nations University-Tokyo), 13(3), Sept 1991/12 pages.

144. Doris M. Meissner *et al.*, **International Migration Challenges in a New Era** (New York: Trilateral Commission, Sept 1993). Triangle Papers: 44.

145. Kevin M. Cahill (editor), **A Framework for Survival: Health, Human Rights, and Humanitarian Assistance in Conflicts and Disasters** (New York: BasicBooks and Council on Foreign Relations, April 1993).

146. Eric Chivian *et al.*, **Critical Condition: Human Health and the Environment** (Cambridge MA: MIT Press, Sept 1993).

*147. Global AIDS Policy Coalition and Jonathan M. Mann, **AIDS in the World** (Cambridge MA: Harvard University Press, Dec 1992).

*148. Stephen S. Morse (editor), **Emerging Viruses** (New York: Oxford University Press, May 1993). Also see *Infectious Diseases in the Age of Change* (Washington: National Academy Press, Oct 1994).

Global Environmental Problems

*149. Mostafa K. Tolba and Osama A. El-Kholy (editors), **The World Environment 1972-1992: Two Decades of Challenge** (London & New York: Chapman & Hall/Routledge, Dec 1992).

150. World Resources Institute, **World Resources 1992-93: A Guide to the Global Environment** (New York: Oxford University Press, March 1992).

151. Andrew Goudie, **The Human Impact on the Natural Environment**, Fourth edition (Cambridge MA: MIT Press, March 1994; Oxford UK: Blackwell, Nov 1993).

152. Elliott A. Norse, **Global Marine Biological Diversity** (Washington: Island Press, Oct 1993).

153. Jon M. Van Dyke *et al.* (editors), **Freedom for the Seas in the 21st Century: Ocean Governance and Environmental Harmony** (Washington: Island Press, December 1993).

154. Robin Clarke, **Water: The International Crisis** (Cambridge MA: MIT Press, March 1993). First published in London by Earthscan in 1991.

155. Kilaparti Ramakrishna and George M. Woodwell (editors), **World Forests for the Future: Their Use and Conservation** (New Haven CT: Yale University Press, April 1993).

156. Peter B. Stone (editor), **The State of the World's Mountains** (London & Atlantic Highlands NJ: Zed Books, June 1992).

157. United Nations Conference on Environment and Development, **The Global Partnership for Environment and Development: A Guide to Agenda 21** (Geneva: UNCED, April 1992).

158. Daniel Sitarz (editor), **AGENDA 21: The Earth Summit Strategy to Save Our Planet** (Boulder CO: EarthPress, March 1993).

*159. Shridath Ramphal, **Our Country, The Planet: Forging a Partnership for Survival** (Washington: Island Press, 1992).

160. David A. Munro and Martin W. Holdgate (editors), **Caring for the Earth: A Strategy for Sustainable Development** (Gland, Switzerland: IUCN—The World Conservation Union, 1991).

161. Al Gore, **Earth in the Balance: Ecology and the Human Spirit** (Boston: Houghton Mifflin, Jan 1992).

*162. Donella H. Meadows et al., **Beyond the Limits: Confronting Global Collapse, Envisioning a Sustainable Future** (Post Mills VT: Chelsea Green Publishing Co, April 1992).

163. Gerald O. Barney, **Global 2000 Revisited: What Shall We Do?** (Arlington VA: Millennium Institute, 1993).

164. Henry Kendall (Coordinator), **World Scientists' Warning to Humanity** (Washington: Union of Concerned Scientists, Nov 1992).

*165. Mostafa K. Tolba, **Saving Our Planet: Challenges and Hopes** (London & New York: Chapman & Hall/Routledge, Aug 1992).

166. Lester R. Brown et al., **Saving the Planet: How to Shape an Environmentally Sustainable Global Economy** (New York: W.W. Norton, Nov 1991).

*167. Lester R. Brown et al., **Vital Signs 1994: The Trends That Are Shaping Our Future** (New York: W.W. Norton, June 1994).

168. Lester R. Brown et al., **State of the World 1994: A Worldwatch Institute Report on Progress Toward a Sustainable Society** (New York: W.W. Norton, Jan 1994).

169. Lester R. Brown et al., **State of the World 1993** (New York: W.W. Norton, Jan 1993).

170. Jim MacNeill et al., **Beyond Interdependence: The Meshing of the World's Economy and the Earth's Ecology** (New York: Oxford University Press, 1991).

171. Harlan Cleveland, *The Global Commons*, *The Futurist*, 27(3), May-June 1993, pages 9-13.

172. Norman Myers, **Ultimate Security: The Environmental Basis of Political Stability** (New York: W.W. Norton, Sept 1993).

*173. Ernst Ulrich von Weizsäcker, **Earth Politics** (London & Atlantic Highlands NJ: Zed Books, Jan 1994).

174. Vaclav Smil, **Global Ecology: Environmental Change and Social Flexibility** (London & New York: Routledge, Dec 1993).

175. Wolfgang Sachs (editor), **Global Ecology: A New Arena of Political Conflict** (London & Atlantic Highlands NJ: Zed Books, Dec 1993).

176. Michael Marien, *Environmental Problems and Sustainable Futures: Major Literature from WCED to UNCED*, *Futures*, 24(8), Oct 1992, pages 731-757. Also in *FUTURESCO* #2-3, July 1992-June 1993.

A New Path for Development

*177. Boutros Boutros-Ghali, **An Agenda for Development** (New York: United Nations General Assembly, Agenda Item 91, May 1994).

*178. United Nations Development Programme, **Human Development Report 1994** (New York: Oxford University Press, June 1994).

179. United Nations Development Programme, **Human Development Report 1993** (New York: Oxford University Press, May 1993).

180. United Nations Development Programme, **Human Development Report 1992** (New York: Oxford University Press, May 1992).

181. James Gustave Speth, *A Post-Rio Compact*, *Foreign Policy*, #88, Fall 1992, pages 145-161.

182. New World Dialogue, **Compact for a New World** (Washington: World Resources Institute, Oct 1991).

183. Harlan Cleveland and Mochtar Lubis, **The Future of "Development"** (Minneapolis: Hubert H. Humphrey Institute, University of Minnesota, 1989).

184. Morris Miller, **Debt and the Environment: Converging Crises** (New York: United Nations Publications, 1991).

185. Alvaro Soto et al., **For Earth's Sake: A Report from the Commission on Developing Countries and Global Change** (Ottawa, Canada: International Development Research Centre, 1992).

186. Serge Latouche, **In the Wake of the Affluent Society: An Exploration of Post-Development** (London & Atlantic Highlands NJ: Zed Books, 1993). First published in 1991 in Paris as **La Planete des naufrages** (Planet of the Shipwrecked).

187. Paul Ekins, **A New World Order: Grassroots Movements for Global Change** (London & NY: Routledge, 1992).

188. Robert O. Slater *et al.*, **Global Transformation and the Third World** (Boulder CO: Lynne Rienner Publishers & London: Adamantine Press, April 1993).

189. Marc S. Miller, **State of the Peoples: A Global Human Rights Report on Societies in Danger** (Boston: Beacon Press, Nov 1993).

190. Julian Burger, **The Gaia Atlas of First Peoples: A Future for the Indigenous World** (New York: Anchor/Doubleday, 1990). Foreword by Maurice Strong.

Women and Children

*191. United Nations, **The World's Women 1970-1990: Trends and Statistics** (New York: United Nations Publications, 1991).

192. Eleonora Masini and Susan Stratigos (editors), **Women, Households and Change** (Tokyo: United Nations University Press, 1991). Prologue by Elise Boulding.

193. Hilkka Pietila and Jeanne Vickers, **Making Women Matter: The Role of the United Nations**, Second edition (London & Atlantic Highlands NJ: Zed Books, July 1994).

194. Nuket Kardam, **Bringing Women In: Women's Issues in International Development Programs** (Boulder CO: Lynne Rienner Publications, 1991).

195. Jill M. Bystydzienski (editor), **Women Transforming Politics: Worldwide Strategies for Empowerment** (Bloomington IN: Indiana University Press, 1992).

196. V. Spike Peterson and Anne Sisson Runyan (editors), **Global Gender Issues** (Boulder CO: Westview Press, Aug 1993).

197. Sue Rosenberg Zalk and Janice Gordon-Kelter (editors), **Revolutions in Knowledge: Feminism in the Social Sciences** (Boulder CO: Westview Press, 1992).

*198. James P. Grant, **The State of the World's Children 1994** (New York: Oxford University Press, May 1994).

199. James P. Grant, **The State of the World's Children 1992** (New York: Oxford University Press, March 1992).

IMPROVING GOVERNANCE AND LEARNING

Globally Shared Values

200. Yehezkel Dror, ***Request for Help with Preparation of a Club of Rome Report on "Governance for the 21st Century"***, Technological Forecasting and Social Change, 40(2), Sept 1991, pages 209-212. [NOTE: *The Capacity to Govern: Report to the Club of Rome* will be published in several languages in 1995.]

201. Seyom Brown, **International Relations in a Changing Global System: Toward a Theory of the World Polity** (Boulder CO: Westview Press, 1992).

202. Vaclav Havel, ***Post-Modernism: The Search for Universal Laws***, Vital Speeches of the Day, 60(20), 1 Aug 1994. Also see Vaclav Havel, **The End of the Modern Era**, The New York Times, 1 March 1992, E15.

203. Corinne McLaughlin and Gordon Davidson, **Spiritual Politics: Changing the World from the Inside Out** (New York: Ballantine Books, Aug 1994).

204. Hans Kung, **Global Responsibility: In Search of a New World Ethic** (New York: Crossroad Publishing Co, 1991). First published in Munich in 1990. Also see Shridath Ramphal, **Our Country, The Planet** (see #159) on the urgent need for a new universal ethic.

205. Ruth Nanda Anshen, **Morals Equals Manners** (Mt. Kisco NY: Moyer Bell Limited, 1992).

206. Rushworth M. Kidder, **Reinventing the Future: Global Goals for the 21st Century** (Cambridge MA: MIT Press, 1989).

207. Rushworth M. Kidder, **Shared Values for a Troubled World: Conversations with Men and Women of Conscience** (San Francisco: Jossey-Bass Publishers, April 1994). Foreword by Harlan Cleveland.

208. Ervin Laszlo, **The Inner Limits of Mankind: Heretical Reflections on Today's Values, Culture and Politics** (London: Oneworld Publications, 1989).

209. Katsuhiko Yazaki (editor), **Why Future Generations Now?** (New York & Osaka: Future Generations Alliance Foundation, May 1994). In English and Japanese.

210. Harlan Cleveland, **The Global Commons: Policy for the Planet** (Aspen CO: The Aspen Institute & Lanham MD: University Press of America, 1990).

211. Harlan Cleveland, *Ten Keys to World Peace*, *The Futurist,* 28(4), July-Aug 1994, pages 15-21.

Expanding and Reshaping the U.N. Role

212. Boutros Boutros-Ghali, *Empowering the United Nations*, *Foreign Affairs,* 71(5), Winter 1992, pages 89-102.

213. James N. Rosenau, **The United Nations in a Turbulent World** (Boulder CO: Lynne Rienner Publishers, Fall 1992).

*214. Erskine Childers with Brian Urquhart, *Renewing the United Nations System*, *Development Dialogue* 1994(1). Available from the Dag Hammarskjold Foundation or the Ford Foundation.

215. Peter J. Fromuth, **A Successor Vision: The United Nations of Tomorrow** (Lanham MD: United Nations Association of the USA and University Press of America, 1988).

216. Harold Stassen, **United Nations: A Working Paper for Restructuring** (Minneapolis MN: Lerner Publications Co, July 1994).

217. Harlan Cleveland and Lincoln P. Bloomfield, **Rethinking International Cooperation** (Minneapolis MN: University of Minnesota, Hubert H. Humphrey Institute, 1988).

218. Christopher D. Stone, **The Gnat Is Older Than Man: Global Environment and Human Agenda** (Princeton NJ: Princeton University Press, April 1993).

219. Lee H. Hamilton, *Reforming the Post-Cold War UN*, *The Christian Science Monitor,* 1 Dec 1992, page 19.

*220. Ruben P. Mendez, **International Public Finance: A New Perspective on Global Relations** (New York: Oxford U Press, 1992).

221. 22nd UN Issues Conference, **The United Nations: Structure and Leadership for a New Era** (Muscatine IA: The Stanley Foundation, 1991).

222. 25th UN Issues Conference, **The UN System and NGOs: New Relationships for a New Era?** (Muscatine IA: The Stanley Foundation, 1994).

223. 26th UN of the Next Decade Conference, **Collective Security and the United Nations: An Old Promise in a New Era** (Muscatine IA: The Stanley Foundation, 1991).

224. 27th UN of the Next Decade Conference, **Changing Concepts of Sovereignty: Can the United Nations Keep Pace?** (Muscatine IA: The Stanley Foundation, Fall 1992).

225. 28th UN of the Next Decade Conference, **The UN Role in Intervention: Where Do We Go From Here?** (Muscatine IA: The Stanley Foundation, June 1993).

226. Peter Juviler and Bertram Gross (editors), **Human Rights for the 21st Century: Foundations for Responsible Hope. A U.S./Post-Soviet Dialogue** (Armonk NY: M.E. Sharpe, Oct 1993).

227. Gerald B. Helman and Steven R. Ratner, *Saving Failed States*, *Foreign Policy,* #89, Winter 1992-93, pages 3-20.

228. John P. Renninger (editor), **The Future of the United Nations in an Interdependent World** (Dordrecht & Boston: Martinus Nijhoff, 1989).

229. J. Martin Rochester, **Waiting for the Millennium: The United Nations and the Future of World Order** (Columbia SC: University of South Carolina Press, June 1993).

230. Richard A. Falk, Samuel S. Kim, and Saul H. Mendlovitz (editors), **The United Nations and a Just World Order** (Boulder CO: Westview Press, 1991).

231. Errol E. Harris, **One World or None: Prescription for Survival** (Atlantic Highlands NJ: Humanities Press, June 1993).

232. James A. Yunker, **World Union on the Horizon: The Case for Supernational Federation** (Lanham MD: University Press of America, April 1993).

233. Hugh McTavish, **Ending War in Our Lifetime: A Concrete, Realistic Plan** (Dixon KY: West Fork Press, Jan 1994).

234. Ha-Sang Yoo, **Planning the UN City** (New York: Vantage Press, 1987).

Culture Lag and UNESCO's Potential Role

235. **Vancouver Declaration. Final Report of the UNESCO Symposium on Science and Culture for the 21st Century: Agenda for Survival** (Ottawa: Canadian Commission for UNESCO, 1990).

236. Willis Harman, **Global Mind Change: The Promise of the Last Years of the Twentieth Century** (Indianapolis IN: Knowledge Systems Inc, 1988).

237. Stephen Toulmin, **Cosmopolis: The Hidden Agenda of Modernity** (New York: The Free Press, 1990).

238. Robert Ornstein and Paul Ehrlich, **New World, New Mind: Moving Toward Conscious Evolution** (New York: Doubleday, 1989; Touchstone paperback edition, 1990).

239. Clark Kerr, **Higher Education Cannot Escape History: Issues for the Twenty-First Century** (Albany NY: State University of New York Press, Jan 1994).

*240. Paul Kennedy, **Preparing for the Twenty-First Century**, (New York: Random House, March 1993/428 pages).

241. Edward O. Wilson, *Is Humanity Suicidal?* The New York Times Magazine, 30 May 1993, pages 24-29.

242. Silvio O. Funtowicz and Jerome R. Ravetz, *Science for the Post-Normal Age*, Futures, 25(7), Sept 1993, pages 739-755.

243. Howard Newby, *One Society, One Wissenschaft: A 21st Century Vision*, Science and Public Policy, 19(1), Feb 1992, pages 7-14.

244. David Orr, *Schools for the Twenty-First Century*, Resurgence, #160, Sept-Oct 1993, pages 16-19.

245. Michael T. Klare (editor), **Peace & World Security Studies: A Curriculum Guide** (Boulder CO: Lynne Rienner, May 1994).

246. Mel Gurtov, **Global Politics in the Human Interest**, Second edition (Boulder CO: Lynne Rienner, 1991). [Textbook]

247. Barry B. Hughes, **International Futures: Choices in the Creation of a New World Order** (Boulder CO: Westview Press, Aug 1993). [Textbook]

248. Lynn H. Miller, **Global Order: Values and Power in International Politics**, Third edition (Boulder CO: Westview Press, April 1994). [Textbook]

249. Charles W. Kegley Jr and Eugene R. Wittkopf, **World Politics: Trend and Transformation**, Fourth edition (New York: St.Martin's Press, 1993). [Textbook]

*250. Ernest L. Boyer, **Scholarship Reconsidered: Priorities of the Professoriate** (Princeton NJ: The Carnegie Foundation for the Advancement of Teaching, 1990)

Part II: ABSTRACTS
Selected from *Future Survey* and **Future Survey Annual**

[Asterisked numbers indicate especially recommended items.]

A. OVERVIEWS

1. Recent Trends and Near-Term Futures

*001
Global Outlook 2000: An Economic, Social, and Environmental Perspective. The United Nations. NYC 10017: United Nations Publications (Room DC2-853; 212/963-8321), May 1990/340p/$19.95.

Revised version of an earlier 1988 study undertaken for the UN General Assembly, drawing on research and projections prepared by many parts of the UN system. The baseline scenario for the 1990s, assuming that government policies will not change, views long-term growth performance of all countries as largely unchanged from recent trends. World GDP per capita will grow at 1.8% per year during the 1990s, up slightly from 1.6% in the 1985-1990 period. Sufficient adjustment will take place to avoid a major economic downturn, but the rich-poor gap will continue to widen. The risk of serious deterioration of the environment will increase unless patterns of production and consumption are radically altered. Regional diversity in economic growth is expected in the 1990s, with negligible growth or absolute decline in many of the heavily indebted countries. The world energy situation may be on the threshold of new problems of geographic concentration of supplies. Food self-sufficiency may not improve, but rapid deterioration of recent years will be checked. No overall reduction in the 500 million malnourished people is expected by 2000. The widening R&D and technology gaps may threaten future North-South trade. Literacy rates are likely to continue increasing in the 1990s, even as the total number of illiterates also increases. National economies will suffer increasingly from the effects of crime, especially new techniques for non-violent but illegal acquisition and use of money. Drug abuse and illicit trafficking are likely to continue. The HIV/AIDS epidemic will continue to spread, with a projection of about 15 million new HIV infections in the 1990s, adding to an estimated 6-8 million infections to date. Reorientation of welfare services towards mutual self-help, prevention, rehabilitation, and income-generating activities will be of special significance in LDCs. Alternative scenarios suggesting policy changes focus on accelerated growth in the developed economies by 0.5% per year brought about by greater policy coordination, increased trade flows, an increase in investment, writing off 30% of LDC debt, increasing capital flows, and a 5% reduction in military expenditures.

Specific chapters are devoted to the world economy, environment, energy, agriculture, new technologies and their diffusion (microelectronics, new materials, biotechnology), structural changes in production and trade, population and labor force issues, human settlements, education, health, and social policy. Concludes that the outlook for the next decade depends vitally on the progress made both in national policy-making and in international cooperation. There are wide limits to the possible, varying from stagnation and environmental disaster to relieving poverty, improving quality of life, safeguarding the environment, stabilizing the world economy, and moving towards a global community. [**NOTE**: Excellent global overview.]
(**world trends in 1990s**)

002
Report on the World Social Situation 1993. UN Dept of Economic and Social Development. NY: United Nations, Aug 1993/226p(8x11")/$24.95pb. (Sales # E.93.IV.2)

The 13th in a series of reports prepared every four years. **Part One: Social Conditions.** *1) Population and Urbanization*: expected world population of 8.5 billion in 2025, changes in immigration flows, growth of refugees, growth of youthful populations without employment; *2) Hunger and Food Supplies*: chronic hunger presently afflicts some 550 million people worldwide; *3) Health*: emerging public health concerns (spread of cholera, malaria, AIDS, TB) in the midst of remarkable advances in medical technology; declining infant mortality rates and rising life expectancy largely due to strong government intervention; *4) Education and Literacy*: despite gains in school enrollment there were 948 million adults aged 15 and over who were illiterate in 1990; the number of book titles published worldwide increased from some 521,000 in 1970 to 834,500 in 1988; educational reforms attracted considerable attention in all countries; *5) Housing and Sanitation*: housing conditions in most countries have deteriorated in recent years, especially in indebted poor countries; *6) Unemployment and Low-Productivity Employment*: a major problem in all world regions, and by far the most important cause of poverty; all countries are affected by the rapid advent of labor-saving technical progress; *7) Income Distribution and Poverty*: increasing—but not uniform—polarization in living conditions; "in both developed and developing countries, women have fallen into poverty at a significant rate"; *8) Government Expenditures on Social Services*: slow economic growth almost everywhere has tightened fiscal constraints; one of the most significant trend has been privatization of social service delivery in all countries; *9) Quality of Life*: notes a "paradoxical combination of material progress and social deterioration."

Part Two: Major Issues and Dilemmas. *10) Major Changes in Economic and Social Institutions*: the State is being divested of means of production, mechanisms for social security are being redesigned, laws are establishing private ownership; *11) Financial Crisis*: social security policies face severe challenges in all countries due to aging populations and slow economic growth; *12) Ethnic Conflicts and National Disintegration*: a "great escalation" of violent conflict in the world since the end of the Cold War, destroying conditions necessary for economic and social development; *13) Environment*: protecting the environment from wasteful production and consumption patterns remains a problem of "momentous importance"; *14) Social Consequences of Advances in Technology*: spread of infotech and biotech; new technologies generally support sustainable development; *15) Drug/Tobacco/Alcohol Use*: data on consumption patterns and trends. [**NOTE**: An outstanding integration of global data and sophisticated analysis, serving as general background to the World Summit for Social Development, to be held in early 1995.] (**UN on world social trends**)

003
Change: Threat or Opportunity for Human Progress? Edited by Üner Kirdar (Director, UNDP Development Study Programme). NY: United Nations Publications, Feb 1992/1209p in 5 vols/$75.00 set.

Essays from the Round Table on Global Development Challenges, meeting in Turkey in September 1990 on the 40th anniversary of the UN Development Programme. Kirdar introduces each volume with an overview of issues and questions.

Vol I: Political Change (329p/$23.50pb). Essays on hopes for peace/justice/democracy/development, globalization and regionalization, new thinking for coping with regional conflicts (by Robert McNamara), the new Cold War within capitalism, Japan in a changing world order (by Saburo Okita), European economic integration, the new market economies in Central and Eastern Europe, Africa between uncertainties and hopes, the coming of global civilization (by Marc Nerfin), and the beginnings of a new global ethics.

Vol II: Economic Change (356p/$23.50pb). Essays on the challenges of global development, a new global development agenda for the 1990s (integrating environment and development, discussing trade and investment, stressing demilitarization and human development), promoting diversification in the world commodity economy, a new strategy for multilateral cooperation, "liberal internationalism" as the only foreign policy philosophy that will enable us to cope with the challenges in the new era, a new philosophy of foreign aid (by Harlan Cleveland and Mochtar Lubis), economic issues of the 1990s, the vision of people-centered development for the South, the extremely serious position of many debtor countries in the near and medium terms, a new institution for debt relief (an International Debt Discount Corporation, proposed by Peter B. Kenen), and recent changes in world trade.

Vol III: Globalization of Markets (161p/$17.50pb). Essays on globalization of financial markets and the monetary system, implications of globalization for the developing world (which does not seem to be benefiting), strengthening the international monetary system, managing exchange rates, coordinating macroeconomic policies, changes in capital financial markets, the role of the IMF in globalized financial markets, and regional integration in Europe and North America.

Vol IV: Changes in the Human Dimension of Development, Ethics and Values (145p/$16.50pb). Essays on the population dimension (by Nafis Sadik), international sci/tech cooperation, education and human development as the key factor in human progress (by Federico Mayor), a strategy for creating value-added services in the Third World, participatory development as a key element for the 1990s, assessment of the Nairobi Forward-looking Strategies for the Advancement of Women to the year 2000, new strategies for the development of culture, culture and knowledge in development, and ethics of leadership.

Vol V: Ecological Change: Environment, Development, and Poverty Linkages (218p/$19.50pb). Essays on UNCED and required global changes (by Maurice Strong), links between poverty and the environment, promoting environmentally sound economic progress (by Robert Repetto), sustainable development through global interdependence, global warming and global development, the likely impact of global warming on LDCs, linking technology and ecology for sustainability (by Heitor Gurgulino de Souza), debt-for-nature and debt-for-scholars swaps, preventive environmental policy, industrial restructuring for sustainability, sustainable development for megacities, a new earth order (by Claes Nobel, who points to five key catalysts: the power of business, the power of the media, the power of women, the power of youth, and the power of earth ethics), and a New World Strategy (based on harmony, cooperation, sharing, and reverence for life). [NOTE: The essays in these volumes are mostly at a very general level.]

(**1990 Round Table on Global Development**)

004
A World Fit for People: Thinkers from Many Countries Address the Political, Economic, and Social Problems of Our Time. Edited by Üner Kirdar (Senior Advisor, UN Development Programme) and Leonard Silk (former economics columnist, *NY Times*). NY: New York U Press, Nov 1993/481p/$40.00.

"The world is now passing through an era of shocks and transformations that are unprecedented in the opportunities and risks they present." The most important change is that the world now has the potential of becoming a far safer and better place. This volume stems from the second Round Table Conference on Global Change, held in Bucharest in September 1992. [See **Change: Threat or Opportunity for Human Progress?** edited by Üner Kirdar (UN Publications, 1992/5 vols; **FS Annual 1993** #11541), for Proceedings of the first Conference, held in Turkey in 1990.] The 55 essays appear in four groups: **1) Political Reconstruction**: the retreat of the West from Third World problems, changing Northern policies and disparate Southern responses, the imperative of effective global governance, the future of democracy, the mixed economy as a practical target (by Nobel Laureate Laurence R. Klein, U of Pennsylvania), the rise in regionalism, development and democracy, lessons for Africa; **2) Economic Development**: the case against unregulated markets (by Paul Streeten), the globalized world economy, imposing conditions on aid, the need for a new vision of development; **3) Human and Ecological Values**: sustainable human development (by Mahbub ul Haq), social justice as a prerequisite for change, the "vital E's of a good international society" (Talat Sait Halman lists them as Equality, Equity, Education, Employment, Energy, Ethnic Equilibrium, Ethics, Equanimity, Environmental Enlightenment, Ecumenism, Enterprise, and Economic Elan), containing ethnic conflict, new religious identities, the role of women in change, self-esteem as a key value for the future, sustainability as the main global issue; **4) Countries in Transition**: overcoming the legacy of the old order in Eastern Europe and the USSR, difficulties in transforming economies, integrating East and West, the contribution of the 35,000 transnational corporations, the emergence of NGOs, the unprecedented process of privatization (by Nicholas Georgescu-Roegen), and trade and payments after the Soviet collapse. [NOTE: Overly generalized.] (**world political/economic issues**)

*005
The First Global Revolution: A Report by the Council of The Club of Rome. Alexander King (former President, CoR) and Bertrand Schneider (Secretary-General, CoR). Foreword by Ricardo Diez-Hochleitner (President, CoR). NY: Pantheon Books, Sept 1991/259p/$15.00pb.

We are in the early stages of forming a new type of world society. The magnitude of changes in the population explosion, world climate, global food security, energy availability, and the geopolitical situation amounts to a major revolution on a worldwide scale. The global revolution has no ideological basis; humanity must grope its way toward an understanding of the new world. Since its founding in 1968, the Club of Rome, comprising 100 independent individuals from 53 countries, has sought a deeper understanding of "the world problematique"—the massive and untidy mix of problems that form the predicament of humanity. This is described in chapters on the whirlwind of change, areas of acute concern, mismanagement of the world economy, the vacuum created by evaporation of generalized religious faith and respect for the political process, and the worldwide human malaise.

A corresponding term, "the world resolutique," is introduced here to connote a coherent, comprehensive, and simultaneous attack on many of the diverse elements of the problematique. Three zones of the problematique that demand immediate attention: 1) reconversion from a military to a civil economy (all governments should institute active policies for their declining arms industries, with freed resources devoted to improving the social structure); 2) rethinking development strategies (with much greater priority to be given to the needs of the marginalized and forgotten millions of the rural poor, and to small-scale projects); 3) creation of an environment for survival (requiring reduction of global CO_2 emissions, reforestation, alternative forms of energy, and greater energy conservation). Suggestions for action on the environment include a Worldwide Campaign of Energy Conservation and Efficiency working with National Energy Efficiency Councils, a competent high-level body to consider in depth and over a long time frame the implications of macropollution, a UN Environmental Security Council parallel to the existing Security Council for military matters, Global Development Rounds (regular meetings of industrial leaders and governments similar to the Tariff Rounds of GATT), creation of National Centers for Clean Technology, a UN scientific meeting to plan a comprehensive World Alternative Energy Project, and concepts of global development integrated into UNESCO educational programs.

Unfortunately, the deficiencies of government are at the root of many strands of the problematique. Some of the more obvious inadequacies of national governments and intergovernmental bodies include retaining the principle of sovereignty in the face of interdependence, priority given to short-term solutions, organization in the form of sectoral ministries with a confused mass of specialized units and vested interests, and swollen bureaucracies. New qualities of governance must include a strategic vision and a global approach, a capacity for learning and innovation, and an ethical perspective. Other "agents of the resolutique" must be the challenge of continuous learning in a transitional society ("Introduction to the Great World Problems" should be a compulsory course for all students), science and technology for development within a human framework, and the mass media (the Club of Rome seeks to engage in a broad debate with journalists and top media leaders). These ideas "are offered as a basis for learning our way into the future." [NOTE: Some important ideas, but with no index, no bibliography, and only a few very abbreviated footnotes, mostly referring to other CoR reports. There is a hint of insular hauteur to this report, rather than reaching out in the spirit of intellectual interconnectedness demanded by our times.]

("world problematique" and "world resolutique")

006
The Great Transition Restated, Alexander King (President, Club of Rome, Paris), *Science and Public Policy*, 18:1, Feb 1991, 15-22.

We seem to be in the throes of a fundamental transition to a new society as different from that of today as the industrial revolution was from the agrarian world. This brief survey of changes since creation of the Club of Rome in 1968 touches on the fading dominance of the two superpowers, the collapse of the Soviet Empire, emergence of three gigantic trading and industrial blocs (a prospect of great concern to other regions), the imperative for restructuring the UN and its agencies, the paradox in world political trends toward creating both larger units for trade and problem-solving and smaller units as ethnic groups become more active in their demands for autonomy, the disappointing results of massive development aid programs (much greater priority must be given to the needs of rural populations), meaninglessness of the "Third World" concept, transformation of the world communication system, awakening of public consciousness to environmental threats, the dramatic increase in terrorism and violence, four major macropollution problems (acid rain, toxics and radioactive wastes, ozone layer, and greenhouse effect), the expected rapid increase in demographic disparities between rich and poor countries, threats to global food security, the fundamental matter of human values, and establishing global solidarity to enable a harmonious passage through this great transition. [NOTE: Outstanding brief overview.] (recent global trends)

*007
Reality Isn't What It Used To Be: Theatrical Politics, Ready-to-Wear Religion, Global Myths, Primitive Chic, and Other Wonders of the Postmodern World. Walter Truett Anderson (Albany CA). San Francisco: Harper & Row, Aug 1990/288p/$18.95.

Author of **To Govern Evolution** (Harcourt Brace Jovanovitch, 1987; #022 in this Guide) discusses the social construction of reality, the belief systems that gave form to the modern world, and the emerging postmodern era in which different groups have different beliefs about belief itself (essentially objectivists vs. constructivists, who hold that the "real world" is an ever-changing social creation). Three major processes are shaping this painful transition: the breakdown in old ways of belief, the emergence of a new polarization between fundamentalists (of religion, science, ideology, or cultural tradition) vs. relativists, and the birth of a global culture with a worldview that is truly a *world*view (globalization provides a new arena or theater in which all belief systems become aware of other belief systems). "Globalizing processes require us to renegotiate our relationships with familiar cultural forms, and remind us that they are things made by people: human, fallible things, subject to revision. Globalism and a postmodern worldview come in the same package; we will not have one without the other."

The problem for those who hope for a true global civilization is figuring out how fundamentalist and postmodern worldviews can coexist. This is a new polarization—not as overriding as the capitalism-communism conflict of the Cold War years, but one more kind of fragmentation and conflict. Six stories are competing for attention and credibility in the postmodern world: the Western myth of progress (with its enthusiasm for technological change and economic development), the Marxist story of revolution and international socialism, the premodern Christian fundamentalist story, the premodern Islamic fundamentalist story, the early post-modern Green story (profoundly reactionary) and the "new paradigm" story (borrowing heavily from 20th century science). "Information makes life difficult for anyone who would like to hold on to a story in its pure form. Information acts upon stories as rain acts upon sand castles.... Faced with information, the believer becomes either a constructivist or a fundamentalist: the former takes stories lightly, changes them, or abandons them entirely when it becomes necessary; the latter deals with troublesome information through psychological denial and/or political repression." There is no likelihood that any of these six political/religious belief systems will go away: these competing ideologies will be part of global civilization.

"The postmodern worldview is becoming the *zeitgeist*, as modernism was in past centuries. It will be a central element in the global culture, but it is hardly likely to be universally accepted in any explicit form or to unite all people." The fundamental characteristics or metatrends of the postmodern worldview: 1) changes in thinking-about--thinking: a growing awareness of the multidimensional, relativistic quality of human experience; 2) changes in identity and boundaries: we live in the age of multiple identities and fading boundaries between nations, races, classes, cultures, and species; 3) changes in learning: we come to accept the centrality of learning and discovery to the life of every individual and society as a necessity for survival; 4) changes in ethics and values: we come to accept morality and moral discourse as a living and central element in human existence; the collapse of belief does not result in a collapse of morality; 5) changes in relationship to traditions, customs, and institutions: we inhabit all kinds of social constructions of reality in new ways. Concludes with a discussion of two mega-issues of "the global not-quite-civilization": the prospect of massive environmental change and worldwide demands for human rights. Both are social constructions of reality, and beliefs about belief will be part of the dialogue. [NOTE: The somewhat flippant title obscures a thoughtful, clearly-written, important, and original work. Anyone who persists in reading this guidebook will find their actions justified here.]

(**constructivism as postmodern worldview**)

008

Reinventing the Condition of a Civilized Life: The Spiritual Search, William Van Dusen Wishard (President, World Trends Research, Reston VA), *Vital Speeches of the Day*, 60:3, 15 Nov 1993, 84-88.

A briefing for Members of Congress by the author of **The American Future: What Would George and Tom Do Now?** (The Congressional Institute, 1992; **FS Annual 1994 #12437**), asserting that so much is happening so fast in so many areas of life that we no longer have a frame of reference within which to understand our times. The key to understanding what is happening to America and the world is the new availability of unlimited technical power being given to a rapidly increasing number of citizens, which vastly increases life's possibility and danger. We're experiencing the death throes of the Modern Age, characterized by the expansion of Europe and the white race, the Newtonian concept of the universe, the ideal of scientific objectivity, the book and the printed word, patriarchal predominance, the mass society, and by progress defined as dominance of nature and the continued expansion of the material realm. All these impulses have run their course.

As we move from one age to the next, a new set of characteristics is at work: 1) certainly, it will be a global future, with greater equality of races and ethnic groups; 2) human activity will evolve within the context of the earth as a whole, which means greater cooperation with earth's systems; 3) interdependence will be a primary operating principle, between individuals, institutions, and nations; 4) the fostering of Life in all its forms—human, animal, environmental—will become a defining ethic by which we judge human activity; 5) the basic reality will not be material but spiritual; our whole understanding of who we are and what the human venture is about will take a quantum leap forward; 6) globalization of technology, finance, and employment is making all economies a sub-set of a global production system; 7) Modernism has deconstructed; all the major currents of 20th century intellectual thought have now dried up—even the belief that science will provide ultimate meaning in life has evaporated; 8) everywhere we see the disappearance of boundaries—national, cultural, and ethnic—that have helped to provide identity; one of the central facts today is the massive spiritual search that's taking place. Political leaders must explain to Americans what's going on, and enlist them in building the next phase of the American experiment. A new cultural climate is needed—one of hope and possibility that encourages young people to reach beyond themselves and grab the edges of a new period of history. "Our task is not only reinventing government, but reinventing the conditions of a civilized life for a new period of history." [ALSO SEE: Vaclav Havel, #202 in this Guide]   (**end of Modern Age**)

009

Transformations: The Eight New Ages of Capitalism, Ernest Sternberg (School of Architecture and Planning, SUNY-Buffalo), *Futures*, 25:10, Dec 1993, 1019-1040.

Author of **Photonic Technology and Industrial Policy: US Responses to Technological Change** (SUNY Press, 1992) observes that momentous transitions are upon us. Eight new ages are occurring at the same time: 1) the new information economy, generating wealth and power through knowledge; 2) the worldwide economy of proliferating images (which become an obstacle to coherent thinking); 3) the age of global interdependence and a globalized economy; 4) the new mercantilism, where advanced technology and manufacturing are becoming strategic national resources; 5) the age of spreading corporate power, where a new global class controls a multinational investment and production apparatus; 6) the age of flexible specialization, with ascendance of more entrepreneurial and adaptable firms; 7) the age of new social movements to protect the environment and promote human rights and other humane concerns; 8) the age of new fundamentalisms that arises as a response, as changes pose ever-greater threats to ethnicities and religions. We do not know which of these transformations, or which combination, will dominate the future. We should not try to obscure these divergent possibilities with a homogenous picture of change. [NOTE: A useful survey that embraces the complexity of our time, rather than insisting on a single view.]

(**eight transformations underway**)

010

WORLD 2000: An International Planning Dialogue to Help Shape the New Global System, William Halal (Prof of Management, GWU), *Futures*, 25:1, Jan-Feb 1993, 5-21.

The WORLD 2000 project, sponsored by the Board of Directors of the World Future Society, seeks to define the emerging global system and to help shape its formation. It hopes to do so by conducting an international planning dialogue that brings together a diversity of views from all sectors—a process of "strategic planning for the planet" that seeks to form a global consensus on how to realize a commonly shared vision of the future. This "white paper" provides background for the strategic dialogue, focusing on three major elements: **1) Key Driving Forces or Supertrends**: a stable population of 10-14 billion people by roughly the mid-21st century, industrial output increasing by a factor of 5-10 over the next few decades [!??], the wiring of the globe, the IT revolution accelerating other technical advances, global integration (a shared international culture, common currency, and some form of world governance), more diversity and complexity (ethnic regions seeking autonomy and splintering of societies), a universal standard of freedom and human rights, striving for higher-order values; **2) Critical Issues Blocking the Passage Ahead**: making the leap to a global order, achieving sustainable development, managing complexity, alleviating the North-South gap, the vacuum of power and ideas; **3) A Master Strategy to Resolve These Issues**: disseminate advanced infotech, integrate economic and social interests in human-centered enterprise, carefully nestle society into its living environment, develop green technology, decentralize institutions to empower individuals, foster collaborative problem-solving. [NOTE: An admirably concise overview of trends, issues, and strategies. The dialogue began with a dozen WORLD 2000 sessions at the June 1993 WFS General Assembly in Washington.] **(world trends and issues dialogue)**

*011

The Highly Probable Future: 83 Assumptions about the Year 2025, Joseph F. Coates (Coates & Jarratt, Washington), *The Futurist,* 28:4, July-Aug 1994/7-page insert ($3.00/copy; quantity discounts).

Statements developed for Project 2025: Anticipating Developments in Science and Technology and Their Implications for the Corporation, sponsored by 18 large organizations [report forthcoming]. *1) Managing Our World:* movement toward a managed environment will have progressed substantially (although this does not imply total control), everything will be smart by embedded microprocessors and responsive materials; *2) Health:* all diseases and disorders will have their linkages to the human genome identified, explicit programs to enhance physical and mental abilities, in-depth personal medical histories on smart cards; *3) Environment and Resources:* substantially less animal protein in diets of advanced nations, synthetic and genetically manipulated foods for individual tastes and needs, use of synthetic soils, wide use of genetically-engineered microorganisms for waste management and pollution cleanup, routine and reliable worldwide weather reporting, per capita energy consumption at 66% of 1990 level in advanced nations (but at 160% of 1990 level in the rest of the world); *4) Infotech and Automation:* a global broadband network of networks, common use of robots, universal on-line surveys and voting in all advanced nations, customized materials, language translation for some vocabularies, expert systems will mimic or surpass human learning, factory-manufactured housing as the norm, self-monitoring infrastructures, widespread interactive vehicle-highway systems; *5) Population:* world population at about 8.4 billion people, birth control widely used, world population divided in three tiers (World 1 living in prosperity, World 2 living comfortably in the context of their culture, World 3 living in destitution), emergence of a worldwide middle class; *6) World Tensions:* internal strife and border conflicts peaking between 1995 and 2010, effective UN peacemaking as well as peacekeeping, widespread contamination by a nuclear device will have occurred (by accident or as an act of political/military violence), epidemics and mass starvation common in World 3, effective supranational government for some functions (environment, war, narcotics, business regulation, disease control), substantial environmental degradation (especially in World 3), migration regulated under new international law; *7) Electronic Global Village:* a global currency in use, lifelong learning effectively institutionalized, national decisions influenced by electronically-assisted referenda, universal smart ID cards; *8) Issues and Values:* a universal health care system in the US, old-age security based on need-only criteria, more leisure time for the middle class, economic health measured in a new way to account for environmental quality and quality of life, sustainability as the key concept in environmental management. [NOTE: A good baseline scenario for anyone who thinks about the future.] **(Coates' trends to 2025)**

012

A Glimpse of the Future: Technology Forecasts for Global Strategists. McKinley Conway (President, Conway Data; founder, World Development Council). Norcross GA: Conway Data Inc (40 Technology Park/Atlanta), Nov 1992/103p(8x11")/$95.00pb.

Compiler of **Site World** (Conway Data, 1991; **FS Annual 1992** #10989), a guide to more than 700 "megaprojects" worldwide, offers pleasant introductory comments about the role of forecasting and futurism, and provides a lengthy checklist of: 1) changes in business strategy (executive outlook, locations and sites, facilities design, human and material resources, growth industries such as sports, fish farms and used human body parts [!]); 2) the global infrastructure (linkages, pipelines, rail, energy, water supply, urban forms); 3) the operating environment (political climate, social changes, catastrophic risks, ecosystem protection, weather); 4) changes in science and technology: biotechnology and health care, information systems, engineering, R&D facilities, space and spaceports, the "new science" of geo-economics). Each forecast is flagged with one of three time spans: 0-10 years, 10-20 years, and 20-30 years, with special flaggings for major developments of greatest global impact.

A summary chapter provides an overview of these major developments in each of the three time periods: **1) 0-10 Years**: genetic science revolution, a global anti-pollution crusade supported by all elements of society, new concepts of loop cities combined with high-speed rail so as to create "super metro areas", global communications with automatic language translation for almost everyone everywhere, a new global society of "globalists" (executives of global firms and globe-trotting government officials); **2) 10-20 Years**: implementation of a realistic global program for controlling population, using solar energy in highly efficient systems for desalinizing seawater in very large volumes (soon after 2000, this exciting development could result in huge new construction projects to deliver desalted water, notably in the Sonora desert, the Baja peninsula of Mexico, and parts of the Sahara desert), smart cars and smart roads (with robot-run vehicles on designated routes), domed cities and bubble farms (in which thousands of acres are covered by dome units), a new generation of SSTs and TAVs (trans-atmospheric vehicles), hydrogen as a fuel becomes cost-competitive with oil and use of solar power is widespread in sunny regions; **3) 20-30 Years**: linking human brains to computers (permitting downloading of wisdom to be shared with others and uploading to revolutionize education), new biotechnology discoveries to elevate millions of dysfunctional people to new roles (artificial eyesight for the blind, hearing for the deaf), effective means for neutralizing old nuclear wastes, rival companies offering inexpensive trips to the moon and space colonies supporting mining and tourism, improved materials enabling human-powered flight for non-athletes, an asteroid warning/defense system (with batteries of huge missiles) to prevent disastrous collisions.

Also includes chapters on dominant centers of R&D activity in the US, a 1986 paper looking back at a list of "geo-economic superlatives" for the 1956-1986 period (introduction of jet aircraft in 1960, construction of the interstate highway system, Mexico's Maquiladora program, inexpensive air conditioning), and a listing of over 600 science parks worldwide (the US leads with 304). [NOTE: Obviously upbeat about mega-technology and mega-construction, but at least some of these forecasts seem likely. This high-tech worldview contrasts markedly with others that are blind to *any* new techno-development, for better and/or worse. The report is addressed to corporate planners and not to scholars (thus the high price), and the documentation is skimpy. But it is a nicely handled synthesis, and very interesting to those who can afford it.] **(global infrastructure in 30 years)**

013
Crystal Globe: The Haves and Have-Nots of The New World Order. Marvin Cetron (President, Forecasting International, Arlington VA) and Owen Davies (Hancock NH; former *Omni* Senior Editor). NY: St. Martin's Press, Oct 1991/430p/$25.00; updated Oct 1992/$14.95pb.

The authors of **American Renaissance** (St Martin's, 1989; **FS Annual 1991** #10564), which hopefully forecasts that the US will be wealthier and more tranquil by 2000 and that we will live better in every way, go global with their forecast that "The world will be a more peaceful and prosperous place in the 1990s than it has been in the decades since WWII." Despite many uncertainties, the outlines of a new and more flexible world order are already [crystal?] clear. Despite local antagonisms and the ambitions of Third World rulers, peace will be restored by the joint effort of the entire world community (this fundamental change will be the guiding theme of the 1990s). No single nation will dominate this new global order. Military powers will be replaced by three powerful regional economic blocs, each group heavily influenced by its largest members: 1) the most powerful of these blocs will be the EC, the "role model for the post-postwar world"; by 2000, the European bloc will include some 23 nations with 520 million people; 2) in the Pacific Rim bloc, Japan will lose its industrial might in the 1990s, due to an aging population (by 2000, Japan will not be among the top ten economic forces); 3) in North America, "Canada will cease to exist as an independent dominion" by 2000 or soon thereafter [elsewhere this is qualified as a 60% probability], replaced by the nation of Quebec and four new US states; Mexico should have one of the most vibrant national economies in the world by 2000. As for the have-nots, the authors see Middle East accord between Israel and its neighbors by 2000 or earlier, more effective measures against terrorism, African economic growth outpaced by population growth and aggravated by AIDS, an end to apartheid in South Africa, "glimmers of hope" and partial economic integration for Latin America, uniformly dismal prospects in the "lands without hope" (Bangladesh, Cambodia, Myanmar, Pakistan), growing instability in India inhibiting its improved standard of living, and a reuniting of the two Chinas. Concludes that, "for much of the Third World, the political and economic changes of the 1990s will go largely unnoticed." [NOTE: A bit light (in the cause of crystal vision) and uneven, but still an interesting and sometimes provocative economics-oriented global tour through American eyes. Appendices provide profiles of 37 countries and describe 90 major trends changing the world.] **(three blocs and the have-nots in 2000)**

014
50 Trends Shaping the World, Marvin Cetron and Owen Davies, *The Futurist*, 25:5, Sept-Oct 1991, 11-21 (single copy $3.00 from WFS, with quantity discounts).

Adaptation of the 90 trends described in Appendix A of **Crystal Globe**. These 50 trends are arranged in 12 categories: **1) Population**: the population bomb still explodes in LDCs; millions dies from AIDS in the 1990s; new medical technologies make life longer and more comfortable in the industrialized world; **2) Food**: the family farm quickly disappears in the US and other developed nations in the 1990s; biotechnology brings new protein to LDCs; water will be plentiful in most regions and cheaper desalinization will make life easier in many desert areas in the next 20 years; **3) Energy**: oil prices will plummet to $7-9 per barrel by 2000, and growing competition from other energy sources will keep the price of oil down; **4) Environment**: air pollution and other atmospheric issues will dominate eco-policy discussions, with more attention paid to soot and other particulates; **5) Science and Technology**: high technological turnover rates are accelerating (today's technical knowledge will be only 1% of that available in 2050); **6) Communications**: networks will grow ever more rapidly in the 1990s; **7) Labor**: the labor force is aging rapidly in many countries; unions will continue to lose their hold; people will change occupations/jobs/residences more frequently; **8) Industry**: multinational companies will continue to grow and many new ones will appear; demands will increase for social responsibility; companies will be increasingly judged on how they treat the environment; government regulation will increase; **9) Education**: literacy will become a fundamental goal in developing societies; **10) World Economy**: world trade will grow 4.5% per year in the 1990s; all national currencies will be convertible around 2000; **11) Warfare**: the world has become "safer" for local or regional conflicts; brushfire wars will be more frequent and bloody; the US and USSR will sign a long procession of arms treaties in the 1990s to cut military expenses; **12) International Alignments**: "Quebec will secede from Canada, probably in 1996;" the remaining Canadian provinces will all be absorbed into the US by 2010; the UN and other major international organizations will become more important; international bodies will take over much of the peacekeeping role now being abandoned by the superpowers; the two Koreas will re-unite before 2000; the Soviet Union will become a confederation of 15 largely independent states. [NOTE: A quick and mostly unsurprising overview that extrapolates trends and conventional wisdoms of the moment.] **(50 world-shaping trends)**

015
Fast Forward: Where Technology, Demographics, and History Will Take America and the World in the Next Thirty Years. Richard Carlson (Spectrum Economics, Palo Alto CA) and Bruce Goldman (San Francisco CA). NY: HarperBusiness, April 1994/246p/$25.00.

Revised edition of **2020 Visions: Long View of a Changing World** (Portable Stanford, 1990; **FS Annual 1992** #11194), with an emphasis on technology as the driver of change, in an era when the chief conflict among developed nations will be economic (World War IV). The nations of the world will lie on a continuum depending on their smooth integration into the global system: taking the lead will be developed countries, followed by some 15 other countries and Southern China which are rapidly modernizing. The Soviet Union's remnants, most of Latin America, and the Arab Middle East are slowly modernizing but at risk; at great risk are much of Northern China, the Philippines, India, and Pakistan. Somalia, Ethiopia, much of Central Africa, Bangladesh, and Haiti are "near collapse." Chapters discuss: *1) The Global Economy*: foundations of globalization include trade, foreign investment, technology, television, and collective responsibility for environmental threats (the dark side of globalization includes Islamic fundamentalism, Maoism, and fanatical environmentalism); *2) Technotopia*: total access through merger of TV/telephones/computers, the rise of the "infostrainment industry" (certifiably independent info consultants comparing producer claims against product performance), many new materials, biotechnology (to rival electronics in dollar volume and social impact by 2020); *3) Demographic Tremors*: aging, migration pressures, ethnic cleansing, resegregation of US; *4) The World to Come*: nation-states will coalesce into megastates (massive confederations with common economic rules and joint military forces), political power will decentralize in large nations, developed nations will continue to be afflicted by terrorism; *5) The Eastern Hemisphere*: "the 21st century will be the European century"; instability in the Middle East, Asia as a headless giant with little regional unity, Japan's success as unsustainable, most of Africa to "slide into decades of chaos"; *6) The Western Hemisphere*: movement toward economic and ultimate political confederation throughout North America and the Caribbean, several Canadian provinces as US states by 2020, an expanding list of Latin American countries with strong growth prospects (with hemispheric free trade by 2020). Other chapters discuss the US economy (we are headed for at least a small-scale trade war in the 1990s), health care, environmental priorities, energy consumption (US consumption will hold steady through 2020; world demand will increase by 50%), housing and infrastructure, the dissolving community, a slow process ahead of decriminalizing drugs, education, and US politics (foreseeing a shift in political power from Federal and local levels to the states, and the rise of ethnic and environmental politics). [**NOTE**: Broad and popularly-written, with generally upbeat forecasts.]   (**US and global trends; megastates**)

016
G-Forces: Reinventing the World. The 35 Global Forces Restructuring Our Future. Frank Feather (President & CEO, Geo-Strategic Opportunity Development Corp, Toronto). Toronto: Summerhill Press (52 Shaftesbury Ave), Nov 1989/438p/Can$27.95 (dist. in Canada by U of Toronto Press; published in US by William Morrow in Aug 1990, and in Japan by Kodansha).

A futurist, consultant, and former international banker asserts that the complexity of persistent global problems, fragmented analyses, widespread disinformation, myths, and prejudice have all combined to form a dense fog of misunderstanding. "This fog obscures the massive global opportunities staring us in the face and creates confusion about the variety of constructive options open to us." Adopting a geo-strategic view will "blow away the fog and bring the real global future into focus—and within our grasp." Western nations have already moved beyond Toffler's "Third Wave" of services (following the 1st and 2nd Waves of agriculture and industry); we must also consider the 4th Wave of information, the 5th Wave of leisure and tourism, and the 6th wave of outer space. The six waves manifest themselves in varying strengths and speeds in different countries and regions, and are influenced by the 35 G-Forces that interact in a "4-STEP" long-wave cycle of global social development: Social, Technological, Economic, and Political. Chapters on each G-Forces are arranged in these four categories.

S) Social Motivation: Satisfying Psychological Drives: 1) stabilizing global population (the population explosion is not a problem; rather, it is one of managing population as a global resource); 2) feeding the future (the problem is inadequate distribution, storage, and packaging); 3) clean water for all (more efficient storage, usage, and disposal can meet the shortage problem); 4) global wellness (an opportunity for basic wellness for all by 2050 if we reinvent medical practice); 5) meaningful work for a globalized labor force ("the human race is succeeding magnificently at reducing its working hours and heading towards a 5th Wave leisure society by the mid-21st Century," if work is redefined, reduced, and redistributed in various ways); 6) housing the future in super-cities (there is no shortage of land or materials; new high-tech and low-tech approaches can meet the challenge; it is possible to have large but efficient and humane cities); 7) sexual and racial harmony (women and "non-white" people will gain visibility and be the primary builders of the future; the end of patriarcy is a major G-Force); 8) globalizing values, beliefs, and culture (movement toward a single global community consciousness, aided by cultural mixing and globalized media); 9) the untapped capability of educated people (education must be geared to a changing future, and instructional productivity boosted by computers.

T) Technological Innovation: Creating the Info-Rich Leisure Society: 10) eliminating hard work (the driving force of technological advance will drastically reduce work hours to 24 hours or less per week by the end of the 1990s for most Western populations); 11) the drive for productivity and efficiency; 12) global sharing of information and technology, boosting the creation of wealth; 13) growing computer power as new microchips are developed; 14) a real-time info-globalized network of information utilities (the global electronic highway of ISDN); 15) the techno-leadership of Japan; 16) pushing back high-tech frontiers (brain/mind research, nanotechnology, biotech, new materials); 17) an info-rich world, substituting information for mass.

E) Economic Modernization: Redistributing Planetary Riches: 18) Atlantic "sunset" and Pacific "sunrise" (Japan as the major economic and political force in East Asia and the world); 19) industrializing the Third World ("if we manage ourselves properly, we should all get rich"); 20) reinventing the global financial system after a Mini-Depression in the early 1990s (based on a 57-year economic mega-cycle); 21) the Planetary Information Economy creating a "growing pie" (the rich-poor gap will not close by 2050, "but it will shrink remarkably"); 22) ending global energy shortages (declining oil intensity, conservation potentials, fusion reactors, solar energy); 23) resource self-sufficiency (through declining resource intensity, recycling); 24) restoring the planet's environment (ecological deficits are temporary, as we learn how to manage better and take a long-term view); 25) reinventing capitalism and communism (neither are suited to the postindustrial Planetary Information Economy, as cooperation replaces competition); 26) converting military waste to earthly eco-development (a shift to sustainable development and the 6th Wave Outer-Space economy will generate great wealth).

P) Political Reformation: Restructuring Political Power: 27) disarming the planet (the need to redefine national security and create a global disarmament governance system for all weaponry); 28) the traumatic rebirth of America (the US is in danger of burning out rather dramatically, but it can revive and economically integrate with Canada and Mexico by 2000 to become "Amexicana"; 29) perestroika (Soviet economic output will at least double between 1985 and 2000, and the USSR will gain much relative economic power as the Western economies suffer from Mini-Depression); 30) Soviet unification of Europe (likely emergence of a "United Soviet States of Europe" in the early 21st century, in accord with the trend toward socialism in Western Europe; a reunified but politically neutral Germany will allow Soviets to politically dominate); 31) Japan as number one in global technology (and cultivator of "global community consciousness"); 32) China's economic modernization for late 21st century super-stardom (politically, though, "China is still ruled by a feudal mentality"); 33) Third World solidarity and independence from the developed countries; 34) informed "partocracy" (participatory democracy) in the Western information society; 35) cooperative globalized governance (the final step in reinventing the world, with restructuring of the UN into four cooperation councils: Social, Technological, Economic, and Political). Concludes that all that is needed is better management, including a Mission Statement for planet Earth. [NOTE: An impressive tour de force, integrating ideas of many leading futurists, sprinkled with interesting data and charts, and aggressively upbeat throughout. All of the G-Forces are iffy, some appear very unlikely (#29 on perestroika), and others overlap (#15 and #31 on Japan, #13, #14, #17, and #21 on infotech). Still, it's a provocative and useful framework.]

(geostrategic view of G-Forces)

017
Megatrends 2000: Ten New Directions for the 1990's. John Naisbitt and Patricia Aburdene (Megatrends Ltd, Washington DC). NY: William Morrow and Co, Jan 1990/384p/$21.95.

"Before us is the most important decade in the history of civilization, a period of stunning technological innovation, unprecedented economic opportunity, surprising political reform, and great cultural rebirth." The new megatrends—"the most important trends of the 1990s"—are the gateways to the 21st century. **1) The Global Economic Boom**: the world is entering a period of economic prosperity; North America, Europe and Japan will form a golden triangle of free trade; there will be an abundance of natural resources throughout the 1990s; there will be no energy crisis. **2) Renaissance in the Arts**: as the affluent information economy spreads, the need to reexamine the meaning of life through the arts has followed; "during the 1990s the arts will gradually replace sports as society's primary leisure activity" [!???]; corporate involvement in the arts will deepen, and arts funding is growing at the state and local level. **3) Emergence of Free-Market Socialism**: the welfare state has been dismantled in the UK and the command economy has been dismantled in the USSR; the world is undergoing a profound shift to economies run by markets. **4) Global Lifestyles and Cultural Nationalism**: a new universal consumer-driven lifestyle is spreading, along with a powerful countertrend to assert the uniqueness of one's culture. **5) Privatization of the Welfare State**: shift of the state sector to private enterprise worldwide; growth of workfare in the US; a shift of focus from class or group to individual empowerment. **6) Rise of the Pacific Rim**: the world's trade center is shifting from the Atlantic to the Pacific; Asia has half the world's population and will have two-thirds by 2000; the driving force is the "economic miracle of Asia;" California is the US gateway to the Pacific Rim—America's Megastate. **7) The 1990s—Decade of Women in Leadership**: "men and women are on an equal playing field in corporate America" [!??]; the proportion of women is increasing in many professions and women dominate the information society; **8) The Age of Biology**: a shift from the models and metaphors of physics to those of biology, as biotechnology becomes a powerful presence in our lives. **9) Religious Revival**: religious belief is intensifying worldwide under the pull of the millennial year 2000; the worldwide charismatic movement has tripled in the last decade to nearly 300 million; in turbulent times of great change, people head for the two extremes of fundamentalism and personal spiritual experience (New Agers represent 5-10% of the US population). **10) Triumph of the Individual**: the great unifying theme at the end of the 20th century, happening simultaneously with globalization; new technologies have empowered the individual (e.g., videocassettes as the ultimate in narrowcasting). Concludes that wealth has not led to increased greed; "The developed world's economic boom will be the foundation for higher evolution and global affluence." And the post-cold war era will see the US and USSR collaborate on the environment and on ending poverty.

[NOTE: It's easy to take potshots at this exhuberant hyperbole, written in digestible short paragraphs. *Time* magazine, for example, calls the book "millennial mega-babble" and views the authors as "foremost of the 21st century ecstatics" (8 Jan 1990, p72). Yet, there are new slants on common ideas (global economy, Pacific Rim) and some fresh and provoking notions here (triumph of the individual, women in leadership, renaissance of the arts), worth considering even though exaggerated in many ways. What should be understood is that this is a prime example of *creaming the future*. Indeed, the authors even acknowledge that "our market niche in the vast world of information is to highlight some of the positive" (p15). It's a fun read, upbeat, provocative, and inspiring to some—and it makes big bucks from New Agish Reagan-Bush yuppies (the ideology is clearly there, although not openly stated). Don't confuse this with even-handed truth-seeking about present trends and likely futures; it tends to infotainment and/or religion. Yet, paradoxically, Naisbitt is widely seen as a—if not *the*—leading US futurist, even as he and his wife deny the label and call themselves social forecasters (the garish book jacket touts both authors as "the world's leading trend forecasters"). And it is this image of the bubbly, hip-shooting pop futurist that complicates the enterprise of serious futures-thinking.]

(Megatrends II)

018
Wild Cards: Preparing for "The Big One," John D. Rockfellow (Senior Fellow, Copenhagen Institute for Futures Studies, Denmark), *The Futurist,* 28:1, Jan-Feb 1994, 14-19.

A major earthquake in California [or in Japan—see **FS Annual 1993 #11622**] is but one example of wild cards, or events with less than 10% chance of occurring. The Copenhagen Institute, along with the Institute for the Future (US) and Bipe Conseil (France) collaborated on a report, **Wild Cards: A Multinational Perspective**. Some possible futures: *1) Hong Kong Rules China:* Hong Kong, Taiwan, and the five special economic zones of mainland China become supernovas and dominate mainland China; *2) Europe Goes Regional:* the nation-state dismantled by 2000 in favor of strong regional representation; *3) The No-Carbon Economy:* a green tax on fossil fuels discourages their use, and many nations agree on a "no carbon" economy by 2050; tax revenues finance new energy sources; *4) The Group of Seventy:* the Group of Seven leading industrial countries becomes the new Group of Seventy and dominates global negotiations over trade; *5) Loss of Financial Underpinnings:* the Japanese real estate market completely collapses around 1995, and foreign investments are repatriated to cover debts; *6) End of the Nation-State:* the success of international organizations results in a power shift away from the nation-state; *7) Third World Exodus:* the rich-poor gap widens, and people migrate en masse from poorer countries by 2000; *8) The New Chernobyl:* a nuclear accident in the Slovak Republic in 1995, involving a Soviet-built reactor, leads to public pressure that forces abandonment of nuclear power. **(global wild cards)**

2. Evolution and Long-Term Futures

019
Evolution: The Grand Synthesis. Ervin Laszlo (Pisa, Italy). Preface by Alexander King (Club of Rome). Foreword by Jonas Salk. Boston: New Science Library/Shambhala (dist. by Random House), May 1987/211p/$10.95pb.

Author of the Club of Rome's 1977 report on Goals for Mankind and former Director of UNITAR offers a "preliminary sketch" of the main elements of a grand synthesis that unites physical, biological, and social evolution into a consistent framework. Evolution is the maker of the future, and the rising evolutionary paradigm is a major step in the advance of contemporary science, marking an era in which evolution is becoming conscious of itself. Laszlo describes fundamental concepts of the new evolutionary sciences (systems in the third or nonlinear state, convergence to higher levels, cross-catalytic feedback loops, etc.), evolution of matter and life, and the evolution of society (subject to the same laws as those governing natural systems). The dynamics of social evolution concern the progressive yet discontinuous development of society's collective information pool (culture broadly defined).

Intervention in the processes of social change is of vital importance. Evolution can be purposively steered, and the future of humanity depends on the success of such steering. All societies today are embedded in a tightening web of increasing interaction and interdependence. But most nation-states are highly specialized and forced into narrow niches in world production systems, markets, and politics. Having much less diversity, specialist species and peripheral countries are increasingly vulnerable to crises as the pace of change accelerates. The way beyond these crises is the acceleration of transnational convergence. Specialized societies need to master transnational flows through coordinated and cooperative regional structures.

(need to steer social evolution)

020
The New Evolutionary Paradigm. Edited by Ervin Laszlo (Rector, Vienna Academy for the Study of the Future). Foreword by Ilya Prigogine. World Futures General Evolution Series, Vol 2 (Keynote Volume). NY: Gordon and Breach Science Publishers, 1991/204p/$33.00.

A joint effort by members of the General Evolution Research Group, formed at a 1986 meeting at the Salk Institute. The common focus for evolution of nature and society is conceived as "irreversible and nonlinear change in domains far from thermodynamic equilibrium." The nine chapters: *1)* **Ralph H. Abraham** on complex dynamical systems theory (a general introduction to the mathematical underpinnings of general evolution theory); *2)* **David Loye** on chaos and transformation (chaos gives birth to order over and over again; in light of this, we need investment in normative social science); *3)* **Gianluca Bocchi** on the changing image of biological evolution (the Darwinian idea of gradual development is increasingly questioned by new thinking from many fields); *4)* **Jonathan Schull** on evolution and intelligence (suggesting a functional model of adaptive behavior); *5)* **Vilmos Csanyi** and **György Kampis** on modelling biological and social change (applying a replicative model to the modern social crisis); *6)* **Robert Artigiani** on a nonequilibrium systems model of social evolution (language and society co-evolving in a mutually reinforcing process); *7)* **Pentti Malaska** on the transformational dynamics approach to economic and social evolution (suggesting a future policy focus on adaptation by means of intensive growth and renewal of needs); *8)* **Mika Pantzar** on linking the evolutionary paradigm to neoclassical economics; *9)* **Riane Eisler** on stages of sociocultural evolution from a gender-holistic perspective (concluding that we are at the threshold of a major societal bifurcation). [NOTE: The leading edge to guiding world futures—or an unnecessary over-complexification that distracts from the tasks at hand?]

[ALSO SEE: Other volumes in the General Evolution Series: Vol 1, **Nature and History: The Evolutionary Approach for Social Scientists** by Ignazio Masulli (1991); Vol 3, **The Age of Bifurcation: Understanding the Changing World** by Ervin Laszlo (1992/126p/$33.00); Vol 4, **Cooperation: The End of the Age of Competition** edited by Allan Combs (1992). For papers and book reviews, see the quarterly edited by Laszlo since 1981, *World Futures: The Journal of General Evolution* ($113/year from G&B, Box 786, Cooper Station, NYC 10276).] **(evolution: new thinking)**

*021
The Choice: Evolution or Extinction? A Thinking Person's Guide to Global Issues. Ervin Laszlo (Montescudaio, Italy). Afterword by Federico Mayor (Director-General, UNESCO). NY: Jeremy P. Tarcher/Putnam, Aug 1994/215p/$17.95.

"Our generation is called upon to make the choice that will decide our ultimate destiny....We are forced to choose, for the processes we have initiated in our lifetime cannot continue in the lifetime of our children." The four parts discuss: *1) The Threat to Survival:* drivers of the grand transition (informatization, and globalization of government and business), the five shock waves of this century (communism, fascism, decolonialization, glasnost, and *global stress* caused by poverty, overpopulation, militarization, and environmental degradation), obsolete beliefs and misguided practices (the "Neolithic illusion" that nature is infinite, economic blind spots, policy specialization and fragmentation); *2) The Imperatives of Perception:* the urgent need for evolutionary literacy, preserving the integrity of the world's cultures within the "culture of interexistence," catalyzing social creativity (the role of science, art, religion, and education); *3) The Imperatives of Action:* three basic rules (think globally, act morally, live responsibly), priorities of human development so as to escape the dinosaur syndrome (providing the necessary minimum of education, free and unbiased channels of communication, relevant and reliable information), strengthening UNESCO (which is active in all of the domains where priority action is called for), creating a functional world order ("a global peacekeeping system, an ecologic authority, and a financial regulatory body would serve every nation's interest; they would not impair the autonomy of national and local decision-making in other

policy domains"), thorough reform of the UN system (better coordination of agencies, and opening membership to regional organizations, multinational business and NGOs);
4) The Outlook: signs of hope (value change, green politics, the shift in corporate culture, the shift toward a systems paradigm in science, articulation of a new theology), the hope for an "evolutionary future" where some societies develop highly advanced environmental technology while others evolve in different ways guided more by social and spiritual goals ("a world of this kind would be diverse, but not inequitable and unjust"). [**NOTE**: Concludes with a selected list of 26 books by Laszlo on evolution, systems thinking, and world problems. Laszlo is a member of The Club of Rome, President of The Budapest Club, and Director of Planetary Citizens.]

(**action for an evolutionary future**)

022

To Govern Evolution: Further Adventures of the Political Animal. Walter Truett Anderson (Albany CA). Boston and San Diego: Harcourt Brace Jovanovich, March 1987/376p/$22.95.

Talk about the need for humanity to live within nature is empty rhetoric. Rather, human power in nature is the ultimate political issue. The central political problem of our time is that we literally do not know what we are doing: we have no concept of a politics that fits the reality of the present situation. Governance is inextricably connected with the growing human responsibility for everything "evolution" implies: the survival and extinction of species, the changing ecology of the planet, and the biological condition of the human species itself. Evolution is no longer a mechanistic process obeying the logic of natural selection: today the driving force in evolution is human intelligence. It is not the case that the human species *ought* to take responsibility, rather, we are already involved. As we increasingly move into an age of human power over the workings of nature, we will have to come to terms with this reality. We have made the transition into acts of evolutionary governance, but we have not yet developed a concept of this governance. The central project of the coming era is to create a global social and political order commensurate to human power in nature. This requires an ethic of responsibility and appropriate ways of thinking about new issues and making decisions. But many are still avoiding responsibility in the belief that they are apolitical: some environmentalists simply think that humans should stop interfering in nature, neo-Darwinists argue that we need not worry because species come and go, and fundamentalist Christians think that we should make maximum use of God's resources. Matters of evolutionary policy must become everyone's business, and Anderson stresses "further adventures" as a way of recognizing danger while carrying a banner of enterprise and hope.

Concludes that the various problems and issues can be seen as a set of evolutionary political adventures or undertakings that have already begun: 1) restoration of the Earth as a global learning project; 2) the eugenics project of guiding human evolution through genetic screening, new reproductive technologies, etc.; 3) the population project that attempts to place a limit on the growth of human numbers; 4) the genetic resources project to maintain a store of genetic information and protect species from extinction; 5) the attempt to promulgate a general idea of the rights of animals and other living things; 6) the genetic technology project of creating new forms of life. We must create a biopolitical culture to raise the level of public awareness and produce well-informed citizens of a biopolitical age. [**NOTE**: A fresh prod in useful directions, although avowedly lacking specifics.]

(**need to consciously govern evolution**)

023

Beyond Natural Selection. Robert Wesson (Senior Research Fellow, Hoover Institute). Cambridge MA: MIT Press, July 1991/353p/$29.95.

A "political scientist who has undergone ecdysis" challenges the limited reductionist view of evolution. The universe is incomprehensibly complex in its foundations, and organisms are the acme of complexity. Evolution is not a single process but a conglomerate of interactions. It involves many kinds of systems, each interacting with innumerable systems at its own and other levels. "It is doubtful that there can be any theory both logically coherent and broad enough to cover the manifold aspects of evolution." Conventional theory, indulging the old daydream of a universe like a great clockwork, is incomplete despite or because of its neatness and the logical charm of building on a few axioms. Adaptation often fails to correspond with habitat, many traits are seemingly independent of adaptive needs, and evolution often has apparently maladaptive outcomes. The thrust of evolution has now become the cultural development of humanity; information stored in nucleic acid has been supplemented or swamped by information humanly produced and symbolically stored. We have thus largely freed ourselves from the givens of the biological past. We have even partly freed ourselves from our own cultural past as we fashion a changing present. As evolution advances, it derives less from chance and more from choice. If wise enough, humans can make their own evolution. "If there is to be a next stage for humanity, it has to rest on new, broader, more humane values, in dedication to common needs of this possibly imperiled species." [**NOTE**: Good for overturning conventional theory. As regards human action, though, a similar argument is made in much greater detail by Walter Truett Anderson in **To Govern Evolution** (above), curiously not mentioned among the 600 references cited.]   (**evolution theory reconsidered**)

024

Invariances and Determinism in Global Forecasting, John Platt (deceased; Prof Emeritus, U of Michigan), *Futures Research Quarterly*, 9:2, Summer 1993, 23-32.

In this generation, the world is passing through the greatest evolutionary jump in human history, a "unique metamorphosis." Technology drives social change today. A "technological determinism" occurs when we rush into an evolutionary valley, when technosocial inventions are feasible and desired by all. Determinism of this kind can be used, within limits, to make social and global forecasts for the next few decades that will be relatively invariant to the turbulence of events. These invariances can be found in three different categories: **1) Ongoing Social Consequences of Present Technologies**: the end of colonialism, the rise of a multi-polar world, global TV penetrating all borders, the increase in refugees and migrants forcing cultural diversity, the increase in health and longevity, an increase of education in all countries, decline of mainline Western religions, perhaps an end to large-scale armies and wars, extinction of species and heightening of environmental concern, the international environmental movement as perhaps the strongest force for global integration; **2) Probable Consequences of New Technologies Just Ahead**: world population may level off or drop due to more efficient contraceptives and abortifacients, new ranges of crime and terrorism made easier by mobility, an ever-growing "informational feast," mounting pressure for global reorganization and integration; 3) **Long-Range Limits and Self-Maintaining Patterns**: limits to growth and adjustment to sustainable patterns, a balancing of interests leading to guaranteed entitlements and ombudsmen in all organizations. In sum, "the human race, if it survives, cannot help but become something like an integrated global organism." It will not be a dictatorship. We will move together because we have to. "After this great shock front has passed, we might go on for generations or centuries in the new world with nothing like this rate of change and reorganization again." [NOTE: A final, thought-provoking overview (albeit somewhat upbeat) from one of America's great futurists.]

(**probable global future in next few decades**)

025
Awakening Earth: Exploring the Evolution of Human Culture and Consciousness. Duane Elgin (Mill Valley CA). NY: William Morrow, Oct 1993/390p/$23.00.

Author of **Voluntary Simplicity** (Morrow, 1981,1993; **FS Annual 1994** #12323) warns that Earth's biosphere is being severely wounded, even crippled, by humanity. Yet through humanity, the Earth is awakening as a conscious global organism. "Pushed by the harsh reality of an injured Earth, the human family is being challenged to realize a new level of identity, responsibility, and purpose." To be sustainable, a civilization must maintain the integrity of its physical, social, and spiritual foundations. To seek only to survive is not sufficient for long-term sustainability—we need a shared and compelling sense of purpose and potential for living together as a world civilization. Two views of evolution are dominant today: *materialism* (where matter is considered the primary reality) and *transcendentalism* (which emphasizes rising above the material world). But these old approaches no longer work in isolation from each other. A third, *co-evolutionary view* is emerging that integrates East and West, viewing reality as comprised equally of matter and consciousness in a mutually supportive spiral of development that can produce a sustainable, planetary civilization.

Our highest potential as a species is our ability to achieve full self-reflective consciousness. Developing our capacity for reflective knowing, both personally and socially, is a paramount evolutionary challenge. To fully coevolve our capacity, humanity must work through major stages of development. Chapters are devoted to: 1) contracted consciousness and the archaic era, beginning roughly 35,000 years ago; 2) surface consciousness and the era of awakening hunter-gatherers; 3) depth consciousness and the era of agrarian-based civilizations (includes most of recorded human history; basic arts of civilization developed, although most individual lived as impoverished peasants); 4) dynamic consciousness and the scientific-industrial era (an era of moral relativism, intellectual absolutism, nation-state egotism, and technological giantism, that separated humans from nature, the divine Life-force, and other persons; 5) reflective consciousness and the era of communication and reconciliation (an epoch of profound stress and challenge, as humanity copes with the problems of the scientific-industrial era, and engages in economic, ecological, political, spiritual, racial, ethnic, gender, and generational reconciliation); 6) oceanic consciousness and the bonding and building era (will begin with great confidence in knowing we made it through a perilous transition and now share a common vision of a workable future; a fermenting global culture will emerge, and a system of global governance could be developed); 7) flow consciousness and the surpassing era (the strength of human bonding enables the world to liberate its creativity); 8) integral awareness and the initial maturity of planetary civilization (emergence of a wisdom culture that balances being and becoming, unity and diversity). Humanity could move very fast through the stages of growth essential to realizing maturity, perhaps within another dozen generations, or roughly 500 years (due to exponential growth in communications technology and the push of global crises). But our future is not predetermined: we can fill out these stages of development in whatever way and with whatever timing we choose. And we are only halfway through the stages of growth to initial maturity.

The problem at the moment is that five different perceptual paradigms coexist on the planet: hunter-gatherers (much less than 1%), agriculturalists (roughly half of the world population), industrialists (those in urban settings, soon to be a majority), communicationists (those influenced by the global consciousness of the new communications), and Gaians (planetary citizens with a strong sense of global family and global bonding). By the mid-21st century, a majority of humanity could begin to coalesce within the Gaian perceptual context as a common organizing paradigm. Pitfalls on the path to maturity include inflexibility and delay, lack of vision, severe ecosystem disruption, resource wars, authoritarianism, lack of rich-poor reconciliation, information wars between authoritarian leaders and hackers, biological warfare (the poor terrorist's nuclear weapon), religious fanaticism, or planetary psychosis. Priority needs for building a sustainable and satisfying future: breaking the cultural hypnosis of consumerism, designing ecological ways of living, sharing a compelling vision of the future, developing a conscious democracy, nurturing a reflective perceptual paradigm, and reconciling our polarities. [NOTE: Challenging, thoughtful, original, well-documented, and plausibly hopeful.]

(**evolution toward a sustainable society**)

026
The Universe Story: From the Primordial Flaring Forth to the Ecozoic Era—A Celebration of the Unfolding of the Cosmos. Brian Swimme (San Francisco) and Thomas Berry (Bronx, NY). San Francisco: HarperSanFrancisco, Dec 1992/305p/$22.00.

The Director of the Center for the Story of the Universe at the California Institute of Integral Studies teams with the author of **The Dream of the Earth** (Sierra Club, 1988; **FS Annual 1990** #9591) to provide a comprehensive story of the universe for modern times. Aimed at the general reader, the authors seek to provide a new unity to the educational process and "the comprehensive context of the future" as we enter the Ecozoic era. Chapters describe the primordial flaring forth 15 billion years ago, galaxies and supernovas, the sun, the first life on Earth 4 billion years ago, plants and animals in the Paleozoic era 550 million years ago, human emergence 2.6 million years ago, Neolithic settlements of 12,000 years ago, classical civilizations, the rise of nation-states, and the change of consciousness toward viewing the universe as an irreversible sequence of transformations. The final chapter describes transition from the Cenozoic era of the last 67 million years to the Ecozoic era where the well-being of the planet is a condition for the well-being of any of the component members of the planetary community. The first law of economics must be to preserve the economic viability of the planet; the first commitment of the medical profession must be to preserve the health of the planet; the basic concern of religion must be to preserve the natural world as the primary revelation of the divine. The dominant issue of the immediate future will be the tension between plunderers and preservers, the mechanistic and the organic, and anthropocentric and biocentric norms. The immediate goal of the Ecozoic is to alter the mode of consciousness that has been responsible for devastation of the planet. The overall objective is to assist in establishing a mutually enhancing human presence on Earth, based on an Earth-centered language. [NOTE: A very ambitious cosmic integration of past, present, and future, based on contemporary science: is there any better "story of the Earth" for our time?] **(transition to Ecozoic era)**

027
Sacred Eyes. L. Robert Keck, Ph.D. (Boulder CO). Indianapolis IN: Knowledge Systems Inc, Dec 1992/297p/ $18.95.

Methodist minister and corporate wellness consultant states that "we are living in an extraordinary time, a crucial juncture in history." To be able to see what is important in a time like this—to envision what is being born and what is dying in the womb/tomb of transformation—we must be able to look deeply into soul-level territory. If we look with cynical eyes we see a truncated vision, bereft of hope. In like manner, pessimistic eyes see only evidence to support despair. "It is with sacred eyes that we can see the larger, more realistic, picture." Sacred eyes can penetrate through the opaqueness of materialism and reductionism, can penetrate the chaos of our current time to see "the pattern that connects," and can envision the emerging values of the 21st century. If we look deeply into humanity's soul we can see a new hope emerging, an epoch-sized transformation of the human psyche, a growth spurt of spiritual maturity. "Many futurists analyze the content of newspapers and the activity on the culture's surface in order to ascertain the trends of today, and then extrapolate them into the future as a means of predicting our tomorrows." A larger and deeper picture can give us a more accurate analysis: "only with Deep Value Trend Analysis can we know the values that will endure into the 21st century so as to really shape our future."

It is clear that humanity is on an evolutionary journey of maturation similar to that of the individual. In Epoch I, we grew up through a childhood in which our purpose was to develop physically, with a value system that was basically feminine. In Epoch II we matured into our collective adolescence in which the purpose was ego and mental development, with an essentially masculine value system. In Epoch III, at the end of the 20th century, we are moving into adulthood and spiritual maturation, defined by five major values: 1) holism and synergy, as we mature beyond the need for patriarchal and hierarchical proclivities; 2) empowerment of people in a "new era of spiritual democracy" (discovery of the power within oneself and within relationships that will transform life as we know it); 3) change as a thoroughly permeating condition of life (and the ability to view change as user-friendly); 4) re-membering human-nature that was dis-membered in the adolescent phase (returning to at-one-ment with nature); 5) historical integrity: discovering anew how our body, mind, and spirit form a unity. Concludes that "the transformation in which we are living is huge—nothing less than the emergence of a new heaven and a new earth and, consequently, a new God and a new humanity." [NOTE: Typically New Age, with the avid embracing of "holism" while in fact taking a rather narrow view that focuses on the middle-class North American individual and ignores society, poverty, resources, and technology. The metaphor of human maturation has been used before in Alfred Korzybski's widely popular **Manhood of Humanity** (Dutton, 1921), and the stage theory is much like the transition from Epoch A to Epoch B proclaimed by Jonas Salk in **The Survival of the Wisest** (Harper & Row, 1973), or the not-yet-realized transition from Consciousness II to Consciousness III espoused by Charles A. Reich in **The Greening of America** (Random House, 1970). Otherwise the book seems amply documented, mentioning such thinkers as David Bohm, Fritjof Capra, Riane Eisler, Willis Harman, Jean Houston, Sam Keen, George Leonard, Ilya Prigogine, and William Irwin Thompson.] **(transformation to Epoch III maturation)**

028
The Creative Imperative: A Four-Dimensional Theory of Human Growth & Planetary Evolution. Charles M. Johnston, M.D. (Director, Institute for Creative Development, Seattle, WA). Berkeley, CA: Celestial Arts (900 Medoc), 1986/407p/$14.95pb.

We stand today at a critical threshold in the evolution of the species, demanding wisdom and maturity beyond any we have ever known. We must find more inclusive and vital ways of comprehending our reality—perspectives large enough to embrace the fact of our being living beings—and place that fact at the center of the human equation. A new model is presented, based on an understanding of creative dynamics, making it possible to think four-dimensionally about any developmental process and to understand our present place in the evolution of culture. Culture is seen as a creative process, organized according to a predictable sequence of formative configurations. In the future, we should see four developments in all spheres: 1) the realization of post-material understanding; 2) the creative integration of traditional polarities; 3) achievement of personal and global identity; 4) creative integration of previous stage-specific realities. These four parameters are applied to general patterns of global change, education, business and economics, the arts, awareness of the whole of our health, participatory governance, science and technology, and spirituality.

(evolution of culture)

029
Tempest, Flute, and Oz: Essays on the Future. Frederick Turner (Prof of Arts and Humanities, U of Texas-Dallas). NY: Persea Books (60 Madison Ave), Aug 1991/ 165p/$19.95.

We stand on the verge of a new epoch of culture and history. Revolutions in Eastern Europe and the movement toward democracy in many countries are signs of an emerging *new cultural worldview*. Turner seeks to assess these changes, and develops an explanatory myth based on Shakespeare's **The Tempest**, Mozart's **The Magic Flute**, and the beloved 1939 movie of L. Frank Baum's **Wizard of Oz**. The mythic story is a renegotiation of the contract that the human race entered into in Eden, as told in countless human mythologies—a story we will need to take us on the next stage of our collective human journey. Some basic traits of the new movement to succeed modernism: environmental consciousness, a desire for world peace (explicitly rejecting the myth of conflict), and scientific ideas such as the evolving universe, the place of human beings in nature, and new knowledge of the brain and of human nature. These ideas overturn the socio-economic determinism of the left, and are fatal to the ethnocentrism, sexism, and racism of the far right. The naturalistic and evolutionary theologies that are emerging are likewise anathema to religious fundamentalism.

Essays discuss the powerful solvents (telecommunications, the global ecological crisis, multinational corporations) that are dissolving the elements of culture throughout the world so as to bring them into contact and even fusion, a new-old synthesis of values (in which economic value, truth value, ethical value, and aesthetic value can all be coherently accommodated), our future evolution as a species, and two proposals for our work as a species in the next millennium: the transformation of the planet Mars into a living ecology and the development of artificial intelligence as a deep cultural and artistic project. Concludes that we are at a remarkable juncture in our own history and of the history of the cosmos: when evolution becomes fully self-aware. The wholeness of the universe is an emergent property, and as more and more sensitive organisms evolve to observe it, so the universe assumes more and more a coherent unity. [**NOTE**: Frontier thinking, best appreciated by those with a humanities background.] **(evolving cultural worldview)**

030
The Revelation: Our Crisis Is a Birth. Barbara Marx Hubbard (Greenbrae CA). Sonoma CA 95476: The Foundation for Conscious Evolution (PO Box 1941), May 1993/363p/$25.00;$16.95pb.

Addressed to those across the face of the Earth with a profound attraction for the evolution of ourselves and our world. "We are a future-oriented family of humanity who sense within ourselves the birth of the Universal Human." This book, based on Hubbard's larger **Book of Co-Creation** (forthcoming), calls on this transcendent community—founders of a New Order of the Future—to fulfill our destiny as catalysts for a planetary awakening to the next stage of our evolution. The text is in three sections: 1) **The Journey**: tells the author's personal story from daughter of a New York toy manufacturer to Connecticut mother of five and homemaker, to discovering Teilhard de Chardin and Bucky Fuller, hearing the inner words to tell the story of the birth of humankind as one body, developing the Committee for the Future in 1970 and the SYNCON (synergistic convergence) process as a tiny microcosm of "synocracy," finding the Christ-light in 1979, encountering the New Testament, and discovering the feminine energy to guide science and democracy toward synergistic co-operation in building new worlds on Earth; 2) **The Revelation**: as an alternative to Armageddon (the scenario of violence), offers a gentle path to the next phase of evolution—a Planetary Birth Experience that can occur in our lifetime by awakening a critical mass of inspired individuals; the next stage is a loving path to the New Jerusalem, a community of natural Christs, the birth of Universal Humanity [with many passages cited from the New Testament, along with the Higher Voices]; 3) **A Call to a New Order of the Future**: a letter of invitation to join the New Order, the Planetary Birth Communion ceremony, a Declaration of Intention to Build a Common Union of Co-Creative Consciousness, a Core Library for Conscious Evolution (about 50 briefly annotated books), also describes TOGETHERNET (Together Foundation, Burlington VT; 802/862-2030) that will share information on a planetary awakening. [ALSO SEE: *An Interview with Barbara Marx Hubbard* (*The Futurist*, 27:5, Sept-Oct 1993, 38-42.] **(Planetary Birth Experience)**

031
The Life Era: Cosmic Selection and Conscious Evolution. Eric Chaisson (Richard Physicist, Lincoln Laboratories, MIT). NY: The Atlantic Monthly Press (420 Lexington Ave), June 1987/259p/$19.95.

Cosmic evolution is the study of the many varied changes in the assembly and composition of energy, matter and life in the Universe—a cosmology wherein life plays an integral role, and the scaffolding for a modern humanism. This companion volume to **Cosmic Dawn: The Origins of Matter and Life** (Atlantic-Little, Brown, 1981) considers our cosmic heritage, the history of the idea of change (demonstrating continuity in the development of the idea throughout the ages), efforts now underway to explain the physical and biological order of our world, and two preeminent changes in the history of the Universe. The first change was from the energy era to the mass era, as matter evolved to control radiative energy. We are now beginning to experience a second great change, as the emergence of technologically intelligent life on Earth enables life to control matter. As we enter the Life Era—an era of opportunity that we ourselves have helped create—matter is now losing its total dominance. Within a few generations, we should be a type-I civilization, capable of controlling the resources of Earth. The next step in the development of a Life Era, a type-II civilization, entails manipulation of one's parent star system, as terrestrial energy resources necessarily become depleted over the next several centuries. A type-III civilization, if possible to achieve, would able to exploit an entire galaxy.

A concluding chapter describes implications for the Life Era, the most important being the rapid development of a global culture that embraces a planetary ethics concerned with what is best for all humankind. A program for evolutionary humanism requires a broadened education (in contrast to our present intellectual efforts, which are "grossly imbalanced against generalization and synthesis"), an ethical synthesis between the two leading politico-economic systems of our planet, and harmonious co-existence between individual humans and the planetary state. **(evolutionary humanism for a Life Era)**

032
Metaman: The Merging of Humans and Machines into a Global Superorganism. Gregory Stock (Visiting Senior Fellow, School of Public and Intl. Affairs, Princeton U). NY: Simon & Schuster, Sept 1993/365p/$24.00.

The Gaia hypothesis of life as a single living organism expresses the connectedness of all living things in our planetary ecosystem and provides a poetic image of earth. But it offers little insight into *our* future because it views human civilization as largely irrelevant. Biophysicist Stock focuses on the biological nature and significance of modern civilization as the key to understanding the future of humankind. "Metaman" is a superorganism—a community of organisms so fully tied together that it is a single living being. It also includes the nonhuman elements and structures (crops, livestock, machines, buildings) that are part of the human enterprise. Human activity has organized itself into large functional patterns that join to sustain the entirety of Metaman. "Metaman is that part of humanity, its creations, and its activities that is interdependent." It is an extension of the animal kingdom, a major evolutionary transition to a new level of complexity, grouping into a social superorganism bound together by technology. Metaman provides human beings with an environment that increasingly enables us to pursue our chosen activities; it lets us express our individuality more fully. As Metaman grows and evolves, human life undergoes a metamorphosis. "One thing is virtually certain: the future is going to be far stranger than is generally imagined." This era of Metaman's birth is not an ending; humanity's future is filled with promise.

Chapters discuss the extension of life's patterns, the fusion of technology and biology, physiology of the superorganism, an evolving global brain created by electronics, global government and global culture, the rites of passage (what is really new is not the existence of environmental problems but the existence of solutions; the challenge to humanity is not to find solutions but to implement them), the control of population growth, dawn of the solar age, human-machine hybrids, biological design, genetic modification, the blurring boundary between natural and manmade, the rising expectations of humanity, challenges to human values, the changing face of evolution ("a profound evolutionary transition is underway"), and extension of Metaman into the solar system and beyond. Concludes that "viewing humans as the germ of Metaman offers a powerful new image of ourselves that is in harmony with the two seemingly opposing realms we must integrate technology and nature." Metaman restores to us a story of the universe that possesses the strength of the ancient myths. It affirms modern civilization when we are still uncomfortable with the new powers of Metaman. "Civilization is not an intrusion into the natural realm, but a harmonious extension of it." [NOTE: Boldly original and intelligently upbeat, supported by 98 pages of notes. A challenging contrast to the evolutionary views of Duane Elgin, and of Brian Swimme and Thomas Berry (#025/026 above).] **(Metaman as evolving superorganism)**

033

The Overview Effect: Space Exploration and Human Evolution. Frank White (Space Studies Institute, Princeton NJ). Foreword by Gerard K. O'Neill. Boston: Houghton Mifflin, Nov 1987/318p/$18.95.

The Overview Effect is the shift in consciousness that can occur in outer space. One can experience it by flying in an airplane, and especially so if one is a space traveller. Satellites and unmanned probes can also contribute. The Overview Effect and related phenomena are the foundations for a series of new civilizations evolving on Earth and in space, in that such explorations are catalysts for social and personal transformation. "At the moment, space exploration is supporting the creation of a planetary overview system composed of the physical system of the planet Earth, the living system that has evolved on Earth popularly known as Gaia, the global human social system known as humanity, and a worldwide technology system." The key to survival is that as a species enters into or becomes aware of a new environment, the quantity of new information may be enough to move the system beyond simple changes and take it into a state of transformation. Chapters discuss the halo spaceflight experience, the early and later orbital missions, the space shuttle, space exploration as a catalyst to biological evolution (speciation), and the embryonic "human space program" to support humanity's understanding and achievement of its purpose as an active partner in universal evolution. Over the next thousand years, we can pursue the vision of a universal civilization, and humanity taking its rightful place as citizens of the universe. Includes interviews with some 20 US astronauts on their overview experiences, plus diary excerpts of Soviet cosmonauts. [NOTE: Very stimulating—the best book yet on the *human* meaning of space exploration.]

(human evolution and space exploration)

034

The SETI Factor: How the Search for Extraterrestrial Intelligence Is Changing Our View of the Universe and Ourselves. Frank White (Space Studies Inst., Princeton NJ). NY: Walker and Co., Aug 1990/250p/$19.95.

Author of **The Overview Effect** (above), and co-author with Isaac Asimov of **The March of the Millennia** (Walker, Jan 1991; **FS Annual 1994** #10928), asserts that SETI may hold the key to becoming citizens of the universe. SETI is far more than an intellectual curiosity, for we may within our lifetimes find an answer to the long-standing question, "Are we alone?" Human thinking about the presence of extraterrestrial intelligence has shifted dramatically in the past 30 years. Earlier researchers confidently but erroneously predicted abundant life and intelligence in the solar system. Based on what is now known, it seems slightly possible that primitive life may be found somewhere in our solar system, but highly improbable that advanced intelligent civilizations will be. The next phase in the detection process is among the stars, which may possibly provide millions of potential life-sites. On the 500th Anniversary Columbus Day in 1992, NASA plans to initiate the Microwave Observing Project, the largest and most sophisticated search ever. Within six years, this project will have conducted a targeted survey of some 800-1000 stars within 80 light years of Earth, and an "All-Sky Survey" of the entire Milky Way galaxy. "According to NASA, the project will have generated more information in its first half-hour of operation than all other searches during the past three decades combined."

Chapters discuss framing the question of extraterrestrial intelligence, the arguments for and against abundant life and intelligence, the past and future impact of SETI ("the SETI factor"), probabilities of success, 12 plausible outcome scenarios for the next 25 years (grouped under no contact, contact within the Milky Way galaxy, and contact with another galaxy), the impact of non-contact, assumptions about long-term impacts of contact, and getting ready for SETI. Concludes by proposing an aggressive "Human Space Program," a global commitment to explore the universe as a tool of human and universal evolution, and to push the boundaries of human thought and presence outward into the cosmos. The SETI component of this program should be seen as a global priority. The view of Earth from orbit and from the moon produced the Overview Effect; "the SETI factor is bringing us to an advanced version of the Overview Effect—a realization of the unity and one-ness of everything in the universe." [ALSO SEE: **SETI, Phone Home** (*The New York Times Magazine*, 21 Oct 1990, 34ff), and a provocative essay by futurist Allen Tough (U of Toronto) on possible positive impacts from contact with extraterrestrials (**FS Annual 1987** #8744).]

(SETI acceleration in late 1992)

035

The Waning of Humaneness. Konrad Lorenz (Austrian Academy of Sciences). Translated by Robert Warren Kickert. Boston: Little, Brown May 1987/250p/$17.95. (First published in Munich by R. Piper & Co, 1983.)

An ethologist and winner of the Nobel Prize for Medicine/Physiology warns that "now, as never before, the prospects for a human future are exceptionally dismal." Most probably the human race will be committed to suicide by use of nuclear weapons; if this does not happen, humans remain in peril through poisoning the environment. And even if this stupid conduct can be checked, humans remain threatened by a progressive decline of those attributes and attainments that constitute their humanity. The route taken by evolution is planless: it can go in any direction whatever, blindly responding to every new selection pressure that turns up. The question of retrograde evolution is of vital importance to humans. Our bodies already show signs of domestication, and retrogression of specific human characteristics and capacities conjures up the terrifying specter of the less than human, even of the inhuman. The technocratic system—the currently dominant societal order—threatens to establish itself as a tyrant over humankind. Social constructs comprising vast numbers of people, even when described as democracies, take on more and more totalitarian aspects. Humans thinking scientifically and technomorphically have forgotten how to come with everything else that is living. Increasing intolerance of the unpleasurable transforms the natural highs and lows of our normal lives into an artificially flattened expanse of monotonous gray. A need to be "entertained" (the exact opposite of creative activity) is a symptom of an extraordinarily pitiable state of the human soul. Various national cultures have largely lost their singularities, and children treat their parents like members of an alien ethnic group. Modern technology, especially drugs, make us slaves to comfort and ease.

Concludes with a justification for optimism that a saving countermovement is underway, and that the culmination of technocratic development has been surpassed. Lorenz identifies an oscillation in public opinion, and argues that we can educate our children to perceive the beautiful and the harmonious, to be antipathetic toward indoctrination, and to show sympathy and compassion for all of our fellow creatures. We should take the stance of "evolutionary epistemology," understanding and accepting the fact that feelings and emotions convey just as valid messages about realities as do measured results. [NOTE: A powerful thesis, with many references to Huxley and Orwell, followed by a weak argument for hope.]

(retrograde human evolution?)

036

What I Believe. Jacques Ellul (retired Prof of Law and of Sociology and History of Institutions, U of Bordeaux). Grand Rapids MI: William B. Eerdmans Publishing Co, 1989/223p/$19.95. (Translation by Geoffrey W. Bromiley of *Ce que je crois*, 1987.)

A summation of beliefs about humanity, history, and the Christian faith by the distinguished author of over 40 books, including **The Technological Society** (Knopf, 1964) and **The Technological System** (Continuum, 1980; **FS Annual 1981-82** #3707). Of interest here is Part II, "The Human Adventure," with essays on chances of history, the prehistoric period, the historic period, and the posthistoric period, where the social environment is being replaced by the technological environment. With historical advance, there is an increasing transition to the voluntary and artificial (or human intervention in nature). Everything is now changing—a total crisis triggered by transition to a new environment, a change much more fundamental than anything the human race has experienced for the last 5000 years. In the last 30 years, technology has begun to impose itself everywhere, to change everything, to take over all social activities and forms. We moderns are unable to live without our appliances and technical gadgets. Previous human adaptation followed the slow rhythm of evolution from generation to generation; today the technological environment develops with ever increasing speed, and we have to adjust rapidly. What is at issue is the danger of what might happen to our humanity. We must formulate what kind of humanity we want and what kind to repudiate.

(transition to technological environment)

037

The Yawning Vacuum: A World Without Alternatives, Rajni Kothari (Founder, Centre for the Study of Developing Societies, Delhi), *Alternatives: Social Transformation and Humane Governance*, 18:2, Spring 1993, 119-139.

The most fundamental change in the current historical situation is that we may be entering a period in which there is little scope for alternatives. It is not just the socialist alternative that has collapsed; in many ways, the Third World as an alternative mode of thinking has also collapsed. There has been consolidation of the imperial era, of world capitalism and techno-hegemony, of the state by the market, of a plurality of cultures by a monoculture, and of a greening of the world by its whitening. The future of the unipolar/corporate/technocratic/globalizing model is by no means assured, but it is undoubtedly on the upswing, and has succeeded in brainwashing the elites of the East and South. A new epidemic of violence seems to be gaining ground everywhere, especially in cities and among unemployed youth. Unemployment is growing worldwide, and the old objective of full employment has long ago been given up. Prospects for economic development are in decline, and an end of any humanitarian vision of dealing with human suffering. Many of the new ethnicities and nationalisms are highly chauvinistic. Many of the bonds that tie human beings together are under stress; there is craving for genuine community, but little idea of where to find it. The range of counterestablishment movements is considerable, but the peace movement has been coopted, the green movement lacks vision and politics, the women's movement is largely elitist, the alternative futures movement remains largely academic, and the human rights movement (which will likely grow) is in danger of being coopted. The biggest failure of these new movements is their inability to become part of a united political movement for democracy. Underlying all is a basic crisis of vision, an end of "alternatives" in the comprehensive sense of the term. A few movements still present a distant hope, "but that hope is getting more and more distant." [NOTE: Remarkably bleak views from a major Third World social thinker. For further Kothari essays, see **FS Annual 1991** #10289.]

(global alternatives in decline?)

038

The End of History and the Last Man. Francis Fukuyama (RAND Corporation, Washington). NY: The Free Press, Jan 1992/418p/$24.95.

While serving as deputy director of the US State Department's Policy Planning Staff, Fukuyama [or his handlers?] created an intellectual sensation with his essay on *The End of History?* in the Summer 1989 issue of *The National Interest* (**FS Annual 1991** #10274). In it, he argued that a remarkable consensus on the legitimacy of liberal democracy has emerged worldwide in the past few years, and that liberal democracy may constitute the "end point of mankind's ideological evolution" and as such constituted the "end of history." This book "is not a restatement of my original article, nor is it an effort to continue the discussion with that article's many critics and commentators." Rather, Fukuyama focuses on an old question, arguing that it makes sense to speak of a coherent and directional Universal History of mankind that will eventually lead the greater part of humanity to liberal democracy. This is due to the unfolding of modern natural science, which has had a uniform effect on all societies that have experienced it, while establishing a uniform horizon of economic production possibilities. "Technology makes possible the limitless accumulation of wealth, and thus the satisfaction of an ever-expanding set of human desires. This process guarantees an increasing homogenization of all human societies, regardless of their historical origins or cultural inheritances." All modernizing countries "must increasingly resemble one another," as they are increasingly linked with one another through global markets and a universal consumer culture. It is not possible to reject technology and modern natural science. The most articulate source of opposition to technological civilization comes from the environmental movement; the most radical have doctrines with a common ancestry in the thought of Rousseau. As degradation of the natural environment becomes more obvious, Rousseau's critique of modernization has great appeal. But "it seems highly unlikely that our civilization will voluntarily choose the Rousseauian option." There is "no doubt that contemporary democracies face any number of serious problems...but these problems are not obviously insoluble on the basis of liberal principles, nor so serious that they would necessarily lead to the collapse of society as a whole, as communism collapsed in the 1980s."

Concludes by addressing the question of the end of history and the creature who emerges, the "last man." As anticipated by Nietzsche, the typical citizen of a liberal democracy is a last man who favors comfortable self-preservation with neither striving nor aspiration. There may be a side of the human personality that remains unfulfilled by the "peace and prosperity" of contemporary liberal democracy. Fear of becoming contemptible "last men" may lead to men asserting themselves in new ways, even to the point of becoming once again bestial "first men" engaged in bloody prestige battles, this time with modern weapons. [**NOTE**: Illustrates why one should not confuse style and substance. The style of this book appears to be eloquent, big-league political theory. The substance is a superficial and wordy view of modern realities, based on many shaky premises. Unlike most conservatives who ignore population/environment/resource issues, Fukuyama at least mentions environmental problems, but his understanding is limited to playing off of Bill McKibbon's **The End of Nature** (Random House, 1989; **FS Annual 1991** #10462), an equally unhelpful appreciation of problems and prospects.] **(triumph of liberal democracy?)**

039
A Short History of the Future. W. Warren Wagar (Distinguished Teaching Prof, Dept of History, SUNY-Binghamton). Afterword by Immanuel Wallerstein. Chicago: U of Chicago Press, Nov 1989/323p/$24.95.

A memoir of post-modern times in the form of a history book written in 2200 by Peter Jensen as a gift to his granddaughter. The book is divided into three time periods reflecting three different world regimes: a megacorporate global economy reigning until the nuclear catastrophe of 2044, the subsequent socialist world commonwealth of the World Party, and a decentralized order of autonomous societies from the 2150s on. Interludes between each chapter provide personal correspondence of the Jensen family, affording a human-level view of everyday life. (In one instance, the interlude takes the form of a scholarly spat between great-grandfather Carl Jensen and a reviewer of his 2033 book on **Technocracy as the Highest Stage of Capital**.)

"Earth Inc." attains its highest form with creation of the Global Trade Consortium in 2008, ultimately comprising the dozen megacorps that have agglomerated the ever-dwindling number of ever-bigger corporate entities. (For example, General Industries was formed in 2003 by a supermerger of three oil companies, two electronics companies, and two auto manufacturers; Hollings-Gray, or HoG, specializes in franchise farming worldwide.) The new rulers employ a judicious blend of "public information management" and "enhanced data control" (centralized collection of data about all citizens). Population growth, pollution, and soil erosion were kept at bay by new technology and bioengineering that produced new food crops such as the King Plant. The "Big Earth" earthburger (a palatable concoction of lentils, tofu, and vegetable adhesives), replaced the hamburger by offering twice the nutrition at one-third the cost. A new worldview arose from the "molecular sciences". However there is a global warming and subsequent flooding of many coastal areas, a startling rise of crime in big cities, a new drug in 15 colors (perfected in the 2010s and known on the streets as "pop"), and a mutation of HIV-1 causing casually acquired immunodeficiency syndrome (CAIDS) that was not eliminated until the late 2020s. The most brutal economic depression in history, reaching a low in 2038 and again in 2043, left half the workers in the core countries unemployed.

World tensions lead to a nuclear war in 2044, with widespread destruction. A democratic red and green World Party comes into power and creates a global commonwealth, featuring a Planetary Restoration Authority, zero population growth by 2110, a centrally managed global economy, a uniform global system of schools, and a Genetic Initiative to enhance intelligence and sociality. Reacting to bigness and bureaucracy, small parties gain prominence in the mid-21st century, and humankind become independent of complex social machinery. Plutomania is almost extinct, and people live in autonomous communities, both on earth (in harmony with nature) and in space. In contrast to "substantialism," the reigning philosophy of the World Party, the philosophy associated with the Smalls is known as "ecomysticism." [**NOTE**:A well-written 3-in-1 scenario that describes the world under three successive regimes. The latter two seem unlikely to a late 20th century sensibility, but sensibilities change. The comprehensive portrayal of the early 21st century (including corporations, technology, government, philosophy and ecology) is the most compelling single scenario presently available of how things might turn out. And it is fun to read, with imaginative details scattered throughout.] **(three world regimes, 1990-2200)**

040
A Short History of the Future. Second Edition. W. Warren Wagar (Distinguished Teaching Prof, Dept of History, SUNY-Binghamton). Chicago: U of Chicago Press, Aug 1992/324p/$14.95pb.

A memoir of post-modern times in the form of a history book written in 2200, divided into three time periods reflecting three different world regimes: a megacorporate global economy reigning until the "nuclear catastrophe of 2044," the subsequent socialist world commonwealth of the World Party, and a decentralized order of autonomous societies from the 2150s on. Interludes between each chapter provide personal correspondence of the Jensen family, affording a human-level view of everyday life. First written in 1987-1988 and published in late 1989, this edition has been rewritten to take into account the "World Revolution of 1989." Chapters describe the management of democracy by the megacorps, formation of the Global Trade Consortium in 2008 and the International Data Storage Center in 2012, dislocation and confusion caused by global warming in the early 20th century, the mutations of HIV-1 (notably "a diabolical virus, HIV-7"), and nuclear proliferation despite some reduction in warheads.
(world future for the next 200 years)

041
The Next Three Futures: Paradigms of Things to Come. W. Warren Wagar (SUNY-Binghamton). Foreword by Edward Cornish (President, WFS). Westport CT: Greenwood Press, Oct 1991/157p/$46.00;$15.00pb.

Following introductory chapters on the state of futures inquiry, past futures from H.G. Wells to the present, and a typology of futurist paradigms (technoliberal, radical, and countercultural), Wagar provides four broadly integrative chapters: **1) The Future of the Earth**: population and food, energy and the environment, growth vs. no-growth; **2) The Future of Wealth and Power**: the distribution of wealth, long-term costs of capitalism, threats to democratization; **3) The Future of War and Peace**: a reminder that a mighty array of weapons still exists and that warfare is endemic in the modern world-system (but with a discussion of the "end-of-war" thesis and new world orders); **4) The Future of Living**: work and leisure, the family, health and human engineering, and the next culture. Technoliberal, radical, and countercultural interpretations in each of these four areas are discussed. Concludes that each worldview—capitalism and bourgeois democracy, democratic socialism, and Ecotopian New Age—is essentially correct: "the human race may be destined to follow all three paths to the future, not simultaneously, but sequentially." The next future is almost surely the one we are building today: globalized liberal democratic capitalism. Exploitation of new markets in the former Second and Third worlds, and the fresh energies released by diffusion of political democracy, will keep the system humming for years. But resentment of the many have-nots will build, and eventually the system will disintegrate from within, perhaps by the end of the next bout of worldwide business expansion, say in the 2030s. This will be replaced by a worldwide republic of working men and women that disarms the nation-states, fully guarantees civil liberties, and restores the environment. At some point, perhaps in the late 21st century, humankind will be ready for its third future of a decentralized classless society and the dying out of the state. [**NOTE**: This provocative thesis is spelled out as an extended scenario in Wagar's **A Short History of the Future** (above). Wagar has taught a highly successful course on "History of the Future" since 1974, and this book can serve as a brief, well-tested, cross-ideological introduction for college students. Many may object, however, to the facile dismissal of the familiar right-left divisions within "technoliberalism."]

(world futures scenarios)

B. EIGHT KEY ELEMENTS

1. Politics in the Post-Cold War Era

*042

Birth of a New World: An Open Moment for International Leadership. Harlan Cleveland (President, World Academy of Art and Science). Foreword by Robert S. McNamara. San Francisco: Jossey-Bass Publishers, April 1993/260p/$25.95.

The key to all the sudden happenings around us is the spread of knowledge—rapidly expanding literacy, rapid growth in the numbers of educated people, and rapid increases in readers, radio listeners, and TV watchers. Spreading knowledge about the advantages of political choice and a worldwide "fairness revolution" that ended totalitarianism. The wet blanket of the Cold War dampened both hopes and fears. Lifting the wet blanket intensified the struggles for human rights and made possible a new war on poverty, but also blew into flame the smoldering embers of religious and cultural conflict.

Chapters consider reconciling cultural diversity with human rights and opportunities, the failure of the nation-states ("the evidence is now overwhelming that every national government is beyond its depth"), the growing list of functions that only credible international organizations or regimes can perform, international arrangements that work (ingredients for success include a consensus on desired outcomes, a win-win game, pooling sovereignty, reliable communication, flexible and uncentralized systems, and the US as a key player), the management of peace (the UN is needed more than ever in a world of bargains and accommodations; "a practical pluralism, not a unitary universalism, is the likely destiny of the human race"), the erosion of superpower in "a new world disorder," managing a world economy with nobody in charge, growth with fairness in world development, and the global commons (outer space, the atmosphere, the oceans, and Antarctica). A new agenda to make the world safe for diversity includes: 1) radical disarmament and durable deterrence of nuclear weapons; 2) deterring use of other weapons; 3) organizing to anticipate, deter, and mediate regional conflict, manage crises, and mediate ancient quarrels (or isolate those that cannot be settled); 4) responding to humanitarian crises in and between countries; 5) developing a wider and more flexible system of world leadership through a "club of democracies" whose members act in different groupings for different situations. This open-ended club as a center of initiative is already in formation. Like it or not, the US is still the only available chair of the executive committee for a club that calls the shots for world order, prosperity, and development. But the US must lead by imagination, consultation, and persuasion. **(club of democracies in formation)**

043

Rethinking International Governance: Coalition Politics in an Unruly World, Harlan Cleveland (Prof Emeritus, U of Minnesota), *The Futurist*, 25:3, May-June 1991, 20-27.

The current cacophony of change—the democracy movement in Eastern Europe, the greening of politics and business, the debating of settled assumptions, and the pushiness of people wanting a voice in their own destiny—is the consequence of getting hundreds of millions of people educated to think for themselves and to learn to use modern information technology. The spread of knowledge brings with it a number of forces for change in world affairs, and the dominant metaphor of our time is now "the right to choose." We have learned much from what worked and what didn't work in this century's first two tries at "world order"—the League of Nations and the UN. We now have a chance to revise the flawed assumptions on which the UN was built. We now know that, under a workable system, no one country or individual is going to be in charge. An informal and open-ended "club" of democracies is becoming the gyroscope for world security, the world economy, and development. The broadening leadership of this group will likely make the global community, even more than it is today, a world with nobody in charge—and thus with many elements of the world's diversity partly in charge. Finances of ongoing international functions, however, must be set free from national legislatures by international taxes on such global functions as transportation, communication, international transactions, and use of the global commons.

(new international governance)

044

After Insularity: Hegemony and the Future World Order, Joshua S. Goldstein (Prof of International Relations, USC) and David P. Rapkin (Prof of Political Science, U of Nebraska), *Futures*, 23:9, Nov 1991, 935-959.

Historically, global leadership has been provided (when provided at all) by hegemonic nations that held military and economic power. These hegemons emerged from the shadow of global wars that weakened other great powers, with geostrategic insularity playing an important role. Now, the development of technology has undermined insularity and brought an increasing globalization of politics, economics, military capabilities, technology, communication, and culture. These trends bring new incentives for international cooperation. In a post-insular world, international security depends more than ever on common security. Four scenarios of the current transition to a new world order are considered: 1) renewed US hegemony (considered unlikely); 2) rapid US decline with the Gulf War as an insignificant counterexample and perhaps even a deliberate diversion; 3) Japanese hegemony (virtually ruled out because of economic vulnerability and a lack of strategic depth); 4) growing great power cooperation under lingering US leadership (most plausible). In the longer term, as the relative power of the US slowly declines, new global structures of coordination should emerge.

(cooperation replacing single-country hegemony)

*045

Governance Without Government: Order and Change in World Politics. Edited by James N. Rosenau (Director, Institute for Transnational Studies, USC) and Ernst-Otto Czempiel (Co-Director, Frankfurt Peace Research Institute). Cambridge & NY: Cambridge U Press, March 1992/311p/$59.95;$17.95pb.

A world government capable of controlling nation-states has never evolved. But governance is not synonymous with government, and considerable governance underlies the current order among states and gives direction to the challenges posed by various problems. Indeed, governance without government is in some ways preferable to governments that are capable of governance. During the present period of rapid and extensive global change, the constitutions of national governments and their treaties have been undermined by the demands and greater coherence of ethnic and other subgroups, the globalization of economies, the advent of broad social movements, the shrinking of distance by IT, and the "mushrooming of global interdependencies" fostered by AIDS, pollution, drugs, and terrorism. Much depends on how the characteristics of the global system are perceived: either as continuing dominance by states or as states within a larger new order. There is no clear-cut evidence to support or reject either of these perspectives, and "a new or reconstituted global order may take decades to mature." Chapters discuss polyarchy in 19th century Europe, the decay of the Westphalian system of states, governance in the international political economy, variables that explain effectiveness of international institutions, international regulatory ventures, strategies to support democratization, and citizenship in the emerging global order. Rosenau concludes that "the proliferation of governance without government, of access points in a polyarchal world, poses huge new challenges to citizenship in the emergent global order." Increasingly people will have to choose between channeling their loyalties to systemic order or subsystemic autonomy. But tendencies toward a pluralist order may be substantially offset by the centralizing tendencies inherent in worsening environmental conditions, which would encourage a cooperative global order. [NOTE: Subtle and important observations.]

(**governance in a polyarchal world**)

046

Turbulence in World Politics: A Theory of Change and Continuity. James N. Rosenau (Prof of Political Science and Director, Institute for Transnational Studies, USC). Princeton NJ: Princeton U Press, July 1990/480p/ $55.00;$14.50pb.

Today's changes are so thoroughgoing as to render obsolete the rules and procedures by which politics are conducted. The anomalies are more pervasive than ever before, and the discontinuities more prominent than the continuities. Theorizing must begin anew, and present understandings of history's dynamics "must be treated as conceptual jails from which an escape can be engineered only by allowing for the possibility that a breakpoint in human affairs is imminent, if not upon us." The very notion of "international relations" seems obsolete, and a new term is needed: "postinternational politics," which suggests the decline of long-standing patterns without indicating where changes may be leading. Five major forces drive today's transformations: the shift to a postindustrial order, the emergence of issues (pollution, terrorism, the drug trade) that are direct products of new technologies, the reduced capacity of states and governments to provide satisfactory solutions to the major issues, the weakening of whole systems (thus fostering tendencies toward decentralization), and feedback from consequences of the foregoing for the orientations of the world's adults (who have enlarged analytic skills and are not as manipulable as were their forebears.")

A major theme is the bifurcation of macro global structures into the two worlds of world politics: the more coherent and structured state-centric world, and its multi-centric counterpart. There are fewer than 200 essential actors in the state-centric world, which seeks to preserve territory and controls armed force. The multi-centric world has hundreds of thousands of essential actors, who seek to increase market shares and operate in temporary coalitions with situational rules and relative equality. The rise of the multi-centric world has brought major changes to the state-centric world. "Global life has turned in decentralizing directions that may make the notion of hegemony in world politics obsolete." International security alliances also seem increasingly anachronistic, because the lines dividing adversaries are now murky. Concludes with four scenarios of the kind of global order that may follow the present period of turbulence: **1) Global Society**: sources of interdependence will progressively deepen and widen to the point where explicit ties develop, and actors in both the state-centric and multi-centric worlds are responsive to worldwide norms such as human rights; **2) Restored State-System**: confronted by disorder from fragmentation, publics may be persuaded that only the nation-state can meet challenges; **3) The Pluralist Scenario**: the dynamics of decentralization comes to predominate, and the multi-centric world dominates its state-centric counterpart; **4) Enduring Bifurcation**: clashes between centralizing and decentralizing dynamics not resolved, and the rapid pace of change becomes a constant. [NOTE: Some academics will find this elegant, original, and important; others will merely find it stilted and wordy. Non-academics will not be interested.]

(**two worlds of post-international politics**)

*047

The End of Sovereignty? The Politics of a Shrinking and Fragmenting World. Joseph A. Camilleri (La Trobe U) and Jim Falk (U of Wollongong). Aldershot UK: Edward Elgar Pub., April 1992/312p/$62.95. (Dist. in US by Ashgate Pub., Old Post Rd, Brookfield VT 05036.)

It is a commonplace that the times are global, yet much of the analysis of what is happening and what should be done is predicated on a completely different worldview of sovereign nation-states. The concept of sovereignty was elaborated in 16th and 17th century Europe to explain and legitimate the rise of the centralized and absolutist state. The intellectual coherence and plausibility of the sovereignty principle have been in steady decline for some time, and reconceptualization is now necessary and possible. Five major influences are discussed at length: the penetration of market relations into almost all aspects of human life (through internationalization of production, trade, and finance), the homogenizing architecture of technological change (the most conspicuous symptom and agent of globalization), the globalization of the security dilemma, the growing sense of impending ecological crisis, and the rise of local and transnational social consciousness. Some key trends: 1) increasing diversity, complexity, and interaction, with a likely proliferation of state structures; 2) failure of national states to make adaptive responses to an increasingly fragile global environment, resulting in further delegation of tasks and resources to international and supranational forums and agencies; 3) rising tensions between national macroeconomic policy and transnational corporations; 4) a deepening contradiction between emerging processes of decentralization and democratization within and between societies, and intensified centralization and bureaucratization of economic and political life; 5) a possible transition to a new concept of civil society grounded in a multiplicity of overlapping allegiances and jurisdictions, where the traditional, the modern, and the postmodern coexist; 6) conflicting tendencies of reasserting cultural identity *and* accepting cultural pluralism as an organizing principle of national and international life. [NOTE: Captures some important subtleties, for those willing to appreciate them.]

(**sovereignty principle reconsidered**)

048

International Society. Evan Luard (Research Fellow, St. Antony's College, Oxford U). NY: New Amsterdam Books, Sept 1990/273p/$25.00.

Brings together some of the main findings of three earlier books on international society. If society is defined in a narrow way (as a compact, closely integrated community), international society clearly could not qualify. But as the world grows smaller, it begins to take on some features of such a society. Various ways in which international society differs from other societies: 1) it is highly decentralized (power at the center is almost non-existent, in contrast to highly centralized power in national societies); 2) links between individuals are more diffuse, tenuous, and uncertain; 3) there is no sense of community or solidarity; 4) it lacks a common value-system; 5) it is complex and diverse; 6) it has very large and growing inequalities in standard of living, education, technology, culture, and amenities. Concludes with a discussion of justice and change. "In a rapidly shrinking world, it is changes in international society and institutions, rather than those within single states, which now matter most." The demand for order must be balanced by an equal concern for justice, since a system which denies justice cannot for long be orderly. **(international society emerging)**

049
Post-Capitalist Society. Peter F. Drucker (Prof of Social Science, Claremont Graduate School). NY: HarperBusiness, April 1993/232p/$25.00.

Further thoughts on the major political divide that we are living through, first described in **The New Realities** (Harper & Row, 1989; **FS Annual 1990** #9571). "The new society—and it is already here—is a post-capitalist society." It will use a free market and the institutions of capitalism will survive. But the center of gravity in the post-capitalist society differs from that which dominated the last 250 years, because the basic economic resource is no longer capital or natural resources, but knowledge. Value is now created by productivity and innovation, and the leading social groups of the knowledge society are knowledge workers, nearly all employed in organizations. Unlike employees under capitalism, they own the tools of production. Capital now serves the employee, where under Capitalism the employee served capital.

In post-capitalist society, worldwide changes in political structure are as great as those in social structure. We do not face a "new world order" but a *new world disorder*—no one can know for how long—in the age of the post-sovereign state. In the late 19th century, the nation-state began to mutate into the Megastate, the Pork Barrel state, the Nanny state, and the Cold War state. The Cold War state has become economically self-destructive, and no longer works even militarily. Today, transnationalism and regionalism challenge the nation-state from the outside, while tribalism undermines it from within. These three vectors of the post-capitalist polity each pull in a different direction: 1) there is a growing need for truly transnational institutions that can take action on protecting the environment, stamping out terrorism, promoting arms control, and enforcing human rights; 2) the irreversible trend toward regionalism was triggered by the EC but will not be confined to it, and there is also a growing movement toward "mini-regions"; 3) "the more transnational the world becomes, the more tribal it will also be," because of the existential need for roots. The next decades will require high government competence. Government must abandon things that do not work (military aid is first on the list), concentrate on things that do work, and analyze its half-successes. A central requirement of the post-capitalist polity is to restore citizenship by fostering autonomous community organizations in the social sector.

(tribalism and transnationalism)

050
Global Paradox: The Bigger the World Economy, the More Powerful Its Smallest Players. John Naisbitt (Telluride CO). NY: William Morrow, Jan 1994/304p/$23.00.

World trends point overwhelmingly toward formation of economic alliances, and toward political independence and self-rule. As the global economy gets larger, the component parts get smaller. Removal of trade barriers has opened the way for smaller companies, and infotech and deregulation have enabled small companies to get an edge on big companies. The almost perfect metaphor for the movement from bureaucracies of every kind to small, autonomous units is the shift from mainframe computers to PCs, with PCs networked together. At the same time, the growth of democracy greatly magnifies and multiplies the assertiveness of tribes: "the more universal we become, the more tribal we act." As English becomes everyone's second language, their mother tongue becomes more important and more passionately held. We hold on to our language and currencies as we become universal in many other ways. Europe's Maastrict Treaty that seeks to create a common currency is doomed to failure: "the EC will not adopt a common currency—in this century and beyond." Rather, with the multiplication of countries, the world will have many more currencies, not fewer (besides, the common currency of electronics already exists). By the beginning of the 21st century we should have at least 300 countries in the world; the old Soviet Union alone is now 15 countries, and on its way to eventually becoming as many as 60 or 70 countries. We are moving toward a world of 1,000 countries, perhaps by the middle of the 21st century (but the US will not split up because it is already very decentralized). "Several decades from now it will be easier to keep track of 1,000 countries and thousands of global networks than it was to keep track of 100 countries two decades ago." Transition to a "free-market democracy" matches the shift from the state to the individual, from vertical to horizontal, as politics and political leaders become less important in people's lives. We are experiencing "the spread of governance without government."

Five additional chapters discuss: 1) how the telecommunications revolution is powering the Global Paradox; 2) globalization of travel—the world's biggest industry—driven as no other by individual decisions; 3) emergence of a universal code of conduct for the 21st century—a global ethical standard to which all politicians and political activity will be held, an emerging global consensus on environmental issues and human rights, and the trend toward greater corporate social responsibility; 4) China as the world's biggest economy by 2000 (if it can sustain current economic momentum, and cope with unemployment, corruption, inflation, and environmental damage); 5) Asia and Latin America as new areas of opportunity, and the decline of the EC in the global economy. In sum, "the Global Paradox tells us that the opportunities for each of us as individuals are far greater than at any time in human history." [**NOTE**: Upbeat as always, and rather disconnected. But an intriguing provocation.]

(a world of 1,000 countries?)

051
Powershift: Knowledge, Wealth, and Violence at the Edge of the 21st Century. Alvin Toffler (Los Angeles CA). NY: Bantam Books, Nov 1990/585p/$22.95. (Very brief version as *Newsweek* Special Report, 15 Oct 1990, 86-92. Also as Bantam audiocassettes, 300 min./$22.95.)

"The third and final volume of a trilogy" that began with **Future Shock** (Random House, 1970), which looked at the process of change, and continued with **The Third Wave** (Morrow, 1980; **FS Annual 1980-81** #2274), which focused on the directions of change. **Powershift** deals with the control of changes still to come—who will shape them and how. This is the dawn of the Powershift Era. "We live at a moment when the entire structure of power that held the world together is now disintegrating. A radically different structure of power is taking form. And this is happening at every level of human society." The crackup of old-style authority and power in business and daily life is accelerating, at the very moment when global power structures are disintegrating as well. Power is being redefined by the spread of a new knowledge economy, an "explosive new force that has hurled the advanced economies into bitter global competition, confronted the socialist nations with their hopeless obsolescence, [and] forced many 'developing nations' to scrap their traditional economic strategies...." Despite inequities of income and wealth, the coming struggle for power will increasingly turn into a struggle over the distribution of and access to knowledge. "This new system for making wealth is totally dependent on the instant communication and dissemination of data, ideas, symbols, and symbolism." It is a super-symbolic economy, serving a de-massified society. It also involves a fundamental change in the mix of violence, wealth, and knowledge employed by elites to maintain control. In smokestack societies, power was exercised by bureaucrats. In transition to the new economy, the new-style "post-bureaucratic" organizations can be called "flex-firms.

Chapters discuss such topics as life in the super-symbolic economy, info-wars (struggles for the control of knowledge), power in the flex-firm, the shift from mass democracy to a fast-moving "mosaic democracy," privatization as the global buzzword, global forces that could sweep us into a new Dark Age (fundamentalist religious movements, eco-medievalists among the Greens, and nationalist movements), and the power triad (Tokyo, Berlin, Washington). Concludes with a chapter on the global gladiators: the new power-seekers "leaping onto the world stage." A Global Council of Global Corporations may arise to speak for the new-style firms and provide a collective counterbalance to nation-state power. The Soviet Union is fast-fracturing, and some pieces will almost surely flake off, to be drawn into a German-dominated Europe or the Japanese sphere of influence in Asia. China could also split up, with new parts becoming a giant new Confucian Economic Community.

[NOTE: Employs the same formula as in earlier books: portentous and exaggerated statements, frenetic narrative, some interesting ideas (baked and half-baked), and cutesy chapter heads and subheads (God-in-a-White Coat, The X-Shaped Desk, Materialismo, The Paradox Bomb, The Cubby-hole Crash, Alfalfa Secrets and Guided Leaks, Fam-Firms of the Future, The Economic Godzilla). Behind all the bells and whistles, there isn't much here that is new. This is clearly the least and narrowest of Toffler's blockbuster triad. Despite many references to **Future Shock**, there is no mention of its important concluding chapters on "Strategies for Survival," including education in the future tense, taming technology, and the strategy of social futurism (which wrongly pronounced the death of technocratic planning that is econocentric and short-range).]

(**new knowledge economy**)

*052

Out of Control: Global Turmoil on the Eve of the 21st Century. Zbigniew Brzezinski (Prof of Foreign Policy, Johns Hopkins U). NY: Charles Scribner's Sons (Macmillan), April 1993/240p/$21.00.

"History has not ended but become compressed." Recognizing the notable acceleration in the velocity of our history and the uncertainty of its trajectory is a necessary point of departure. Discontinuity is the central reality of our contemporary history, demanding an intensified debate regarding the meaning of our era. But our ability to understand the wider ramifications of the present and the future is impeded by the massive collapse of almost all established values. Totalitarian doctrines have been discredited. The role of religion in defining moral standards has also declined. Humanity's capacity to control itself and its environment has been expanding exponentially and our material expectations ("permissive cornucopia") even more so. The interaction between the acceleration of our history, our increased capacities to shape the world, our rapidly expanding material desires, and our moral ambiguity is generating unprecedented dynamics of uncontrolled change. There is a "danger that world politics—both in terms of international affairs and of internal societal conditions—could simply spiral out of control, generating massive political disorder and philosophical confusion." The critical challenge that America now faces in the postutopian age is to recognize that "only by creating a society guided by some shared criteria of self-restraint can it help to shape a world more truly in control of its destiny."

Chapters discuss our "century of megadeath" (in which 170 million human beings were destroyed by wars and totalitarian genocide), the emergence of mass political awareness, the abortive attempts at coercive utopia (the challenge of 20th century totalitarianism was the challenge of utopian hubris carried to an extreme), the opposite condition of "permissive cornucopia" in the West (the good life defined by the cultural pornography of television), America as the peerless global power (but the value content of America's message to the world threatens to undermine its special role as global leader), a checklist of 20 American shortcomings (indebtedness, low savings, poor education, urban decay, a deepening race and poverty problem, spiritual emptiness, etc.), the transformation of America from a largely European culture to a global mosaic (leading to perhaps further loss of social cohesion), potential impacts from the end of the Russian empire (multimillion migrations, ethnic and border conflicts, a Russian variant of fascism), concerns over global ecology dramatizing the mounting salience of global inequality (a major issue of 21st century politics), and China's future role. The needed correction can only emerge from "a prolonged process of cultural self—reexamination and philosophical reevaluation, which over time influences the political outlook both of the West and of the non-Western world." [NOTE: Timely and thoughtful.]

(**need for cultural reexamination and restraint**)

053

Pandaemonium: Ethnicity in International Politics. Sen. Daniel Patrick Moynihan (D-NY). NY: Oxford U Press, Feb 1993/221p/$19.95.

The 1991 Cyril Foster Lecture at Oxford University, arguing that ethnicity as a subject has been slighted, if not ignored. At the outset of the 20th century, two large ideas predicted the steady or even precipitous decline of ethnic attachments. "The liberal expectancy" saw ethnic identities as recessive and transitional, while Marx predicted that ethnicity would give way to proletarian internationalism. Far from vanishing, ethnicity has been and will be an elemental force in international politics. Today's struggles have been going on for generations and explain much of modern history. The evils of ethnic politics that have returned with redoubled vengeance, notably in what was Yugoslavia, suggest Pandaemonium, the capital of hell in **Paradise Lost**.

Had the US considered the force of ethnicity in the former USSR, "the Cold War might have come to an end on its own without the US having become a debtor state in the process. Had we seen what was coming, the West would have conducted its affairs differently." As early as 1979, Moynihan wrote that the Soviet Union was about to disintegrate due to rising ethnic tensions. In 1980, he forecasted that "The defining event of the decade might well be the break-up of the Soviet Empire." In 1984, he announced that "The Cold War is over...The Soviet Union is a failed society and an unstable one...The place has collapsed." Soviet scholars in the US, as well as the CIA, by and large dismissed or ignored this ethnic dimension.

"*Now* what story will we tell ourselves?" We are at the end of the 75 year crisis of the European state system. "The age of totalitarianism is ended." Yet states are the basic building blocks of international law. At the turn of the century, some 50 acknowledged states constituted the world community. This number is now approaching 200, with most of the newer states created from ethnic conflict. In the next 50 years, will another 50 or 150 new states be added? "Primal fissury" is to be expected. "Most of these new states will be badly off, not least from the point of view of ethnic homogeneity. Nor will they have much in the way of a civic culture." We should not expect very much free enterprise in states created to give one or another ethnic group a realm of its own. The larger states, associations of states, and the UN must fashion responses to conflicts concerning self-determination. "These will not be pretty events, and expect a fair degree of compassion fatigue on the part of the donors and the peacekeepers." But with luck there will be examples of successful adaptation, compromise, and evolution (e.g., Catalonia in Spain). The dynamics of ethnic conflict can be understood, anticipated, and moderated. "The challenge is to make the world safe for and from ethnicity, safe for just those differences which large assemblies, democratic or otherwise, will typically attempt to suppress. The idea deserves attention. As does the whole question of sovereignty."

(**ethnicity as key force in world politics**)

054

The Coming Anarchy, Robert D. Kaplan (Contributing Editor), *The Atlantic Monthly*, 273:2, Feb 1994, 44-76.

"To understand the events of the next 50 years, one must understand environmental scarcity, cultural and racial clash, geographic destiny, and the transformation of war." West Africa is becoming the symbol of worldwide demographic, environmental, and societal stress, in which criminal anarchy emerges as the real strategic danger. "Disease, overpopulation, unprovoked crime, scarcity of resources, refugee migrations, the increasing erosion of nation-states and national borders, and the empowerment of private armies, security firms, and international drug cartels are now most tellingly demonstrated through a West African prism." This region introduces us to the issues that will soon confront our civilization—the way the political earth will be a few decades hence. Malthus is the prophet of West Africa's future, "and West Africa's future, eventually, will also be that of most of the rest of the world." Other observations: 1) West Africa is reverting to the Africa of the Victorian atlas: a series of coastal trading posts and an interior that is again becoming blank and unexplored owing to violence and disease; 2) as many internal African borders crumble, a denser boundary is being erected that threatens to isolate the continent: the wall of disease (of the 12 million HIV-positive people worldwide, 8 million are in Africa); 3) post-modernism will be "an epoch of themeless juxtapositions, in which the classificatory grid of nation-states is going to be replaced by a jagged-glass pattern of city-states, shanty-states, and nebulous and anarchic regionalism"; 4) as small-scale violence multiplies at home and abroad, state armies will continue to shrink, replaced by private security and urban mafias (especially in the former communist world); 5) future wars will be those of communal survival, aggravated or in many cases caused by environmental scarcity. [**NOTE**: Notably bleak and rambling argument that fails to make the case of Africa's distress as a model for the future. It offers no positive trends or prescriptions for this seemingly hopeless situation.]

(**West Africa as model for future world?**)

055

Minorities at Risk: A Global View of Ethnopolitical Conflicts. Ted Robert Gurr (Prof of Government, U of Maryland). Washington: US Institute of Peace Press, July 1993/427p/$32.95;$19.95pb.

The first comprehensive report of the Minorities at Risk project, a global survey of 233 politically active communal groups, involving 915 million people (17% of world population). Every form of ethnopolitical conflict has increased sharply. Among the groups studied, nonviolent political action has more than doubled between 1950 and 1990, and violent protest and rebellion both quadrupled. Some forecasts for the 1990s: 1) the immediate potential for escalating ethnopolitical conflict is greatest in the Soviet successor states; 2) South Asia is likely to suffer the most severe escalation of communal conflicts in the Third World (long-standing regional conflicts in India are intensifying, and Pakistan's politics are rent by communal divisions); 3) indigenous activism is likely to escalate throughout the Americas, especially in the Latin American societies that have been most resistant to claims of native peoples; 4) Western European and North American democracies face a resurgence of ethnic conflict (some of it based on regional claims by people like the Québecois and the Scots, but most due to tensions between dominant groups and minorities of Third World origin). Although some propose changing the state system so that territorial boundaries correspond more closely to social and cultural boundaries, a more constructive and open-ended answer is to pursue positive-sum coexistence of ethnic groups and plural states. This means both recognizing and strengthening ethnic groups within the existing nation-state system.

(**increasing ethnopolitical conflict**)

056

Nation Against State: A New Approach to Ethnic Conflicts and the Decline of Sovereignty. Gidon Gottlieb (Prof of International Law, U of Chicago; Visiting Senior Fellow, CFR). NY: Council on Foreign Relations Press, Dec 1993/148p/$22.95;$14.95pb.

Serbs, Croats, Bosnian Muslims, Armenians, Azerbaijanis, Georgians, Sikhs, Kurds, and Palestinians are currently consumed by cruel wars to realize national aspirations. Making room for nations trying to break loose from states that rule over them is a pressing issue for world stability; so is avoiding global fragmentation. A territorial approach to ethnic conflicts, granting self-rule or statehood to those who want it, would result in scores of new sovereign states; it offers a clean and simple solution, but also seeds new conflicts. The tried and tested alternatives to this approach, involving international protection of human rights and creation of special minority rights regimes, have shown little promise. Gottlieb outlines a third "states plus nations" approach for addressing ethnic conflicts, rendered possible by changing attitudes to the sovereignty of states. It involves: 1) extending the international system of states to make room also for a system of nations; 2) deconstructing the sovereignty of states and redistributing some attributes to different hands; 3) having a variety of boundary lines and functional borders for different purposes; 4) recognizing the concept of a "national home" (an entity that can exist beyond state limits); 5) establishing functional associations of peoples beside associations of states. **("states + nations" approach)**

057
The New Tribalism: Notes on a Difficult Problem, Michael Walzer (Co-Editor, *Dissent*), *Dissent*, Spring 1992, 164-171.

"All over the world today, but most interestingly and frighteningly in Eastern Europe and the Soviet Union, men and women are reasserting their local and particularist, their ethnic, religious, and national identities." It is now apparent that popular energies mobilized against totalitarian rule were fueled in good part by "tribal" loyalties and passions. The left has never understood the tribes: their first response is to argue for containment in democratically transformed multinational states. The impulse of the left is to cling to whatever unities exist and make them work, similar to those who firmly oppose divorce of husband and wife. But despite its difficulties, we have to think about divorce among nations. We should aim at protected spaces of many different sorts, matched to the needs of different tribes. If some sort of union or confederation is our goal, the best way to reach it is to abandon coercion and allow the tribes first to separate and then to negotiate their own voluntary and gradual, even if only partial, adherence to some new community of interest. "Our common humanity will never make us members of a single universal tribe. The crucial commonality of the human race is particularism. With the end of imperial and totalitarian rule, we can at last recognize this commonality and begin the difficult negotiations it requires." **(new tribalism)**

058
Savages and Civilization: Who Will Survive? Jack Weatherford (Prof of Anthropology, Macalester College, St. Paul MN). NY: Crown Publishers, Jan 1994/310p/ $24.00.

Neither the classless society of communism nor the global village of capitalism managed to homogenize the world during the 20th century. Despite an international pop culture of sports and entertainment icons, ethnic and cultural identities have grown stronger everywhere. In the struggles among cultural groups in world history, the victors usually seized the title of "civilized," and the defeated bore the stigma of being savages, barbarians, and heathens. But just as civilization seems to have defeated the tribal people of the world, it seems to be in worse danger than ever before. No longer in fear of enemies from outside, civilization now seems vulnerable to enemies from within. After relating the conditions of various tribal cultures around the world, Weatherford concludes that nowhere in the world did he see as much savagery, crime, and cruelty as on the streets of Washington DC. Similar patterns hold throughout the urban world, as new gangs organize around tribal principles: "the most savage way of life is now found in the centers of our most modern cities. Civilization has produced a savagery far worse than that which we once imputed to primitive tribes.... The cities and institutions of civilization have now become social dinosaurs." The challenge now facing us is to live in harmony without living in uniformity, and to share some values such as basic human rights and basic rules of interaction. [**NOTE**: A marked contrast to the "zones of peace" (#066).] **(savagery of urban civilization)**

059
The Coming Clash of Civilizations: Or, the West Against the Rest, Samuel P. Huntington (Prof of Govt, Harvard U), *The New York Times* (Op-Ed), Sunday, 6 June 1993, p19. (Adapted from *The Clash of Civilizations*, Foreign Affairs, 72:3, Summer 1993, 22-49.)

"World politics is entering a new phase in which the fundamental source of conflict will be neither ideological or economic. The great divisions among mankind and the dominating source of conflict will be cultural." Nation-states have been the principal actors in world affairs for only a few centuries. The broader reaches of history have been the history of civilizations; the world is returning to this pattern. World politics will be shaped in large measure by the interactions among 7 or 8 major civilizations: Western, Confucian, Japanese, Islamic, Hindu, Slavic-Orthodox, Latin American, and possibly African civilizations. The fault lines between civilizations will be the battle lines of the future, because: 1) differences among civilizations are basic, involving history, language, culture, and religion; these differences are the product of centuries and will not soon disappear; 2) the world is becoming smaller and interactions between peoples are increasing, thus intensifying civilization consciousness; 3) economic and social changes are separating people from long-standing local identities, with religion moving in to fill the gap; 4) the growth of civilization consciousness is enhanced by a return-to-the-roots phenomenon in non-Western civilizations ("Asianization" in Japan, "Hinduization" in India, "re-Islamization" of the Middle East); thus, "the central axis of world politics is likely to be the conflict between 'the West and the rest'"; 5) cultural differences are less mutable and hence less easily compromised than political and economic ones; 6) economic regionalism is increasing; if successful, it will reinforce civilization consciousness. Western policy should thus seek to promote more cooperation and unity in its own civilization, maintain close relations with Russia and Japan, strengthen international institutions, limit the expanding military strength of potentially hostile civilizations, and accommodate non-Western modern civilizations. [**NOTE**: A compelling analysis, but one that may well establish a dangerous paradigm emphasizing differences and conflict. Huntington's notion of reverting to "civilization consciousness" is diametrically opposed to Elgin's paradigm (#025) of evolving consciousness and transition to sustainability. Pressures for a sustainable world are not considered by Huntington.]

(civilizations as basic future conflict)

*060
The New Cold War? Religious Nationalism Confronts the Secular State. Mark Juergensmeyer (Prof of Religion and Political Science, U of Hawaii). Berkeley: U of California Press, May 1993/292p/$25.00;$15.00pb.

The longing for an indigenous form of religious politics free from the taint of Western culture appeared to be an anomaly when the Islamic revolution in Iran challenged secular politics in 1979. In the 1990s, it has become a major theme in international politics. "Proponents of the new nationalisms hold the potential of making common cause against the secular West, in what might evolve into a new Cold War." The new religious revolutionaries are concerned not so much about the political structure of the nation-state as with the political ideology undergirding it. They reject the notion that what draws people together as a nation and what legitimates their political order is a rational compact that unites everyone in a geographical region. Many religious people outside of America and Europe do not take such secular nationalism for granted, and dismiss it as bereft of moral or spiritual values. Religious nationalism has become popular at this moment of history because religion provides the only stable point in a time of social turbulence and political confusion. It is one way of reconciling heretofore unreconcilable elements—traditional religion and modern politics. Moreover, "The material expectations offered by secular ideologies often cause frustrations because they cannot be fulfilled in one's own lifetime; the expectations of religious ideologies do not disappoint in the same way because they are not expected to be fulfilled in this world."

"It is possible to imagine that the current situation could get far worse, and a global state of enmity could settle in, surpassing the hostility of the old Cold War. One can foresee the emergence of a united religious bloc stretching from Central and South Asia through the Middle East and Africa. With an arsenal of nuclear weapons at its disposal and fueled by American fear of Islam, it might well replace the old Soviet Union as a united global enemy of the secular West. Such a conflict might be compounded by the rise of new religious radicals in Europe and the US." But, *it is equally likely* that religious nationalists are incapable of uniting with one another, and that they will greatly desire an economic and political reconciliation with the secular world. A grudging tolerance might develop between religious and secular nationalists, and each might admire what the other provides: communitarian values and moral vision on the one hand, and individualism and rational rules of justice on the other. The new synthesis between religion and the secular state can be incendiary, but may also be necessary for the essential elements of democracy to be legitimated.

Whether or not a new Cold War develops depends on how religious nationalism behaves, and how it is perceived. Our first task is coming to terms with the phenomenon and accepting the fact that, in one form or another, it is here to stay. We should then sort out which aspects of religious nationalism should be opposed (e.g., abuses of human rights, irresponsible international behavior), which aspects we can live with or even admire (appreciation of tradition, grounding of public institutions in morality), and aspects that we might have to learn to coexist with (the views of divine justification for human laws, certain lands as the province of only one religion, and exalting communitarian values over individualistic ones).
[NOTE: A fair-minded treatment of a very important but unpleasant possibility. Amply documented, with 45 pages of notes, some 500 bibliographic references, and a list of about 100 political, religious, and intellectual leaders interviewed in the 1988-1992 period.]
(religious nationalism vs. secular nationalism)

061
The New World Order. Pat Robertson (Chairman, Christian Broadcasting Network, Virginia Beach VA). Dallas TX: Word Publishing, Sept 1991/319p/$16.99.

The new world order is seen as the quest to eliminate national sovereignty, to destroy the Christian faith, and to establish a world government, a world police force, world courts, world banking and currency, and a world elite in charge of it all. Dominant forces espousing this view are the Council on Foreign Relations and the Trilateral Commission: the behind-the-scenes Establishment. Other forces include various global issues and world order programs at major universities. "Consistently, the view is futurist, applying alternative visions, imaging, and other fanciful means of exploring the promised globalist world-view which they believe is just ahead of us. Supporting the research and development of all these programs are some 150 foundations, funding agencies, and research councils, ranging from Amnesty International to the World Future Society." (p152) Specifically mentioned villains include Richard Falk, Norman Cousins, Fritjof Capra, Willis Harman, the New Age world religion, the UN Treaty on the Rights of the Child, and "the Club of Rome—the notorious pro-death group that preaches the doctrine of Zero Population Growth." The one thing the utopian dreamers always omit is the sinful nature of man. Peace will only come when its source is flowing from the benign influences of Almighty God. "There is absolutely no way that government can operate successfully unless led by godly men and women operating under the laws of the God of Jacob." Robertson has formed the Christian Coalition to rebuild the foundation for a free, sovereign America and to wage the "epic struggle" between "people of faith and people of the humanistic-occultic sphere."

[NOTE: Such fevered distortions from almost anyone else could be quickly dismissed. But Robertson heads a fairly sizable media empire, and hosts "The 700 Club" on TV, seen in 86 countries. What sells in today's America? As of late 1991, this hysterical tract was #1 on the *Publishers Weekly* Religious Bestsellers list *and* among the top ten on the secular nonfiction bestseller list. Hoping for public crucifixion, Robertson predicts that "Anyone who gets involved in the struggle for freedom can be assured of being branded by the Establishment as being narrow-minded, provincial, obstructionist, a defender of fortress America, out of touch with the global realities, unskilled in foreign policy and, of course, the usual 'bigoted, fundamentalist Christian, right-wing zealot.'" (p263) Pat says it all. But evangelical Christianity need not be hostile to intelligent futurism: note **Wild Hope** by Tom Sine (**FS Annual 1993**, #11821) from the same publisher!] **("new world order" denounced)**

062
The Rise of the Nonprofit Sector, Lester M. Salamon (Director, Institute for Policy Studies, Johns Hopkins U), *Foreign Affairs*, 73:4, July-Aug 1994, 109-122.

A striking upsurge is under way around the globe in organized voluntary activity and creation of private, nonprofit, or non-governmental organizations. "We are in the midst of a global *associational revolution* that may prove to be as significant to the latter 20th century as the rise of the nation-state was to the latter 19th." The upshot is a global third sector: a massive array of self-governing organizations pursuing public purposes outside the formal apparatus of the state. For example, in the developing world, some 4,600 Western voluntary organizations are now active providing support to some 20,000 indigenous NGOs. Bangladesh alone boasts some 10,000 registered NGOs. In the UK, there are some 275,000 charities, with income near 5% of GNP. This flourishing of third-sector activity has been encouraged by the crisis of the modern welfare state, the crisis of non-participatory development efforts, the global environmental crisis, the failure of socialism, the communications revolution making it far easier to organize, and the bourgeois revolution (a new urban middle class whose leadership is critical to nonprofit organizations). The proliferation of these groups may be permanently altering the relationship between states and citizens. Most decisive for further third-sector growth will be the relationship that nonprofit organizations can forge with government. They must find sufficient legal and financial support, while maintaining a meaningful degree of autonomy.

(rise of global third sector)

063
The Nonprofit Sector in the Global Community. Kathleen D. McCarthy (Director, Center for the Study of Philanthropy, CUNY Graduate School), Virginia A. Hodgkinson (VP, INDEPENDENT SECTOR), and Russy D. Sumariwalla (former VP, United Way Strategic Inst.). San Francisco: Jossey-Bass, Feb 1992/520p/$49.95.

A new paradigm of the global community is emerging, due to communication technology and a worldwide push toward democratic forms of government. Creation of an international "public" is heralded by growing international movements in nonprofit organizations, notably the peace, environment, and world hunger movements. This book is an initial attempt to understand these organizations, with 28 essays in four parts: 1) **Global Comparisons**: tax policy toward non-profits in 10 countries, public vs. private provision of social services, a Japanese perspective on private philanthropy; 2) **Modern Developed Democracies**: non-profits in Britain, Northern Ireland, the Netherlands, France, Germany, Sweden, Australia, Japan, Israel; 3) **Eastern Europe and the Soviet Union**: the independent sector in Hungary, Poland, Bulgaria, USSR; 4) **Developing Countries**: voluntarism in Argentina, Chile, Uruguay, Egypt, Palestine, India, Indonesia, Singapore, China. Concludes by proposing a "new social order" with a larger share of responsibility for the nonprofit sector in many nations, which would enhance public responsibility and increase empowerment, self-help, and the use of human talent. The editors also propose a "global organization that represents the nonprofit sectors of all nations and parallels the UN as a global organization." [NOTE: Suggests the growing importance of NGOs worldwide, but makes no mention of the Union of International Associations (Rue Washington 40, Brussels), which encompasses part of the global non-profit sector. ALSO SEE: *At Rio, NGOs Were Again Out Front* by Hazel Henderson (*Christian Science Monitor*, 25 June 1992, p19), remarking on the key role of the 13,000 non-governmental organizations represented at the Earth Summit.]

(non-profit organizations worldwide)

2. Democratization and Peacemaking

064
The Third Wave: Democratization in the Late Twentieth Century. Samuel P. Huntington (Prof of Government, Harvard U). Norman OK: U of Oklahoma Press, Sept 1991/366p/$24.95.

Expansion of the Julian J. Rothbaum Lectures at the U of Oklahoma, on the third wave of democratization in the 1974-1990 period—perhaps the most important global political development of the late 20th century. The first wave of democratization (minimally defined as free and fair election of top leaders) had its roots in the American and French revolutions, lasting from 1828 to 1926. This was followed by a reverse wave away from democracy (1922-1942), a second wave of democratization (1943-1962), and a second reverse wave toward authoritarianism (1958-1975). The third wave began in Portugal in 1974, and had led to transition of some 30 countries from non-democratic to democratic systems. This may be followed by a third reverse wave, and then a fourth wave of democratization sometime in the 21st century. The two key factors affecting the future stability and expansion of democracy are economic development and political leadership. Most poor societies will remain undemocratic as long as they remain poor. "Economic development makes democracy possible; political leadership makes it real." [NOTE: A narrow study with a useful reminder of potential reversal of recent democratic gains. No reference is made to Alvin Toffler's **The Third Wave** (Morrow, 1980; **FS Annual 1980-81** #2274), a much broader view of evolution beyond industrial civilization.]

(third reverse wave of democratization ahead?)

065
Grasping the Democratic Peace: Principles for a Post-Cold War World. Bruce Russett (Prof of Intl. Relations, Yale U; editor, *J. of Conflict Resolution*). Princeton NJ: Princeton U Press, Sept 1993/173p/$19.95.

Scholars and leaders now commonly say that democracies almost never fight each other. When they do get into disputes, they are less likely to let the disputes escalate. The more democratic each state is, the more peaceful their relations are likely to be. Understanding that democracies rarely fight each other has great consequences for policy in the contemporary world. It should affect the kinds of military preparations believed to be necessary, and encourage peaceful efforts to assist the emergence and consolidation of democracy. "Perhaps most important, understanding the sources of democratic peace can have the effect of a self-fulfilling prophecy." The literature on requisites for democracy is vast, but much of it is deeply flawed—ethnocentric and too enamored of economic preconditions. Yet some things have been learned and stated with some modesty. [Among several "good efforts," Russett notes **The Third Wave** by Huntington (above).] "The emergence of new democracies with the end of the Cold War presents an opening for change in the international system more fundamental even than at the end of other big wars." In 1992, for the first time, a majority of states approximated democratic standards, with another 35 in some form of transition to democracy. "If the chance for wide democratization can be grasped and consolidated, international politics might be transformed." **(new politics of a democratic majority?)**

066
The Real World Order: Zones of Peace/Zones of Turmoil. Max Singer (Chevy Chase MD) and Aaron Wildavsky (died 1993; ex UC-Berkeley). Chatham NJ: Chatham House Pubs., Fall 1993/212p/$25.00;$16.95pb.

Former Presidents of the Hudson Institute (Singer) and the American Political Science Association (Wildavsky) argue that the key to understanding the real world order is to separate the world into two parts: one part (with about 15% of world population) is zones of peace, wealth, and democracy; the other is zones of turmoil, war, and development. The countries in the zones of peace and democracy will have most of the power in the world, and will not face a serious threat to their national survival or freedom, because modern democracies do not go to war with one another. The zones of peace are something new in the world. In the zones of turmoil, democracy is likely to recede in the next few years before advancing again, "because the shallow or questionable democracies that initially took the place of communist governments do not have strong roots and face tremendous ethnic and economic problems." Very gradually, though, the number of people living in stable democracies will become a larger share of the world's population. Some proposals: 1) a UN Democratic Caucus of democratic member countries, to coordinate participation in UN decisions and to bind some marginally democratic countries to the stable democracies; 2) a broader view of Europe to include Slavs, the eastern branches of Catholicism, and some Moslems (a broad Europe would speed development of those countries outside of "narrow Europe"); 3) creating competitive subnational units of government in countries with more than 20-30 million people (in that countries within the zones of peace no longer have to be large to protect themselves against attack), which would lead to smaller and better governance. US foreign policy should seek to keep international trade as open as possible, and to limit violence and encourage democracy in the zones of turmoil, so that the zones of peace will be extended as soon as possible. In sum, "the spread of wealth, democracy, and peace...(has) a good chance to cover most of the people of the world by the end of the next century." [NOTE: An interesting and guardedly optimistic view designed to counter "fashionable pessimism" over international affairs. But blind spots abound, with no mention of population growth, terrorism, or global environmental problems. ALSO SEE: **Passage to a Human World** by Max Singer (Hudson Institute, 1987; Transaction Books, 1989; **FS Annual 1988-89** #8870).]

(**extending zones of peace and democracy**)

067
The Global Resurgence of Democracy. Edited by Larry Diamond (Hoover Institution) and Marc F. Plattner (National Endowment for Democracy). Baltimore MD: Johns Hopkins U P, March 1993/336p/$50.00;$14.95pb.

The 29 essays, first published in the *Journal of Democracy* (co-edited by Diamond and Plattner), are arranged in four sections: **1) The Democratic Moment**: democracy's third wave by Samuel P. Huntington [see #064 above], rethinking African democracy, the culture of liberty; **2) Problems of Democratic Institutionalization**: paradoxes of democracy, comparing democratic systems, constitutional choices for new democracies; **3) Political Corruption**: the rise of standards, strategies for reform, Nigeria's perennial struggle; **4) The Global Democratic Prospect**: the new world disorder, why democracy can work in Eastern Europe (due to the civic legacy of dissent), prospects for a democratic transition in China, Latin America's fragile democracies (resumption of economic growth would contribute most to restoring confidence in democratic rule; it will take years of struggle to secure democratic stability in most countries), the rebirth of political freedom in Africa. **Leszek Kolakowski** (U of Chicago; Oxford U) concludes by warning of continuing threats to democracy: the growth of malignant nationalism, religious intolerance and theocratic aspirations, terrorism and criminal violence (compelling democratic governments to combat them with non-democratic measures), and—perhaps most important—the mentality of endless expectations in a world of overpopulation and shrinking resources that is likely to require many undemocratic restrictions.

(**new fragile democracies as problematic**)

068
Democracy and Democratization: Processes and Prospects in a Changing World. Georg Sørensen (U of Aarhus, Denmark). Boulder CO: Westview Press, June 1993/170p/$49.50;$13.95pb.

In recent years, the swift progress of democracy in many countries has raised hopes for a better world. But there are questions as to whether democratic advancement will continue, and whether potential positive effects of democracy will be forthcoming. The large majority of the current transitions are restricted, frail, and unconsolidated, and plagued by acute social and economic problems. The only encouraging element is that popular organization in the struggle for democracy has reached record levels. And, with the end of the Cold War, the Western excuse for supporting authoritarian regimes is no longer valid. Still, "the odds seem to weigh heavily against the further development and consolidation of the frail democratic openings that have taken place in recent years." Nor do transitions to democracy guarantee improved development and human rights. Transitions can lead to unstable conditions involving greater human rights violation than before. Concludes with two polar scenarios: **1) Springtime of Democracy**: trend to democratization continues both in countries and the international system; the rise of democracy in developing countries is supported by demilitarization and solution of a number of perennial conflicts ("perhaps even a peace settlement in the Middle East is conceivable"); **2) Democratic Decay**: non-representative organizations (transnational corporations, the Group of Seven) become more powerful in the international system, accompanied by democratic decay on the national level (growing lack of interest in politics, public debate bereft of significant issues, an increasingly empty shell of formal political practices); trend to rising economic and social inequality leads to greater political inequality; decreasing support for democratic institutions reduces the perceived costs of authoritarian solutions. Author's conclusion leans toward the pessimistic scenario. "Support for elite-dominated, restricted democracies will not be enough. Without a more solid, popular basis, today's fragile democracies may well be tomorrow's authoritarian dictatorships."

(**new fragile democracies as problematic**)

069
Low Intensity Democracy: Political Power in the New World Order. Edited by Barry Gills (U of Newcastle upon Tyne), Joel Rocamora (Transnational Institute), and Richard Wilson (U of Essex). London and Boulder CO: Pluto Press (dist by Westview), Dec 1993/264p/$47.50; $19.95pb.

The struggle to define "democracy" has become a major ideological battle. "Democracy" has replaced "development" as the buzzword for the 1990s, and seems to be sweeping the globe. Some have tried to explain this wave of political change as the historical triumph of an idea. But there are grounds to be skeptical. Although they have instituted some of the trappings of Western liberal democracies such as periodic elections, in a real sense these new democracies have preserved ossified political and economic structures from the past. Four case studies in this book (Argentina, Guatemala, the Philippines, and South Korea) "demonstrate that democracy as understood in the West is basically incompatible with societies characterized by extreme concentration of wealth in the hands of a tiny elite." Participatory progressive democracy is the only answer to this low intensity democracy. Also included are essays by Andre Gunder Frank on marketing democracy in an undemocratic market, Samir Amin on the offensive of the West that is really against socialism rather than pro-democracy, Noam Chomsky on the emerging capitalist world order and the remote but emerging possibility of more meaningful democracy, and Roger Burbach on America's thin democracy. [ALSO SEE: **The New Ideology of Imperialism** by Frank Furedi of U of

Kent (Pluto Press, April 1994/140p/$51.50;$17.00pb), on the renewed onslaught against the Third World by the major Western powers that fear resurgent nationalism.]

(low intensity democracy in Third World)

*070

The Transformation of War. Martin van Creveld (Dept of History, Hebrew U of Jerusalem). NY: Free Press, Jan 1991/254p/$22.95.

Contemporary "strategic" thought is rooted in a "Clausewitzian" worldview that is now obsolete or wrong. And the view that war may not have a future is incorrect. Large-scale conventional war may be at its last gasp, but war itself is about to enter a new era of conflict between ethnic and religious groups. The state's attempt to monopolize violence is faltering, and the rise of low-intensity conflict may end up destroying the state. Nuclear weapons make it impossible for large sovereign territorial units (states) to fight each other in earnest without running the risk of mutual suicide. Large heterogeneous empires such as the Soviet Union are disintegrating (China and India are also likely candidates; both countries are afflicted by an expanding population and powerful centrifugal forces). If low-intensity conflict continues to spread, 1) future war will not be waged by armies, but by groups now called terrorists, guerrillas, bandits, and robbers; their organizations are likely to be built on charismatic lines and motivated by ideology; 2) attempts to assassinate or otherwise incapacitate leaders will be regarded as part of the game of war; 3) the distinction between soldiers and civilians will blur, as well as differences between "front" and "rear" (practices that had been considered uncivilized, such as capturing civilians and entire communities for ransom, "are almost certain to make a comeback"); 4) cultural monuments and religious shrines will no longer enjoy immunity; 5) weapons such as gas that are prohibited today will be increasingly used because they are cheap, easy to make, and well-suited for closed urban space; 6) existing distinctions between war and crime will break down, as is already the case in Lebanon, Sri Lanka, El Salvador, Peru, and Columbia; 7) many of today's weapons systems will be assigned to the scrap-heap; "in the not too distant future, major military-technological R&D as we have known it since the industrial revolution will grind to a halt" (at present, it largely serves as a welfare system for engineers); 8) war will not take place in the open field but in complex environments; it will be a war of listening devices and car bombs—protracted, bloody, and horrible; 9) war will be waged for the souls of men, rather than territorial control; 10) individual glory, profit, and booty gained at the expense of civilians will once again become important; 11) "However unpalatable the fact, the real reason why we have wars is that men like fighting, and women like those men who are prepared to fight on their behalf;" 12) thus in vast parts of the world no man, woman, or child will be spared the consequences of the newly-emerging forms of war. [**NOTE**: Important, depressing, and provocative.]

(new era of low-intensity conflict)

071

War and Anti-War: Survival at the Dawn of the 21st Century. Alvin and Heidi Toffler (Los Angeles CA). Boston: Little, Brown and Co, Oct 1993/302p/$22.95.

"The way we make war reflects the way we make wealth—and the way we make anti-war must reflect the way we make war." We are speeding toward a totally different structure of power that will create not a world cut in two, but sharply divided into three contrasting and competing civilizations symbolized by the hoe, the assembly line, and the computer. In this trisected world the First Wave supplies agricultural and mineral resources, the Second Wave provides cheap labor and does the mass production, and a rapidly expanding Third Wave sector rises to dominance based on the new ways in which it creates and exploits knowledge. In Third Wave brain-based economies, there are shifts to de-massified production, heterogeneity, ever more information exchange, smaller work units, constant innovation, and a speed-up of daily life.

These changes are reflected in warfare. Knowledge is now the central resource of destructivity, as well as that of productivity. We are moving toward the de-massification of destruction (e.g., by using a laser to designate an individual target). Smart tools produce smart weapons. The Third Wave military requires a vast electronic infrastructure, and, as illustrated in the Gulf War, the velocity of warfare is increased. There will be a radical diversification of the kinds of wars we are likely to confront in the future: separatist wars, ethnic/religious violence, coups d'etat, border disputes, civil upheavals, and terrorist attacks. In the wired global economy, many of these seemingly small conflicts trigger strong secondary effects in nearby or even distant countries. The maximization of lethality has reached its outer limits, and a new arms race may seek to reduce lethality with such weapons as infrasound generators that cause nausea and diarrhea, protective devices built into buildings, calming agents that cause drowsiness, laser rifles that temporarily blind opponents, and technologies that incapacitate hardware or software. (These weapons could, however, be used by terrorists, criminals, or repressive states.) Info-terrorism will be a major arena; one consultant warns that "an electronic Pearl Harbor is waiting to happen." Tomorrow's military leaders will also employ knowledge strategies, such as spin doctor tools to influence the media.

The crisis the world faces today is the absence of a Third Wave peace-form that corresponds to the realities of the Third Wave war-form. With a world fast-dividing into First, Second, and Third Wave civilizations, three distinctly different forms of warfare need to be averted or limited. The variety of wars requires a variety of anti-war forces. One might even imagine "Peace Corporations" contracting to limit war in a region. And the "UN dinosaur" should be transformed to a more flexible Third Wave organization that represents nonstate actors, global corporations, and other entities. [**NOTE**: Glib and self-important as usual, but interesting. Despite the pomposity, though, there isn't much here on peace-making, or "anti-war."]   **(Third Wave war and peace)**

072

Global Mafia: Crime Goes International (Special Report), Michael Elliott, *Newsweek*, 13 Dec 1993, 22-31.

Several trends have met to form a new space for organized crime: 1) development of infotech, making it easy to transfer billions of dollars around the globe within seconds; 2) the collapse of communism in the former USSR and Eastern Europe ("the rebirth of the profit motive has combined with weak governments to form a devastating mixture"); in China, the government has decreed that it is good to grow rich but "has been unable to control the genies of crime and corruption that it has unleashed"; 3) the declining significance of national borders; 4) the rich world's appetite for narcotics, especially cocaine ("never before has one form of criminal activity generated such enormous sums of ready money for investment"). The drug cartels' new global reach, mated with the post-communist world economy, has bred the new organized crime. There is no single worldwide criminal conspiracy, but criminal cooperation is growing (e.g., East European and Russian gangs sell arms to the Sicilian Mafia; Japanese and Italian gangsters held a conference in Paris in 1992). Roy Godson (National Strategy Information Center, Washington), estimates annual worldwide profits of organized crime at $1 trillion. Tim Worth (US Undersecretary of State for Global Affairs) warns that "We have a problem that is accelerating far beyond the ability of our current institutions." Sen. John Kerry (D-Mass) states that "Organized crime is the new communism, the new monolithic threat." Indeed, the CIA is investigating whether oranized-crime groups could get nuclear weapons. Elliott notes that "until recently, the West feared the old conspiracy of Russian-led international communism. Now there are signs that a network of Russian criminals is circling the globe just as effectively as the cadres and ideologues ever did. And the Chinese chapter of this tale is no less frightening." Keys to combating this trend: internationally enforced rules against money laundering, more police officers who can speak foreign languages, coordinating the activities of police bureaus and national-security agencies, and legal systems that protect investors and punish white-collar crime in post-communist countries. [**NOTE**: The sub-head to this report announces that "The new global mafia poses the most serious criminal threat in history." Real or potential, this threat deserves consideration in thinking about security, the global economy, sustainability, and world futures. Similar to eroding national borders, the boundaries to these topics should be reconfigured. ALSO SEE: **Thieve's World**, by Claire Sterling, **FS Annual 1995, #13177.**]   (**global mafia: the new communism?**)

073
Enforcing Restraint: Collective Intervention in Internal Conflicts. Edited by Lori Fisler Damrosch (Prof of Law, Columbia U). NY: Council on Foreign Relations Press, Oct 1993/403p/$17.95pb.

A perennial criticism of international law is that the system has too often failed to restrain states from violations of norms. More recently, the complaint has been turned inside out— that legal rules are a spurious form of restraint, giving states and organizations an excuse to stand by and do nothing while conflict rages within a state's borders. Fortunately, the dramatic changes of the last few years give cause for optimism that both criticisms can be overcome. Instead of the view that interventions in internal conflicts must be presumptively illegitimate, "the prevailing trend today is to take seriously the claim that the international community ought to intercede to prevent bloodshed." Legal arguments now focus not on condemning or justifying intervention, but on how best to mobilize collective efforts. Case studies here (on Yugoslavia, Iraq, Haiti, Liberia, Somalia, and Cambodia) show large segments of the international community willing to endorse strong collective action, although capabilities are still far from optimal. If unacceptable behavior is to be deterred, the international community must identify thresholds that will elicit response if crossed, and clarify what responses will be forthcoming. [ALSO SEE: **International Law and the Use of Force** by Anthony Clark Arend and Robert J. Beck (Routledge, Aug 1993/$65.00;$19.95pb), on the transition to a pro-democratic paradigm—an emerging legal obligation regarding use of force.]

(**growing legal support for intervention**)

074
Laser Weapons: The Dawn of a New Military Age. Bengt Anderberg (Major General, Swedish Armed Forces) and Myron L. Wolbarsht (Prof of Ophthalmology, Duke U). NY: Plenum Press, Nov 1992/243p/$24.95.

Most battlefield weapons are extremely noisy, and give off a flash and some smoke when fired, thus giving the soldier's position away. The ammunition from current weapons has a curved trajectory requiring adjustments. Consumption of huge amounts of ammunition leads to logistical problems. A laser weapon firing a beam of light has a flat trajectory and limited logistical problems, and is silent and less detectable when fired. High-energy laser weapons are now being studied for antiaircraft and antimissile use. Low-energy laser systems may become even more useful against sensors and the human eye. An anti-eye low-energy laser (LEL) weapon may very well be hand-held, used alone or in combination with a rifle or machine gun. They would be relatively cheap and very cost-effective, with the "ammunition" stored in batteries. "Low-energy laser weapons will soon be deployed and used within all branches of the military service in every country.... Most nations will be able to mass-produce cheap and effective anti-eye laser weapons in the future." Some consequences: 1) there will surely be many armed conflicts during this and following decades where small, cheap, anti-eye laser weapons may very well be used; this "most terrible weapon on the future battlefield" will have the power to cause mass blindness, resulting in "devastating postwar problems"; 2) ground soldiers will have tremendous psychological problems watching their friends go blind; they will thus avoid looking at the enemy, which will severely reduce their combat efficiency (efficient protection against the laser threat at this time is not possible without degrading vision unacceptable); 3) aircraft pilots will be the highest priority target for LEL weapons; present aircraft and helicopters should be retrofitted with a means of indirect viewing, which will certainly be very expensive; 4) it will be very costly to build up even a limited capability to handle the expected increase in eye casualties; 5) much R&D will be devoted to creating countermeasures and counter-countermeasures. [**NOTE**: A sober volume on a worrisome development.]

(**anti-eye low-energy laser weapons**)

075
The Military in New Times: Adapting Armed Forces to a Turbulent World. Edited by James Burk (Assoc Prof of Sociology, Military Studies Inst., Texas A&M). Boulder CO: Westview Press, Feb 1994/212p/$44.95.

The end of the Cold War was a welcome event, but it has confused international relations, rather than clarifying them. It aggravates long-term changes in technology, attitudes toward authority, and transnational organization. Operating together, these changes have: 1) multiplied the threats to which the military might have to respond, while at the same time limiting the usefulness of armed force as an instrument of national policy; 2) made the successful exercise of authority more difficult (perhaps part of the evolution of liberal democratic societies), while increasing demands for competent leadership in a variety of spheres; 3) encouraged the expansion of multinational peacekeeping forces, while discouraging the use of armed force outside the framework of international coalitions. The absence of a clear focal enemy in the new "multicentric world" complicates the task of military planning. The multi-centric world encompasses not only the new organization of interstate relations, but a new realm of sovereignty-free actors (corporations, ethnic groups, NGOs, social movements). Of major importance is a general decline in the willingness of people to uncritically trust and follow the direction of institutional authorities. Clients, especially those with power, are less willing to accept professional judgments as final. And war is no longer the principal means of resolving conflicts, at least among developed countries. The armed forces of Sweden, Switzerland, and Canada best illustrate the postmodern trend toward tolerating heterogeneous values and lifestyles. The problem faced by the postmodern military is not the lack of things to do, but the absence of a consensus on what is most important. It also faces a problem of cultural lag associated with the peacekeeping role: while world structures currently favor increased reliance on multinational peacekeeping, national cultures supply meager resources to the peacekeepers. [**NOTE**: Timely and sophisticated. Includes contributions by James N. Rosenau on the transition to a multi-centric world and by Charles C. Moskos on the postmodern military.]

(**postmodern military in a multi-centric world**)

076
World Military and Social Expenditures 1993 (15th Edition). Ruth Leger Sivard (Director, World Priorities). Washington: World Priorities Inc, Nov 1993/56p (8x11")/ $7.00pb.

The 15th accounting of the use and misuse of the world's resources. Total world military expenditures have declined from the peak year of 1987, but are still "well over $600 billion a year" in 1987 dollars. [**NOTE**: Total military expenditures have been recalibrated downward for recent years due to new calculations of Soviet Union GNP (p55). Higher figures were used in the 14th edition of **WMSE** (**FS Annual 1992** #11044).] Military spending in the West has, so far, been slow to adjust to sudden dissolution of the Cold War threat. Overall NATO military spending in 1992 was about 10% below the peak in 1987 (but in real terms it was one-third higher than before the big run-up of the 1980s). Two precursors of future military trends, NATO expenditure on R&D and on military equipment, were still 50% above levels that were common before the 1980s surge in spending. On the Soviet side, expenditures took a nose dive in 1991 and 1992: "by 1992, the military budget of the former USSR had apparently slipped to about half the level of 5 years earlier." Over the same 5-year period, the US cutback was less than 10% in inflation-adjusted terms. After a modest drop in 1990, military expenditures of developing countries appeared to head upward again, led by increased spending in the Middle East and the Far East. Since 1987, the overall reduction in military outlays appears to have produced an average annual savings worldwide of about $14 billion—a relatively minor "peace dividend."

Sections of the **WMSE** report are devoted to nuclear arsenals (even after planned reductions, "future nuclear stocks would still contain 10,000-20,000 warheads, representing more than 900 times the six million tons of TNT expended in World War II"), the costs of dismantling nuclear weapons, war-related deaths in the 1945-1992 period (23.1 million total; the 29 "major wars" underway in 1992 are an all-time record high), military control and repression in the Third World, the challenges of social development (i.e., improving health and education), the status of various arms control agreements, US military and social expenditures, and the usual statistical annex. [**NOTE**: A concise array of timely and valuable data, presented in user-friendly charts, tables, and maps—along with a dollop of social outrage.]

(**world military spending: slow decline**)

077
Nuclear Winter in the Post-Cold War Era, Carl Sagan (Cornell U) and Richard P. Turco (UCLA), *Journal of Peace Research*, 30:4, Nov 1993, 369-373.

An update of "nuclear winter" thinking, following two earlier papers in *Science* (23 Dec 1983 & 12 Jan 1990; **FS Annual 1985** #6602 & **FS Annual 1991** #10419). A small-scale test of something like nuclear winter has been recently performed. The oil well fires ignited in Kuwait in January 1991 by the retreating Iraqi army produced about one ten-thousandth of the soot expected in a nuclear war. Nevertheless, the darkening of the sky and the cooling of the ground by about 5°C are just what is predicted by nuclear winter theory. Now that the Cold War is over, the START I treaty mandates a build-down to 6,000 accountable strategic warheads by each side. With START II, each side would settle down to 3,500 strategic warheads by 2003. But this is not nearly enough. Residual arsenals after START II will still endanger almost everyone. Moreover, nuclear technology is now more widely available, and manufacturing methods have become cheaper. "If we wish to arrange a world in which no miscalculation, no technological error, no fit of ethnic or religious passion, and not even a conspiracy of madmen could bring about a global environmental catastrophe, we must arrange a world with fewer than several hundred nuclear weapons."

(**nuclear winter threat continues**)

078
Strengthening Nuclear Nonproliferation. Kathleen C. Bailey (Center for Security and Technology Studies, Lawrence Livermore National Laboratory). Boulder CO: Westview Press, Dec 1993/132p/$35.95; $14.95pb.

The nuclear nonproliferation regime is a set of policies and agreements designed since the 1960s to prevent the further spread of nuclear weapons, roll back weapons programs, and pursue disarmament. A key component of the regime is the 1968 Nuclear Nonproliferation Treaty, due for renewal in 1995. The most serious problem with the treaty is nonmembership by key countries (China, France, Israel, India, Pakistan). Other nations have joined the NPT, but have failed to adhere to its letter or spirit (North Korea, Iran). Whether or not a nation is party to the NPT, there are no significant repercussions if they do acquire nuclear weapons. New problems could pose a major threat to extending NPT past 1995, and create new stimulus for proliferation: 1) a very serious question is whether the three former Soviet republics now with nuclear weapons—Ukraine, Belarus, Kazakhstan—will give them up; 2) nuclear weapons or their components could be sold for high sums to terrorists or proliferant nations; sales of spent nuclear fuel, a source of plutonium, may also be lucrative; 3) as budget priorities are shifted in weapons programs, there is wide concern about the potential of a Russian "brain drain" in which key scientists and technicians would sell their expertise ("there may be even greater danger that US nationals will begin to market their skills elsewhere"); 4) the dissolution of the Warsaw Pact and drastic changes in NATO may stimulate proliferation in Europe. In the future, the nuclear non-proliferation regime will face more challenges than in the past. A new NPT should improve safeguards, develop detection and verification technologies, provide security assurances, and educate publics and governments on the costs of nuclear weapons possession. Military intervention should be considered, as when Israel bombed Iraq in 1981, in cases where proliferation presents a clear threat to international stability and other means have failed.

(**nuclear proliferation: new stimuli?**)

079
The Plutonium Genie, George Perkovich (Director, Secure Society Project, W. Alton Jones Foundation), *Foreign Affairs*, 72:3, Summer 1993, 153-165.

Plutonium is one of the most dangerous materials on earth: ten pounds can make a crude nuclear weapon, and one-thirty-thousandth of an ounce will cause cancer if inhaled. Since its creation as a war child of the 1942 Manhattan Project, 22 countries now possess or control separated plutonium in various forms and amounts. About 260 tons of the material are in nuclear weapons. Roughly 530 tons are in untreated spent reactor fuel, and some 120 tons are stored in weapons-usable form or recycled as fuel awaiting potential future use. To cope with the problem, an international regime is proposed to manage the storage and reduction of existing plutonium through direct disposal as waste or (more expensively and insecurely) through irradiation in power reactors. By regulating and facilitating waste disposal and other environmental and safety matters, the international regime would go beyond current arrangements. A major inducement for participation would be the promise of international cooperation in solving the disposal problems that confront all countries.

(**international plutonium regime proposed**)

*080

How Nuclear Weapons Spread: Nuclear-Weapon Proliferation in the 1990s. Frank Barnaby (Chilbolten UK; former Director, Stockholm Intl. Peace Research Inst.). London & NY: Routledge, Dec 1993/144p/$55.00.

The world's nuclear arsenals total nearly 50,000 weapons (the ex-Soviets have about 27,000; the US has about 20,000). If promises are implemented, the ex-Soviet and US arsenals will be reduced to about 9,000 nuclear warheads. Doing so will make the arsenals of China, France, and the UK relatively more significant. All three are modernizing their weapons. And there is also concern about proliferation of nuclear weapons to countries that do not have them. Nuclear programs in India, Pakistan, Israel, Iraq, Iran, North Korea, Argentina, Brazil, and South Africa are discussed. Israel is very secretive about its nuclear weapons and continues to deny their existence. This myth is crucially important, because the US government cannot under law "continue giving economic aid to Israel if it acknowledges that Israel has nuclear weapons."

It is increasingly recognized that the risk of proliferation of nuclear weapons to countries may be decreasing. But the risk of nuclear weapons spreading to sub-national groups such as terrorists may be increasing. As plutonium becomes more available, it is increasingly likely that a sub-national group will acquire it by theft or other means, and construct its own nuclear explosive device. The disintegration of the Soviet Union and the instability of Eastern Europe may make the theft of plutonium produced in Soviet-supplied reactors more likely. There is a very serious danger that authorities in these countries will protect fissile material poorly, or give it low priority. Only a small number of competent people is needed to fabricate a primitive nuclear device producing explosions equal to 100-1000 tons of TNT. Such a device can easily fit into a medium-sized van, and could destroy the center of a relatively large city. Even if the device did not produce nuclear fission, the dispersion of small particles of deadly plutonium (the most likely danger) would make a significant area of a city uninhabitable for some time. This would be threat enough by a group known to have fissile material. In addition, more and more countries are acquiring ballistic missiles. "Sub-national groups may, in the future, acquire and use ballistic missiles as delivery systems for nuclear weapons."

The 35-year-old International Atomic Energy Agency has about 930 nuclear facilities under safeguards in about 60 countries. But more inspections will be required in the next few years, at a time when the IAEA is cutting its budget. There are good arguments for a new international agency with the authority and resources to conduct surprise inspections of undeclared nuclear facilities in any country. A strong international agency to deal with nuclear smuggling is also needed. [**NOTE**: Authoritative, readable, and restrained. The "suitcase bomb" discussed by a few others in the 1980s is not mentioned here (presumably not feasible). But there is much else to worry about. Barnaby was editor of **The Gaia Peace Atlas** (Doubleday, 1988; **FS Annual 1990** #9728), still a valuable overview of the peace problem in its broadest dimensions.] (**nuclear weapon use by terrorist groups**)

081

Preventing a Biological Arms Race. Edited by Susan Wright (Director, Science and Society Program, U of Michigan). Cambridge MA: MIT Press, June 1990/446p/$25.00.

In theory, the menace of biological warfare should no longer be with us. Developing, producing, and stockpiling biological and toxin weapons—which deploy living organisms and natural poisons to spread disease and debilitation in humans, animals, and plants—are unconditionally banned by treaty. The US, the USSR, and most other nations have signed, ratified, and apparently complied with the 1972 Biological Weapons Convention. But East-West military rivalry and confrontations in the Middle East have eroded confidence in the treaty regime. The advent of genetic engineering and other new biotechnologies has stimulated renewed military interest, and there are "ominous signs of increasing military development of the biological sciences, a trend which if continued could provoke a biological arms race." This race could come about from the synergistic interaction of accusations directed toward biological and chemical warfare activities in other countries, military development to counter perceived threats, and other nation's perceptions of those activities. Concludes with proposals on strengthening barriers to biological weaponry, addressed to national governments in general, the US government, the USSR, the organized international community, scientists and corporations responsible for R&D in the biosciences, and individual citizens. (**biological arms race ahead?**)

082

Biological Weapons: Weapons of the Future? Edited by Brad Roberts (Center for Strategic and International Studies; editor, *The Washington Quarterly*). Boulder CO: Westview Press, 1993/101p/$13.95pb.

Biological weapons are munitions or other delivery systems, such as spray tanks, filled with biological agents of warfare—living organisms, or infective materials derived from them—that are intended to cause disease or death among humans, animals, and/or plants. Western intelligence agencies have detected 10 or 11 countries engaged in offensive *bw* programs, up from 4 in the 1960s (this compares with roughly 20 states involved with the proliferation of chemical weapons). Bioweapons are a major challenge for the post-Cold War era because: 1) *bw* of the former Soviet military might trickle out to other states or non-state entities, or the scientific expertise can be readily purchased; 2) difficulty of acquiring nuclear capabilities and the costs of chemical weapons encourages interest in *bw*; 3) the revolution in the biological sciences makes it possible to create novel organisms (conceivably, the technology might in the future create agents that harm only specific racial groups); 4) bioscience now makes it easier to do a number of things that in the 1960s seemed difficult or risky (e.g., significant quantities of biological agent can be produced much more quickly, obviating the need to stockpile large amounts for long periods); 5) "the increasing availability of biotech and advanced expertise means that perhaps as many as 100 countries have the means of making their own biological weapons"; 6) better agents matched to more effective delivery systems, notably cruise missiles, may make their tactical use more likely; 7) the prospects for *bw* terrorism have probably increased; 8) deepening doubts about the effectiveness of the existing treaty regime in detecting and responding to non-compliant actions by states. Concludes that the US must give priority to improving the full range of *bw* defense.

(**bioweapons: growing threat**)

083

The International Missile Bazaar: The New Suppliers' Network. William C. Potter and Harlan W. Jencks (both Monterey Institute of International Studies). Boulder CO: Westview Press, Jan 1994/340p/$59.00.

As recently as the mid-1980s, the threat of missile proliferation seemed remote if not fanciful. The discovery of missile proliferation in the late 1980s was a shock for many observers. The number of states capable of selling ballistic missile technology, missile components, and missiles themselves is large and growing. Detailed histories of 11 national missile programs are provided here: Argentina, Brazil, India, Pakistan, North Korea, South Korea, Iran, Iraq, Israel, Egypt, and China. The motivations of Third World states to acquire missiles and focus their limited resources on missile development: 1) perceived threats from regional neighbors; 2) national prestige (India's Agni missile is seen as a confidence-builder and symbol of self-reliance); 3) potential economic benefits of exporting missiles and missile technology (North Korea, for example, has little of value to sell except weapons and desperately needs foreign exchange); 4) missile capability buys a "place at the table" in international fora that make important decisions; 5) lack of respect for the Missile Technology Control Regime (widely regarded in the Third World as a neo-imperialist mechanism). The availability of established modern technologies has made it possible for newcomers in rocketry to advance much faster, skipping some stages altogether. However, most Third World missile proliferation has involved copying and modifying the Soviet SCUD, which is a relatively primitive rocket (although still good enough to terrorize or deter neighbors). The military utility of ballistic missiles is questionable in the absence of nuclear warheads. Thus nuclear proliferation is more important than ever.

(**missile proliferation in Third World**)

084

Preventing Weapons Proliferation: Should the Regimes Be Combined? Leonard S. Spector and Virginia Foran (both Carnegie Endowment for International Peace). Muscatine IA: The Stanley Foundation, Feb 1993/37p(8x11")/free.

A report drawn from ideas presented at the 33rd Strategy for Peace conference, convened at Airlie House in October 1992. Today, six broad-based international regimes seek to limit the expansion of various military capabilities: The Nuclear Nonproliferation Regime, The Biological Weapons Regime, The Chemical Weapons Regime, The Missile Technology Control Regime, The Coordinating Committee for Multilateral Export Controls, and a possibly emerging new global regime for limiting transfers of advanced conventional weapons (but there is little consensus on whether such transfers should be curbed, and how). Integrating these regimes would improve overall efficiency, lead to more consistent involvement to address violations, help to address existing conflicts among some of the regimes, and enhance the possibility of cross linkages (e.g. offering incentives to states that accept all of the nonproliferation regimes). Potential drawbacks include encouraging an unduly uniform strategy, giving equal weight to each of the regimes (many observers think that nuclear arms control should continue to receive foremost consideration), and enhancing the appearance that the advanced states were seeking to impose a cartel on LDCs. Concludes that initiatives for wholesale consolidation appear impractical and undesirable. But important steps can be taken in multilateral verification, export controls, sanctions, and UN monitoring to harmonize and strengthen the regimes. A permanent or ad hoc UN inspectorate capability could serve all of the major regimes and provide an additional link among them. And connections between global and regional regimes are growing, strengthening both.

(**enhancing weapons proliferation regimes**)

085

Security Without War: A Post-Cold War Foreign Policy. Michael H. Shuman (Executive Director, Institute for Policy Studies, Washington) and Hal Harvey (Executive Director, Energy Foundation, San Francisco). Foreword by Sen. Paul Simon (D-IL). Boulder CO: Westview Press, Nov 1993/318p/$59.50;$18.95pb.

For 45 years, the centerpiece of US security policy was the Cold War, undergirded by five principles: a focus on military threats and a single armed villain, a response to adversaries by intimidation, an emphasis on tough military action instead of "soft" alternatives of conflict prevention and resolution, unilateral action, and exclusive reliance on foreign policy experts to craft security policies. These principles have become obsolete. "If the US is to be secure from foreign threats, it must assess *all* these threats and address them with policies that emphasize nonprovocation, conflict prevention, multilateralism, and democracy." The five new principles: 1) recognize multilateral, multidimensional threats (a dozen "hot spots" around the world, the global march of weapons technology, the growth of illegal drug trafficking, the worsening trade deficit, assaults on the global environment, etc.); 2) emphasize conflict prevention and resolution (a key objective for security planners must be to avoid war, because the costs of war are becoming unacceptable as advanced weapons spread to more countries); 3) make security policies nonprovocative, in that a key cause of war is insecurity (US national security depends on freeing nations across the globe from all kinds of insecurity); 4) favor multilateral approaches (a stronger UN can offer every nation a way to lower defense expenditures without compromising its security); 5) promote democratic policies by opening US foreign and military policy to meaningful democratic participation. The key to security without war is not some magic weapons system or a clever formula for arms reduction, but an entirely new framework of international relations in which offensive force postures are gradually replaced. [**NOTE**: Eminent good sense.]

(**new post-Cold War principles**)

086

Non-Offensive Defence for the Twenty-First Century. Edited by Bjørn Møller and Hakan Wiberg (both Centre for Peace and Conflict Research, Copenhagen). Boulder CO: Westview Press, March 1994/248p/$49.95.

Non-offensive defense (NOD) seeks to (re)structure armed forces and military postures to maximize their defensive capacities while minimizing their offensive capacities. Doing so can facilitate arms control and disarmament by eliminating reciprocal fears, strengthen peace by ruling out preemptive and preventive wars, and provide effective yet non-suicidal defense. NOD principles could be applied to regional arms control in potential conflict spots such as Eastern Europe, India-Pakistan, the Persian Gulf, and North and South Korea. An arms control regime could seek to limit international trade in weapons lending themselves in offensive use, while leaving trade in weapons of a strictly defensive nature largely unconstrained. **(non-offensive defense)**

087
Global Engagement: Cooperation and Security in the 21st Century. Edited by Janne E. Nolan (Sr Fellow, Brookings Foreign Policy Studies). Washington: The Brookings Institution, April 1994/623p/$39.95;$19.95pb.

The character of international security has changed markedly in the past few years, so that past strategy based on preparing for massive military confrontation is no longer adequate or appropriate. This volume explores the premise that "cooperative engagement is the appropriate principle for security relations under the new international circumstances that have emerged." The central purpose of *cooperative security* is to recognize and articulate how the character of security has changed. It replaces preparations to counter threats with the prevention of threats, or with actions to make preparation more difficult. It differs from *collective security*, which seeks to deter aggression through military preparation and defeating aggression when it occurs (but both strategies are mutually reinforcing). Cooperative security has five major elements: strict controls and security measures for nuclear forces, a regime for conversion of excess defense industries, agreements regulating size and composition of forces, agreement on a concept of legitimate and effective intervention, and promotion of transparency and mutual interest as the basis for monitoring agreed-on constraints.

An initial chapter discusses imperatives for cooperation: global diffusion of civil and military technology, shrinking military budgets and export markets, the collapse of the USSR, internationalization of economic activity, the surge of civil violence, and the extensive evolution of practical collaboration. Other chapters consider regime architecture, the political economy of nonproliferation, when to use military action and how to insure its effectiveness (by William J. Perry, now US Secretary of Defense), the role of a reformed UN in promoting cooperative security (with a warning that latent tensions in the system, especially regarding the authority of the Security Council, are likely to escalate in the next five years or so), cooperative security in various world regions, and the critical necessity of US support for a cooperative security regime. A transition strategy for the 1990s is outlined, including denuclearization of the former USSR, new security partnerships, controlling technology diffusion, conflict prevention and mediation, and a new US leadership role. [**NOTE**: Could well be an authoritative leading-edge volume.]

("cooperative security" as key principle for 1990's)

088
Collective Security in a Changing World. Edited by Thomas G. Weiss (Associate Director, Watson Institute for International Studies, Brown U). Boulder CO: Lynne Rienner Publishers, March 1993/232p/$35.00.

The roots of the concept of collective security reach back several centuries through a long series of proposals for maintaining international peace. The central idea has remained the same: the governments of all states would join together to prevent any of their number from using coercion to gain advantage, notably conquering another. The extraordinary changes of the past several years in international politics suggest the possibility that collective coercion to keep the peace, as foreseen in the UN Charter, could at last become practical. Also, the balance of power has been so transformed that the US would be well advised to rethink totally the bases for its national security policies. Chapters discuss legal issues, institutional and operational issues, the "two other Cs" in the debate about security (Common Security proceeds from the need to reduce the insecurity of adversaries; Comprehensive Security stresses nonmilitary dimensions of stability), the relativity of sovereignty, the unprecedented opportunities for the UN to take the lead in building a sounder basis for lasting peace, characteristics of successful military cooperation in Operation Desert Storm, and regional collective security arrangements. Concludes that collective security does not imply the disappearance of states or transfer of a wide range of decisionmaking to another institution; it does imply "an added tempering element in a world of decentralized authority." There will be no dramatic change in the UN constitution to transform it into a full-blown collective security system responsive to all crises. But significant incremental measures could promote more and better collaborative actions. At the same time, larger security roles for regional organizations will no doubt emerge.

(new opportunities for collective security)

089
Keeping the Peace in the Post-Cold War Era: Strengthening Multilateral Peacekeeping. John Roper *et al*. Report #43. NY, Paris, and Tokyo: The Trilateral Commission (distributed by Brookings Institution), Dec 1993/101p/$12.00pb.

The end of the Cold War lifts a central obstacle to strengthening multilateral peacekeeping and extending multilateral operations beyond traditional peacekeeping tasks. This strengthening is in the broad interests of the Trilateral countries, especially in that the new era is so far one in which disorder is spreading in many corners of the world. This report provides four essays, each with proposals. **John Roper** (Director, Institute for Security Studies, Western European Union, Paris) notes the recent expansion of UN tasks and recommends planning for three levels of UN forces: a highly-trained standing ready force of 4-5 battalions (600-700 troops each), rapid deployment forces from the armed forces of member states (ten countries or groups of countries should each provide a brigade group of about 5,000 troops each), and earmarked troops with special training to deal with serious aggression by a regional power. **Enid C.B. Schoettle** (Council on Foreign Relations, NYC) explains the continuing UN financial crisis and proposes that UN assessments be paid in full and on time ("above all a challenge for the US"), that increases are needed in UN reserves (e.g. a Peacekeeping Reserve Fund), and that serious thinking should begin about new sources of UN financing. **Masashi Nishihara** (Research Institute for Peace and Security, Tokyo) seeks greater effectiveness of multilateral operations by agreeing on a target number of forces available for UN operations, developing human and material resources fully (for peacekeeping, peace-enforcing, and humanitarian operations), and sharing training facilities. **Olara Otunnu** (President, International Peace Academy, NYC) suggests three basic prerequisites for intervention: situations of massive and systemic suffering, situations able to elicit a strong response from a wide spectrum of the international community, and intervention by the UN only as a last resort. Four consensus scenarios for intervention are emerging: to provide military protection of humanitarian relief, to provide direct protection to populations under siege, to enforce monitoring of agreements, and to rebuild a collapsed state. **(enhancing UN peacekeeping)**

090
International Peacekeeping. Paul F. Diehl (Associate Prof of Political Science, U of Illinois). Baltimore MD: Johns Hopkins U Press, Aug 1993/211p/$36.50.

The termination of war has always provided a fertile environment for the growth and development of international organizations. The end of the Cold War is also ushering in a new era for international organizations, as major powers retrench in various areas of the world. Into that vacuum, the UN may encourage the peaceful settlement of disputes, and a new security apparatus for the UN or regional organizations is likely to emerge. The most prominent operational approach to international peace and security is peacekeeping operations, distinguished by a noncoercive mission, lightly armed forces, and neutrality. Peacekeeping operations, in contrast to collective security and peace observation missions (which may share some commonalities), include observation, interposition, maintaining law and order, and humanitarian activity. Alternatives to the present ad hoc system (which has performed reasonably well): 1) a permanent UN peacekeeping force, which has some advantages (but its marginal utility is not substantial); 2) regional peacekeeping organizations (their overall record is mixed; OAS has been successful, while the League of Arab States has consistently been ineffective); 3) multinational forces drawn from groups of states, with no ties to the UN (problems include organizing and maintaining neutrality). Concludes with the caveat that peacekeeping operations are not a panacea for all threats, and the conditions for success are limited. Still, they can be expected to assume a prominent role in the next decade and beyond. **(peacekeeping to expand)**

091
The Wave of the Future: The United Nations and Naval Peacekeeping. Robert Stephens Staley II (Research Fellow, International Peace Academy, NYC). IPA Occasional Paper Series. Boulder CO: Lynne Rienner Publishers, Nov 1992/63p/$6.95pb.

Former professor of strategy at the US Naval War College notes that the breakup of the USSR, as well as numerous disruptive changes in inter- and intra-state relations worldwide, may increase the need for peacemaking and collective security forces with military capabilities within the UN. Many nations recognize the importance of common maritime security, a role that could be played by individual nations, or a consortium of nations. But a powerful UN Maritime Agency for overseeing all UN maritime concerns seems to be the most efficient and productive option. Its objectives would include peacekeeping, enforcement, and observation. Under such an agency, nations will agree ahead of time to supply personnel and equipment for various UN requirements. Such forces would be constituted and employed only when the UNMA is directed by specific Security Council resolutions. Land-based peacekeeping is complicated and expensive, but the situation at sea is far more complex because navies are expensive and require a well-developed support structure. Staley goes on to describe various regional maritime challenges (Middle East, Mediterranean, Indian Ocean, Caribbean, etc.), and several organizational models. **(UN Maritime Agency proposed)**

092
Critical Juncture: The Future of Peacekeeping. Michael Renner (Sr. Researcher, Worldwatch Institute). Worldwatch Paper 114. Washington: Worldwatch Inst, May 1993/74p/$5.00.

The traditional rule for regulating conflict and providing security was expressed by an old Roman maxim, "if you want peace, prepare for war." This has been a guiding principle of nations for some 2,000 years. The vast bulk of all preparations for war has been concentrated in the 20th century, which has also had 75% of all war deaths since the rise of Rome. Since 1945, some 135 wars have killed more than 22 million people, with civilians as a rapidly growing share of the victims. Worldwide, there were 18 million officially recognized refugees in 1992 (up from 2 million in 1951), and another 20 million displaced within their own countries. Since the mid-1980s, the number of major armed conflicts has gradually declined (from 36 in 1987 to 30 in 1991), but "the future may well bring a surge of new warfare." Unrestrained production and trading of arms has resulted in enough weapons to insure that fighting can continue for a long time, and the ready availability of arms encourages governments to rely on them in settling disputes. Violent conflict will not diminish unless the world community confronts the root causes, directing adequate attention and resources to conflict prevention at the earliest stages possible.

A new principle of conflict resolution is needed: "if you want peace, prepare for peace." The international community is edging toward a greater reliance on "collective security," but UN moves toward an alternative security system have been tentative, inconsistent, and weak—undermined by lack of agreement on what should be done, underfunded by refusal of key members to pay their dues, and overwhelmed by demands for services. UN finances can be improved by giving the Secretary-General authority to borrow on commercial markets, to charge interest on overdue assessments, and/or to issue bonds. Other proposals to consider: taxes on military spending, the profits of arms manufacturers, and/or the international arms trade. Some steps toward a collective security system can be taken immediately: setting up an early warning office (the Iraq-Kuwait dispute and the violence in Yugoslavia could have been prevented), recruiting individuals for a pilot permanent peacekeeping unit, and establishing a peacekeeping/peacemaking fund. [**NOTE**: Surprisingly, the linkage to creating a sustainable society is not made.] **(improving collective security)**

093
Struggles for a Just World Peace: A Transition Strategy, Saul H. Mendlovitz (Co-Director, World Order Models Project, NYC), *Alternatives: Social Transformation and Humane Governance*, 14:3, July 1989, 363-369.

A Movement for a Just World Peace is in formation, seeking to transcend the images, norms, and concerns of the nation-state system and to promote the WOMP values of peace, social justice, economic well-being, ecological balance, and positive identity. Illustrative actions supporting system transformation (rather than mere system reform) include: **1) Short-Term (1991-93)**: establishing a critical mass of national and sectoral cadres in the US and linking them to like-minded people in other societies, peace and justice agendas for local and national politics, targeting egregious state behavior that violates human rights, an annual 5% reduction in defense budgets over a 10-year period; **2) Mid-Term (2001-03)**: establishing a small but permanent UN peacekeeping force, a global food agency to implement the right to food, and a court to deal with individuals who commit crimes against humanity; **3) Long-Term (2011-13)**: a global tax scheme to maintain a basic needs regime for global society, complete and general disarmament with alternative security system in place, political decision-making authority given to an ecological regime. **(agenda for a just world peace)**

094

Who Will Pay For Peace? Mark Sommer (Peace and Conflict Studies, UC-Berkeley), *The Christian Science Monitor*, Wed, 19 Feb 1992, p18.

In many parts of the world, peacekeeping is beginning to supplant unilateral military action as a means of settling disputes between nations. Eight peacekeeping missions have been established in the past three years, while just 13 were mounted in the previous 43 years. But while world leaders have gratefully delegated these tasks to the UN, they have failed to appropriate essential funds. Member nations currently owe the UN $377 million in back peacekeeping dues and have committed the UN to an additional $1 billion of peacekeeping obligations in the coming year. (The chief debtor is the US, which owes $141 million assessed according to its relative wealth.) The world still spends three times as much in a day preparing for war as it does in a year protecting the peace—an annual ratio of nearly 1000 to 1. World military expenditures currently total nearly $1 trillion a year, of which about $300 billion is spent on procuring weapons and equipment. A 1% tax imposed on every traceable purchase of military weapons and materials could finance all current peacekeeping operations, build a rigorous global verification system, and contribute substantially to the UN's general operating budget. A 2% tax would finance a conversion fund to help nations adapt to nonmilitary activities. A 3% tax could underwrite a global Earth Corps for environmental rescue and sustainable development. Like "vice taxes" on cigarettes and alcohol, a global arms tax would serve as a mild restraint on the arms trade by making it more visible.

(global arms tax proposed)

3. Globalizing Information

095

Global Communications & International Relations. Howard H. Frederick (Dept of Politics, U of California-Irvine). Belmont CA: Wadsworth Publishing Co, March 1993/287p/$20.25pb.

A textbook with chapters on global communication trends (greater centralization of control, information explosion, geopolitics now Gaiapolitics, greater democracy, increased cross-cultural contact, changes in technology), the history of long-distance communication, communication within and between national societies, technological channels of global communication, international communications organizations, issues in global communication (the war of ideas, national sovereignty, deregulation, the controversy over "flow" from rich to poor countries, media imperialism, trade in services, protecting journalists, codes of ethics, the status of women), information and "new world orders," contending theories of global communication, communication in war and peace (noting that, with better communications, The War of 1812 need not have happened or could have ended sooner), international communication and information law, and the growing perception that the right to communicate should be added to the Universal Declaration of Human Rights. Concludes that there is evidence for the emergence of *world public opinion* forming around global problems and widespread national problems. It desires peace through international law, opposes torture and discrimination, and supports action to eliminate poverty and preserve a sustainable environment. **(global communication trends)**

096

Information Technology and World Development, Majid Tehranian (Dept of Communications, U of Hawaii), *InterMedia*, 16:3, May 1988, 30-38.

The world economy is currently driven by the massive application of new information technologies. Four perspectives on the impace are identified: the Technophilic optimists, the Technophobic pessimists, the Technoneutrals (who have little theoretical pretension and considerable interest at stake not to alienate their clients), and the Technostructuralists who argue that technologies by themselves are neither good nor bad. Four global trends are also identified: 1) transnationalization of the world economy at the centers, with a growing disjunction between world economic and political systems; 2) tribalization of politics at the peripheries as a reaction to the forces of transnationalization, resulting in such slogans as small is beautiful, self-reliant development, and neither East nor West; 3) growing democratization of values at the semi-peripheries, as the electronic media reach the illiterates of the world; and 4) totalitarianization of surveillance throughout the world. Concludes with four scenarios of Continuity (inexorable transition to information societies), Reform (a new world economic and communication order), Collapse (due to contradictions and failures of capitalism), and Transformation (advent of Green movements and communitarian democracy facilitated by infotech). **(infotech and world development)**

097

The Race to the Intelligent State: Towards the Global Information Economy of 2005. Michael Connors (BZW Investment Mgt Ltd, London). Oxford UK & Cambridge MA: Blackwell Business, July 1993/221p/$29.95.

Describes the evolution of the information infrastructure or "infostructure," starting from the premise that far-reaching change is inevitable in the long-run. The information technology of 2005 will include huge computing power in very small packages at very low cost, a hybrid network of optical fiber and improved satellites providing enormous data transmission capacity to much of the world, a massive capacity of optical memory devices, computers of all kinds much more accessible to the general public, and expert systems providing decision support for professionals in a much wider range of applications than is presently considered. A long chapter is devoted to the future of the information superpowers, the US and Japan (in Japan, the information sector is estimated to grow at a compound rate of 9%, and to increase fivefold in value between 1986 and 2005).

Some conclusions and forecasts for 2005: 1) the positive effects of the information revolution will be far more noticeable in the developing world; 2) purchasers of electronic gadgetry will be much more circumspect: they will better understand what they are buying and will buy only what they understand; 3) "the information electronics industry, which is already showing signs of maturity, will be palpably mature by 2005;" a far greater proportion of the electronics market will be a replacement market than today; 4) the most significant change will probably be that most households and virtually all offices in the developed world will be connected to an integrated digital broadband wide area public network of some kind; 5) video conferencing will be commonplace and the range of information available over networks will be incomparably wider than today; 6) "mobile personal communications equipment will be commonplace, with perhaps one-third of the population of the developed world carrying mobile telephones"; 7) an information revolution of sorts is likely to have run its course by 2005 and an intellectual revolution might be built upon the foundations which it creates; 8) the world will shrink still further, and a larger and culturally richer international society will continue to grow. Concludes with an Information Access Index ranking 136 countries on five indicators; by 2005, this Index "will show a considerable narrowing of the spread between the highest and lowest scores." [**NOTE**: A bland and benign view.]

(**information society in 2005**)

098
Programmed Capitalism: A Computer-Mediated Global Society. Maurice Estabrooks (Senior Economist, Federal Government of Canada). Armonk NY: M.E. Sharpe, Dec 1988/205p/$24.95.

"When the history of the 20th century is written, it will be seen as an age of revolution and transformation that, in terms of its speed, pervasiveness, and technological complexity, was greater than any in the history of civilization." It will be seen as a metamorphosis on the grandest of scales that gave rise to a new social and economic order in which intelligent machines emerged to mediate all essential activities of the new global society. With financial, economic, and political integration, historians will call this *the age of programmed capitalism*. There is a correspondence between the nature of an economic system and its technological underpinnings used to record, communicate, and process information, money, and capital. Based on this relationship, four great economic transformations can be described: 1) when mankind began to trade and barter goods and services; 2) the use of precious metals such as gold or silver as a medium for exchange; 3) the industrial society system, when country-denominated paper money replaced its predecessor as a more efficient medium for exchange; 4) computer replacement of paper money so that money can now be traded freely, inexpensively, and instantly anywhere in the world. Conversion to a computer-mediated economic system requires new institutions unique to a new global-centered society. "Growing computerization is integrating all national markets and fusing financial institutions and political states into one economic identity and sovereignty. It is altering the location and structure of economic activity and investment throughout the world." (p176) The result is a "rapidly changing, increasingly obsolete, complex, hyperactive society," where rampant technological change increases the demands on our workers and managers. We deploy armies to produce more knowledge and information, even as it becomes obsolete at an increasingly rapid pace. The new horizontally-organized society demands a much greater capacity of its citizens to function intelligently: stronger abstract thinking, more rapid learning, and the ability to communicate large quantities of information. The danger is that the majority of our citizens will not be capable of coping with this new society. And the new world system cannot operate any longer without a new set of rules, regulations, and institutions. The global computer-based hyperstructure holds the possibility of generating tremendous synergies and wealth in the global economy, but this potential can only be realized by cooperation among governments. [**NOTE**: This is not a great book, but it does point out the important globalizing influence of the computer as well as any other. Some sections seem exaggerated in an Alvin Toffleresque way and about half of the references come from *Business Week, The Economist, Fortune,* and the *Toronto Globe and Mail*. There are no references to Toffler, Bell, or other post-industrial society thinkers, nor to Canadians (other than Harold Innis) who have made original contributions to thinking about communications (Marshall McLuhan, Orrin Klapp, and Arthur J. Cordell). Interestingly, it seems to be a Canadian strength!]

(**computer-mediated global society emerging**)

*099
Governing in an Information Society. Steven A. Rosell (Parliamentary Centre for Foreign Affairs and Trade, Ottawa), *et al*. Montreal H3A 1T1: Inst. for Research on Public Policy (1470 Peel St), Fall 1992/167p/Can$14.95pb. (Order from Renouf Publishing, 1294 Algoma Rd, Ottawa K1B 3W8; 613/741-4333.)

"We are in the midst of a fundamental economic and social transformation whose extent and implications we only partially grasp." The transformation is being driven by an interplay of developments in infotech, the emergence of a more educated and informed population, the increasing role and reach of the mass media, higher degrees of specialization in a more knowledge-based economy, and a much richer infrastructure of public and private organizations. This progress report from a group of 14 Canadian public servants seeks to make sense of the implications for governance of the emerging global information society, and to develop more appropriate and effective approaches to governing in that new environment. Multiple factors contribute to today's global crisis in governance, but a persuasive case can be made that "many of the roots of the current crisis are to be found in new patterns of human interconnection." Indeed, the hallmark of the information society is the growing degree of interconnection, both within the state and across national boundaries. As society becomes more interconnected, we are facing a loss of boundaries, which throws into question basic conceptual distinctions we use to make sense of the world. And, as society becomes more complex and takes on more variety and configurations, the capacity of existing regulatory (governance) systems is being overwhelmed.

The discussions of the Governing in an Information Society Roundtable were organized around three themes: **1) Information-based Ways of Organizing**: the general pattern is to establish and manage an overall framework of interpretations and objectives, enabling a wide range of players to innovate and learn (this may argue for the need to privatize or contract out as many functions as possible, leaving the public sector to focus on setting the framework for these functions); **2) Forging Consensus**: a recurring theme was the critical importance of generating shared frameworks, visions, myths, stories, and interpretations in the context of which a consensus can be generated; consensus was expressed about the extent to which it was possible and desirable to control the information society with traditional legal and regulatory mechanisms (new consensus-shaping mechanisms include stakeholder summits, market-based approaches, faster regulation, alterative dispute resolution); **3) Strategic Use of Information**: the process of learning appears to be central to governing in an information society; both within and outside government, it is self-defeating to try to control data and information—the real challenge is to provide leadership in the continuing process by which people interpret and make sense of that information. [**NOTE**: Astute reflections based on leading-edge literature and thinkers, notably Harlan Cleveland and Donald N. Michael, who both presented papers to the Roundtable. An Appendix reprints these papers along with three others.]

(**information society impact on governance**)

100
Managing in the Information Society: Releasing Synergy Japanese Style. Yoneji Masuda (President, Institute for the Information Society; Professor, Aomori U). Foreword by Ronnie Lessum (City U Business School, London). Oxford UK and Cambridge MA: Basil Blackwell, June 1990/168p/$24.95.

New edition of **The Information Society as Post-Industrial Society** (IIS, 1980; World Future Society, 1982; **FS Annual 1981-82** #4250), with the first two chapters of the original deleted and a new chapter added on the transformation of the human species to *Homo intelligens*. Other chapters consider the spirit of the information society as the spirit of globalism, four stages of computerization, formation of structurally organic information networks, the transition from closed to open educational environments (with lifetime self-learning as the leading form of education), the future global information utility combining computer and communications networks (whereby anyone, anywhere, at any time will be able to easily, quickly, and inexpensively get any information), transformation to a new synergetic economic system and participatory democracy, how the issue of privacy invasion will ultimately lose its historical significance, an international ecological order based on pollution-free and material-saving technology, synergistic feedforward based on common goals, building voluntary communities, and "computopia" as a rebirth of theological synergism. [**NOTE**: In the Foreword, Ronnie Lessum likens Masuda to a latter-day Henry Ford—a man ahead of his time. The mix of upbeat naivete, high-tech, and humanistic idealism on a global scale is also reminiscent of the late Buckminster Fuller.] (**information society as globalism**)

101
Global Networks: Computers and International Communication. Edited by Linda M. Harasim (Associate Prof of Communication, Simon Fraser U). Cambridge MA: MIT Press, Aug 1993/411p/$29.95.

Examines the issues raised by the new networking technology of electronic mail, computer conferencing, and televirtuality (virtual reality). The 21 chapters are in four sections: **1) Overview**: networks as social space, shaping networks into "networlds," the global matrix of minds (stimulated by interconnected computer networks), reflections by a member of the Whole Earth 'Lectronic Link (WELL); **2) Issues**: jurisdictional quandries, information property, computer networks and work, integrating global organizations through task/team support systems, cross-cultural communication and computer-supported cooperative work, global networking for local development, OECD initiatives on information security [also see #12668]; **3) Applications**: building a global network at the Western Behavioral Sciences Institute, computer conferencing in Europe, global education through learning circles, capacity building in Africa and Latin America, cognitive apprenticeship on global networks, computer networks and the emerging global civil society (perhaps leading to a Charter of Communication Interdependence); **4) Visions for the Future**: social and industrial policy for the International Public Network, co-emulation in a global hypernetwork society, informatization as transition to post-modern civilization, guidelines to reconstructing cyberspace in humane form (civility, conviviality, reciprocity, edification, artfulness, spirituality), the global authoring network process (this book is the product of such a process). (**networking issues and prospects**)

102
Telepower: The Emerging Global Brain, Joseph N. Pelton (Director, Interdisciplinary Telecom. Program, U of Colorado), *The Futurist*, 23:5, Sept-Oct 1989, 9-14.

Former policy director for INTELSAT asserts that the human use of communications contains the key to our future, and the "global electronic machine" is where it starts. The machine contains hundreds of millions of tons of coaxial cable, electronic switches and exchange equipment, satellites orbiting the earth, billions of telephones and TV sets, etc. Each year this colossal machine grows as new capacity is added, in turn making the global village a reality. In the 20 years since the moon landing, the number of people able to see global events on TV has expanded from 0.5 to 3 billion. Our ability to share information is creating global trade and culture; it will soon begin to form a global brain—a global consciousness. The global electronic machine—a multitrillion-dollar universal linkage—is already redefining work as a result of the emerging 168-hour workweek of the global society, where the movement of the sun and the economy never stops. A new type of global worker is being created—the "electronic immigrant"—who can telecommute to work over great distances. "The ability to recruit and electronically import shape professional services into the US, Japan, and Europe could become the top international trade issue of the 21st century." Other problems of the age of telepower are technological unemployment and invasion of privacy; on the bright side, tele-education and tele-health may be the only hope for progress in the services-starved Third World. Ultimately, the combination of converging technologies or "tele-computer-energetics" may replace *Homo sapiens* with *Homo electronicus*. [**NOTE**: H. G. Wells was the first to use the notion of "world brain", but merely in terms of organizing academic knowledge (**World Brain**. Doubleday, Doran, 1938), rather than *all* information for more diverse audiences. ALSO SEE Pelton's **Global Talk** (1981; **FS Annual 1981-82** #4236) for more ideas on the emerging "global village."]

(**global electronic machine**)

103
The Emerging Worldwide Electronic University: Information Age Global Higher Education. Parker Rossman (Niantic CT; Vice President, Global Systems Analysis and Simulation Project/USA). Westport CT: Greenwood Press, Sept 1992/169p/$42.95.

Former Dean of the Ecumenical Education Center at Yale University describes signs of an emerging global classroom, whereby students in one country take courses in another via computer conference and/or TV, catalogs from many universities are available electronically to prospective students in many countries, the world's research libraries are connected, on-line electronic bookstores are available for students, electronic faculty meetings and training can be shared across national borders, special event lectures are shared from country to country, and students and faculty meet in "hyperspace." Chapters describe courses offered on computer networks and cable TV, administration of distance education, the

University of the World project [**FS Annual 1991** #10832], the GLOSAS Global University project, education for all ages and needs worldwide, the global matrix of computer networks, the emerging global encyclopedia and world brain (first proposed by H.G. Wells in 1938), the virtual reality classroom, electronic and multimedia textbooks, the global student, and regional resource centers. Concludes that we have come to the end of an era in which colleges can be bounded by a wall with a narrow gate (keeping out all but a few who can afford high costs), when all students are kept in one place at one time (sharing finite resources and faculty), and when students leaving the campus stop their education. [**NOTE**: Many grand, exciting, and upbeat ideas—both potential and (slowly?) emerging.]

(**global classroom emerging**)

104
Life After Television. George Gilder (Tyringham MA; Senior Fellow, Hudson Institute). New York: W.W. Norton, June 1992/126p/$19.95.

Author of **Microcosm: The Quantum Revolution in Economics and Technology** (Simon and Schuster, Sept 1989; **FS Annual 1991** #10837) asserts that television is giving way to the much richer, interactive technologies of the computer age. The age of television is over; the new system will be the telecomputer, a personal computer adapted for video processing and connected by fiber-optic threads to other telecomputers around the world. "The telecomputer will surpass the television in video communication just as the telephone surpassed the telegraph in verbal communication." The telecomputer will enhance individualism, promote creativity, and enrich and strengthen democracy and capitalism around the world. It could revitalize public education by bringing outstanding teachers to classrooms everywhere, and by making home schooling feasible and attractive and thus competitive. In contrast, TV at its heart is a top-down totalitarian medium, squeezing the consciousness of an entire nation through a few score channels. To date, the culture we have created with our infotech is dreary at best, because of the need to achieve mass appeal. By radically changing the balance of power between the distributors and creators of culture, the telecomputer will forever break the broadcast bottleneck. TV manufacturers are holding out the promise of high-definition TV, which is simply the old medium dressed up with a bigger screen and sharper pictures. Centralized on-line database services are also obsolete, and are apt to be replaced by a scanning system that allows customers to pay only for information used. If the US does not act soon, the telecomputer network will be built by Japan, and made of Japanese fiber and optoelectronics and possibly Japanese computers. The key to advancing a national integrated services digital network (ISDN) of fiber optics is the removal of government obstacles to its rapid deployment by the Baby Bells.

(**telecomputer age to replace TV and HDTV**)

105
Technology 2001: The Future of Computing and Communications. Edited by Derek Leebaert (Director, Future Technology Inc, Bethesda MD). Cambridge MA: MIT Press, Feb 1991/392p/$29.95.

After a brief Foreword by Arthur C. Clarke, the 13 chapters discuss such matters as **1) The Forward Drive of Computer Technology**: progress in bi-polar and field-effect transistors, beam-controlled technologies for fabrication of microelectronics, ever-easier user interfaces; **2) Supercomputing**: evolving "the most powerful computers at any point in time" will soon enable the fully integrated computational environment; **3) Changes in the Microprocessor**: device miniaturization will continue, with performance improvements in process technology and multiple processor architectures; **4) Harnessing the Tides of Information Abundance**: by the mid-1990s we will view personal computers as knowledge sources rather than knowledge processors—as gateways to vast amounts of information; knowledge systems will progress from "smart" to "brilliant" in the 1990s; **5) The Future of Networking**: "In the 1990s, networking will evolve to the point where people will be able to electronically communicate anything (voice, data, image, video), anytime, anywhere in the world" (William R. Johnson Jr, VP, Digital Equipment Corp); **6) The Future of On-Line Technology**: the trend to move information on-line so as to improve productivity and reduce costs will continue as a dominant theme in the 1990s; by 2001, on-line technology will be as pervasive as the telephone is today; **7) Document Processing**: future systems will be characterized by transparency, decentralization, and modularity; entirely new forms of electronic documents will be created; **8) Optical Storage**: storage capacity places limits on the amount of information available; optical storage multiplies the capabilities of the computer; **9) Imaging Capabilities in the 21st Century**: advances in the 1990s will enable integrating of images into computer-based info systems, leading to "integrated information environments" that make full use of text, graphics, images, and voice; at some point, image synthesizers will assume roles analogous to music synthesizers; **10) The Awakening of Human Possibility**: the computer accelerates history and enhances the sense of possibility; **11) Human Interface**: the future will bring human-machine communication that mimics the way humans interact with one another; tomorrow's HI will be able to train itself to recognize user gestures; **12) Evolution of Telecommunications**: development of ISDN to bring together the computer and voice-telephone environments; the evolution of cellular telephony to the point of complete mobility; **13) Public Policy for the Information Age**: excellence in education as a national priority; programs to upgrade skills of math and science teachers; tax incentives for R&D; open trade policy; global harmonization of industry standards. In the Introduction. Leebaert states that "Everything is being melted in the furnace of the new." And he adds: "Civilization is about the externalization and cross-breeding of knowledge—the tapping of other people's skills." [**NOTE**: A swaggering Grand Tour of infotech frontiers. As a balance to this upbeat acritical perspective, read the bleak criticism of Jacques Ellul's **The Technological Bluff** (#109 below).]   (**infotech in the 1990s**)

106
The Information Technology Revolution: Computer Hardware, Software, and Services into the 21st Century, William E. Halal (Prof of Management, GWU), *Technological Forecasting and Social Change*, 44:1, Aug 1993, 69-86.

Combines a literature scan, a Delphi survey of 11 authorities, and interviews with IT specialists. The Delphi panel assessed 14 emerging ITs and applications: 1) small computers most people commonly use to manage work and personal affairs (.85 probable by 2002, with a $19 billion market); 2) parallel processing widely available, using thousands of chips in networks (.71 probable by 2003, with a $42 billion market); 3) public networks permitting access of all people to libraries of data, programs, etc (.84 probable by 2007, with a $35 billion market); 4) optical computers that boost computation speed by 1000 times go commercial (.86 probable by 2000, with a $37 billion market); 5) sophisticated software for personalized teaching, managing medical care, controlling corporations (.95 probable by 1996); 6) expert systems commonly used (.88 probable by 1998); 7) voice access computers permitting more convenient interaction (.84 probable by 2002); 8) routine parts of most software generated automatically (.82 probable by 2003); 9) computers that learn by trial and error (.86 probable by 2004); 10) access to library materials via computer (.87 probable by 2000); 11) half of all workers perform jobs partly at home using computers (.52 probable by 2009); 12) education commonly conducted with computer teaching and interactive TV (.69 probable by 2002); 13) teleconferencing replaces majority of business travel (.40 probable by 2006); 14) half of all goods sold by electronic shopping (.43 probable by 2007). Concludes that, in the 2000-2010 period, "the IT revolution may produce not only a dramatic shift in the technological base of modern societies but a dramatic social revolution as well," as portable computers and smart appliances create an interactive environment of ubiquitous computing. But the toughest challenge may be "finding our way through the looming avalanche of data that even now threatens to engulf us. It is supremely ironic to discover that people increasingly feel more ignorant." [NOTE: Excellent overview, despite being starry-eyed up to the conclusion, where the super-conundrum of infoglut is briefly faced.]

(**infotech revolution through 2010**)

107

Mass Communications and American Empire (2nd Edition, Updated). Herbert I. Schiller (U of California-San Diego). Boulder CO: Westview Press, Oct 1992/214p/$45.95;$14.95pb.

A reprint of the First Edition (1969), with chapters on electronics and economics serving The American Century, the rise of commercial broadcast communications, the domestic communications complex, the Global American Electronic Invasion, the international commercialization of broadcasting, the developing world under electronic siege, the structure of international communications control, and a proposed democratic reconstruction of mass communications. A new 43-page introduction looks back on seismic shifts over the past 25 years. In the information age as presently structured, a few thousand corporations operate adventurously on a global scale, utilizing the most up-to-date infotech. The domestic costs contribute to the downgrading of America's well-being and its lessened international strength. In the 1960s it was accurate to refer to American media and cultural imperialism. In the 1990s, there is no diminution of American popular cultural exports, but the producers of these products have become huge, integrated, cultural combines, not exclusively US-owned, offering a total cultural product to a global market. American cultural imperialism is not dead, but, today, "it is more useful to view transnational corporate culture as the central force."

(**advent of transnational corporate culture**)

108

The Technology Gamble. Informatics and Public Policy: A Study of Technology Choice. Cees J. Hamelink (Institute of Social Studies, U of Amsterdam). Norwood NJ: Ablex Publishing Corp, Oct 1988/117p/$29.50.

Informatics is the systematic management of information through electronic systems. It has applications in households, education, industry, public administration, law enforcement, medicine, and the military. Much of the present debate on informatics concentrates on the question of social impact. The general tone of most voices is positive, even euphoric. Most decision-makers view technology as an autonomous force which is difficult to stop. Technology optimism erects obstacles for improving technology choice, with a "boom" scenario seeing decentralized production, improved democracy, increased access to information, and vast amounts of leisure time. The "doom" scenario of critics projects centralized control, a pseudo-democracy of nominal participation in marginal decision-making, and leisure time exploited by a global entertainment industry. Most countries do not have a coherent policy on informatics, as illustrated by the growth of ISDN (Integrated Services Digital Network) in the European communities—the largest public work without any public consultation. The main driving force of ISDN is technology opportunity, with error cost (the cost of not having it) as the major concern, rather than potential social cost. "The ISDN project is a major exercise in flying blind toward a sophisticated and expensive highway system with no idea as to who will ride the roads, at what price, and with how many traffic accidents." (p45) Most European countries are intent on implementing ISDN plans irrespective of warnings that it is the Concorde of the telecommunications industry, and that ISDN may stand for "Innovations Subscribers Don't Need."

The available tools for improving technology choice are evaluated (learning from history, product testing, analysis of present impacts, risk analysis, and technology forecasting and assessment.) All of these tools of inference have serious flaws, and there is always imperfect information. Our technology choices are gambles, but there seems resistence to admit this. The notion of "gamble" keeps awareness of potential hazard alive. The obsessive gambler wants to exert control over chance, and is unrealistic in estimating possible losses. Many processes of choice are afflicted by this "gambler's syndrome" (e.g., the launch of the Challenger space shuttle in 1986, when signals of serious risk were not taken seriously). Technology choice can be improved by a shift from irresponsible obsessive gambling toward a responsible type of social gambling which accepts that we cannot know the outcomes of our choices. This requires moral courage. "The problem of technology choice is, finally, a moral problem." (p103) (**improving technology choice**)

*109

The Technological Bluff. Jacques Ellul (Prof Emeritus of Law and the Sociology and History of Institutions, U of Bordeaux). Translated by Geoffrey W. Bromiley. Grand Rapids MI: William B. Eerdmans Publishing Co (255 Jefferson SE), Oct 1990/418p/$24.95.

Author of over 40 books, including **The Technological Society** (1954; Knopf, 1964), **The Technological System** (Continuum, 1980; FS Annual 1981-82 #3707), and **What I Believe** (Eerdmans, 1989; #036 in this Guide) argues that he is not anti-technique, but is working out a theory of the technical society and system, and the point we have reached today. Technological bluff is the gigantic bluff in which discourse on techniques envelops us, making us believe anything, and rearranging everything in terms of technical progress. Chapters discuss: **1) The Great Innovation**: the proliferation of techniques, mediated by communications and changed human discourse, has encircled and outflanked people and society, and suppressed moral judgment (an excursus attacks the "astounding" ignorance of Julian Simon); **2) Ambivalence**: technical development is a complex mix of positive and negative elements; all technical progress has its price, and a great number of harmful effects; **3) Unpredictability**: looking ahead has become an absolute necessity, but the different methods of forecasting meet with almost constant failure; "foresight ought to replace forecasting if we have the least sense of responsibility;" **4) Contradictions of the Technical System**: thresholds of reversal from the rational to the irrational; fragility of big organizations; **5) Humanism**: all technodiscourse seeks to be discourse about humanity and human primacy; **6) Technical Culture**: enthusiasts for technical culture promote acquisition of technological knowledge and adapting the young to the technical environment; technique is creating a new culture of ever-greater speed; **7) Human Mastery**: an essential aspect of technodiscourse holds that we enjoy full mastery over technique; **8) Rationality**: technique obeys rationality and becomes an instrument of human reason, plunging us into a world of irrationality; **9) The Ideologies of Science**: evolution of ideology from scientism to science in the service of the national economy and national greatness; **10) Technical Progress**: techniques developed in the last decade (principally in computers and telematics) are leading to absurdity; "it is the flood of techniques that makes us absurd"; the constant replacement of weapons is a techno-economic absurdity in its purest form; **11) Unreason**: the whole problem is that our modern way of thinking is reductionist and one-dimensional; paradigms at work in this descent of the technical world into unreason include the desire to normalize everything, growth and change at all costs, and forcing life into increasing speed; **12) Costs**: technique is now a driving force for the economy, creating "stupefying expenditures that no one can control"; **13) The World of Gadgets**: technique produces more technique whether it is needed or makes sense; basic needs are swamped by others; **14) Waste**: the ineluctable consequence of a technical system in constant development; **15) The Bluff of Productivity**: "what produces enthusiasm for computers is not that they are useful and efficient but that they give the illusion of being intelligent;" **16) Fascinated People**: we are fascinated by modern technique—fixated on an object, with hypnotic obedience; **17) From Information to Telematics**: we are deluged today by a flood of data that is incoherent and useless, producing disorganization; television is a screen between us and reality; **18) Advertising**: on every TV channel, advertising plunges us into the world of an idealized and stylized technique; **19) Diversions**: we are diverted from thinking about ourselves and our human condition by the computer, TV, technical games and amusements that lead us into an unreal world, sport that has become technicized and professionalized, the motorizing of society, mechanistic art, the Eurodisneyland project (the prime manifestation of the deculturizing of France); **20) Terrorism in the Velvet Glove of Technology**: the discourse on technique, which is never subjected to criticism, is a terrorism that places people in subjugation; the totally technicized and computerized society is inevitable—the ineluctable outcome is dictatorship and terrorism; **21) The Great Design**: the complete integration of humanity into the technical system. Concludes that balance and cohesion are increasingly difficult to maintain; the gigantic bluff is self-contradictory, and we may thus expect enormous global disorder. "This must be made to cost as little as possible."

[NOTE: An update and extension of decades of thinking, providing an outstanding, broad-ranging critique of technology and where it is taking us, backed up with extensive documentation of French and American sources.]

(**technique as driving force creating unreason**)

4. The Globalizing Economy

110

The New Global Economy in the Information Age: Reflections on Our Changing World. Martin Carnoy *et al*. University Park PA: Penn State U Press, July 1993/170p/$25.00;$12.95pb.

The world economy is becoming more competitive, more global, and more dominated by information and communications technology. The first political casualty of the information age was the communist state system, based on an inflexible 1920s-model hierarchical state and production system. Investment, production, management, markets, labor, information, and technology are now organized across national boundaries. **Manuel Castells** (Prof of Planning, U of California-Berkeley) argues that "the Third World is no more—rendered meaningless by the ascendance of the newly industrialized countries mainly in East Asia, by the development process of large continental economies on their way to integration in the world economy (China, and, to a lesser extent, India), and by the rise of a Fourth World, made up of marginalized economies in the retarded rural areas of three continents and in the sprawling shantytowns of African, Asian, and Latin American cities." **Martin Carnoy** (Stanford U) discusses the continuing growth of large multinational enterprises, and the crucial role of the nation-state in creating an innovation society. **Stephen S. Cohen** (UC-Berkeley) comments on the new nature of international competition, high-volume flexible production, and America's mistakes. **Fernando Henrique Cardoso** (Prof of Sociology, U of São Paulo) argues that globalization of the economy has had a negative and disintegrating effect on the Third World: there is no longer a South on the periphery of the capitalist core in a classical relationship of dependence. We are dealing with a crueler phenomenon: either the South enters the democratic-technological-scientific race, or it becomes "unimportant, unexploited, and unexploitable." Concludes that: "Instead of thinking globally and acting locally... political leaders of the 1990s will have to think locally, relating to their own people, while acting globally to reach out to the flows of power and wealth."

(**new global information-based economy emerging**)

111

Global Shift: The Internationalization of Economic Activity. Second Edition. Peter Dicken (Prof of Economic Geography, U of Manchester). NY: The Guilford Press, Feb 1992/492p/$30.00pb.

The notion that something fundamental has happened to the world economy is now increasingly accepted. Economic activity is becoming not only more internationalized but, more significantly, it is becoming increasingly globalized. These terms are not synonymous: globalization is a more advanced and complex form of internationalization, a much more recent phenomenon, and the emerging norm in a growing range of economic activities. We also live in an era of turbulence and volatility, in which economic life in general is being restructured rapidly and fundamentally. Chapters discuss global trends in production and trade, the growth and spread of transnational corporations, the costs and benefits of TNCs, technological changes in products and processes, the changing position of nation states, dynamic global networks within and between business firms, the textiles and clothing industries (the first manufacturing industries to take on a global dimension, and the most geographically dispersed of all industries), the automobile industry (an industry of giant organizations, many increasingly organized on international lines), the electronics industries (with far-reaching implications for the long-term evolution of all economies), internationalization of services (increasingly the major source of employment in all developed economies and many LDCs as well), and problems of adjusting to global shift (unemployment, protecting domestic industries, Third World countries). [**NOTE**: Good overview of TNCs and key industries, but ignores tourism/travel and environmental problems that will offer constraints and new opportunities.] **(globalizing economic activity)**

112

Trade Lessons from the World Economy, Peter F. Drucker (Prof of Social Science, Claremont Graduate School), *Foreign Affairs*, 73:1, Jan-Feb 1994, 99-108.

In recent years the economies of all developed nations have been stagnant, yet the world economy has still expanded at a good clip. From this seeming paradox there are lessons to be learned, and they are quite different from what nearly everyone asserts: 1) too many economists and politicians treat the external economy as something separate and safely ignored when they make policy for the domestic economy; 2) the segments that comprise the world economy are rapidly merging into one transaction, increasingly representing different dimensions of cross-border alliances (the strongest integrating force in the world economy); 3) information flows in the world economy are probably growing faster than any category of transactions in history (they may already exceed money flows in the profits they generate); 4) contemporary money flows do not respond to attempted government restrictions such as taxes on money-flow profits; the trading just moves elsewhere; 5) US trading activity is more or less in balance: the trade deficit bewailed in the media is in merchandise trade, but the services trade account has a large surplus (many statisticians acknowledge gross underreporting of service exports by as much as 50%); 6) formal and informal alliances are becoming the dominating form of economic integration in the world economy; 7) "for developed economies, the distinction between the domestic and international economy has ceased to be a reality...an unambiguous lesson of the last 40 years is that increased participation in the world economy has become the key to domestic growth and prosperity;" 8) the evidence is clear that both advocates of managed trade and conventional free trade are wrong in their prescriptions for economic growth; 9) investment abroad creates jobs at home; 10) "the world economy has become too important for a country not to have a world-economy policy."

(world economy lessons to be learned)

113

Managing the World Economy: The Consequences of Corporate Alliances. Edited by Peter F. Cowhey (Prof of Intl. Relations, UC-San Diego) and Jonathan D. Aronson (Prof of Intl. Relations, USC). NY: Council on Foreign Relations Press, March 1993/343p/$18.95pb. (Brief version in *Foreign Affairs*, 72:1, 1993, 183-195.)

The way the world economy works has changed dramatically in the past 45 years. In general, firms have adapted faster than governments. Over time the gap between existing regulations and reality has grown so large as to interfere with effective management of global commerce and discourage economic growth. Academics and policymakers cling tightly to the old, comforting rhetoric of free trade and the six pillars on which it was built. But these pillars have eroded and are being replaced by the pillars of a "market access regime." The six key transitions are: 1) from the US model to a hybrid model of industrial organization; 2) from separated systems of governance to internationalization of domestic policies; 3) from services produced and consumed domestically to the globalization of services (and eroding boundaries between goods and services); 4) from universal rules to sector-specific codes as the norm; 5) from trade and investment as distinct areas of concern to investment as an integrated coequal with trade; 6) from the concept of national comparative advantage to that of regional and global advantage (Japan and other Asian countries are openly discussing the creation of global blueprints for the international division of labor). The emergence of international corporate alliances is an indicator of the deep changes currently transforming the world economy. As firms change, they are making national economies more interdependent. But an activist government policy does not imply an end to an open, integrated world economy; indeed, governments may have to intervene to maintain open markets. [ALSO SEE: **Networking in Multinational Enterprises: The Importance of Strategic Alliances** by Bernard Michael Gilroy (U of South Carolina Press, Feb 1993/236p/$29.95).]

(transitions in world economy)

114

The Secret Empire: How 25 Multinationals Rule the World. Janet Lowe (Del Mar, CA). Homewood IL: Business One Irwin, April 1992/248p/$24.95.

"The old world believed in political ideology; the new world believes in economics." The new theology is capitalism, and the high priests are the multinational corporations. Through a natural process of business evolution, a select group of multinationals—called the "meganationals"—lead the procession. Ranked in size by bank assets or industrial sales, they include Dai-Ichi Kangyo Bank ($470 billion), Mitsui Taiyo Kobe Bank ($439 billion), Sumitomo Bank ($429 billion), Mitsubishi Bank ($420 billion), Deutsche Bank ($267 billion), Citicorp ($217 billion, **Exxon** ($116 billion), General Motors ($107 billion), Royal Dutch/Shell ($106 billion), IBM ($69 billion), British petroleum ($64 billion), GE ($58 billion), Daimler-Benz ($57 billion), Hitachi ($52 billion), Philip Morris ($51 billion), Fiat ($50 billion), Matsushita ($44 billion), Siemens AG ($42 billion), Du Pont ($40 billion), Unilever ($40 billion), AT&T ($37 billion), Nestle ($36 billion), Bristol-Myers Squibb ($10 billion), Coca-Cola ($10 billion), and Merck ($8 billion). In all, there are 11 US, 6 Japanese, 3 German, 2 Anglo-Dutch, and 1 each British, Swiss, and Italian meganationals. Through mergers, acquisitions, joint ventures, and other business practices, the network of dominant corporations has built exceptional strength, as the world economy becomes dominated by a limited number of companies in most major industries. New regional alliances such as the EC seem to be a counteraction to these massive corporate machines, to safeguard the right to govern. The meganationals are also becoming leaders in the "greening" of industry. When big companies fall into compliance, standards are set for others in the industry. [**NOTE**: Even-handed, despite the lurid title. Membership in the "top 25" can be disputed (e.g., the omission of Ford Motor), but description of emerging networks of economic rule is useful.] **(meganational firms)**

115

International Business and Governments: Issues and Institutions. Jack N. Behrman (Distinguished Prof of Business, U of No. Carolina) and Robert E. Grosse (Dir., Intl. Business and Banking Inst., U of Miami). Columbia SC: U of South Carolina Press, Nov 1990/434p/$29.95.

Governments relate to transnational corporations (TNCs) at three levels: **1) Local**: cities and states/provinces seek to attract foreign investors and offer incentives (often more than necessary); **2) National**: governments set rules for the conduct of foreigners, and sometimes for the conduct of nationally-based companies operating abroad; **3) International**: rules among members of regional associations (OECD, ASEAN) and efforts to create common rules for the world economy. Chapters discuss concerns of national governments, characteristics of TNCs, policies of home governments and host governments, legal issues and international law, and TNC relations with seven regional associations and with UN organizations.

Two groups of issues must be faced cooperatively: economic issues and social/ethical/political issues. The first group concerns location of production, amount and skill level of employment, technology transfer, ownership and control, capital flows, dividends, and location of R&D. The second group involves consumer and environmental protection, discrimination by sex and race, and illicit payments or bribes (new issues likely to arise include maintaining national language and dress, international accounting standards, commercial use of outer space, and economic development of regions that cross national boundaries). A chapter on recent policy shifts discusses three major departures from free trade during the 1980s: industrial policies to guide a specific sector, coproduction that links companies in two or more countries (raising issues of local-content requirements), and countertrade that links export of one commodity to the import of another (it has been estimated that such trade under bilateral arrangements ranges from 5-20% of total world trade and will rise to 20-50% by 2000).

Concludes that increased industrial, technological, financial, and cultural integration in the world economy is binding nations closer together, even though they are psychologically and intellectually unprepared. Along with pressures from environmental problems, this points to a new vision involving closer cooperation, unification of attitudes, and harmonization of principles of law and conduct. But most recent calls for new leadership initiatives are vapid, with no suggestion of which initiatives to take or how they would meet multiple criteria of acceptability. Despite emphasis on economic national goals, Japan appears to have no desire to lead the world. Assertion of American leadership is hampered by its adversarial relationship between business and government, rigidity in international conduct, and a low degree of understanding world problems. Britain is not in a position to assume world leadership, and Germany refuses to step forward. The TNCs themselves are a potential source of leadership, but their managers are not necessarily prepared for this role. [**NOTE**: Excellent overview of issues.]

(**governments and transnational corporations**)

116
Global Scenarios: Geopolitical and Economic Context to the Year 2000, Michel Godet (CNAM, Paris), Pierre Chapuy, and Gérard Comyn, *Futures,* 26:3, April 1994, 275-288.

A pessimistic May 1993 vision by a group of European IT experts who were being questioned on the international context through 2000. Key variables were grouped into five subsystems (international geopolitics and economics, technology, IT infrastructure, strategies, and market trends), and each subjected to morphological analysis of various environments. Major trends: disruptive demographic imbalances, uncertainties due to the lack of a global regulating force, uncertainty about the future of Europe, relentless competition, and slow and irregular growth ("it is to be expected that there will be new oil shocks from now up to 2005"). Summarizes with four scenarios: *1) Black and Gray Scenarios* (over 60% chance): recessionary setback, regional wars, failed European integration, protectionism, and GNP growth of less than 0.5% (black) or 1.5% (gray); *2) Blue Scenario* (15% chance): limited conflict, unequal development, regional protectionism, GNP growth of 2.5%; *3) Pink Scenario* (7% chance): multipolar and interdependent world, economic convergence of East and West Europe, extended free trade, intensive globalization, GNP growth of more than 3%. [**NOTE**: A blizzard of scenarios (S28, S61, S4) and variables (H1, H6, C1, G4) that may deter many readers. Gloomy bottom line contrasts with more upbeat scenarios, below.] (**global scenarios for 2000**)

117
The Global Economy: America's Role in the Decade Ahead. Edited by William Brock (President, Brock Group, Washington) and Robert D. Hormats (Vice Chairman, Goldman Sachs International). The American Assembly (Columbia U). NY: W. W. Norton, Jan 1990/264p/$19.95.

Contributions from the 76th American Assembly, held in April 1989, on the increasingly interdependent, multipolar, and vulnerable world economic system. Essays discuss changes in the 1950-1990 period (the changed position of the US in the international economy, new technology), European integration, improving US-Japan economic relations, major technological thrusts and US competitiveness, changes in the Third World and the emerging "global agenda" of interrelated problems, regional trading blocs, and US leadership. An Appendix by Jan Dauman (CEO, InterMatrix Group) summarizes driving forces and key facts, and offers four Year 2000 scenarios: **1) Toward a Global Economy**: world GDP growth averages 3.5-4.5%, capital flows encourage development, currencies are stable, trade wars virtually disappear (probability considered *"low"*, because nationalism and regionalism are stronger than globalism); **2) Competitive Accommodation**: effective compromises on debt rescheduling, growth of inter-regional alliances such as Europe with Japan and North America with developing Asia (*"moderate"* probability because of need to stimulate growth); **3) Regional Self-Interest**: world GDP growth averages 2.5-3.0% per year, oil prices fluctuate, capital flows are sluggish, the US still faces major deficits, fortress Europe becomes a reality to many countries (*"high"* probability because global leadership appears to be dormant); **4) National Self-Interest**: world GDP growth at 1.5-2.5% per year, the world financial system hovers on the edge of collapse, currencies fluctuate wildly, many trade wars (*"low"* probability). The final report of the Assembly urges a "Global Compact" whereby the US puts its economic house in order, Japan opens its borders and increases development assistance, the EC pledges to reduce trade barriers, and the Third World debt burden is eased. (**Global Compact urged**)

118
Long-Term Prospects for the World Economy. Organisation for Economic Co-operation and Development. Paris: OECD, Aug 1992/193p/145ff. (English and French editions at OECD outlets worldwide, or from OECD Publications, 2 rue Andre-Pascal, 75775 Paris.)

Papers from an OECD "Forum for the Future" conference in June 1991, examining "the main developments which are likely to affect the evolution of the world economy and its major regions over the next decade or so." Overall projections for the global economy in the 1990s and beyond are "by and large optimistic." Estimates for average annual growth in world output up to 2000 are broadly in the 3% range. North America and OECD Europe are likely to grow between 2.5-3% per year, Japan is set to grow between 3-4%, and the Asia-Pacific region as a whole at well over 5.5% (slightly higher for the Asian NIEs). Latin America is expected to grow at around 3%, and Africa at a somewhat lower rate (but Africa's standard of living will not rise significantly because of rapidly increasing population). Creation of NAFTA should be a source of new strength for North America. Still, the Asia-Pacific region's share of world income should continue to rise, from 24% in 1989 to 35% in 2010 and over 50% by 2040. Four major issues other than environment-related questions ("not addressed at the meeting") appear to be particularly important at the global level: the shift of economic gravity to the Pacific Basin (especially with the gradual emergence of China as a major player), regional trading blocs, saving and investment imbalances (resulting in excess demand for financial resources and high interest rates), and increasing competition.

In addition to the summary by Michel Andrieu, Wolfgang Michalski, and Barrie Stevens, there are seven additional papers: **1) Long-Term Scenarios of the World Economy to 2015**, by Andre de Jong and Gerrit Zalm (Central Planning Bureau, The Netherlands), elaborates on Global Shift to the Pacific Basin, European Renaissance, Global Crisis (the world more and more trapped in a "vicious circle," with mounting tensions), and Balanced Growth (the environmental challenge evokes a shift to the coordination perspective and a "virtuous circle," mitigating the strong free-market emphasis of the 1980s without destroying its positive impact); **2) Long-Term Prospects for the US Economy**, by Maurice Ernst and Jimmy W. Wheeler (Hudson Institute), provides a central Surprise-Free scenario of GNP growth ranging between 2.3-2.7% in the 1990s, a Virtuous Circle scenario of good luck and good management yielding 3.2% growth, and a Slow Growth scenario of only 1.8% growth (or 1% per year per capita); **3) North American Economic Integration** by Wendy Dobson (U of Toronto), with three scenarios of Base Case, Freer Trade resulting from NAFTA (accelerating economic growth in all three countries), and further evolution in the longer term to a common market or economic union; **4) European Economic Integration** by Emilio Fontela (U of Madrid) offers the Conventional Wisdom scenario, the Scenario of Deepening (additional impulses towards a United Europe), and a Scenario of Widening (additional members added to the EC); **5) The Evolution of Europe** by Jacques Lesourne (*Le Monde*) considers many possible futures; **6) Japan and the Asia-Pacific Region** by Masaru Yoshitomi and Naohiro Yashiro (Japan Economic Planning Agency), on Japan's aging population, labor shortage, impacts of CO_2 emission controls, and continuing globalization of Japanese firms; **7) The Asia-Pacific Region** by Steven Wong (ISIS, Malaysia) considers the move toward Asia-Pacific cooperation. [NOTE: Thoughtful scenarios and trend analysis, but few authors touch on environmental issues, and none explain their omission. The notions of "vicious-" and "virtuous circles" are useful.]

(**world economy trends and scenarios**)

119
World Economic Survey 1993: Current Trends and Policies in the World Economy. UN Dept of Economic and Social Information and Policy Analysis. NY: United Nations, Aug 1993/258p/$55.00. (Sales # E.93.II.C.1)

The 46th annual report of the UN Secretariat on major developments and issues, beginning with the statement that, as of early 1993, "The world economy remains listless." Growth of world output is expected to expand from 0.2% in 1991 to 0.6% in 1992 and 1.5% in 1993. But the recovery "is delicately poised," as projected growth is balanced by considerable risks and uncertainties. Moreover, "the statistics of the world economy fail to convey the appalling increase in human suffering for which there is no single measure." Developing countries as a group have been growing at an almost constant rate of 3.5% since 1989; in 1992, their growth accelerated to 5%, the highest rate since 1979 (much of this growth occurred in Asia and parts of Latin America). Resumption of growth remains the overriding issue: urgent social concerns in LDCs will remain unaddressed in the absence of growth. Sustainable development, a smooth reallocation of resources from military to civilian uses, increasing employment opportunities, and economic recovery in industrialized countries are all closely linked. The importance of this interrelationship is increasingly recognized. Sections of the report discuss serious weaknesses in developed economies, developments in trade, transfer of resources, oil market trends, carbon tax proposals, famine and undernourishment, and development of the non-state sector in China.

(**world economic trends**)

120
The Great Reckoning: Protect Yourself in the Coming Depression. Revised and Updated. James Dale Davidson (Strategic Advisors Corp) and Lord William Rees-Mogg (Vice-Chair, BBC). NY: Simon & Schuster/Touchstone, Dec 1993/607p/$14.00pb.

The first edition (August 1991) spelled out in comprehensive detail how the world will change in the depression of the 1990s. In a new 40-page introduction, the authors argue that this forecast has come true. Britain is clearly in depression, and slumps are being experienced by Canada, New Zealand, Australia, and Scaninavia. The containment of depression which appeared to have been successful through the end of 1992 cannot ultimately work: it is a policy of postponement, not of prevention. The multi-trillion-dollar losses resulting from malinvestments in the 1980s are real, and can only be disguised until the good credit of governments is exhausted. Budget deficits, lax monetary policy, credit guarantees, and palliatives such as make-work employment will continue to offer short-term gains. But debt cannot go on compounding faster than output forever. Either an economic deflation will cause the financial system to implode, or an extreme political inflation will obliterate much of the value of debts. One way or another, "we expect a great reckoning," due to the compounding debt crisis, insolvent financial institutions in many parts of the globe, the collapse of state-dominated economies, the crash of Asian stock markets, saturation of many markets, and the downturn in the long-wave economic cycle. "We expect the 1990s to be a decade of escalating economic and political disorder unparalleled since the 1930s." Chapters discuss the megapolitics of progress and decline, the information revolution, the new North/South division in world politics, rational living in an age of crisis, and hedging techniques. [NOTE: Far more substantial than the average "depression is coming" book. The authors edit *Strategic Investment* newsletter.]

(**world depression ahead**)

*121
The Death of Money: How the Electric Economy Has Destabilized the World's Markets and Created Financial Chaos. Joel Kurtzman (Westport CT). NY: Simon & Schuster, April 1993/256p/$22.00; Boston: Little Brown Back Bay Books, April 1994/256p/$11.95pb.

Executive Editor of the *Harvard Business Review*, former editor of the Sunday Business section of *The New*

York Times, and author or editor of 13 other books (7 of them with Ervin Laszlo), asserts that money, as a store of value and a unit of account, met its demise about two decades ago. It is no longer a thing, but a system—a network of hundreds of thousands of computers wired together. The new network is much more volatile than the 5000-year-old monetary system it replaced, and supply and demand has little to do with price changes. The death of money has also splintered the world into two economies: the "real economy" where products are made and services rendered, and the "financial economy" of speculation (somewhere between 20 and 50 times larger). The financial economy moves several trillion dollars a day between the major and minor nodes on the network, and is largely unregulated. Chapters describe megabyte money (which has displaced governments in importance), how mathematicians and rocket scientists have replaced stock pickers and traders and shortened the time frame for investing, the prescience of Marshall McLuhan as concerns the new electronic environments, why megabyte money behaves differently than gold-backed money (and why economists fail to recognize it), how information overload caused the electric economy to go haywire in October 1987, how the electric economy is adding to social as well as economic instability (a world of complete impermanence is "a world where the future is vague, undefined, and marked by anxiety"), how concentrated technology leads to speed and vulnerability, how the global electronic market is fueled by fads and rumors to create shorter time horizons and more volatility (making our "real economy" companies especially vulnerable to the ups and downs of the electronic economy), and social costs ("nearly every country in which globalization is proceeding rapidly is besieged by the rise of provincialism and racism," as citizens rebel against the loss of identity and national sovereignty). Concludes with a discussion of how volatility can be buffered to prevent widening chaos and upheaval ("in a vast, free-form, center-less megabyte economy, deregulation may be the opposite of what is needed"). Volatility can be dampened by fixed exchange rates, a stable dollar (perhaps linked to the single European currency of 1997 or to a market basket of goods), stabilized interest rates, perhaps a stock transfer tax, and an environment in which the long-term investor is rewarded. **(stabilizing a volatile electric economy)**

122
Service Industries in the World Economy. P.W. Daniels (Prof of Geography, U of Birmingham). Oxford UK & Cambridge MA: Blackwell Publishers, Aug 1993/210p/ $39.95;$17.95pb.

The geographical domain of service industries now extends far beyond local or national boundaries to embrace the international stage. Daniels identifies the significant processes that have enabled service industries to internationalize at rapid rates in recent years. Service industries such as telecommunications have enabled this process to take place, while themselves being active participants. Chapters discuss explanations for growth, tradability of services, the globalization of retailing, international trade and foreign direct investment in services, services and the global urban system, services and the restructuring of cities, and the desirability of service-dominated economies. **(globalization of services)**

123
The Global Restructuring of Agro-Food Systems. Edited by Philip McMichael (Director, International Political Economy Program, Cornell U). Ithaca NY: Cornell U Press, July 1994/303p/$42.50;$16.95pb.

Agro-food systems are undergoing restructuring in an era of declining national regulation. Flexibility in production and marketing that characterizes industry has also emerged in agro-food. Growing specialization in food systems is apparent in the global expansion of niche markets for fresh and processed foods. Agribusiness corporations have revitalized contract farming on a global scale, and transnational fruit and vegetable distributors serve proliferating metropolitan markets. The content of agricultural politics is inexorably shifting from the (nationalist) agrarian question to the (internationalist) food and green questions. Essays discuss state-level restructuring (Japan, South Korea, Sweden, Australia), the US meatpacking industry, campesinos in rural Mexico, changing production relations in the Dominican Republic, the globalizing of the fresh fruit and vegetable industry, and the shaky foundations of the world food economy.
(globalizing of agro-food industry)

124
Globalization and the Future of Cities, J. N. Behrman (Distinguished Prof of Business, U of North Carolina), *Futures Research Quarterly*, 8:1, Spring 1992, 41-74.

Globalization of business will induce cultural and economic shifts which some nations are already undergoing, willing or not. Worldwide integration of businesses and finance will occur even in the face of political disintegration or decentralization. This relaxation at the center will give cities major roles in decision-making as to the structure of industry and service sectors. Globalization will thus have serious consequences for the concentration of peoples, the way they live, and the development of cities. Cities that prepare themselves to welcome globalization will be more attractive to global actors. The major elements of communities (and lifestyles) that are attractive to foreign TNCs include educational opportunities, wide career choices, recreation, healthy environment, health programs, tolerance toward foreigners, and a local concept of "total community." Cities that respond to the new world economy will be dominated by achievers, the socially-conscious, "integrateds," and leaders who know how to act on the strengths of the community.

(globalization and cities)

125
World Travel and Tourism Review: Indicators, Trends and Forecasts. Vol. 1, 1991. Edited by Donald E. Hawkins (Director, International Institute for Tourism Studies, GWU) and J.R. Brent Ritchie (Director, World Tourism Education and Research Centre, U of Calgary). Wallingford, Oxon UK: C.A.B. International (distributed in US by U of Arizona Press), April 1991/243p(8x12")/ $170.00.

1) Indicators: data on tourist arrivals and receipts in the world, six major regions, and 33 selected countries. The travel and tourism industry is now the world's largest industry, employing over 100 million people, with gross sales of $2 trillion (5.5% of world GNP). **2) Trends and Forecasts**: world tourism outlook for the 1990s (4% annual tourism growth expected in the 1990s; the world's stock of hotel rooms expected to grow from 10.5 million to 18.4 million by 2000), projections of world tourist arrivals (to rise from 463 million in 1992 to 666 million in 2000), tourism and the environment (by Joseph F. Coates), World Tourism Model simulations for Germany, airline traffic forecast (total passengers projected to expand at 5.7% per year for the next 15 years), cruise industry trends (the industry has enjoyed nearly 11% annual growth in the past decade), tourism and the handicapped, the expanding international convention and meeting market, the resort timesharing industry, the senior travel market, the youth market, and business travel (51% of air trips by Americans in 1990 were for business). **3) Global Tourism Policy Issues for the 1990s**: the physical environment takes center stage ("green tourism has arrived", recognizing the limits to tourism development (sustainable development and "low impact tourism" as new paradigms), "the paradoxical situation in which cultural diversity is thriving in a sea of homogenization," emerging health and security concerns as a major deterrent to tourism, preventive legal care concerning the legal rights of travelers.

(**world tourism trends**)

126
The Management of International Tourism. Stephen F. Witt (Prof of Tourism Studies, U of Wales), Michael Z. Brooke (Brooke Associates), and Peter J. Buckley (Prof of Managerial Economics, U of Bradford). London & Boston: Unwin Hyman, Dec 1991/209p/$55.00;$17.95pb.

Tourism is playing an increasingly important role in the world economy. International tourism receipts already comprise 7% of the value of world exports. "One thing can safely be said of tourism in the future: it will increase. Current forecasts suggests a 5% yearly growth in inter-national tourist flows through the 1990s."

But tourism receipts and expenditures are far greater—in volume and in profit—for Europe than North America: in 1987, Europe received $95.1 billion and spent $85.5 billion for a net balance of +$9.6 billion; North America received $19.3 billion and spent $26.6 billion for a negative balance of -$7.3 billion. Chapters discuss the international tourism industry, tourism demand, operating methods, marketing, finance, organization, research, and corporate strategies. Some concluding forecasts: 1) many nations and suppliers will be encouraged to enter the holiday market, and it is likely that supply will move ahead of demand; 2) against the pressure towards expansion stands the possibility of a world slump (much depends on economic growth: "a 1% growth in private consumption leads to 0% growth in tourism; but a 2.5% increase leads to 4% more tourism, while a 5% figure adds up to a 10% growth); 3) product innovation is more likely to be about unpackaging rather than packaging, with more personalized arrangements; 4) the market for holidays tailored to special segments (birdwatchers, hikers) is large and growing rapidly; 5) the argument between economic growth and limits to growth is rapidly becoming universal, as locals worry about over-visiting; 6) rival pressures for more professionalism and cheap labor will increase the trend toward a two-tier labor force (ultimately, mechanization of menial tasks may reduce the lower tier, and "it is not improbable that self-service will move up-market"); 7) large companies are likely to put much effort into anticipating or finding new tourist centers (the facilities sector, as in other industries, is concentrated at the high end and fragmented at the low end); 8) the "tourism backlash" will probably spread, centered on local issues such as culture and environment; 9) the growth of travel will persuade governments to look hard at reducing frontier formalities; a world currency would be a boon to tourism; 10) 21st century technical developments enhancing air travel: a new generation of short-take-off aircraft, a solution to aircraft noise, and space technology applied to international travel. [ALSO SEE: *Wide Horizons: Travel and Tourism in the Coming Decades*, The Futurist, 26:5, Sept-Oct 1992, 28-32.]

(**world tourism trends in 1990s**)

127
Millennium: Winners and Losers in the Coming World Order. Jacques Attali (President, European Bank for Reconstruction and Development, London). Foreword by Alvin Toffler. NY: Times Books, Sept 1991/130p/$17.00. [First published in French in slightly different form as **Lignes d'horizon** (Librarie Artheme Fayard, 1990).]

Former special advisor to President Mitterrand and author of 15 books (boosted by Alvin Toffler as "one of Europe's premier intellects") describes the acceleration of history. Change is now the only constant in a world in upheaval, as a new geopolitical order is being born. In the next century, Japan and Europe may supplant the US as the chief superpowers. They will preside over a world with a common ideology of consumerism, bitterly divided between rich and poor, threatened by a warming and polluted atmosphere, and girdled by a dense network of airport metropolises for travel. The "rich nomads" of the world's privileged regions will roam the planet, seeking ways to use their free time, shopping for information, sensations, and goods only they can afford. These wealthy wanderers will everywhere be confronted by roving masses of "poor nomads"—boat people on a planetary scale—seeking to escape the destitute periphery where most of the earth's population will continue to live.

Conflict is more likely now that the Cold War has ended and the market has triumphed. Industry is the only lasting foundation of a nation's power, and, in this sense, signs of America's relative decline are everywhere. Japan has become the dominant pole of the Pacific sphere, one that increasingly embraces the US. In ten years, half of world trade will occur in the Pacific rim, deepening Japan's leading role. If hypersonic airplanes are successful (they are being studied), they will be able to reach any point in the Pacific in less than two hours from Tokyo. America may become Japan's granary (more US land is devoted to agriculture for Japan than the entire land surface of Japan). Each sphere will continue to extract profits from its underdeveloped periphery, but "the periphery of the Pacific sphere is infinitely more promising than that of the European sphere." The Asian countries are growing rapidly, whereas Africa is a lost continent, whose economic plight will only grow worse. However, the real loser of the next millennium will be the planet itself if the imperative of the market is allowed to run rampant. "Never before have people held as much power to shape their future as they do today. And never before have there been so many urgent decisions to be taken by a single generation." [**NOTE**: Fresh and important; especially useful for notions of nomads, spheres and peripheries, and evolution of market forms.]

(**a world of rich and poor nomads**)

128
Global Work Force 2000: The New World Labor Market, William B. Johnston (Senior Research Fellow, Hudson Institute), *Harvard Business Review*, 69:2, March-April 1991, 115-127.

Co-author of **Workforce 2000** (Hudson Institute, 1987; **FS Annual 1988-89** #9295) states that human capital—once considered to be the most stationary factor in production—increasingly flows across national borders as easily as cars, computer chips, and corporate bonds. Just as managers speak of world markets for products and capital, they must now think of a world market for labor. In the 1990s, the world's work force will become even more mobile. Movements of workers will be driven by the growing gap between the world's supplies of labor and demands for it. While much of the world's skilled and unskilled human resources are being produced in the developing world, most of the well-paid jobs are being generated in the cities of the industrialized world. This mismatch will trigger massive relocations of people (especially young, well-educated workers), lead some industrialized nations to reconsider their protectionist immigration policies (Japan less so than others), boost the fortunes of nations with surplus human capital (the Philippines, Egypt, Poland, Hungary), and lead to a gradual standardization of labor practices in developed countries (by 2000, European standards of vacation time—five weeks—will be common in the US, and world standards governing workplace safety and employee rights will emerge). Just as the automobile triggered suburbanization, which took many decades to play out, so will jumbo jets shape the labor market over many years. This comes at a time when LDCs will produce a growing share of skilled human capital: **1) High School Enrollees**: between 1970 and 1986, the US, Canada, Europe, Japan, and USSR saw their share shrink from 44% to 30%; if current trends continue, their share will drop to 21% by 2000; **2) College Students**: between 1970 and 1985, the share of college students in the developing world leaped from 23% to 49%; by 2000, the share from LDCs will be 60%—not counting LDC students in Western universities.

(global labor market emerging)

129

The End of Jobs, Richard J. Barnet (Senior Fellow, Institute for Policy Studies, Washington), *Harper's Magazine*, Sept 1993, 47-52.

"Across the planet, the shrinking of opportunities to work for decent pay is a crisis yet to be faced." The ranks of the unemployed, the unemployable, the underemployed, and the subemployed are growing so fast that "the worldwide job crisis threatens not only global economic growth but the capitalist system itself." Some 47 million new job seekers enter the already overcrowded labor market each year, 38 million of them in Asia, Africa, and Latin America. "Within the next 20 years throughout the underdeveloped world, more than 750 million men and women will reach the legal working age, adding to the 700 million people currently unemployed or underemployed in poor countries." The feminization of the work force is also changing job prospects everywhere. As traditional cultural barriers begin to give way, large numbers of women take jobs that pay them much less than men, thus exerting downward pressure on job prospects and wages. Unless wages and working conditions in poorer countries improve, global corporations will use the threat of relocation to bargain down working conditions in richer countries. At the same time, the drive for "global efficiency" means that the numbers of Chinese, Mexicans, and others who land a job in the system, while growing rapidly, will still barely make a dent in the ranks of the jobless.

There are no national solutions to the job crisis. Coordinated strategies at the global level are needed to avoid flooding the planet with goods and services far in excess of what people want or the planet can afford. However, such cooperation seems improbable at this time. The recent trend toward greater inequality in the US and in much of the world means that the vast majority of the 8 billion people living in the first quarter of the 21st century will be neither producers nor consumers in the new global economy. The global economic system is fragile because it depends on growth fueled by expansion of consumption, but the fierce drive to eliminate work and cut wages works against this. Steady jobs for good pay are becoming poignant memories or just dreams for more and more people. Until we rethink work and decide what human beings are meant to do in the age of robots, and what basic economic claims on society human beings have by virtue of being here, there will never be enough jobs. "The lack of decently compensated jobs under decent working conditions is a global deficit so vast as to require fundamental rethinking about the global economic system itself." [**NOTE**: There is surely a growing problem, but is it as bad as portrayed here? Not mentioned is the growing numbers who make a living in the underground or informal economy. As noted by Kempe Ronald Hope, Sr in *Growth and Impact of the Subterranean Economy in the Third World* (*Futures*, 25:8, Oct 1993, 864-876), the subterranean sector is directly responsible for improving the standard of living of large numbers of people and contributes significantly to the bettering of life in general. Besides, was there ever a time when most people had "decently compensated jobs under decent working conditions?"] **(global jobs deficit growing)**

130

An Introduction to the World-System Perspective. Thomas Richard Shannon (Prof of Sociology, Radford U, Radford VA). Boulder CO: Westview Press, Oct 1989/208p/ $38.50;$19.95pb.

World-system theory is a continuation of the central concerns of Marx, Weber, and Durkheim, and is also part of a general theoretical development in sociology that began in the 1970s. World-system theory was initially formulated by Immanuel Wallerstein (SUNY-Binghamton), and has become a major subfield within US sociology. Many world-system theorists, notably Wallerstein, view their work as an extension of Fernand Braudel and the *Annales* school of French historical thought. It is also the outgrowth of dependency theory, notably the work of Andre Gunder Frank, which looks at the exploitative relationship between advanced capitalist countries and the periphery. World-system theorists reject the structural-functionalist theory of modernization, which considered societies relatively stable systems of interrelated parts. Critics of modernization theory also reject its attribution of a benign role to the core countries, which ignores centuries of abuse and exploitation. World-system theorists share with Marx the notion that the nature and functioning of capitalism is fundamental to understanding society, but they do not accept many of the details of Marx's theory. Chapters discuss world-system structure, the contemporary world-system, world-system dynamics (economic cycles, cycles of hegemony) and various criticisms of the theory. Concludes that world-system theory is valuable because it addresses a set of issues that are essential to understanding the modern era. In doing so, the theory has helped to refocus the sociological study of large-scale social change (most previous theorizing was virtually ahistorical). Nevertheless, there are major inconsistencies among various theorists, and the theory does not yet constitute a generally satisfactory account of modern social change. Alternative theories include the rise and fall of great powers (Paul Kennedy; **FS Annual 1988-89** #8862/8863), long-term economic cycles (W.W. Rostow), and long cycles of world leadership (George Modelski). [**NOTE**: A fair-minded introduction and assessment, although largely of interest to sociologists. Another criticism of world-system theory, not mentioned here, is that it is confined to social structures and pays no attention to population/environment problems, and questions of sustainability.]

(world-system theory assessment)

131

Global Formation: Structures of the World Economy. Christopher Chase-Dunn (Prof of Sociology, Johns Hopkins U). Cambridge MA: Basil Blackwell, 1989/419p/$45.00.

"The motivation behind this work is the feeling that we don't really understand the nature of the social system in which we are living, a world of our own creation and yet beyond our control." Chase-Dunn proposes a structural approach to the study of the modern world-system (in contrast to the position of Wallerstein and others). The modern world-system is a capitalist "world-economy" with dominant core states, dependent peripheral areas, and intermediate semi-peripheral states. A "world-economy" contains multiple societies, multiple states, and a single economic division of labor (in contrast to a "world-empire" where a single state apparatus rules over multiple cultures). The main structures of the world-economy are the world class system, the core/periphery hierarchy, the interstate system, and the world market. Chapters discuss a reformulation of Marx's theory of capitalist accumulation in world-system terms, systemic cycles and trends, stages of capitalism (or cycles of world-system development), the world-system since 1945 (the transnationalization of capital, the new international division of labor), the trend toward world cultural integration, geopolitics and capitalism, the rise and decline of hegemonic core powers, recent trends, core/periphery cycles, and problems of building world-system theories. Concludes that support for further world-state-formation is likely from capitalists and their political allies, and it will at first be dominated by capitalist muddling through. But as the world political system becomes relatively centralized and the gap between core and periphery begins to diminish, "the logic of socialism will eventually gain the upper hand." This will not be the utopian end of history, but simply the next progressive step. **(world-system theory)**

132

World Investment Report 1991: The Triad in Foreign Direct Investment. UN Centre on Transnational Corporations. NY: United Nations Pubs. (Room DC2-0853), Oct 1991/108p(8x11")/$25.00pb. (Sales No. E.91.II.A.12).

The first substantial attempt by UNCTC to examine the global structure of foreign direct investment and related policy implications, focusing on the role of the Triad (US, EC, Japan) during the 1980s. Foreign direct investment has become an increasingly important factor in international economic relations, growing much faster than world trade and output. After having nearly tripled between 1984 and 1987, worldwide outflows of foreign direct investment increased by another 20% in both 1988 and 1989, reaching an absolute level of $196 billion. By 1989, the total worldwide stock of this investment stood at about $1.5 trillion. But developing countries remain relatively marginalized, receiving only $30 billion of this investment in 1990. Between 1985 and 1989, their share in total investment fell from 25% to 18%, and it is unlikely that this declining share will be reversed in the near future, despite efforts by nearly all countries to open up their economies. Further, flows to developing countries are highly concentrated, with 10 countries accounting for three-fourths of the total inflow. The international community should try to reach consensus on ways and means to attract a greater flow of foreign direct investment to developing countries, with special attention to technology, trade, and finance.

(foreign direct investment trends)

133

How Credit-Money Shapes the Economy: The United States in a Global System. Robert Guttman (Prof of Economics, Hofstra U). Armonk NY: M.E. Sharpe, June 1994/561p/$68.00;$27.95pb.

How well or poorly our economy functions depends to a significant degree on the modalities that guide the creation, distribution, and circulation of money. An important evolution in money forms occurred during the Great Depression when the US and other industrial nations abandoned the gold standard ("commodity-money") in favor of a payments system based on central bank notes and private bank checks. Introducing such inconvertible paper money, which is created in acts of credit-extension ("credit-money") gave domestic economies an elastic currency. This innovation revolutionized the ways in which the advanced capitalist economies worked, and greatly contributed to the economic expansion of the first two postwar decades. The boom ended in the late 1960s, and gave way to gradually intensifying stagflation. The US economy is now forced to undergo long-term restructuring, involving a transformation of our credit system at a time when a new money form ("electronic" money) is altering the ways in which our credit system operates. As the dollar's world-money status erodes, three scenarios suggest the new system: 1) continuing the route begun in the mid-1980s, when the leading powers decided to cooperate in managing the merging multicurrency system (but efforts in this direction have recently faltered); 2) in the absence of renewed cooperation, it is quite possible, even likely, that the world economy will gradually disintegrate into three competing blocs imposing their respective currencies; 3) the only satisfactory solution, but by far the most difficult, is to replace all key currencies with a supranational form of credit-money ("a logical step in the evolution of contemporary capitalism"). Rather than reaching for the most difficult and utopian version, a single currency for the entire world economy, it would be much more realistic to conceive of this new form of world money—"supranational credit-money" (SNCM)—as used solely in international transactions between countries, with national currencies confined to strictly domestic circulation. Two chapters describe at length how SNCM could work. [**NOTE**: Addresses the mysteries of money with remarkable clarity.]

(new form of world money needed)

5. Population Growth and Health Threats

*134

The Future of World Population. Wolfgang Lutz (Director, Population Project, IIASA, Austria). *Population Bulletin*, 49:1, June 1994/47p/$7.00 single copy.

Brief version of a forthcoming report, **The Future Population of the World: What Can We Assume Today?**, based on a late 1992 meeting of demographers at the International Institute of Applied Systems Analysis. Current trends are discussed in the three components of population change—fertility, mortality, and migration—and scenarios are presented on these components for 12 world regions. *Three major certainties* are apparent: world population will continue to grow (increasing at least 50% and perhaps even doubling by 2030), developing countries will account for a greater share of world population (rising from 78% in 1990 to 85-87% by 2030), and the average age in all world regions will increase under all scenarios (the share of people age 60 and over will rise from today's 9%

to 13-17% in 2030). Some other projections: 1) world population under the IIASA central scenario will grow to 8.96 billion in 2025 [contrast with lower PRB projection of 8.38 billion, below] and 12.56 billion in 2100; 2) the high migration scenarios through 2030 assume annual net migration gains of 2 million in North America, 1 million in Western Europe, and 350,000 in the Japan/Australia/New Zealand region; 3) by 2030, under the central scenario, Western Europe will increase in population by 10%, North America by 35%, China by 50%, South America by 75%, and Sub-Saharan Africa by 298%; 4) AIDS may not reduce population growth significantly if fertility remains high; in sub-Saharan Africa, a three-year decline in life expectancy per decade is the worst case and a three-year-per decade increase is the best case; 5) life expectancy in Japan, Europe, and North America will increase one year per decade through 2030 (low scenario), two years per decade (central scenario), or three years per decade (high scenario). [**NOTE:** Excellent array of scenarios and discussion of uncertainties and assumptions. The upper limit of mortality improvement reflects the cautious view of demographers, not of biologists on the frontiers of aging research.]   (**world population at 12.6 billion in 2100**)

135
1994 World Population Data Sheet. Carl Haub and Machiko Yanagishita (PRB). Washington: Population Reference Bureau, May 1994/one page (20x28")/$4.00.

Demographic data and estimates in 15 categories for the countries and regions of the world, using the new UN geographical definitions of Europe and Asia, forced by dissolution of the USSR. *1) World Population:* 5.61 billion in mid-1994, with a projection of 7.02 billion in 2010 (up 25.2%) and 8.38 billion in 2025 (up 49.4%); *2) Regional Population Growth (1994, 2010, 2025):* Africa from 700 million to 1.08 and 1.54 billion; Latin America and Caribbean from 470 million to 584 and 679 million; Asia from 3.39 billion to 4.25 and 5.02 billion; Europe from 728 million to 738 and 731 million; *3) Growth in Selected Countries (1994, 2010, 2025):* US from 261 million to 300 and 338 million; Canada from 29 million to 33 and 36 million; Mexico from 92 million to 119 and 138 million; Brazil from 155 million to 180 and 200 million; China from 1.19 billion to 1.38 and 1.50 billion; India from 912 million to 1.16 and 1.38 billion; Indonesia from 200 million to 250 and 289 million; Nigeria from 98 million to 162 and 246 million; Russia from 148 million to 145 and 142 million; Germany from 81 million to 78 and 73 million; *4) World Population Doubling Time:* at the current rate of growth, population will double in 43 years (the doubling rate was 42 years in 1993, 41 years in 1992, 40 years in 1991, and 39 years in 1989 and 1990); *5) Regional Population Doubling Time:* 24 years in Africa, 26 years in Western Asia/Middle East, 29 years in Central America, 33 years in South Central Asia, 37 years in South America, 65 years in East Asia, 98 years in North America, and 1,025 years in Europe; *6) Annual Change:* about 90 million people are added to world population every 12 months, 97% of them in the Third World. [**NOTE:** As always, an essential reference in a handy format, at a modest price. Don't think about the future without it!]
(**world population up 25% by 2010**)

136
World Access to Birth Control. Edited by Sharon L. Camp (VP, Population Crisis Committee). Washington: PCC (1120 19th St NW; 202/659-1833), Oct 1992/one page (25x22")/$5.00.

A wall chart with analysis on the reverse side, rating the availability of family planning information and services in 124 countries. Several hundred individual country experts contributed information on over 120 measures of family planning program strength. This was consolidated into ten indicators related to the range of birth control choices available (60% of total score), the competence of those providing family planning services (20% of total), and the convenience of services and the amount of information available to contraceptive users. Countries are scored from 0 to 100. Top countries were Denmark (97 out of 100), The Netherlands (95), Sweden (95), and Norway (93). China rated 90 and India 73. The US was given a total score of only 75. Canada rated 71 and Japan 43. Seven countries received a 0 score: Gabon, Iraq, Kuwait, Liberia, Libya, Saudi Arabia, and Somalia. Overall, the 1992 assessment showed "a dramatic increase in access to birth control around the world, reflecting the expansion of organized family planning programs in developing countries and much better program implementation." Of the 87 developing countries studied in both the 1987 and 1992 editions, 57 improved their scores by 10 points or more (of these, 33 gained 20 points or more). But some 12 countries appear to have moved backwards with lower 1992 scores (including Brazil, Columbia, Jamaica, and the Philippines). In 22 countries scoring less than 25 points, couples still have virtually no access to birth control information or services. If the world is to reach population stabilization in the next century at less than double the current 5.4 billion people, the proportion of couples practicing contraception must increase from about 50% to 75%.   (**access to birth control increases**)

137
Population Policies Reconsidered: Health, Empowerment, and Rights. Edited by Gita Sen (Harvard Center for Population and Development Studies), Adrienne Germain (International Women's Health Coalition, NYC), and Lincoln C. Chen (Director, Harvard Center). Cambridge MA: HCPDS/IWHC (dist. by Harvard U P), July 1994/280p(8x11")/$14.95pb.

Modern population policies, begun four decades ago, have sought to manage rapid population growth in high-fertility countries, largely through family planning programs. About half of all couples in the world now use contraception, but contraceptive services are by no means universally accessible or affordable. As many as one-third of all pregnancies end in abortion, often illegally and with great hazard to women's health. Many family planning programs exclude youth, the unmarried, and even men from information and services. Reconsideration of population policy is urgently needed to re-establish a strong consensus for public action. Three major themes are addressed: 1) population policies should be transformed to reflect a fundamental commitment to ethics and human rights; 2) rather than concentrating simply on fertility control, population policies can only be effective and humane as part of broader human development approaches; 3) strategies for change should focus on empowering women at many levels of society, and promoting reproductive and health services that include broader information and encourage men's responsibility. "Investing in people's health, empowerment, and human rights is not only worthy in its own right, but would probably be more conducive to population stabilization than narrowly conceived policies of population control." The new population approach would complement approaches to sustainable development, and shift state actions to promote quality of life. [ALSO SEE: **Power and**

Decision: The Social Control of Reproduction edited by Gita Sen and Rachel C. Snow (HCDPS/Harvard, July 1994/348p/$14.95pb), on gender bias in technology and policy.] **(broader population policy needed)**

138
The Population Explosion. Paul R. Ehrlich and Anne H. Ehrlich (both Stanford U). NY: Simon & Schuster, April 1990/320p/$18.95.

In 1968, when there were only 3.5 billion human beings, Paul Ehrlich wrote **The Population Bomb**, warning of impending disaster if the population explosion was not brought under control. "Then the fuse was burning; now the population bomb has detonated...a largely prospective disaster has turned into the real thing." Today's population is now 5.3 billion, with 95 million people added each year, and per capita global food production declining since 1984. Chapters discuss "Why Isn't Everyone as Scared as We Are?" (the slow motion of the early stages of exponential population growth, failure to make connections between disparate events, a taboo against frank discussion of the population crisis in many quarters), the depletion of natural capital (squandering our inheritance), the impact of humans on the environment (I= Population x Affluence x Technology), food as the ultimate resource (and how Africa and Latin America are falling behind), how overpopulation is rapidly degrading earth's ecosystems, connections between population and public health, the shortsightedness of most economists, environmental threats to national security, and the Bang and the Whimper (if we escape the nuclear Bang, "the Whimper simply is the way that civilization will end if current population/resource/environment trends continue").

Concludes that *Homo sapiens* has brought its old mind into the new world, and the slow pace of biological evolution has kept us from adjusting our perceptual apparatus to world-scale problems [see **New World, New Mind: Moving Toward Conscious Evolution** by Robert Ornstein and Paul Ehrlich. Doubleday, Jan 1989; *FS* 12:1, #90-017]. Moving to a directed cultural evolution must be the first part of dealing with the human predicament. We must then deal with the I=PAT equation by reducing all three sources of impact through population control in both poor and rich nations, energy conservation, and renewable energy sources. The problems that loom in humanity's future demand a stronger management system, and a Global Commons Regime is proposed, using the Law of the Sea as a model. **(overpopulation disaster)**

139
Population, Resources and the Environment: The Critical Challenges. Norman Myers (Oxford UK). NY: United Nations Population Fund (220 E 42nd St), Dec 1991/154p/$24.75pb.

The unprecedented rapid growth in human numbers, plus their distributional patterns and urbanization trends, induces critical constraints on the development process, as well as unsustainable burdens on the environmental resource base that underpins much economic activity. Based on the latest UN projections, world population is expected to grow from 5.3 billion in 1990 to 6.3 billion in 2000, 7.2 billion in 2010, and 8.5 billion in 2025. (These figures are rather higher than those projected until recently, due to a slowing in the decline of fertility in a number of countries.) The medium-level projection for eventual world population in 2100 is 11.3 billion, with a high projection of 14.2 billion and a low projection of just under 8 billion. Although the global rate of population growth has declined from a high of 2.1% in the late 1960s to 1.7% today, the number of people added each year is higher than ever, and is projected to keep on climbing, reaching an annual peak of 97 million by 2000. In 1989, the number of people estimated to be living in absolute poverty totalled 1.2 billion, or 23% of world population.

The growth in human numbers and in consumption, along with growth of environmentally adverse technology, combine to precipitate a downturn in the capacity of environmental resources to sustain human communities. The problem of land shortages, accompanied by farmland fragmentation, is becoming widespread in many if not most developing countries. Water deficits are already a serious constraint on development in 88 developing countries with 40% of world population. Chapters discuss environment and the quality of life, and seven case studies of population carrying capacities (Pakistan, India, Philippines, Ethiopia, Kenya, Mexico, and El Salvador). The effort to establish a sustainable future will require major changes in our economic, political, and social structures. We know what to do: the scientific understanding is there, the relevant technologies are available, the policy imperatives are established. "What is generally missing is the political will to get on with the task, but this may well reflect an inadequate grasp of the concealed costs of inaction." Proposed policies include, first and foremost, governments learning to integrate population factors into development planning; also, nationwide information/education campaigns, human resource development to improve quality of life, and policies to combat growing problems of population distribution and to upgrade women's status.
(population/environment challenges)

140
Environmental Refugees in a Globally Warmed World, Norman Myers (Visiting Fellow, Green College, Oxford U), *BioScience*, 43:11, Dec 1993, 752-761.

Much has been written about the physical impacts of global warming, but little attention has been directed to the human impact, notably the emergent issue of environmental refugees. According to recent estimates, there are at least 10 million environmental refugees today (roughly half of them in Sub-Saharan Africa), compared with 17 million refugees under the conventional definition. The first figure is certainly on the low side because governments often take little official account of this unconventional category. In any event, we can assume that the number of environmental refugees is likely to swell rapidly as burgeoning throngs of poor people press ever harder on overloaded environments. Some estimates are made of key world regions, assuming a global population of 10 billion people in 2050 and a sea level rise of 30cm (about one foot): **1) Bangladesh**: by 2050, expected hazards would destroy homes and holdings in an area containing 7% of today's population, affecting 15 million people; **2) Egypt**: the country could well lose 12-15% of its scarce arable land, now containing 14% of the population; sea-level rise would thus displace more than 14 million people by 2050; **3) China**: the government estimates that 30 million people would be displaced by coastal flooding (a highly conservative estimate, in that 525 million Chinese will be living in the coastal plain by 2050); **4) India**: the total of flood-zone refugees could range from 20 to 60 million; **5) Caribbean Island States**: may eventually become subject to tropical storms of increased intensity over a longer season, "sufficient to reduce greatly the suitability of parts of the islands for permanent human habitation." Overall, "the total of environmental refugees as calculated here for a greenhouse-affected world is about 150 million." This amounts to 1.5% of the world population in 2050, compared with only 0.2% of the global population today. [**NOTE**: An important speculation by a prolific author best known for his estimates of future species extinctions (**FS Annual 1991** #10517).]

(**150 million environmental refugees in 2050?**)

141

Beyond Charity: International Cooperation and the Global Refugee Crisis. Gil Loescher (Prof of International Relations, U of Notre Dame). A Twentieth Century Fund Book. NY: Oxford U Press, Dec 1993/260p/$35.00.

"The stark fact must be faced that the world is witnessing a huge growth in forcibly displaced people"—those driven from their countries by civil war, famine, grave social injustice, political oppression, and individual persecution. The total number of refugees has grown from 2.8 million in 1976 to 8.2 million in 1980 and nearly 18 million at the end of 1992. "It is likely that the number will exceed 20 million during this decade. In addition, at least another 20 million people are displaced inside their own country." [**NOTE**: In **Protecting the Dispossessed** (below), Francis M. Deng estimates 25 million people displaced within their own countries.] The growth in numbers and the complexity of refugee flows have presented enormous challenges to the UNHCR (UN High Commissioner for Refugees), which is chronically underfunded and understaffed. At the same time, "governments all over the world have become less tolerant toward refugees and feel that there is no more room for immigrants of any kind." A steady erosion has occurred in even the minimal protections afforded refugees by international law. In sum, the international community is not meeting its legal and ethical obligations.

The time has come to move beyond charity and to broaden the scope of approach to the growing refugee problem. A comprehensive program would include: 1) establishing an independent UN monitoring body to provide good intelligence that can lead to effective prevention; 2) strengthening regional emergency relief and conflict resolution machinery; 3) establishing a basis for collective intervention in internal conflicts (mass expulsions of people should be seen as analogous to military invasions of neighboring countries); 4) insuring international access to areas experiencing humanitarian crises; 5) encouraging governments to assure asylum to refugees (of critical importance to maintaining human rights protection); 6) resolving the problem of long-staying refugee populations (short-term relief for returnees must be complemented with national development efforts and careful reintegration). [**NOTE**: Environmental refugees are not mentioned here, but can only add to the problem (see above).]

(**refugee crisis growing**)

142

Protecting the Dispossessed: A Challenge for the International Community. Francis M. Deng (Senior Fellow, Brookings Institution). Washington: The Brookings Institution, Sept 1993/175p/$26.95;$9.95pb.

About 25 million people worldwide are reported to be displaced within their own countries—a number that far exceeds the estimated 18 million refugees. Like refugees, the displaced are victims of civil wars, natural disasters, forced relocation, and gross violations of human rights. Deng, formerly a UN Human Rights Officer and Sudan's Minister of State for Foreign Affairs, was appointed Special Representative of the UN Secretary-General. This book is derived from Deng's report to the UN Commission on Human Rights in March 1993, finding that there is no adequate system of protection and assistance for displaced people. Responsibility for assisting such persons lies in the first instance with the home country, but if a country is unwilling or unable to meet minimum standards of humanitarian or human rights law, protection becomes a matter of international attention to override traditional prerogatives of sovereignty. There is much that the international community and especially the UN can do. It does not have to wait until conditions have deteriorated as badly as in Somalia and the former Yugoslavia before acting decisively. And much preventive action can be taken to make international involvement far more cost-effective than the massive intervention that crises always require. Needed documents include a compilation of existing rules and norms, a code of conduct to guide treatment of displaced persons, and a UN declaration. Internally displaced persons should be added to the mandates of the High Commissioner for Refugees or the Department of Humanitarian Affairs, or an equivalent body should be established. [ALSO SEE: **Refugees: Rationing the Right to Life. The Crisis in Emergency Relief** by David Keen of St. Antony's College, Oxford (Zed Books, Sept 1992/86p/$49.95/$15.95pb), on the six-fold increase of refugees in the last two decades. Rising numbers and shrinking relief budgets are straining the current system of relief to the breaking point.]

(**displaced people and refugees**)

143

Cities in the 21st Century: The Urban Half. *Work in Progress* (United Nations U), 13:3, Sept 1991/12p(14x10")/free. (Available from UNU-Tokyo in English, French, Spanish, and Japanese editions, or from Jerome C. Glenn, Executive Director, American Council for the UNU, 4421 Garrison St NW, Washington DC 20016; 202/686-5179.)

Materials largely from a Symposium on the Mega-City and the Future, held in Tokyo in October 1990, to be eventually published in book form. By 2000, it is estimated that there will be 24 mega-cities around the globe with populations in excess of 10 million; 18 of them will be in the Third World. These mega-cities often tend to have more in common with each other than their rural hinterlands—a kind of urban pathology that crosses ideological, economic, and cultural lines. The 11 essays discuss the pathology of the city (the gap between the very rich and the very poor is widening in all mega-cities), the retreat of the "metropolitan solution" of the mid-1960s, crime and homelessness, new strategies to cope with worsening urban poverty, lopsided modernization (by Ignacy Sachs and Dana Silk, who stress that urbanization is by far the most important social transformation of our times, and that world urban population will rise from 34% in 1960 and 40% in 1980 to 48% in 2000 and 62% in 2025), urban transport and urban growth, Tokyo as role model for the mega-city of the future, the growth of Seoul (projected to be the world's 7th largest metro area in 2000), Asia's growing urban rings, the positive aspects of urbanization (immigrants from the countryside are generally assimilated into urban labor markets), and the emerging world city system. [**NOTE**: Published in book form as **Mega-city Growth and the Future** (UNU Press, June 1994, *Future Survey*, 16:11, #94-509).]

(**UNU Mega-City and the Future Symposium**)

144

International Migration Challenges in a New Era. Doris M. Meissner (Project Director; Carnegie Endowment for International Peace), Robert D. Hormats (NYC), Antonio Garrigues Walker (Madrid), and Shijuro Ogata

(Tokyo). A Report to the Trilateral Commission (Triangle Papers: 44). NY: The Trilateral Commission, Sept 1993/116p/$12.00pb.

With the end of the Cold War, we are moving to a new, as yet undefined era. But it is certain that recent changes are unleashing powerful processes of social and political fragmentation at the same time that nations are increasingly interdependent. "With growing migration pressures occurring in this time of extraordinary change and uncertainty, large numbers on the move can be the source of political instability and dangerous upheavals." International migration is thus emerging as a critical concern for peace and stability. Chapters discuss categories of migrants (legally admitted immigrants, contract labor migrants, illegal immigrants, asylum-seekers, the growing number of refugees), Canada's immigration policies (with a population of just over 27 million, Canada's annual target of 250,000 immigrants from 1992 to 1995 is nearly 1% of its population), US immigration policy (nearly 9 million newcomers came to the US in the 1980s), immigration in EC countries (Europe today stands at the crossroads of international migration pressures, but with growing intolerance and public disapproval), Japan's recent opening to foreign workers (a new foreign worker trainee program will accept about 100,000 foreigners a year, and the number of illegal workers is growing). Concludes that a broad consensus is developing in Trilateral countries that receiving countries must be attentive to pre-refugee, pre-migration circumstances in sending countries. This requires a broad mix of measures: 1) fostering an international migration regime; 2) foreign policies and international priorities that emphasize broad-based improvements in human rights and democracy; 3) aggressive pursuit of population stabilization and sustainable development in poor countries; 4) national policies and systems for orderly admission of immigrants and refugees, and for effective integration of newcomers. [NOTE: Soon after completing this project, Meissner became Commissioner of the US Immigration and Naturalization Service.]

(**migration pressures growing**)

145
A Framework for Survival: Health, Human Rights, and Humanitarian Assistance in Conflicts and Disasters. Edited by Kevin M. Cahill (Director, Ctr for Intl Health and Cooperation, NYC). NY: BasicBooks and Council on Foreign Relations, April 1993/340p/$25.00pb.

Focusing on health, human rights, and humanitarian assistance offers an innovative approach to foreign policy that may be more effective in many cases than the conventional military and economic "solutions" that have so often been flawed. By building on common objectives and universally accepted values, by defining the core needs of all human beings and proposing ways to satisfy those needs, we may be able to create a better framework for survival in a new century. These essays from a September 1992 CFR symposium in NYC are grouped in four parts: **1) Legal and Economic Issues**: Richard Falk on human rights and the sovereignty of states, obligations of donor nations, concerns of recipient nations; **2) Health Issues**: why relief efforts didn't work in Somalia, casualties of mine warfare, responding to sudden population displacements, the need for a US international health corps to facilitate overseas work; **3) Private Voluntary Response**: the greatly increased roles of NGOs in disaster and conflict situations, shaping effective relief responses to disasters (they must be multi-dimensional and well-coordinated), the experience of Médecins sans Frontières (one of the world's leading private emergency assistance organizations), making the humanitarian system work better (through better coordination, a better division of labor, increased professionalism); **4) UN Response**: mobilizing international relief, aid to children caught in war, the plight of refugees. In an introductory essay, **Cyrus Vance** discusses six imperatives for the year 2000: peace and security, sustainable economic development, curbing population growth and environmental degradation, democracy and human rights, strengthening key international institutions, and providing adequate global health care. (**humanitarian assistance**)

146
Critical Condition: Human Health and the Environment. Edited by Eric Chivian (Harvard Medical School), Michael McCally (U of Chicago), Howard Hu (Harvard School of Public Health), and Andrew Haines (London Medical School). Cambridge MA: MIT Press, Sept 1993/244p/$29.95;$15.95pb.

A report by Physicians for Social Responsibility, which has led the effort to educate citizens about the medical consequences of nuclear war since 1961, and shared the 1985 Nobel Peace Prize with its international umbrella organization, International Physicians for the Prevention of Nuclear War. "The world now faces a similar threat to human health and survival from changes to the global environment...and there is a similar lack of understanding about the consequences." The problem of environmental degradation, however, is more complex by orders of magnitude than that of nuclear war, and its solution will demand much greater change in the way people will lead their lives. This report seeks to gather the best available medical information about the environment. Chapters discuss: **1) Risk Assessment and the Physician**: the training of physicians ought to shift from a bioengineering to an ecological model; all physicians should understand the relationship of environment to health; **2) Urban and Transboundary Air Pollution**: criticizes the current US approach to air pollution for inadequate control of ozone and lead, and for failing to address indoor air pollution; **3) Drinking Water Pollution**: "the number of different industrial and agricultural chemicals that threaten public and private water supplies is enormous;" nitrates, heavy metals, pesticides, and volatile organic compounds are of greatest concern; **4) Food Contamination**: the integrity of food is threatened by many man-made pollutants; most of these toxins are invisible and not easily detected by consumers ("moreover, the processing or cooking of food is generally not effective in neutralizing their impact"); **5) Occupational Exposures**: it is estimated that occupational disease is responsible each year for 50,000-70,000 deaths in the US, and for about 350,000 new cases of illness; **6) Radiation**: medical concern about nuclear power plants centers on four distinct public health problems: catastrophic accidents, nuclear waste containment, weapons proliferation, and hazards to workers and surrounding populations from routine operation; **7) War-Induced Environmental Damage**: the escalating numbers of weapons and the diverse technologies of destruction and delivery place the environment in greater jeopardy than ever before from aerial bombardment, land mines, toxic pollution, and despoliation; **8) Loss of Stratospheric Ozone**: increase in ultraviolet-radiation reaching the earth is expected to have direct health effects on humans (skin cancer, aging skin, cataracts, sunburn of the cornea, impacts on the immune system) and to result in food shortages; **9) Possible Effects of Climate Change**: more summer deaths from high temperature, increased threats from communicable diseases, impacts on the availability of food and water, impacts on mental health; **10) Population Growth**: physicians should have a major role in population control efforts, due to clear evidence of the threats to human health, the environment, and socioeconomic development; **11) Species Extinction and Biodiversity Loss**: massive species extinctions forecloses the possibility of understanding and treating many diseases. [NOTE: Authoritative and readable overview. ALSO SEE: **Your Health, Our World: The Impact of Environmental Degradation on Human Wellbeing** by Diane Wiesner (Prism/Unity, distributed in US by Avery, 1992/337p/$14.95pb).]

(**health and environmental problems**)

*147
AIDS in the World. The Global AIDS Policy Coalition. Jonathan M. Mann (General Editor and GAPC Coordinator; Director, Intl. AIDS Center, Harvard U). Cambridge MA: Harvard U Press, Dec 1992/1,037p/$45.00;$19.95pb.

The first annual global report from GAPC, founded in 1991 to track the evolving HIV/AIDS pandemic, critically analyze the global response, and encourage policy analysis and advocacy. Chapters discuss the HIV pandemic, the AIDS pandemic, interactions of HIV and other diseases such as TB (it is highly likely that new disease interactions will be discovered and none are likely to be beneficial), economic and social impacts of AIDS, research achievements (it is generally hoped that safe and effective vaccines will be developed in the 1990s), national AIDS programs in 37 countries (in 13 of these countries, the head of state has yet to make a statement on HIV/AIDS), prevention activities over the past decade (three elements are essential: information/education, health and social services, and a supportive social environment), providing care, the widely varying cost of care and prevention, funding the global AIDS strategy, AIDS and human rights, global vulnerability to HIV infection (57 Third World countries are at high risk), and various policy issues.

Overall, the global HIV/AIDS pandemic is volatile and dynamic, and its major impacts are yet to come. "The pace of the pandemic is fast outgrowing the pace of the response, and the gap is widening rapidly and dangerously.. It is essential, for our common future, that we not shrink from sounding the alarm." In early 1992, 12.9 million people worldwide had been infected with HIV (including 7.1 million men, 4.7 million women, and 1.1 million children). Some 21% of this number has thus far developed AIDS; of these, over 90% (nearly 2.5 million) have died. AIDS is spreading to new communities and countries around the world, repeatedly demonstrating its ability to cross all borders. A modified Delphi survey of 22 HIV/AIDS experts was conducted to obtain adjustment factors for underreporting of AIDS, estimate 1991 prevalence for each of 10 geographic areas, and to make projections to 2000. Adult HIV infections are projected to grow from 11.8 million in January 1992 to 17.5 million in 1995 (with 11.4 million in sub-Saharan Africa). Delphi estimates for 2000 range from 38 million to 109 million worldwide (with a range of 21 to 34 million in sub-Saharan Africa, 11 to 45 million in Southeast Asia, 2 to 8 million in North America, 1.6 to 8.5 million in Latin America, 0.5 to 7.0 million in the Caribbean, and 1.2 to 2.3 million in Western Europe). Concludes with a chapter on the danger of newly emerging viruses in the Global Village, stressing that "HIV is but one of a long series of microbes that have recently surfaced, and will be followed by more." [NOTE: Important and authoritative global overview of a major factor in the world, for the next few decades at least. The next edition of **AIDS in the World** will examine successful interventions to prevent HIV infection, future demands on health and social service systems, the political economy of tests and drugs, and the impact of women's status on AIDS.]

(**38-109 million HIV infections in 2000**)

*148
Emerging Viruses. Edited by Stephen S. Morse (Rockefeller U, NYC). NY: Oxford U P, May 1993/317p/$39.95.

Many of the deadliest, most feared, and most common diseases have been viral, e.g.: AIDS, influenza, smallpox, and shingles. AIDS and influenza also typify the emergence of "new" diseases, often manifested explosively as epidemics. "Viral traffic," the movement of viruses to new species or new individuals that is often abetted by human actions, is the major factor in viral emergence. Anticipating and limiting viral emergence is more feasible than previously believed; to do so, the essential first step is global disease surveillance. *William H. McNeill* (U of Chicago), author of **Plagues and People** (Anchor/Doubleday, 1976), notes that our billions of human bodies offer "a magnificent feeding ground" for a hungry virus or bacterium. *Thomas E. Lovejoy* (Smithsonian Institution) points to the potential of global climate change to affect biological systems and create epidemiologic effects. *Llewellyn J. Legters* (Uniformed Services University of the Health Sciences, Bethesda) *et al.* provide a scenario in the form of a "News Report of the Future" covering the "super-Ebola" Pandemic of 1994-95 that spreads rapidly to every continent in the world, illustrating how ill-prepared we are to detect such global epidemic threats in a timely fashion and to respond appropriately. *Donald A. Henderson* (Office of Science and Technology Policy, Executive Office of the President) laments that "we are not today well-structured or staffed on a global level to detect either new or emerging viral diseases," and proposes a global surveillance system based on 15 broadly-based tropical medicine centers. Other essays discuss such topics as viral hemorrhagic fevers emerging because of accelerating ecologic changes, the coevolution of virus and host, new technologies for virus detection, case studies of animal viruses that recently crossed species, and how viruses evolve. [NOTE: A major warning that should be on every serious futurist's short list of nasty possibilities. ALSO SEE: **The Coming Plague** (Farrar, Strauss & Giroux, Oct 1994, *FS*, 16:11 #94-549), **Infectious Diseases in the Age of Change** (National Academy Press, Oct 1994), and **Emerging Infections: Microbial Threats to Health in the United States** (National Academy Press, 1992; **FS Annual 1994** #12581), a similar warning of potential global epidemics that also advocates more global surveillance. **Where Are 'New' Diseases Born?** (*Science*, 6 Aug 1993, 680-681), reports on the "emerging viruses" meeting that gave rise to Morse's book, and a test (now underway at a logging operation in Papua New Guinea) of the hypothesis that changing environments are the main cause of emerging infectious diseases.]

(**global viral epidemic threat**)

6. Global Environmental Problems

*149
The World Environment 1972-1992: Two Decades of Challenge. Edited by Mostafa K. Tolba (Executive Director, UN Environment Programme, Nairobi) and Osama A. El-Kholy (Cairo U, Egypt). London & NY: Chapman & Hall (div of Routledge), Dec 1992/884p/$89.95;$29.95pb.

Reviews trends over the past 20 years, with progress in some areas offset by accelerating destruction in others. **The Issues**: 1) air pollution (perception has broadened tremendously in the past two decades); 2) ozone depletion (once a matter of scientific curiosity, it has become an urgent policy question); 3) climate change (an issue raising important questions of international equity); 4) fresh water (due to growing population and per capita use, "it is highly likely that water, like energy in the 1970s, will become the most critical resource issue in most parts of the world by the late 1990s and the early 21st century"); 5) coastal and marine degradation (pressures on coastal zones are leading to continuing degradation, likely to be exacerbated by climate change and sea level rise); 6) land degradation ("if the process of desertification is not arrested soon, the world shortage of food will increase dramatically"; meanwhile, the cost of anti-desertification measures is escalating); 7) deforestation and habitat loss (increasing recognition of the economic value of forests and wetlands has added impetus to their conservation, and new global initiatives are underway after UNCED); 8) biodiversity (current measures to slow losses are valuable but insufficient); 9) environmental hazards (frequencies of major natural disasters have increased); 10) toxic chemicals and hazardous wastes (proliferation in many areas).

Causes and Consequences: 11) agriculture and fisheries (sustainable agriculture requires institutional mechanisms to give correct signals of emerging scarcities of land and water); 12) industry (the challenge is in restructuring for sustainable production); 13) energy (reviews production, consumption, and environmental impacts); 14) transport (one of the major contributors to environmental degradation; a coordinated global strategy for this sector is outlined); 15) tourism (now the second largest item in world trade; the concept of sustainable development should be applied to it worldwide); 16) population pressure on resources (caused by increased numbers, poverty, overconsumption, and unsustainable production technologies); 17) settlements (urbanization in poor countries and counter-urbanization in OECD countries); 18) health (infant and child mortality rates have declined steadily and life expectancy has increased, but the overall picture is still alarming in many respects); 19) peace and security (continuing military expenditure implies a lack of conviction for disarmament; a planned conversion process is needed to reverse environmental degradation).

The Response: 20) understanding the environment (all branches of science deepened tremendously since 1972, but new knowledge is not quickly applied in policies); 21) perceptions and attitudes (public concern is much greater than in 1972); 22) national responses (environmental policy is now a concern of virtually all nations and has become increasingly cross-sectoral and integrated, but laws and programs have grown haphazardly; governments are increasingly joining in international agreements and committing scarce resources to their implementation); 23) international responses (models for cooperation within the UN and between UN agencies and other bodies).

Concludes that the overriding message of this review is that human beings and human institutions wait too long before taking action. "On nearly every issue we have failed to apply the precautionary principle when it was appropriate—indeed prudent—to do so. We have had more than enough talk about environmental problems.... Despite the very real achievements and advances of recent years, the state of the world environment and the living conditions of many of its people have continued to get worse...we no longer have the luxury of picking and choosing what to do next: the state of the world environment demands that we take action simultaneously on a broad front, with no further delay.... It is no exaggeration to say that the ability of the biosphere to continue to support human life is now in question." [**NOTE**: A massive, authoritative overview, well-organized and clearly-written. Especially valuable for Chapters 20-23 on "The Response."]

(**environmental trends, impacts, and responses**)

150
World Resources 1992-93: A Guide to the Global Environment. World Resources Inst (Allen L. Hammond, Editor-in-Chief), in collaboration with the UN Environment Programme and UN Development Programme. NY: Oxford U P, March 1992/385p (8x11")/ $29.95;$15.95pb.

Fifth edition of a biennial series, with editions in eight languages. **Part I**, in support of the UNCED meeting, focuses on sustainable development with four special chapters. The overview chapter, providing an extensive definition of sustainable development, concludes that it requires simultaneous progress along at least four dimensions: economic, human, environmental, and technological. The three other chapters provide case studies on what sustainable development might mean in industrial countries, poor countries (breaking the cycle of poverty and environmental degradation), and rapidly industrializing countries. **Part II**, as in previous editions, focuses on a particular region, in this case the severe problems faced by Central Europe. (The fourth edition focused on Latin America; the third edition on Asia.)

Part III reports on basic conditions and trends, key issues, and recent developments. **1) Population and Human Development**: declining growth rates and increasing numbers; human development measures; children's health; urbanization; **2) Food and Agriculture**: despite disincentives, many farmers are finding it profitable to invest in sustainable agriculture; agro-chemical taxes should be imposed to control off-site impacts; **3) Forests and Rangelands**: an area about the size of China and India combined—almost 11% of the Earth's vegetated surface—has suffered moderate to extreme soil degradation in the past 45 years; **4) Wildlife and Habitat**: biodiversity is more threatened now than at any time in the past 65 million years; up to 15% of Earth's species could be doomed over the next 25 years; **5) Energy**: global energy production has increased by about 50% over the past two decades, with fossil fuels accounting for over 90% of production; **6) Freshwater**: resources are under severe and increasing stress; by 2000, withdrawals for agriculture will increase slightly and industrial withdrawals will probably double; "shortages could reach crisis proportions in the Middle East and North Africa"; **7) Oceans and Coasts**: only a small fraction of the world's wastewater is treated; trends show rising coastal pollution and accelerated destruction of coastal marine habitats; **8) Atmosphere and Climate**: includes estimates of emissions for the major greenhouse gases by source and country (the US accounts for 18.4% of global emissions, followed by the USSR at 13.5%, China at 8.4% and Japan at 5.6%); **9) Policies and Institutions**: discusses evolution of NGOs and grassroots organizations. **Part IV** provides 52 data tables for the countries and regions of the world. Concludes that "the world is not now headed toward a sustainable future, but rather toward a variety of potential human and environmental disasters.... Sustainable development will require a fundamental change in existing policies and practices." [**NOTE**: A major collaborative effort; the authoritative source for data and analysis on global environmental issues. ALSO SEE: Sixth edition, published in May 1994 (*FS* 16:11 #94-501), **Teacher's Guide to World Resources 1992-93** (142p looseleaf/$4.95), and **World Resources Data Diskette** ($119.95).]

(**sustainable development defined**)

151

The Human Impact on the Natural Environment (4th Edition). Andrew Goudie (Prof of Geography, Hertford College, U of Oxford). Cambridge MA: MIT Press, March 1994/454p/$40.00;$19.95pb.

Trends in human manipulation of the environment: 1) the ways in which humans affect the environment are proliferating; 2) environmental issues that were once locally confined have become regional or even global problems; 3) the complexity, magnitude, and frequency of impacts are probably increasing; 4) compounding the effects of rapidly expanding human population is a general increase in per capita consumption and environmental impact. Chapters describe the human impact on vegetation (deforestation, fires, air pollution), animals (domestication, dispersal, extinction, expansion, contraction), soil (salinity, erosion, acidification), water (pollution, river flow, lake levels), geomorphology (new landforms, accelerated sedimentation and coastal erosion, river-channel changes), and climate and the atmosphere (pollution, urban climates, the CO_2 problem). A concluding chapter on the future discusses the spatial patterning of change, consequences of global warming, projected sea-level rise, and environmental uncertainty. [NOTE: Offers background on what has happened and is happening, but no guidance on the human response.] **(human impact on environment)**

152

Global Marine Biological Diversity: A Strategy for Building Conservation into Decision Making. Elliott A. Norse (Chief Scientist, Center for Marine Conservation, Washington). Washington: Island Press, Oct 1993/383p/$50.00;$27.50pb.

This companion document to the **Global Biodiversity Strategy** (World Resources Institute, 1992; **FS Annual 1993** #11768) is sponsored by CMC, IUCN, WWF, UNEP, and the World Bank. It argues that conserving biodiversity in the sea has been even more neglected than on land. Despite their importance to us, humankind is destroying marine species and ecosystems, not only in estuaries and coastal waters, but in the open seas. We harm marine biodiversity by overexploiting living things, altering the physical environment, polluting the sea, introducing alien species, and adding substances to the atmosphere that increase ultraviolet radiation and alter climate. The root causes underlying these threats to marine life are too many people consuming too much, institutions that degrade rather than conserve, lack of knowledge, and insufficient valuation of nature. Chapters discuss the importance of marine biological diversity, impediments to marine conservation (national sovereignty, North-South divisions, jurisdictional gaps and overlaps, fragmented decision making, etc.), the key strategy of building conservation into decison making (best done by institutionalizing sustainability into laws and actions, and providing incentives to choose sustainability over other options), tools for conserving marine biodiversity (expanding the knowledge base, planning, regulating threats, economic tools, protecting and restoring areas), and lessons from existing institutions and instruments. Concludes with about 150 recommendations for implementing *"The Strategy,"* such as: 1) nations should sign and implement the Convention on Biological Diversity; 2) UNEP, IUCN, WRI, and WWF should produce biennial reports on the state of biological diversity; 3) the UN should establish 1995 to 2004 as the International Biological Diversity Decade and establish a Global Biodiversity Forum; 4) the UN should establish an Early Warning Monitoring Network on threats to marine biodiversity; 5) UNEP and others should establish an International Marine Conservation Network to link decision makers worldwide; 6) coastal countries should have a management agency responsible for protecting marine resources; 7) nations should push for a new, binding climate convention to replace the one signed at UNCED. **(marine biodiversity strategy)**

153

Freedom for the Seas in the 21st Century: Ocean Governance and Environmental Harmony. Edited by Jon M. Van Dyke (Prof of Law, U of Hawaii), Durwood Zaelke (President, Center for International Environmental Law), and Grant Hewison (Greenpeace New Zealand). Washington: Island Press, Dec 1993/504p/$55.00;$27.50pb.

The image of the limitless sea has dominated Western thought for the past millennium. Because the seas have been viewed as a frontier territory, an "anything goes" attitude has been accepted as appropriate. Legal terminology to justify this approach is "freedom of the seas"—a concept developed by the major maritime powers during the age of imperialism. This freedom has historically included the freedom to pollute, assuming that oceans have a limitless capacity to assimilate wastes. Technological developments such as drift nets on the high seas demonstrate that "anything goes" is no longer acceptable. Most of these essays, based on a December 1990 meeting in Honolulu, argue that the governing notion should be "freedom *for* the seas," whereby the key goal will be to protect ecological vitality. The 29 essays are in six parts: *1) Ocean Governance*: principles for a comprehensive regime, the process of creating an international ocean regime (by Elizabeth Mann Borgese), potential contributions from indigenous peoples (who generally believe that the sea is not simply a resource for humans to exploit), principles of a new Law of the Sea; *2) Pacific Approaches*: five essays on how Pacific Islanders have begun to build a regime for the South Pacific area based on high environmental consciousness; *3) Controlling Ocean Pollution*: mending the seas through a Global Commons Trust Fund, what is needed in international agreements, protected marine areas and low-lying atolls; *4) Living Resources*: problems of unregulated fisheries, legal issues concerning drift net fishing, trade restrictions of a conservation measure; *5) The 1982 Law of the Sea Convention*: environmental ethics and deep seabed mining; *6) Military Activities*: security regimes for the oceans, denuclearizing the seas, naval operations, military exclusionary zones. In sum, five brands of idealism are reflected here: environmentalism, structuralism, humanism, nonstatism, and transnational bureaucratism. [ALSO SEE: **Global Marine Environment: Does the Water Planet Have a Future?** by Herman Prager of NE Louisiana U (University Press of America, March 1993/161p/$42.50;$18.50pb), on the ocean pollution crisis and the role of international organizations and INGOs in protection.] **(ocean governance)**

154

Water: The International Crisis. Robin Clarke (Consultant, UNEP). Cambridge MA: MIT Press, March 1993/193p/$30.00;$15.95pb. (First published in London by Earthscan, 1991.)

In 1940, total water use was about 1,000 cubic kilometers. Usage doubled by 1960 and doubled again to 4,138 cubic km by 1990, and is projected to be 5,189 cubic km by

2000. Chapters discuss water and climate, degradation of land and water, spreading deserts, growing water scarcity, the neglect of water issues in development planning, the enormous potential for international conflict over water, the high costs of high-tech schemes (diverting rivers, desalting the sea, moving icebergs, large dams), traditional solutions (run-off farming, flooding the fields, small-scale irrigation), new twists to old solutions (changing crops, small dams, micro-irrigation, rainwater harvesting), and water security as a key to food security.

(**water crisis: global overview**)

155

World Forests for the Future: Their Use and Conservation. Edited by Kilaparti Ramakrishna and George M. Woodwell (both Woods Hole Research Center). New Haven CT: Yale U Press, April 1993/156p/$18.50.

Papers from an October 1991 workshop at Woods Hole MA. Woodwell discusses the global need for forests to stabilize heat-trapping gases and protect biotic potential, and calls for "immediate cessation of deforestation and an increase on the order of 10% or more in the forested area of the earth." Richard A. Houghton looks at global deforestation and the impact on global warming. Darrell A. Posey points to the value of indigenous knowledge for new models of sustained natural resource use. Herman E. Daly notes the evolution of the human economy from an era in which manmade capital was the limiting factor in economic development to an era in which increasingly scarce natural capital has taken its place. Robert Repetto points to the role of governments in forest usage. Jagmohan Maini and Ola Ullsten describe approaches to sustainable development of global forests and propose "Project Green Globe" to establish realistic targets for global forest cover. Ramakrishna proposes an "International Commission on the Conservation and Use of World Forests."

The introduction states that the continuous global destruction of forests is a major factor in the warming of the earth. There is a possibility that this warming may soon reach a point where "additional release of heat-trapping gasses that it induces from accelerated decay of organic matter in forests and soils will exceed the extent of control possible through curtailing use of fossil fuels and improving forest management. The warming will feed on itself by destroying forests more rapidly than they can be regenerated. The effect will be a rapid and progressive reduction in the capacity of the earth to support life, including human beings. There is no proof of this potential catastrophe. There will be no proof until it is far too late to deflect the process."

(**global warming to feed on itself?**)

156

The State of the World's Mountains: A Global Report. Edited by Peter B. Stone (Director of Information, Brundtland Commission). London & Atlantic Highlands NJ: Zed Books, June 1992/391p/$60.00;$25.00pb.

A report on "the mountain problematique" as background for the UNCED Earth Summit, prepared by Mountain Agenda (c/o Institute of Geography, U of Berne, Hallerstrasse 12, CH-3012 Berne), with support of the Swiss and German governments. Mountain areas are viewed as the backbone of civilization: they are water towers for human consumption, weather makers for large parts of the world, a source of biological diversity, and privileged places for spiritual and physical recreation. Their major problems include the growing contradiction between marginalization and integration (industrial and political centers are on the plains, but easier access enables integration of remote mountain areas), threats and hopes from agriculture and forestry (the frontier of forest destruction is inexorably moving up the mountains, driven by rapid population increase), new economic opportunities with harmful side effects (mining, large-scale construction, tourism), the impact of climate change (global warming will have a pronounced effect on mountain ecosystems, which can serve as sensitive indicators of the slightest change). Three major steps toward sustainable mountain development: 1) study and support the efforts of mountain inhabitants to reverse present trends and institute new patterns of management (many examples can be found in the hills of Nepal); 2) create more global awareness of the many dangers looming over the mountains, and build an effective global constituency; 3) build a cooperative network of national, regional, and international institutions concerned with sustainable mountain development. Two brief chapters discuss mountain protected areas and climate change in the mountains, with the bulk of the report on specific areas: African mountains and highlands, the Alps, the Himalaya (the most populous and fragile of the world's mountains), the Andes, mountains of the former Soviet Union, and the Appalachians of North America. Briefer attention is given to the eastern Canadian Arctic, Hawaii, Sierra Nevada, Scottish highlands, Pyrenees, the Japanese alps, and six other areas. [**NOTE**: Nothing on the US or Canadian Rockies; otherwise, a thorough and authoritative report. Includes photos and charts.] (**mountain problematique**)

157

The Global Partnership for Environment and Development: A Guide to Agenda 21. UN Conference on Environment and Development. Geneva: UNCED, April 1992/116p/$9.95pb. (Available from UN Publications, 2 UN Plaza, NYC 10017; #E.92.I.15.)

Sustainable development is an imperative, in both environmental and economic terms. The difficult but feasible transition will require a major shift in priorities for governments and people, "involving the full integration of the environmental dimension into economic policies and decision-making in every sphere of activity and a major redeployment of human and financial resources at national and international levels. This global partnership is essential to set the world community onto a new course for a more sustainable, secure and equitable future" (Maurice F. Strong in Foreword).

This summary guide to Agenda 21, the UNCED action plan for the 1990s and beyond, is organized around seven themes: **1) The Prospering World**: revitalizing growth with sustainability; **2) The Just World**: sustainable living that combats poverty, changes consumption patterns, and meets basic health needs; **3) The Habitable World**: developing sustainable human settlements with safe water supplies, sound management of solid wastes, and appropriate air pollution control; **4) The Fertile World**: efficient use of land and water, sustainable agriculture and forest development, managing fragile ecosystems, conserving biodiversity, sound management of biotechnology; **5) The Shared World**: protection of the atmosphere and oceans, sustainable use of living marine resources; **6) The Clean World**: managing toxic chemicals and hazardous and radioactive wastes; **7) The People's World**: enhancing participation and responsibility through education and training, and by strengthening the role of major groups (women, children and youth, indigenous people, NGOs, farmers, local authorities, trade unions, business and industry, and the sci/tech community). Essential means to attain these objectives include better information for decision-making, national capacity building, international legal instruments, sci/tech for sustainability, and improved international institutions.

(Agenda 21 summary)

158

AGENDA 21: The Earth Summit Strategy To Save Our Planet. Edited by Daniel Sitarz. Introduction by Sen. Paul Simon (D-IL). Boulder CO: EarthPress (800/748-1175), March 1993/321p/$24.95. (Quantity discounts available; also distributed by National Book Network.)

An abridgement by a lawyer/environmentalist of the final official text of AGENDA 21, as adopted by all 172 nations (including the US) attending the UN Conference on Environment and Development (UNCED) in June 1992. The first paragraph of the final unedited version of the Preamble reads as follows: *Humanity stands at a defining moment in history. We are confronted with a perpetuation of disparities between and within nations, a worsening of poverty, hunger, ill health and illiteracy, and the continuing deterioration of the ecosystems on which we depend for our well-being. However, integration of environment and development concerns and greater attention to them will lead to the fulfillment of basic needs, improved living standards for all, better protected and managed ecosystems and a safer, more prosperous future. No nation can achieve this on its own; but together we can—in a global partnership for sustainable development.*

The initial chapter, "Understanding AGENDA 21," describes the strategy as a blueprint for action in all areas of human activity, with 40 separate sections of concern and 120 action programs. Subsequent chapters are devoted to seven key themes: the quality of life on earth (controlling population growth, eradicating poverty, changing consumption patterns, improving health), efficient use of natural resources (land, fresh water, energy, agriculture, forests, deserts, mountain areas, biodiversity, biotechnology), protection of our global commons (atmosphere, oceans), managing human settlements, chemicals and waste management, sustainable economic growth (trade policies, decision-making, transfer of environmentally sound technology), and implementation (the role of women, youth, children, indigenous people, private organizations, farmers, local authorities, workers and unions, business and industry, the sci/tech community, and education). "The secretariat of the Earth Summit has estimated the average annual costs (1993-2000) of implementing all of the activities in AGENDA 21 in developing countries to be over $540 billion." Concludes that, for the far-ranging programs of AGENDA 21 to be successful, "a concern for the environment must begin to be integrated into every human action and every personal decision." Humanity must begin the difficult task of taking responsibility for its actions. [ALSO SEE: the full text, **AGENDA 21: The UN Programme of Action From Rio** (UN document E.92-38352 in 3 volumes) from UN Publications, 2 UN Plaza, NYC 10017.] **(AGENDA 21 abridgement)**

*159

Our Country, The Planet: Forging a Partnership for Survival. Shridath Ramphal (President, World Conservation Union-IUCN). Foreword by Seymour Topping (President, American Society of Newspaper Editors). Washington: Island Press, May 1992/291p/$15.00pb.

Former foreign minister of Guyana and secretary-general of the 50-nation Commonwealth (1975-1990), and a member of all the major international commissions that reported in the 1980s (including the Brandt and the Brundtland Commissions), prepared this personal statement on the agenda of the Earth Summit at the request of Maurice Strong. Chapters focus on: 1) **A Fragile World**: "the crisis of survival we face arises from the propensity for destruction, including self-destruction, our species has displayed;" 2) **Air and Water**: an overall picture of unsustainable demands on the planet's natural resources; 3) **Earth and Fire**: on desertification, deforestation, impacts of burning fossil fuels; 4) **The Profligate Rich**: the 25% of the human species in the OECD countries account for 70% of world fossil fuel consumption, 90% of automobiles, 85% of chemical products, and 85% of military expenditures; 5) **The Powerless Poor**: the great majority of the poor subsist in the Earth's less productive, more fragile, and most disaster-prone locations; 6) **Population Pressures**: world population has grown 42% in just 20 years, and will increase by a further 3 billion by 2025; 7) **A Feudal World**: a feudal system holds people in permanent subordination and most of today's developing countries still suffer from the days of colonialism; sustainable development—that which is guided by environmental considerations—requires greatly enlarged flows of aid; "the integration of development and environment is the major issue confronting human society... the rich must improve the quality of their development and so relieve the stress they now place on the planet, while the poor must develop on a basis of growth that respects the Earth's capacity to sustain life. There really is no other way;" 8) **Ethics of Survival**: "We urgently need a new universal ethic and a reordering of global priorities;" such an ethic would teach that all life is sacred and promote a sense of human identity transcending national loyalties.

Concludes with three scenarios: 1) **Muddling Through**: continuing the present pattern of inadequate ad hoc responses to developments as they become critical; by 2000 there is slow transition to renewable energy, further global warming, an expanded and deepened ozone hole, continued land degradation and deforestation, etc.; 2) **An Ordered World**: economic control increasingly wielded by IMF and the World Bank; a glaring failure in tackling global environmental issues due to imposing external values and methods on human communities that often have more understanding about how to manage resources than outsiders; 3) **Enlightened Change**: the path of shared responsibility for our common future; a significant degree of multilateral commitment to environment and development; ascendancy of democratic values worldwide; an enlarged role for internationalism and the UN; a middle path on lifestyle issues ("between ascetic self-denial and complacent self-indulgence"); a multilateral fund to finance sustainable development financed by an international tax. [**NOTE**: An eloquent globalist/Third World view, referring to seemingly all of the recent and important writing on global environmental affairs.]

(Third World view of global environment)

160

Caring for the Earth: A Strategy for Sustainable Living. IUCN/UNEP/WWF (edited by David A. Munro and Martin W. Holdgate). Gland, Switzerland: IUCN-The World Conservation Union, Oct 1991/228p/$19.95. (Distrib in US by Island Press.)

World Conservation Strategy: Living Resource Conservation for Sustainable Development was published in 1980 by the International Union for Conservation of Nature, the UN Environment Programme, and the World Wildlife Fund, resulting in conservation strategies in over 50 countries. This report re-states current thinking about conservation and development, seeking to secure widespread commitment to a new ethic for sustainable living. "Living sustainably must be a guiding principle for all the world's people." The change to living sustainably and caring for the Earth will be a major one for most people. To live within the limits of the Earth, population growth must stop everywhere, and the rich must stabilize (and in some cases reduce) their consumption of resources; ways exist to do this without reducing the real quality of life. Legal, social, economic, and technical measures aimed at sustainability must be integrated in planning and action at all levels, particularly in national governments.

Chapters are organized in three parts: **1) Principles for Sustainable Living**: respect and care for the community of life, development as improving the quality of human life, conserve the Earth's vitality and diversity, minimize depletion of non-renewable resources, keep within Earth's carrying capacity, enable communities to care for their own environments, provide a national framework for integrating development and conservation, create a global alliance to help poor countries develop sustainably, environmental education as an integral part of formal education at all levels; **2) Additional Actions for Sustainable Living**: develop explicit national energy strategies for the next 30 years, build concern for the Earth into the whole apparatus of business and industry, adopt high environmental performance standards backed up by economic incentives, develop efficient national and global systems for waste management, develop a sustainable urban transport policy, create a national strategy for agricultural sustainability, strengthen community management of forests, improve information for sustainable water management; **3) Implementation and Follow-Up**: promote the Strategy for Sustainable Living through broad-based publicity, reorder budget priorities, monitor and evaluate the Strategy, and finance new investment through Earthcare bonds, reduced military expenditure, and greater corporate sponsorship. In all, 132 actions are recommended, and targets are recommended for 1995, 2000, and 2010. [**NOTE**: A free 24-page summary is available from Thaddeus C. Trzyna (CIPA, Sacramento; Chairman of the IUCN Commission on Environmental Strategy and Planning), 916/442-2472.]

(ethic for sustainable living)

161
Earth in the Balance: Ecology and the Human Spirit. Senator Al Gore (D-Tenn). Boston: Houghton Mifflin, Jan 1992/407p/$22.95.

"Our ecological system is crumpling as it suffers a powerful collision with the hard surfaces of a civilization speeding toward it out of control." The damage is remarkably sudden and extensive, but most of us act as if we don't perceive a collision at all (partly because the crunching and shattering take place over a longer time span that we associate with a violent collision, say of automobiles). "The potential for true catastrophe lies in the future." The downslope that pulls us toward it is becoming steeper, and sooner or later our momentum will take us beyond the point of no return. We need a positive feedback loop to accelerate the pace of changes now so urgently needed.Chapters discuss the history of climate and civilization, the political struggle to control atmospheric pollution at the global level, threats to the earth's water system, deforestation, the threat of genetic erosion to the global food system, the floodtide of garbage, the deep crisis of our political system that dumps huge mountains of debt and pollution on future generations, forces working against stewardship, the blindness of classical economics, the crisis in education coinciding with the flood of information, our dysfunctional civilization (we seem increasingly eager to lose ourselves in technology, media, and consumption rituals; the price we pay is the loss of our spiritual lives), and the common environmental threads of world religions.

Concludes that "we must make the rescue of the environment the central organizing principle for civilization." This means securing widespread agreement that it *should* be the organizing principle, and embarking on an all-out effort to use every policy and program to preserve and nurture our ecological system. Toward this end, a Global Marshall Plan is proposed, which, like the post-WWII plan for European recovery, focuses on strategic goals and emphasizes actions likely to remove bottlenecks. The five strategic goals that must inform our efforts: **1) Stabilizing World Population**: ensure that birth control devices are ubiquitously available, fund carefully targeted functional literacy programs for sustainable agriculture; **2) Developing and Sharing Appropriate Technologies**: a worldwide Strategic Environment Initiative is needed (similar to SDI) to develop a series of breakthroughs for environmentally appropriate technologies in agriculture, forestry, energy, building technology, waste reduction, and recycling; **3) A New Global Eco-Nomics**: redefine definitions of GNP and productivity, eliminate government use of inappropriate discount rates and subsidies, full disclosure of corporate responsibility for environmental damage, more and better information on environmental impacts, an Environmental Security Trust Fund with payments based on the amount of CO_2 put into the atmosphere, a Virgin Materials Fee imposed on products at the point of manufacture or importation based on the quantity of nonrenewable virgin materials, tree planting programs as part of community workfare programs; **4) A New Generation of Treaties and Agreements**: the US must take a leadership role, with the Montreal Protocol on phasing out CFCs as a prototype; **5) A Cooperative Plan for Educating the World's Citizens**: a comprehensive program for monitoring changes now under way, a massive effort to disseminate information on local and regional threats, establishing environmental training centers throughout the world. It is also urged that the Plan should have as a general and integrating goal the establishment of social and political conditions most conducive to emergence of sustainable societies: social justice, human rights, adequate nutrition and health care, high literacy rates, political freedom and participation. [**NOTE**: Remarkably sophisticated and well-informed thinking by a world-class political leader for the 21st century. ALSO SEE: **World on Fire: Saving an Endangered Earth** by Senate Majority Leader George J. Mitchell of Maine (Scribner's, Jan 1991; **FS Annual 1992 #11106**), which has similar ideas, but no focus on technology and education; and **Global Environmental Politics** by Gareth Porter and Janet Welsh Brown (Westview, Dec 1991/208p/$43.50;$10.95pb).]

(Global Marshall Plan for environment)

162
Beyond the Limits: Confronting Global Collapse, Envisioning a Sustainable Future. Donella H. Meadows (Environmental Studies, Dartmouth College), Dennis L. Meadows (Prof of Mgmt Studies, U of New Hampshire), and Jörgen Randers (Prof of Policy Analysis, Norwegian School of Mgmt). Post Mills VT: Chelsea Green Pub. Co (Box 130; 802/333-9073), Apr 1992/277p/$19.95.

In 1972, under the auspices of the Club of Rome, the three authors (along with William W. Behrens III) published **The Limits to Growth**, concluding that the physical limits to human use of materials and energy were somewhere decades ahead. The conclusion of this 20th anniversary update: in spite of improved technologies, greater awareness, and stronger environmental policies, many resource and pollution flows have grown beyond their sustainable limits. "The human world is beyond its limits. The present way of doing things is unsustainable. The future, to be viable at all, must be one of drawing back, easing down, healing." Without significant reductions in material and energy flows, there will be in the coming decades an uncontrolled decline in per capita food output, energy use, and industrial production. Chapters discuss overshoot (if a correction is not made, a collapse of some sort is certain "within the lifetimes of many who are alive today"), exponential growth of population and capital as the driving force (which simply cannot and will not go on for long), sources and sinks as limits, dynamics of growth in a finite world (the World3 model, also used 20 years ago, indicates four possible behavior modes: continuous growth of carrying capacity and population/economy, sigmoid growth where population/economy limits itself, overshoot and oscillation, and overshoot and collapse), the Montreal Protocol on ozone as an example of learning about overshoot and backing off from a clear limit, and why technology and markets alone cannot avoid overshoot (an answer to the most common criticisms of putative World3 model oversights).

Concludes that the human world can respond in three ways to signals that resource use and pollution emissions have grown beyond sustainable limits: 1) deliberately disguise, deny, or confuse the signals (build higher smokestacks, dump toxics in someone else's territory, control prices trying to rise in response to scarcity); 2) alleviate the pressures with technical or economic fixes without changing underlying causes (search for more resources, use resources more efficiently, recycling); 3) acknowledge that the human socioeconomic system as currently structured is unmanageably headed for collapse, and change the structure by shifting perceived costs and benefits, increasing the time horizon, and seeing the social whole. Thirteen scenarios are sketched, including that of a sustainable society of 7.7 billion people in the early 21st century, with enough food, consumer products, and services to support everyone in comfort—provided that appropriate policies are begun in 1995. Similar to the Agricultural Revolution and the Industrial Revolution, the Sustainability Revolution could lead to enormous gains and some losses. Everyone can contribute to this necessary revolution, "already well underway." Five tools to facilitate the transition: visioning what is really wanted, networking to inform and sustain us, truthtelling to overcome verbal traps in public discourse, learning, and loving.

[NOTE: A more urgent message than the 1972 **Limits**, with a more sophisticated vision of "sustainable society" replacing the easily misunderstood 1972 call for "the equilibrium state." The authors do not favor zero growth, but "forms of growth that are equitable, affordable, and sustainable." To support this important analysis, 70 figures are employed. But every attempt is made to keep the argument non-technical. Incidentally, the 1972 book was not the first to highlight the limits. **Resources and the American Dream: Including a Theory of the Limit of Growth**, by Samuel H. Ordway Jr (Ronald Press, 1953), criticized the "Cornucopian Faith" and advocated a "Balanced Civilization." In the same year, Fairfield Osborn published **The Limits of the Earth** (Little, Brown, 1953). Five years earlier, in **Road to Survival** (William Sloane Associates, 1948), William Vogt warned of a falling carrying capacity over most of the earth. The earliest intimations of these problems are widely attributed to George Perkins Marsh's **Man and Nature** (1864). Will enough of us ever learn?] **(overshoot of earth's limits)**

163
Global 2000 Revisited: What Shall We Do? Gerald O. Barney (Executive Director, Millennium Institute). Arlington VA: Millennium Institute, 1993/105p (8x11")/ $20.00pb; 16p summary, $8.00. (Order from Public Interest Publications, PO Box 229, Arlington VA 22210; 800/537-9359.)

A brief, updated version of **The Global 2000 Report to the President** (1980; FS Annual 1980-81 #1620), prepared for the 1993 Parliament of the World's Religions held in Chicago. [Barney was the Study Director of the first G2000 report, which sold 1.5 million copies in eight languages.] The overall conclusion: "If present beliefs and policies continue, the world in the 21st century will be more crowded, more polluted, less stable economically and ecologically, and more vulnerable to violent disruption than the world we live in now. Serious stresses involving inter-religious relations, the economy, population, resources, environment, and security loom ahead. Overall, Earth's people will be poorer in many ways than they are today." Critical issues highlighted: our growing numbers and basic needs, food and the loss of arable land, the need to double agricultural yields, loss of biodiversity, global energy for sustainable development, greenhouse gases and ozone loss, and poverty and violence.

To avoid a tragic wasteland and create a just, sustainable future, North and South must build a new world order, including: 1) new participatory mechanisms to replace those of the Cold War era such as the UN Security Council; 2) make development peace and focus on successful transfers; 3) a strong, non-discriminatory body of international law; 4) a continuing forum for global discussions of the whole human mega-problem (the agenda must cease to be limited to a few narrow topics); 5) replace the outmoded and misleading UN System of National Accounts with a new set of national indicators that measure the degree to which a nation is living sustainably; 6) establish everywhere social conditions that actively resist corruption and favoritism; 7) accelerate transfer of up-to-date, socially and environmentally beneficial technologies. The North should make its primary contribution to global sustainability by stabilizing its resource consumption and using "defense" funds to invest in the South; the South can make its primary contribution by achieving population stability.

Questions are also addressed to spiritual leaders about the adequacy of their traditions (Barney doubts "that there is a faith tradition on Earth today that can provide the moral foundation needed for the 21st century"). Over the next five years, humanity "must prepare to die to 20th century ways of thinking and being," while preparing to see the opportunities in our new condition. For our entry into the 21st century, we need a new symbol, such as crossing a stream or river to a new place and a new way of being. [NOTE: Of special interest are 20 charts showing long-term trends from 1600 to 2200, highlighting expected changes in the 75-year lifetime of a child born today.]

(need to build new world order)

164
World Scientists' Warning to Humanity. Coordinated by Henry Kendall (Chairman, UCS). Washington: Union of Concerned Scientists (1616 P St NW, Suite 310), Nov 1992/2p (202/332-0900).

A statement signed by 1,575 scientists from 69 countries and sent to 160 national leaders. Signers include 99 of the 196 living scientists who are Nobel laureates, as well as senior officers from many of the most prestigious scientific academies worldwide.

The warning emphasizes that "human beings and the natural world are on a collision course." If harmful human activities are not checked, the future will be put at serious risk. Critical stress is apparent in the atmosphere, water resources (some 80 countries with 40% of world population have serious shortages), the oceans (total marine catch is now at or above maximum sustainable yield), soil, tropical and temperate forests, and living species. "Much of this damage is irreversible on a scale of centuries or permanent...we are fast approaching many of the earth's limits." A great change in our stewardship of the earth and the life on it is required if vast human misery is to be avoided. Five linked areas must be addressed simultaneously: 1) bringing environmentally damaging activities under control; 2) managing resources crucial to human welfare more effectively; 3) stabilizing population; 4) reducing and eventually eliminating poverty; 5) ensuring sexual equality and guaranteeing women control over their reproductive decisions. Developed nations are the largest polluters in the world today and must greatly reduce their overconsumption while providing aid and support to the developing nations. Developing nations must recognize the grave threat of environmental damage and unchecked populations. A new ethic is required in discharging our responsibility for ourselves and the earth. We need the help of scientists, business and religious leaders, and the world's people. **(1,575 scientists warn humanity)**

*165
Saving Our Planet: Challenges and Hopes. Mostafa K. Tolba (Executive Director, UN Environment Programme, Nairobi). London & NY: Chapman & Hall (29 W 35th St), Aug 1992/287p/$25.00pb. (Also in French and Spanish.)

Outlines trends for the 10 major environmental issues of the past two decades: urban air pollution (lower in most developed world cities but markedly worse in LDCs), rapid advances in understanding stratospheric ozone depletion, increased understanding of causes and possible effects of climate change, increased marine pollution from land-based sources (about 60% of world population lives within 100 km. of coastal areas), assuring quantity and quality of freshwater, growing desertification and degradation of arid lands, deforestation and wetland destruction, loss of biological diversity, reducing the risk of human-caused disasters, and control of hazardous wastes and toxic chemicals. Chapters also discuss sustainable development (in agriculture, industry, energy, transport, and tourism), human well-being (population growth, settlements, health, peace and security), and public perceptions and attitudes. Some priorities for the next two decades: **1) Regulation**: by 1995, a global agreement on reforestation targets for each decade of the 21st century, a global plan to combat marine pollution from land-based sources, agreement to ban all exports of hazardous wastes to LDCs, an international code of conduct for technology transfer; **2) Assessment**: by 2000, comprehensive assessments of urban air quality, freshwater resources, land and soil degradation, and impacts of new technologies; **3) Environmental Management**: by 2000, a 30% reduction from 1990 levels in hazardous waste generated, environmental and natural resource accounting in the national accounts of every country, natural resource imports and exports included in international trade statistics, an end to net global deforestation; **4) Environment and Economics**: by 1995, estimates of the global costs of failing to deal with various problems, and of resources needed for transferring information and technology to LDCs. [**NOTE**: Valuable and concise global overview.]

(global trends and priorities)

166
Saving the Planet: How to Shape an Environmentally Sustainable Global Economy. Lester R. Brown, Christopher Flavin, and Sandra Postel (Worldwatch Institute). NY: W. W. Norton & Co, Nov 1991/224p/$19.95;$8.95pb.

The first in a new Worldwatch Environmental Alert Series, edited by Linda Starke. Chapters describe the June 1992 UNCED conference in Brazil (and the hoped-for Earth Charter as a Magna Carta for the planet), and compare the general inability to comprehend the scale of the ongoing degradation of the planet to passengers on the *Titanic* who could not imagine the altered reality of a sinking ship. The still widely-held belief that the global economy can continue along the path it has been following stems in part from a narrow economic view of the world. "The Shape of a Sustainable Economy" is described in six brief chapters devoted to the energy efficiency revolution, building a solar economy, reusing and recycling materials, protecting the biological base for food and raw materials (croplands, grasslands, forests, and fisheries), adequately feeding a world population 50% larger than today's 5.4 billion people (the authors believe that human numbers can go no higher than 8 billion; the World Bank now projects at least 12 billion people late in the 21st century), and stabilizing world population. Chapters are also devoted to five "Instruments of Change:" 1) abandoning "growth" as an overriding goal and seeking "sustainable progress" instead; 2) better indicators of human welfare that recalculate and go beyond GNP; 3) reshaping government incentives that work against sustainability (underpriced irrigation, below-cost timber sales, subsidized road-building, subsidies for pesticides); 4) green taxes (eight potential taxes are described, e.g.: carbon content of fossil fuels, hazardous wastes generated, pesticide sales, SO_2 emissions, etc.); 5) ecologically sound banking (a new generation of reforms at the World Bank).

Concludes that the goal of a sustainable society depends on redirecting the engine of economic development. "Unless nations address the twin problems of growing Third World poverty and increasing international inequity, global economic and environmental decline are certain to accelerate." And, as national governments begin to take action, new measures of international leadership (rather than size of military or GNP) will likely be developed. The UN will have to assume a more prominent role; most of its environment programs are underfunded or staffed by people with little training. [**NOTE**: The educational task remains immense: as can be readily seen, only a few of the world futures and global economy views even hint at the "sustainable progress" perspective. **Saving the Planet**, as well as **Healing the Planet** by Paul and Anne Ehrlich are both reviewed in *The New York Times Book Review* (15 Dec 1991, p23) as the work of "apocalyptic environmentalists." Citing past forecasts-not-realized by both sets of authors, the reviewer questions present warnings and "the call to governments to take massive and expensive actions based on admittedly incomplete scientific evidence." This indicates the reviewer's inability to read a book, and the authors' problem in getting their oft-repeated message across to those with learning problems. Perhaps the message should give much greater emphasis to explaining costs, benefits, risks, what is scientifically known or strongly—and widely—suspected, and acting on incomplete evidence. The US, after all, invested trillions of dollars on "worst-case" scenarios of the Soviet threat far more dubious than the degradation (not "apocalypse") foreseen by environmentalists.]

("sustainable progress" goal needed)

*167

Vital Signs 1994: The Trends That Are Shaping Our Future. Lester R. Brown, Hal Kane, and David Malin Roodman (Worldwatch Institute). NY: W. W. Norton & Co, June 1994/160p/$22.00;$10.95pb.

The third in an annual series, looking at "how we are doing in creating an environmentally sustainable economy." Key indicators are discussed in signed two-page essays: *1) Food*: 1993 world grain harvest down by nearly 5%, world soybean crop down almost 4%, meat production up slightly, fish catch stable, aquaculture output in 1991 almost double that of 1984, grain stocks projected to drop sharply; *2) Agricultural Resources*: world grain yield down from 1992 high, world fertilizer use in 1993 down 14% from 1989 high, slowing expansion of irrigated areas; *3) Energy*: oil production flat since 1989, wind power up 13% from 1992, total installed nuclear generating capacity up 3% to an all-time high, slowing growth in shipments of photovoltaic cells, natural gas (now providing 21% of world primary energy) at record high production, coal use declined from peak in 1989, sales of compact fluorescent lamps quadrupled in the past five years; *4) Atmosphere*: CFC production continues to drop from 1988 high, global temperature rises slightly, carbon emissions unchanged from 1992; *5) Economic Trends*: world economy expanded by 2.2% over 1992, Third World debt up to all-time high of $1.77 trillion, world trade up 3.3% from 1992, global paper production up 1% to all-time high, gold production (and associated wastes) at record high due to cyanide heap leaching technology; *6) Transportation*: bicycle production at a record high (outstripping auto output by nearly 3 to 1), world auto production essentially flat for the past decade; *7) Environment*: resistance to pesticides growing ("at least 520 insects and mites, 150 plant diseases, and 113 weeds have developed resistance to one or more pesticides meant to control them"), sulfur and nitrogen emissions resume rise after a 1990 drop; *8) Social Trends*: total population increase drops slightly, world cigarette production up (but per capita smoking is down from a peak in 1988), HIV/AIDS cases rise steadily, immunization rates soar, refugee flows at an all-time high of 19 million; *9) Military*: worldwide arms exports declined 36% in 1991, expenditures for UN peacekeeping up 69% over 1992, nuclear warheads declined by 6% in 1993.

In the introduction, Lester Brown interprets and clusters some of the indicators, observing that: 1) of the 9,600 species of birds, populations of 6,600 species are in decline ("of all the available indicators, this may give the clearest sense of the earth's health"); 2) stratospheric levels of free chlorine appear to be peaking in the mid-1990s; if CFC production is phased out as scheduled, free chlorine levels will increase until around 2000 and then slowly diminish; 3) three food supply systems are under mounting pressure: rising demands on *fisheries* are becoming excessive worldwide, *rangelands* are being grazed at or beyond their sustainable yield almost everywhere, and *croplands* are also becoming unsustainable in many countries, leading to soil erosion; 4) stocks of all grains have declined; 5) water scarcity is becoming common; 6) "the world is entering a new phase in the era of rapid population growth, one where fishers and farmers can no longer expand output fast enough to keep up with population"; 7) the ratio of military spending to UN peacekeeping was about 2000 to 1 a few years ago, but is now closer to 250 to 1. [**NOTE**: Fascinating and important. The mix of indicators varies each year, and some (such as bicycle production and UN peacekeeping expenses) cannot be found anywhere else.]

(**key indicators on sustainability**)

168

State of the World 1994: A Worldwatch Institute Report on Progress Toward a Sustainable Society. Lester R. Brown *et al*. NY: W. W. Norton, Jan 1994/265p/ $22.00;$11.95pb.

The 11th annual assessment, now published in 27 languages, with a first printing in English of 100,000 copies. The theme of this year's *SOTW* is carrying capacity. The initial essay by **Sandra Postel** states that, as a result of population growth, consumption patterns, and technology choices, "we have surpassed the planet's carrying capacity. This is plainly evident by the extent to which we are damaging and depleting natural capital." If current trends in resource use continue, and world population grows as projected, by 2010 per capita availability of rangeland will fall by 22%, irrigated land by 12%, cropland by 21%, forestland by 30%, and the fish catch by 10%. The days of the frontier economy are over: we have entered an era in which global prosperity increasingly depends on using resources more efficiently, distributing them more equitably, and reducing consumption levels overall. "Unless we accelerate this transition, powerful social tensions are likely to arise from increased competition for the scarce resources that remain."

Building on this chapter, **Lester R. Brown** warns that we are facing an era of food insecurity. Whereas per capita grain production rose by 40% in the 1950-1984 period, grain output per person fell 11% in the 1984-1993 period. "At present, there is nothing in sight to reverse the worldwide decline in grain output per person." There are many opportunities for expanding food production, but all the identifiable ones are small; no large jumps are in prospect, comparable to those following expanding use of fertilizer or the hybridization of corn. Since WWII, economic policies dominated the evolution of the global economy; during the next four decades ("the environmental era"), environmental limits interacting with population growth will have far more influence. In the past, national security was defined by the Cold War; in the next 40 years, food and job security will dominate, often driving hungry and jobless people across national borders.

Eight other chapters, largely adaptations of recent Worldwatch papers, discuss redesigning the forest economy, safeguarding oceans, reshaping the power industry into a service-oriented industry committed to demand-side management, reinventing transport to emphasize less destructive modes, using computers for the environment, assessing environmental health risks, destroying or dismantling military weapons and materials in an acceptable manner, and building a new World Bank to serve today's world (by measuring success in terms of quality of lending and not quantity, reorienting lending away from large infrastructure projects toward smaller efforts, reducing debt burdens, revamping the criteria for success, more widespread use of natural resource accounting, and more accountability to the public). [ALSO SEE: **Mortgaging the Earth: The World Bank, Environmental Impoverishment, and the Crisis of Development** by EDF attorney Bruce Rich (Beacon Press, Feb 1994/376p/ $29.00).]

(**food insecurity ahead**)

169

State of the World 1993: A Worldwatch Institute Report on Progress Toward a Sustainable Society Lester R. Brown *et al*. NY: W. W. Norton, Jan 1993/268p/ $19.95;$10.95pb.

The 10th annual assessment, now published in 27 languages, with a first printing each year in English of 100,000 copies (in 1989, SOTW was used in more than

1000 courses in some 600 US colleges and universities). Worldwatch President Lester Brown notes intensifying global interest in the planet's future and countless examples of local gains; nevertheless, "the broad indicators showed a continuing wholesale deterioration in the earth's physical condition." Environmental problems are partly caused by an economic accounting system that misleads and a biological accounting system that is largely non-existent. Until we have an accounting system that incorporates natural capital depreciation and losses, we cannot accurately measure real progress or decline, and policymakers must rely on GNP, which overstates progress. Yet "every country is practicing the environmental equivalent of deficit financing in one form or another" by overstocking grasslands, overcutting forests, overplowing, and overfishing. Every society pays a hidden price for environmental pollution (e.g., one study estimates that air pollution may cost the US as much as $40 billion/year in health care and lost productivity). Whereas economic debts are something we owe each other, environmental debts can often be repaid only in the deprivation and ill health of future generations. Environmental decline can no longer be a peripheral issue. "The bottom line is that the world is entering a new era, one in which future economic progress depends on reversing environmental degradation."

"Getting off the deterioration/decline path requires an enormous effort, one akin to mobilizing for war." The overriding need is for a new worldview that reflects environmental realities and redefines security. The question is not only what we must do, but how we can do it quickly before the entire world is caught in "the downward spiral that already has roughly one-sixth of humanity in its grip." Among the principal policy instruments that can convert an economic system from self-destruction to sustainability are regulations and tax policy. Governments have heretofore relied heavily on regulation, which is not a winning strategy. The more effective instrument by far is tax policy, especially partial replacement of income taxes with environmental taxes. It would foster productive activities and discourage destructive ones such as burning fossil fuels, using pesticides, producing hazardous chemical waste, generating nuclear waste, and using virgin raw materials. A carbon tax to discourage burning of fossil fuels is now being considered in the EC and Japan.

Other chapters (largely adaptations of recent Worldwatch Papers) discuss widespread signs of water scarcity and how to move to water security, reviving coral reefs, closing the gender gap in development, supporting indigenous peoples, providing energy in developing countries, rediscovering the benefits of rail transportation, preparing for peace instead of war, reconciling trade and the environment, and the new industrial revolution toward sustainable practices that could be furthered by "a green industrial strategy" (environmental protection itself is already a major industry, accounting for $200 billion in goods and services worldwide in 1990, projected by OECD to grow to $300 billion by 2000). [NOTE: As always, a fresh focus on key ideas, notably green taxes (also discussed in *SOTW 1991*, FS Annual 1992 #10922).]

(new era of environmental concern)

170
Beyond Interdependence: The Meshing of the World's Economy and the Earth's Ecology. Jim MacNeill (Inst for Research on Public Policy, Ottawa), Pieter Winsemius (McKinsey & Co, Amsterdam), and Taizo Yakushiji (School of Poli Sci, Saitama U, Japan). Intro by Maurice Strong (Secy-Gen, UNCED). A Trilateral Commission Book. NY: Oxford UP, Aug 1991/159p/$24.95;7.95pb.

Since 1900, the world's population has multiplied more than three times, and its economy has grown twentyfold. Consumption of fossil fuels has grown by a factor of 30, and industrial production by a factor of 50. "If current forms of development were employed, a further five- to tenfold boost in economic activity would be required over the next 50 years to meet the needs and aspirations of 10 billion people." Since WWII, governments have been preoccupied with economic interdependence. "But the world has now moved beyond economic interdependence to ecological interdependence—and even beyond that to an intermeshing of the two... This is the new reality of the century, with profound implications for the shape of our institutions of governance, national and international. It raises fundamental questions about how economic and political decisions are made, and their implications for sustainability." The maxim of sustainable development is not "limits to growth," but "the growth of limits." We must learn to recognize, and live within, limits of physical impact beyond which degradation of ecosystems are inevitable. "The environment and the economy must be integrated in our major institutions of decision-making: government, industry, and the home. This is perhaps the most important condition for sustainable development."

The June 1992 Earth Summit in Rio seeks to launch a global transition to sustainable development. The summit will address a range of reform proposals, many of which are discussed in this volume: 1) integrating environment into economic decision-making; 2) correcting perverse interventions in the market (OECD's 24 member countries spend over $250 billion a year on agricultural subsidies that encourage overproduction and depletion of basic farm capital); 3) reforming economic accounting systems ("the single most important change in public-sector incentives"); 4) comprehensive indicators on sustainable development; 5) broadening the concept of national security (an environmental interpretation is simply an extension of the economic interpretation); 6) global bargains (helping certain countries eliminate the use of CFCs to protect the ozone layer is one of the most promising and timely strategies); 7) reducing greenhouse gas emissions (an increasing number of studies show substantial potential reductions through energy efficiency and other measures that could return a profit or at least break even); 8) reforming our great international institutions; 9) new global structures such as a World Environment and Development Forum that bring signatories together at least once a year to evaluate progress and decide on necessary actions. Concludes that the 1992 UNCED summit could place the world community on a new course toward a sustainable future. "The Earth Summit will likely be the last chance for the world, in this century at least, to seriously address and arrest the accelerating environmental threats to economic development, national security, and human survival." [NOTE: Important background on UNCED. MacNeill was the main author of the seminal Brundtland Commission report on **Our Common Future** (Oxford, 1987; FS Annual 1987 #8090), and former director of environment for OECD.] (UNCED: background issues)

171
The Global Commons, Harlan Cleveland (President, World Academy of Art and Science; former Dean, Humphrey Institute, U of Minnesota), *The Futurist*, 27:3, May-June 1993, 9-13.

The acts of individuals are producing a pervasive threat to the global environment and creating a new class of problems that are not only global, but behavioral. They are behavioral because they require literally hundreds of millions of people to do something or stop doing something. We need to treat the global environment not as a series of separable puzzles, but as parts of an integrated Global Commons, with hundreds of millions of people [not billions??] responsible for its health. Four enormous environments, still mostly unexplored, are already treated in international law and custom as parts of a Global Commons: outer space, the atmosphere, the oceans, and Antarctica. The problem is not "managing the Global Commons," but managing human behavior in the Commons by stabilizing population, pricing products at their full social cost, and reducing wasteful consumption (and thus pollution). An organization to protect and supervise the "common heritage of mankind" is needed. It could be a revitalized version of the UN Trusteeship Council, which the success of decolonization has now left without a function. The now-dormant Council could readily form a Global Commons Trusteeship Commission to negotiate norms, standards, and guidelines for exploring and exploiting the Global Commons. The Commission would keep the health of the Commons environments under open and continuous review, and make room in its work for the views of major NGOs. It might be empowered to ask governments, NGOs, and individuals to serve as "centers of initiative" on various problems. The new genre of problems depends on wide participation: the Global Commons will be governed pluralistically or not at all. [**NOTE**: Further thoughts based on Cleveland's two recent books: **Birth of a New World** (#042) and **The Global Commons: Policy for the Planet** (#210).]

(**a Global Commons Trusteeship Commission?**)

172
Ultimate Security: The Environmental Basis of Political Stability. Norman Myers (Oxford UK). NY: W.W. Norton, Sept 1993/308p/$25.00.

"Whereas the past 40 years have been dominated by the Cold War, the next 40 years will surely be dominated by environmental conflicts. They will add up to a variant of World War III, a war we are waging against the Earth... It is a war of us all against us all." Moreover, any New World Order must reflect the new situation where the principal threat to security and peace stems from environmental breakdown, plus the need for access to natural resources that are increasingly scarce as more people make greater demands upon them. National security is no longer about fighting forces and weaponry alone: it relates increasingly to watersheds, croplands, forests, genetic resources, climate, and other factors as crucial to a nation's security as military prowess. Not all environmental problems lead to conflict, and not all conflicts stem from environmental problems. But there is ample evidence that environmental factors contribute to security in its all-round sense, security for all, security forever. "It all adds up to a new fact of global living."

Developed nations should be concerned with environmental security in the developing world because of: 1) major interests in exports and imports; 2) the need to maintain political stability; 3) environmental problems that often spill over borders; 4) environmental degradation that triggers mass migrations of people. Chapters are devoted to case studies (each with a negative and a positive scenario) of water in the Middle East, hunger in Ethiopia, food insecurity in sub-Saharan Africa, deforestation and destitution in the Philippines, carrying capacity in India, population growth and ruined environment in El Salvador and other nations of Central America, and population growth and migration in Mexico. Additional chapters describe global population, global warming and ozone-layer depletion, mass extinction of species, environmental refugees (with an estimate of some 150 million future refugees in a mid-21st century world of 10 billion people), synergistic connections, trade-offs with military security (e.g., $12 billion a year, or four days of military spending, could reverse desertification and bring agricultural benefits of $30 billion a year), and ethical aspects of policy. [ALSO SEE: **Redefining National Security** by Lester R. Brown (Worldwatch Paper 14, Oct 1977), and **Defining National Security** by Joseph J. Romm (**FS Annual 1994** #12272).] (**environment as "national security"**)

*173
Earth Politics. Ernst Ulrich von Weizsäcker (President, Wuppertal Institute for Climate, Energy and Enviroment, Wuppertal, Germany). Foreword by Ricardo Diez-Hochleitner (President, Club of Rome). London & Atlantic Highlands NJ: Zed Books, Jan 1994/234p/$60.00;$19.95pb.

To make sustainable development a reality, we need a new set of values, a new culture, and a new set of incentives to make millions of actors in the North and the South act differently. The days of the Economic Century are numbered; we are now entering a Century of the Environment, where the hallmark of the realist must be regard for the environment. "In the Century of the Environment it is the ecological imperative which will become the dominant determinant for law and administration, for city planning and agriculture, for the arts and for religion, for technology and indeed for the economy." The political task associated with this impending transformation is Earth Politics. Chapters are in four parts: *1) Setting the Framework*: the rape of nature in the economic century, classical environmental policy as pollution control, EC environmental policy, emerging global visions (Club of Rome, UNCED); *2) Five Key Issues*: truth-telling prices for energy and materials, ecological transport policy, breaking the vicious circle in agriculture, a new model of wealth and progress for the Third World, endangered biodiversity; *3) Towards Coherent Solutions*: prices that tell the truth, limits to command and control, ecological tax reform [see **FS Annual 1992** #11717 for book coauthored by von Weizsäcker], economy-friendly environmental policy, cooperation with business instead of harassment, urban environmental policy (requiring cities to pay full-cost prices for their pollution); *4) New Models of Wealth*: environmental technology (characterized by cleanliness, productivity, information intensity, error friendliness, and suitability for the informal economy), redefining productivity, responsible science, thinking less about the formal economy, a new role for adult education, and further development of human rights to include rights of future generations. [**NOTE**: A rich package of original, leading-edge ideas. The author is a Club of Rome member, and former President, U of Kassel, and Prof of Interdisciplinary Biology, Essen U.]

(**politics for the Century of the Environment**)

174
Global Ecology: Environmental Change and Social Flexibility. Vaclav Smil (Prof of Geography, U of Manitoba). London & NY: Routledge, Dec 1993/240p/ $59.95;$17.95pb.

"What is the justification of yet another look at environmental troubles and solutions?" Smil tries to separate essential environmental needs and impacts from confusing myths as the only sensible basis for informed decision-making, and argues that the still considerable gaps in our knowledge of the environment should not delay remedial action. The potential for slowing down, stabilizing, and eventually reversing every degradative environmental trend is promising, but actual execution of such shifts will be generally very difficult. "We are not facing marginal adjustments manageable by simple technical fixes, some temporary tax and spending increases, and a few changes in personal habits. We will need profound socio-economic transformation which will demand not only new ways of doing things but also not a few genuine sacrifices." Chapters discuss existential necessities, dimensions of environmental change, effective strategies (an economics for the biosphere, paying the real price, reducing consumption, doing things better), uncertainties and constraints, planetary management, and global compacts (the grandest of which would be a planetary agreement between rich and poor countries). [NOTE: Same title as Sachs (above), but a quite different and supportive view of planetary management. ALSO SEE: Smil's harsh view of **China's Environmental Crisis** (Sharpe, April 1993; **FS Annual 1994** #12258).] **(profound transformation needed)**

175

Global Ecology: A New Arena of Political Conflict. Edited by Wolfgang Sachs (Institute for Cultural Studies, Essen, Germany). London & Atlantic Highlands NJ: Zed Books; Halifax NS: Fernwood Publishing, Dec 1993/262p/ $59.95;$25.00pb.

Nearly everybody has now turned environmentalist, and the conflicts of the future will center on who stands for what kind of environmentalism. These 17 essays probe critically the new language put forth by the rising breed of environmental professionals who push for a worldwide rationalization of life-styles, provide survival strategies for the powers that be, and promote the aspirations "of a rising eco-cracy to manage nature and regulate people worldwide." **1) In the Wake of Rio**: Wolfgang Sachs on the dangers of linking environmentalism to development thinking (sustainability is thus conceived of as a challenge for global management), Nicholas Hildyard on putting the corporate foxes in charge of the chickens, Matthias Finger on the failed politics of the UNCED process, Tariq Banuri on North-South conflicts at UNCED, Klaus Meyer-Abich on the growing North-South gap due to climate change; **2) Confusion Over Sustainability**: Paul Ekins on how to genuinely attain sustainable development, Christine von Weizsäcker on competing notions of biodiversity, Donald Worster on deep flaws of the sustainable development ideal; **3) Against Global Environmental Management**: Vandana Shiva on the greening of the global reach or "green imperialism," Larry Lohmann on resisting green globalism, Eduardo Gudynas on the fallacy of eco-messianism (critiquing the scientific superiority complex, the North's pedagogic tendency, and the new ecocratic discourse), Guy Beney on Gaia as "the globalitarian temptation"; **4) Ecology from Below**: Frédérique Apffel Marglin on regenerating the land and the community, a plea for cultural and ecological pluralism in India, Anil Agarwal and Sunita Narain on green villages. [NOTE: Crypto-anarchist critiques similar to those in **The Development Dictionary**, also edited by Sachs (Zed Books, 1992; **FS Annual 1994** #12225).]

(global environmentalism questioned)

176

Environmental Problems and Sustainable Futures: Major Literature from WCED to UNCED, Michael Marien (Editor, *Future Survey*), *Futures*, 24:8, Oct 1992, 731-757. (Also published in *FUTURESCO*, #2.)

A bibliographic essay on environmental literature reported in *FS* during the five years bounded by the 1987 report of the World Commission on Environment and Development and the 1992 UNCED Earth Summit. Attention is focused on a framework for assembling the literature, based on two major categories: **1) Environmental Problems**: global overviews (planet earth in peril, regions and nations, human population growth), global climate change, endangered resources (overviews, biodiversity, deforestation, protected land areas, freshwater, wetlands, oceans), pollution (air and water, other), waste and hazards (solid and toxic waste, nuclear waste and radiation, natural hazards); **2) Toward a Sustainable Future**: new environmental thinking (ecophilosophy), elements of a sustainable society (general overviews and agendas, ecological economics, green business, ecological agriculture, green technology and transportation, energy, cities and communities, other sectors), actors and environmental movements, government, and information frontiers. In all, 312 items are cited in 255 footnotes, each with *FS* or **FS Annual** reference numbers. An appendix lists 81 English-language periodicals relevant to environmental futures. The 68 strictly environmental titles are listed by date of first publication; the median date is 1982, suggesting a doubling in the past 10 years. Concludes that green infoglut is a neglected problem.

(green infoglut underappreciated)

7. A New Path for Development

*177

An Agenda for Development. Boutros Boutros-Ghali (Secy-General of the UN). NY: UN General Assembly, Agenda Item 91 (A/48/935), May 1994/50p. (Brief version in *The Christian Science Monitor,* 29 July 1994, p18.)

This report is "intended as a first contribution to the search for a revitalized vision of development." Development as a common cause is in danger of fading from the forefront of our agenda. The poorest nations fall further behind, and many of the poor are dispirited. Development must be seen as a fundamental human right, and the most secure basis for peace. It has five major and interlinked dimensions: **1) Peace as Foundation:** development cannot proceed easily where military concerns are at or near the center of life; traditional approaches to development presuppose that it takes place under conditions of peace, but this is rarely the case; **2) Economic Growth as the Engine of Development:** without economic growth there can be no increase in public capital, health, welfare, or security, but this growth must be sustained and sustainable, and requires a supportive national and international climate; **3) Environment as Basis for Sustainability:** the environment permeates all aspects of development, and one cannot be addressed without reference to the other; "sustainability must be strengthened as a guiding principle of development"; **4) Justice as Pillar of Society:** a vigorous civil society is indispensable to lasting and successful social development, and popular participation at all levels of society is vital; **5) Democracy as Good Governance:** democracy must be regarded as a process that grows and must be sustained over time; it is the only long-term means to regulate the tensions that threaten to tear societies apart; without democracy, "development will remain fragile and be perpetually at risk."

Addressing the global development challenge requires building a common awareness of the many dimensions of development, and a better appreciation of the importance of the various actors in development. Each of the five dimensions of development is vital to the success of all others, as well as the core concept of human-centered progress. "A culture of development, in which every major dimension of life is considered as an aspect of development, is emerging." It can encompass the goals of peace, justice, and progress in a single, comprehensive vision and framework for action. Development has to be oriented not only to each person in the world, but also generations yet to come ("the welfare of future generations must not be compromised"). "Signs of a global era of development can be observed... (yet), progress is not inherent in the human condition; retrogression is not inconceivable." [NOTE: Important background for the 1995 World Summit for Social Development; Boutros-Ghali hopes that it "could be a synthesizing event of world significance."]

(development: a broad and revitalized vision)

*178
Human Development Report 1994. UN Development Programme. NY: Oxford U Press, June 1994/226p/$29.95; $17.95pb.

Fifth in an important annual series, focusing on The World Summit for Social Development to be held in March 1995. "The world can never be at peace unless people have security in their daily lives." The search for security lies in sustainable development, not in arms. For too long, the concept of security has been shaped by the potential for conflict between states, and by nations seeking arms to protect their security. "To address the growing challenge of human security, a new development paradigm is needed that puts people at the center of development, regards economic growth as a means and not an end, protects the life opportunities of future generations as well as present generations, and respects the natural systems on which all life depends." Such development should be pro-people, pro-jobs, and pro-nature. It will require foreign assistance linked to common goals, assistance channeled to the poorest nations as a global social safety net, greater attention to freer movement of non-aid flows (especially trade, investment, technology, and labor), possible payment by rich nations for damage to poor nations, new sources of international funding such as global taxation, and a new framework of global governance.

A six-point agenda is offered for the Social Summit: *1) A New World Social Charter,* to give clear expression to the emerging concept of human security (an illustrative social charter is proposed on p.6); *2) A 20:20 Compact for Human Development,* whereby all nations pledge to ensure provision of basic human development levels for all their people (developing countries and donors should both earmark at least 20% of their budgets to human priority concerns); *3) Turning from Arms to Human Security,* by agreeing on a targeted reduction in military spending of 3%/year for the next decade, making an explicit link between reduced military spending and increased social spending, and persuading all nations to allocate perhaps 10-20% of the peace dividend to a global human security fund; *4) A Global Human Security Fund,* financed by the peace dividend, fees on important global transactions and polluting emissions, and official development assistance (these three sources could raise $250 billion a year); *5) A Strengthened UN Umbrella for Human Development,* to cope with the increased responsibility; *6) Creating an Economic Security Council,* a decision-making forum at the highest level to review threats to global human security and agree on necessary actions.

As in the first four Reports, **HDR 1994** discusses trends in human development, and supplies 101 pages of human development indicators, including a composite Human Development Index. Canada reclaims top place from Japan, and the US fell from #6 to #8. The top ten performers in human development in the 1960-1992 period: Malaysia, Botswana, South Korea, Tunisia, Thailand, Syria, Turkey, China, Portugal, and Iran. [NOTE: A trove of viable ideas for global betterment.]

(new world social charter proposed)

179
Human Development Report 1993. UN Development Programme. NY: Oxford U Press, May 1993/230p/$29.95; $17.95pb.

The fourth in an annual series. **HDR 1992** focused on the international dimensions of human development (**FS Annual 1993** #11551). This year's Report focuses on the democratic transition in many countries, such that "people's participation is becoming the central issue of our time." Many new windows of opportunity are opening, as global military spending declines for the first time since WWII, ideological battles of the past are being replaced, and the rising environmental threat prompts cooperation for common survival. Five new "pillars of a people-centered world order" are explored in detail: 1) new concepts of human security that stress the security of people, not only of nations; 2) new models of sustainable human development that promote investing in human potential and creating an enabling environment; 3) new partnerships between the state and market to combine market efficiency with social compassion; 4) new patterns of national and global governance to accommodate the rise of people's aspirations and the steady decline of the nation-state (decentralization of power can be one of the best ways of empowering people); 5) new forms of international cooperation that focus directly on the needs of people rather than the preferences of nation-states (at least 20% of total aid should be allocated to human priority concerns—three times the present 6.5%—and assistance should go where the need is greatest). The implications of placing people at the center of political and economic change are profound, challenging traditional concepts of security, development, the role of the market, and international cooperation. They call for a revolution in our thinking, if the 1990s are to be a new watershed in peaceful development. A chance to focus on the building blocks for a "new people-centered world order" will occur in 1995, when all nations are committed to meet at a World Summit on Social Development. It will be a time to agree on a concrete agenda of national and global actions—the theme of **HDR 1994**.

Since **HDR** first appeared in 1990, several countries have prepared comprehensive human development strategies, and more than 20 other countries are undertaking related initiatives. These efforts are likely to include 10 significant steps: preparing a national HDR, preparing a short statistical profile showing progress achieved and distance to be traveled, improving human development statistics, setting human development targets (e.g., in children's health and education), costing the targets, clarifying who does what, establishing who will pay, designing a national strategy, seeking external cooperation, and building political alliances. As in earlier Reports, **HDR 1993** discusses trends in human development, and supplies 92 pages of *human development indicators*, including a composite Human Development Index. Japan reclaims its place at the top from Canada. The #3-#10 countries remain at last year's ranking: Norway, Switzerland, Sweden, USA, Australia, France, Netherlands, and #10 UK. [NOTE: Original, sophisticated, important.]

("people-centered world order" advocated)

180
Human Development Report 1992. United Nations Development Programme (Inge Kaul, Project Director). NY: Oxford U Press, May 1992/216p/$29.95;$16.95pb.

The first two Reports (**FS Annual 1992** #10996/10997) showed how national budgets could be redirected from military spending into priority areas of human development such as basic health and universal primary education. This third Report concentrates on the international dimensions of human development. Five major conclusions: 1) Economic growth does not automatically improve people's lives, either within nations or internationally. Indeed, income disparities are widening, such that "the richest 20% of the world's people get at least 150 times more than the poorest 20%." This disparity is persisting and widening because world trade generally works to the benefit of the strongest, and market rules are often changed to prevent free and open competition to those areas where developing countries may have a competitive edge. 2) Rich and poor countries compete in the global marketplace as unequal partners; to be more competitive, LDCs will require massive investments in human capital and technology. 3) Global markets do not operate freely; together with the unequal partnership, this costs LDCs $500 billion a year—10 times what they receive in foreign assistance. 4) The world community needs policies in place to provide a social safety net for poor nations and poor people (the closest the world comes to such a safety net is official development assistance, which is fatally flawed in quantity, equity, and allocation.) 5) With the Cold War over, the time has come for a *global compact on human development*—an agreement to put people first in national policies and in international development cooperation.

A new global compact would help developing countries meet basic human goals such as primary education and safe water, create new job opportunities, and accelerate GDP growth. Industrial countries might also want the new compact to address drug trafficking, pollution, immigration, and nuclear threats. All countries might agree to: reduce military expenditures by at least 3% a year (yielding a peace dividend of $1.5 trillion by 2000), reform the official development assistance system (to make it progressive, predictable, and equitable), strike a new bargain with severely indebted nations (to halt the current debt-related net transfer of $50 billion a year from poor to rich countries), and liberalize global markets in goods and services to accelerate growth and insure better distribution.

"The world needs a new vision of global cooperation for the next century." New global institutions might include a global central bank, a system of progressive income tax, an international trade organization, and a greatly strengthened UN system—politically, managerially, and financially. In sum, the world now has a unique opportunity to use global markets for the benefit of all. [**NOTE**: Challenging new frontiers. **HDR92** also includes an update of the "Human Development Index" (based on 46 tables of comparative data), whereby Canada has displaced Japan at the top, followed by Norway, Switzerland, Sweden, USA, Australia, France, Netherlands, and UK in the top ten.]

(**new global compact proposed**)

181
A Post-Rio Compact, James Gustave Speth (Pres, World Resources Inst), *Foreign Policy*, #88, Fall 1992, 145-161.

With the end of the Cold War, the goal of diplomacy is shifting from conflict management to common endeavor. The UNCED Earth Summit suggested that the new axis of world affairs is not East-West, but North-South. America's policy toward developing countries has been in disarray for years, and is due for reinvention. The US should declare a new international mission committing itself to a new era of concerted international action against poverty and environmental deterioration. The Foreign Assistance Act should be totally rewritten. Seven elements of a new US program that reflects the needs of the developing world and America's long-term interests: 1) the prime objective must be to promote sustainable development through effective family planning, sustainable agriculture and forestry, sustainable energy production, and effective pollution control; 2) traditional development assistance must be extended to such critical areas as access to capital and technology; 3) the US should concentrate on building human and institutional capacities needed for sustainable development; 4) overall financial support for development assistance should be increased, perhaps doubled; 5) the US program should directly address global environmental threats to all countries; 6) efforts to promote wise investments must be coupled with internal reforms such as unwise subsidies and waste of water and energy; 7) the new US program should promote multilateral approaches where possible. A new Global Policy Council should replace the National Security Council, and the Agency for International Development (AID) should be replaced by a Sustainable Development Cooperation Agency (SDCA), which would include a Sustainable Development Foundation to make grants and an Institute for Scientific and Technical Cooperation.

(**new US approach to developing countries**)

182
Compact for a New World. New World Dialogue. Washington: World Resources Institute, Oct 1991/26p/free.

An Open Letter to the heads of state and government and legislators of the Americas, by the 28 members from 11 countries of The New World Dialogue On Environment and Development in the Western Hemisphere. Signatories from the US and Canada include Gov. Bruce Babbitt, Sen. John Chafee, Sen. Al Gore, Kathryn S. Fuller, Alice M. Rivlin, James Gustav Speth, Arthur C. Eggleton (Mayor of Toronto), and John David Runnals (IRPP). Eight initiatives are proposed: **1) Forestry**: major assistance from the US and Canada to reverse deforestation and maintain biological heritage in both temperate zones and tropical forests; **2) Energy**: rapidly boosting the efficiency with which energy from any source is used and promoting non-polluting energy sources throughout the hemisphere (the US and Canada should commit to reducing per capita emissions of CO_2 by 30% by 2005); **3) Pollution Prevention**: all governments should revamp improper incentives that reward despoiling the environment; **4) Anti-Poverty**: governments should seek to eliminate hunger by 2000 at the very least and to eradicate poverty throughout the hemisphere by 2020; **5) Population**: each government should seek to reduce population growth to 1% by 2020 and to zero by 2050; **6) Science and Technology**: a network of strong regional research and training institutes to advance sustainable development; includes government support for the new discipline of "ecological economics" which *seeks to reinvent the economics of public policymaking*; **7) Trade and Investment**: environmental standards for new free trade and international investment regimes will be raised to levels required for sustainable development, rather than seeking a "lowest common denominator"; **8) Finance**: sustainable development strategies will create wealth over the long term; in the short term, military budgets should be reduced by at least 20% over the next five years, funds should be redirected away from unsustainable activities, proper incentives should encourage private-sector investment, a new "ecofund" should be managed by a hemispheric agency, etc. [**NOTE**: Big league leading-edge ideas for sustainability.]

(**Western Hemisphere sustainability compact**)

183

The Future of "Development." Harlan Cleveland (U of Minnesota) and Mochtar Lubis (Djakarta, Indonesia). Rethinking International Governance Project. Minneapolis: U of Minnesota, Hubert H. Humphrey Institute, 1989/16p/free.

The project brought together 28 people form 22 countries combining insights from South and North to devise new patterns of international behavior that might enable "development" to conquer poverty. "The underlying crisis of inequity is destined to become a dominant issue in world politics." Development is defined as "the conscious promotion of economic growth with social fairness." Development is not just economic growth, but should be undertaken as a holistic endeavor to cover all human needs and aspirations to live in human dignity. Three kinds of institutional changes might help: 1) An International Development Tax: some tax on the use of the global commons and perhaps on international air travel or passports; 2) International Review of National Development Strategies: each developing country that expects help from the rest of the world should develop a serious plan for doing something about poverty and basic human needs, and have it reviewed by other developing countries; 3) Extranational Institutions: creating a new form of international organization such as the EC. **(rethinking development)**

184

Debt and the Environment: Converging Crises. Morris Miller (Faculty of Administration, U of Ottawa). NY: United Nations Publications, Sept 1991/347p/$19.95pb. (Sales No. E.91.I.17)

Former World Bank Executive Director warns that the debt and environmental developments of the 1980s are "symptomatic of a massive dysfunctioning of the prevailing global system" that threatens breakdown of institutional arrangements governing trade and capital flows, a widening of already large rich-poor income gaps within and between nations, an increased likelihood of a major worldwide depression, and a lessening of the capacity to address environmental damage on a planetary scale. Chapters discuss the growing debt overhang (developing country external debt rose from $838 billion in 1982 to an estimated $1,319 billion in 1990, and the fragile US economy and banking system add to the problem), global environmental degradation (and the "operational vacuity" of the sustainability banners under which the environmental movement marches), debt relief as a necessary condition for Third World cooperation in global environmental programs, the potential and limitations of financial assistance, contending with the "second debt crisis" of the US, barriers to institutional change (inertia, aversion to risk-taking, vested interests in the status quo), the role of multilateral development banks in the environmental crisis, and the role of UNDP and other UN agencies. Concludes that "the major onus must be placed on the industrialized nations to re-establish a congenial milieu for the trade and capital flows that are a necessary condition for global recovery and for implementing environmental programs of the necessary scope and scale." An appendix lists a matrix of 82 debt crisis proposals by various leaders.

(debt and environmental crises intertwined)

185

For Earth's Sake: A Report from the Commission on Developing Countries and Global Change. Alvaro Soto (Exec Secty) *et al.* Ottawa K1G 3H9: Intl Devel. Research Centre (PO Box 8500), 1992/145p/CA$14.95pb.

The Commission was established with support from IDRC and the Swedish Agency for Research Cooperation with Developing Countries. Its seven members include Alvaro Soto (Latin American Environmental Network, Columbia), Anil Agarwal (Director, Center for Science and Environment, New Delhi), Julia Cabias (Ecology Laboratory, Mexico), Martin Khor Kok Peng (Third World Network, Malaysia), Thandika Makandawire (Council for Development of Economic and Social Research, Senegal), Adolfo Mascarenhas (Director of Graduate Studies, U of Dar-es-Salaam, Tanzania), and Erna Witoelar (founder of Indonesia Environmental Forum). The Commission is based on three key propositions: 1) global environmental problems have potentially catastrophic implications for many developing countries; 2) Third World perspectives must be integrated into the international agenda on global environmental change; 3) social dimensions of these issues must be understood and resolved.

The environment worldwide is in crisis at the same time that most parts of the Third World are facing a severe economic and social crisis. In many cases, the socio-economic crisis is the result of development styles that destroy both human potential and the environment. The two crises are the result of unsustainable systems of production and consumption in the North, inappropriate development models in the South, and a fundamentally inequitable world order. To date, Northern concerns have directed the global environmental debate; they reflect a definition of sustainability in which the physical environment is the primary focus and long-term intergenerational issues are key. But the major message from virtually all quarters of the South is that social concerns, economic issues, and *intra*generational equity are the keys to resolving the environment/development crisis. "It is critical to any meaningful approach to sustainable development that environmental issues be integrated with issues of equity, social justice, human rights, and development." Whereas Northern concerns focus primarily on long-term impacts of climate change and ozone depletion, the most immediate and pressing environmental problems in the South relate to depletion and degradation of the biomass base, on which the majority of the population continues to be directly dependent. An additional priority is pollution and resulting health impacts associated with inadequately controlled industrial development and misapplication of chemical technologies. The North tends to frame many of its concerns in the context of the "global commons," but extension of this concept to nationally-based resources threatens Southern sovereignty. Although the economic debt of the South has received abundant attention, the environmental debt of the North has been greatly underplayed. The North bears primary responsibility for many global environmental problems, but the South is likely to experience greater hardships as a result of these problems. "The issue of how the burden of adjustment will be distributed is critical to any meaningful global environmental negotiations." Concludes with a proposed research agenda on eight interacting themes: resource depletion, pollution, natural disasters, poverty and basic needs, economic development models, politics and participation, appropriate technologies, and processes of cultural change (e.g., the population issue should be seen as one of women's rights and women's development). [ALSO SEE: The South Commission report (Oxford, 1990; **FS Annual 1992 #10992**).]

(North/South differences on environment)

186

In the Wake of the Affluent Society: An Exploration of Post-Development. Serge Latouche (Prof of Economics, U of Paris XI). Introduced and Translated by Martin

O'Connor and Rosemary Arnoux (U of Auckland, NZ). London and Atlantic Highlands NJ: Zed Books, 1993/ 256p/$19.95pb. First published 1991 in Paris as **La Planete des naufragés** (Planet of the Shipwrecked).

Author of **L'Occidentalisation du monde** (1989) describes the foundering of the "grand society" and the collapse of the development myth. Twenty years ago a somewhat romantic *tiers-mondisme* could capture the imagination, but now it is dead. People in the West behave as if the end of a simplistic ideology of worldwide transformation—its credibility destroyed by practical complexity—has wiped the reality of poverty away. The fall of socialism and the widening belief in the marketplace work together to increase the myopia towards the worsening realities of exclusion. Development's castaways have come to make up the Fourth World of marginalized people. The new poor include some 40 million in Western Europe, 20-30 million North Americans living below the poverty line, 200-350 million native minorities throughout the world, and several billion people in the least advanced countries. "It seems that the grand society, whose own rationality decrees all other societies to be irrational and which acts the self-fulfilling prophet by exterminating them, has ended up by creating and nourishing a new irrational which, refusing to be abolished, must be recognized as incarnating an *other* reason."

Chapters describe the myth of a world of winners (the enticing message of the grand society is access to abundance for all), the ambivalence of modernity (the noble democratic ideal in practice has been implemented hand in hand with the destruction of cultures through the rise of technology and the market), the price of opulence (public demoralization), the ineffectiveness of giving aid, the informal as the embryo of a new society (its discovery in the 1970s is due primarily to the failure of development), the ambiguity of "assistance policies" in the informal sector, the ambiguities of food self-sufficiency policies (is the target to be the individual, the family, the village, the region, or the nation?), the ambiguities of basic needs and appropriate technologies, the "standard of living" as the dominant reference point in economic policy and in perceiving social reality and thus underdevelopment ("the currently dominant accounting categories represent a radical form of cultural imperialism"), the denied social richness of the other ("the poor are far richer than they are said to be, or than they believe themselves"), the new society of the castaways who have been misled and abandoned by their master, how the population explosion stems from deculturation and Westernization (the former destroys social structures which once worked to limit new births; the latter removes the cultural rationale for these limits), and the informal sphere as "a rough sketch of what could be a new and authentically *post-modern* society." [NOTE: Lucid, profound, and well-informed criticism; a worthy successor to Ivan Illich and Jacques Ellul. The back cover blurb lauds Latouche as "France's most boldly original thinker about the process of global modernization."] **(myths of development)**

187

A New World Order: Grassroots Movements for Global Change. Paul Ekins (Research Director, Right Livelihood Award; Research Fellow, Dept of Economics, Birkbeck College, U of London). Foreword by Jakob von Uexkull (Founder and Chmn, Right Livelihood Award). London & NY: Routledge, March 1992/248p/$74.50; $15.95pb.

It is now increasingly recognized that humanity faces four interlocking crises of unprecedented magnitude: the spread of weapons of mass destruction and the high level of military spending, the affliction with hunger and absolute poverty of some 20% of the human race, environmental pollution and ecosystem destruction, and intensifying human repression. Each of these problems reinforces the others into a single global problematique. Ekins reviews major reports of three UN commissions: the Palme report (various omissions or misplaced emphases are pointed out), the two Brandt reports ("hopelessly flawed"), and the Brundtland report ("pure, conventional developmentalism"). Institutions of interdependence and forced cultural conversion serve to exploit the poor and are fundamental contributors to unsustainability. These conventional approaches do not seem to be containing, far less reversing, the four chief trends. New approaches are needed. The bulk of this book describes case-study material from the nomination files of the Right Livelihood Award, started in 1980 and known as the Alternative Nobel Prize. This includes chapters on people and groups working for peace through public pressure and real security (Petra Kelly, Johan Galtung), defending human rights (Amnesty International, Survival International), seeking "another development" (the Sarvodaya movement of Sri Lanka), promoting development by people (the Bangladesh Rural Advancement Committee), regenerating the environment (India's Chipko Movement), and promoting human development with a holistic model (Finbland's Village Action Movement).

Concludes that the common thrust of the new movements for social and economic change is toward democratization of knowledge, development, and the state. This new articulation of people-to-people and people-to-nature relations promotes cultural diversity, an ecocentric perception, development of people in the round, and governance that promotes autonomy, initiative, and social justice. This "people's alternative, a future that works through a new world order, will prevail." [NOTE: Certainly no relation to George Bush's "New World Order." An Appendix lists 1980-1990 recipients of the Right Livelihood Award, including Eric Dammann, Bill Mollison, Leopold Kohr, Amory and Hunter Lovins, Robert Jungk, Hans-Peter Dürr, Frances Moore Lappé, José Lutzenberger, and Alice Tepper Marlin. More information from Right Livelihood Awards, PO Box 15072, S-10465 Stockholm, SWEDEN.] **(Right Livelihood Awards)**

188

Global Transformation and the Third World. Edited by Robert O. Slater (National Security Education Program), Barry M. Schutz (Defense Intelligence College, Washington), and Steven R. Dorr (DIC). Boulder CO: Lynne Rienner Publishers & London: Adamantine Press, April 1993/380p/$45.00;$22.00pb.

Papers on the trend toward democratization, emerging global economic interdependence, and changing patterns of conflict and conflict mitigation. Some observations: 1) the processes of fragmentation and reordering of state boundaries and identities are likely to continue unabated; 2) as these processes unfold in Europe and the former Soviet Union, it becomes increasingly likely that the Third World will experience greater marginalization, insulating it from outside meddling but also isolating it from an increasingly interdependent and highly competitive international system; 3) we will continue to see more experimentation with different forms of democratic rule, but the depth and breadth of the process is in doubt; 4) we will see a "world of rampant conflict," with an international and regional system ill-prepared to mediate and mitigate; 5) the "Third World" as a concept derives from the past international system; although it was never a monolithic entity, "the structure of the emerging global system renders it even less meaningful." [**NOTE**: Regrettably, the authors do not suggest any alternative to the out-dated term "Third World."] (**"Third World" marginalization**)

189
State of the Peoples: A Global Human Rights Report on Societies in Danger. Edited by Marc S. Miller (Project Director, Cultural Survival, Cambridge MA). Boston: Beacon Press, Nov 1993/262p/$35.00;$18.00pb.

Jason W. Clay, founding editor of *Cultural Survival Quarterly* and director of a database on the languages of the world, notes that there are now more than 190 states in the world, up from only 50 before WWII and 170 as recently as 1989. By contrast, the world's 6,000 or so indigenous groups (defined by a unique language, a long-term relationship to a homeland, and one-time exercise of political control over their destinies) have been around for centuries, even millennia. At the heart of the matter is the state-building, nation-destroying process, founded on the belief that indigenous peoples and states can't coexist. "More than half the world's 15,000 known languages have disappeared already; only 5-10% of the remaining 6,000 to 7,000 are likely to survive another 50 years." Despite this history of cultural destruction, indigenous peoples account for some 10-15% of the world's population, and have traditional claims over some 25-30% of the earth's land area and resources. This report summarizes overall conditions in ten world regions, and the major groups within them. It also includes the Draft Declaration on the Rights of Indigenous Peoples, created by the UN Working Group on Indigenous Populations, specifically recognizing rights to self-determination and protection against cultural genocide. When adopted by the UN General Assembly, it will form the basis for a new relationship of indigenous peoples with states and with the UN. **Julian Burger** notes that, whereas indigenous peoples were once considered a remnant of the past, destined to inexorable assimilation by the mainstream society, the second World Conference on Human Rights has asked the General Assembly to proclaim a decade for indigenous peoples.

(**protecting the rights of indigenous peoples**)

190
The Gaia Atlas of First Peoples: A Future for the Indigenous World. Julian Burger (UN Center for Human Rights). Foreword by Maurice Strong (Secretary-General, 1992 UN Conference on Environment and Development). NY: Anchor/Doubleday, Oct 1990/191p/$15.95pb.

As we reawaken our consciousness that humankind and the rest of nature are inseparably linked, we must look at the world's more than 250 million indigenous people (5% of the global population, living in over 70 countries, in some 5,000 distinct groups). In recent decades, they have suffered from some of the most destructive aspects of "development." They have been separated from their traditional lands and ways of life, deprived of their means of livelihood, and forced to fit into alien societies. Part One, **Ways of Life**, briefly describes various groups such as the Inuit in the Arctic, Pacific Islanders, the Taureg of West Africa, and the Hopis of North America. Part Two, **Crisis**, offers sketches of modern colonialism, deforestation, damming, mining, militarization, and cultural collapse. Part Three, **Alternative Visions**, presents options such as resistance, the indigenous movement (there are over 1000 indigenous organizations worldwide, most established in the last 20 years), coalitions such as the Anti-Slavery Society, self-determination as the key to survival, survival schools, treaties for fishing rights, action by international organizations, and the campaign to get the UN to proclaim a Declaration of Indigenous Rights. Concludes with data on indigenous people in the nation-states of the world (0.5% of US population, 4% of Canada, 40% of Peru, 66% of Bolivia, 7% of India, 10% of New Zealand, etc.), and a map of the "Fourth World", a term used by the World Council of Indigenous Peoples (555 King Edward Ave, Ottawa) to distinguish this way of life from that of the First, Second, and Third Worlds. [**NOTE**: Excellent introductory overview, with numerous photos and maps. The Fourth World term is also used to designate the poorest countries of the world (see **FS Annual 1992** #10984). ALSO SEE in the lushly-produced Gaia Future Series, **The Gaia Peace Atlas** (Anchor, 1988; **FS Annual 1990** #9728), **The Gaia Atlas of Green Economics** (Anchor, 1992, **FS Annual 1993** #11913) and **The Gaia Atlas of Cities** (Anchor, 1993, **FS Annual 1995** #13142).]

(**Fourth World quest for self-determination**)

8. Women and Children

*191
The World's Women 1970-1990: Trends and Statistics. United Nations. NY: UN Publications, May 1991/120p(8x11")/$19.95pb (Sales No. E.90.XVII.3).

An "innovative and experimental" report bringing together indicators on families and households, domestic violence against women (an underreported problem in all regions, classes, and cultures), public life and leadership (only 3.5% of the world's cabinet ministers are women), education and training (the number of illiterate women rose from 543 million in 1970 to 597 million in 1985, in contrast to a minuscule rise in men, from 348 million to 352 million), health and child-bearing (women's life expectancy increased faster than men's in every region), urbanization and sanitation, and women's work and the economy (much of the work women do is still not considered to be of any economic value and is not measured; if unpaid housework and family care were counted, "measures of global output would increase 25-30%").

Some regional trends in the past 20 years: **1) Latin America and Caribbean**: significant gains for women in urban areas but little change in rural areas; **2) Sub-Saharan Africa**: some improvement in health and education, but indicators are still far from minimally acceptable in most countries; fertility remains very high; rapid population growth and serious economic decline is undermining modest gains in health and education; **3) Northern Africa and Western Asia**: gains in health and education; fertility declined slightly but remains very high; **4) Southern Asia**: health and education improved somewhat, but indicators are far from minimally acceptable and very far from men's; **5) Eastern and South-Eastern Asia**: improvements in levels of living, with many male/female inequalities reduced; **6) Developed Regions**: health of women is generally good and their fertility low; "everywhere occupational segregation and discrimination in wages and training are in favor of men."

"Resounding throughout the statistics in this book is one consistent message: major gaps in policy, investment, and earnings prevent women from performing to their full potential in social, economic, and political life." **Policy Gaps**: governments seldom integrate the concerns and interests of women into mainstream policies; development policies typically neglect the informal sector and subsistence agriculture—the usual preserve of women; many laws deny women equality with men in their rights to own land, borrow money, and enter contracts. **Investment Gaps**: households and governments almost always invest less in women and girls than in men and boys; families often give lower priority to health care of girls than boys; governments give little or no support to activities in which women predominate. **Pay Gaps**: occupational segregation and discrimination relegate women to low-paying and low-status jobs; and even when women perform the same work as men, they typically receive 30-40% less pay on average worldwide.

Almost everywhere, access to and use of family planning are increasing, but not as rapidly as they might (giving women means to regulate child-bearing enhances their ability to shape their own lives). In all regions, women now spend less time married and fewer years bearing and rearing children; in most regions, women's share of the total labor force is increasing. Concludes that the cost of policy changes to narrow gaps in the 1990s, especially when weighed against the benefit, would be small. [**NOTE**: Outstanding global survey. Reiterates and updates the perspectives of **Women: A World Report** (Oxford, 1985; **FS Annual 1986** #7381) and **Women...A World Survey** (World Priorities, 1985; **FS Annual 1986** #7382).]

(**women and men: global trends**)

192
Women, Households and Change. Edited by Eleonora Masini (Gregorian U, Rome) and Susan Stratigos. Prologue by Elise Boulding. Tokyo: United Nations U Press, 1991/241p. (Sales No.E.91.III.A.3)

Synthesis volume of the UNU Household, Gender, and Age project initiated in the early 1980s to establish the nexus between macro-level historical events and the micro-level of the household, showing how women are affected by change and how they affect change. These case studies examine the demographic transition in Columbia, textile workers in Brazil and Argentina, women's employment in Chile, social structure in Sri Lanka, economic development and rural women in China, and change on plantations in Kenya. Concludes that decision-makers are frequently not fully aware of women's actual needs (often traced to a dearth of good reporting) and of the practical impact of macro-changes on households. Boulding notes in the prologue that "although much of the edifice of development has been erected on the backs of women living at the lowest economic levels, these women themselves experience little change in their own lives, except for the worse." One constant in the lives of women is domination by men as fathers, husbands, employers, and authority figures in the community—a patriarchy that persists in the great variety of national settings studied here. If poor societies are to develop, attention must be paid to the maldistribution of resources. Improved wages and working conditions, and availability of child care, should be a priority, followed by skill training and community-based adult education. (**impact of change on women**)

193
Making Women Matter: The Role of the United Nations (Updated Edition). Hilkka Pietilä (Helsinki) and Jeanne Vickers (Geneva). London & Atlantic Highlands NJ: Zed Books, July 1994/198p/$49.95;$17.50pb.

Women and their contribution really do matter in building a better future for humanity. The UN can no longer escape recognition of the half of humanity who bear more than half the sky on their shoulder. Member governments have given firm promises to rectify imbalances between men and women in the UN as well as in global and national development. "Now the issue is the keeping of those promises." First published in 1990, this book reviews the "radical new inclinations within the UN system" as background to the UN Fourth World Conference on Women (Beijing, Sept 1995). Chapters discuss the 1985 Nairobi conference and its Forward-looking Strategies for the Advancement of Women, the World Surveys on the Role of Women in Development, the System-wide Medium-term Plan for Women and Development for 1990-1995 ("the most impressive commitment of the UN System to the realization of the Nairobi Strategies," seeking to eliminate all sex-based discrimination in the UN System by 2000), the annual **Human Development Reports** [see #178/180], the truism of emerging rights of women as human rights, and two important issues for the 1990s (violence against women, and the relationship between the status of women and the state of the natural environment).

(**UN role in advancing women**)

194
Bringing Women In: Women's Issues in International Development Programs. Núket Kardam (Dept of Government, Pomona College). Boulder CO: Lynne Rienner Publications, Jan 1991/137p/$26.50.

The women's movement, along with the environmental movement, is changing the way development issues are defined. In the 1970s, an international social movement emerged, working toward more gender-sensitive policies. Kardam analyzes attempts to alter the norms of the development assistance regime, and how three development agencies (UNDP, World Bank, Ford Foundation) have responded. She concludes that the women's movement has been able to affect existing norms in relatively weak and decentralized development assistance regimes, but is constrained by organizational traits from turning general ideas into specific, clear, and implementable policies. [ALSO SEE: **Women, International Development, and Politics**, edited by Kathleen Staudt (Temple U Press, July 1990/320p/$39.95), on issues faced by women interacting with Third World bureaucracies and development organizations.] (**women and development**)

195
Women Transforming Politics: Worldwide Strategies for Empowerment. Edited by Jill M. Bystydzienski (Franklin College of Indiana). Bloomington IN: Indiana U Press, April 1992/229p/$35.00;$19.95pb.

The concept of "politics" is more than the exercise of power in the public realm. Central to the feminist definition of politics is the concept of "empowerment" as the process by which oppressed persons gain some control over their lives. These 13 case studies examine women's culture and movements in Norway, the US, Spain, Japan, Greece, Britain, Mexico, Canada, Uganda, Palestine, Nicaragua, Poland, and rural India (where the Comprehensive Health Project is an effective lever for grass-roots change). Concludes that certain strategies in combination with particular societal conditions result in successful empowerment: 1) getting more women into political bodies works best where voting structures are relatively open, left-wing parties exist, and where cultural values of equality and group rights are embedded (Norway, Japan); 2) where access to official governance structures is difficult, women develop other strategies to voice their concerns, derived from traditional women's culture (Spain); 3) women's movements worldwide are directly related to urbanization, economic expansion, and the growth of the middle class; 4) in countries where access to official governance has been denied to women and to most men as well (Uganda, Palestine, Nicaragua, Poland, India), women have joined with men in nationalist and economic development movements; 5) small consciousness-raising groups can empower women to change their condition.

(women's empowerment strategies)

196

Global Gender Issues. V. Spike Peterson (U of Arizona) and Anne Sisson Runyan (SUNY-Potsdam). Boulder CO: Westview Press, Aug 1993/202p/$38.50;$12.95pb.

An exploration of how world politics looks when seen through a gender-sensitive lens, enabling a view of how the world is shaped by gendered concepts, practices, and institutions. Chapters cover the social construction of gender and gender hierarchy, global gender inequality (fewer than 5% of heads of state and cabinet ministers are women; more than 65% of work hours are performed by women), gendered divisions of power and violence, economic and ecology issues, and women as nonstate and transstate actors. General proposals: *1) Ungendering Power and Politics*: adding women to existing world political structures and transforming these structures and their agendas; *2) Ungendering Violence*: more women in state- and UN-sponsored military bodies; encouraging domestic violence legislation in all states; *3) Ungendering Labor*: include women's reproductive labor and their informal work as part of national economic accounting systems, equal pay for equal work, national child care policies, more women in male-dominated occupations; *4) Ungendering Resources*: increasing the presence of women in decision-making bodies that control resource use; ending the gendered dichotomy of culture (or man) vs. nature. Concludes that "ungendering world politics requires a serious rethinking of what it means to be human and how we might organize ourselves in more cooperative, mutually respectful ways."

(ungendering world politics)

197

Revolutions in Knowledge: Feminism in the Social Sciences. Edited by Sue Rosenberg Zalk (Director, Center for the Study of Women and Society, CUNY) and Janice Gordon-Kelter. Boulder CO: Westview, Mar 1992/170p/ $44.00.

The social changes feminists seek involve aspects of culture and thought that are absolutely central to the social, political, and economic organization of societies. Intellectually and morally, feminists envision societies in which gender stratification has been overcome. This vision means specifically targeting those aspects of society that promote and sustain inequities. Feminists seek a world founded on feminist principles: societies where all people are free and equal and live with respect and dignity, where power and resources are widely dispersed, and where institutions promote such values as nurturing, caring, mutual concern, and cooperation. The new feminist challenges to knowledge reflect the larger feminist movement. The social sciences were largely developed by a homogeneous group of white, middle-class, Western men. The traditional academic disciplines have evolved assuming maleness as the norm of human behavior. Reconceptualizing disciplines holds the promise of a true revolution in knowledge. These essays discuss feminist perspectives on philosophy, psychology, sociology, anthropology, political science, economics, and history.

(feminist critique of social science)

*198

The State of the World's Children 1994. James P. Grant (Executive Director, UNICEF). NY: Oxford U Press, May 1994/87p(8x11")/$8.00pb.

Reports on recent progress in reducing diseases that today still kill over 8 million children a year, and the malnutrition which holds back the mental and physical development of one child in three in LDCs: *1) Polio*, which cripples children for life, declined from about 400,000 cases in 1980 to about 140,000 in 1992, with a reasonable chance that it can be eradicated by 2000; *2) Iodine Deficiency*, the major cause of preventable mental retardation in 120,000 children per year, could soon be brought to an end; *3) Vitamin A Deficiency*, which blinds some 250,000 children a year, could be almost eliminated; *4) Neonatal Tetanus*, preventable by immunization of pregnant women, should soon become a rarity; in ten years, infant deaths have been cut from more than 1 million a year to just over half a million ; *5) Measles*, which still kills more children every year than all the world's wars and famines put together, has declined from over 2.5 million deaths in 1980 to 1 million in 1992 (nonfatal cases of measles have fallen from 75 million to 25 million). The internationally agreed target of 80% immunization against the major vaccine-preventable childhood diseases was reached several years ago by almost half of LDCs. The Convention on the Rights of the Child has been ratified by 150 nations, of which 28 have so far reported on the steps taken toward full implementation.

New goals for the year 2000 undertaken by many nations include a one-third reduction in under-five mortality rates, the halving of child malnutrition, 90% immunization coverage, control of major childhood diseases, primary school education for at least 80% of children, safe water and sanitation for all communities, and family planning information and services available to all. The total extra cost of reaching all of these goals is about $25 billion a year. Some 86 governments have drawn up national action programs for reaching the goals, and another 56 countries are in the final stages of drawing up such plans. However, "there is a clear and growing danger that both present potential and past achievements may be overwhelmed, in the years ahead, by the growing crises of absolute poverty, rapid population growth, and increasing environmental pressures." This "PPE problem" will not be resolved without a sustained national and international effort to overcome the worst aspects of poverty, which is the root of the population and environmental crisis—and the most accessible point at which to break the powerful synergisms which form the downward spiral of PPE problems. An adequate response to PPE problems must include four basic kinds of investment: prevention of common diseases and disabilities, primary education for all children (especially for girls), an effort to improve the lives of women in poor communities, and making family planning available.

("PPE problem" to negate child health advances?)

199

The State of the World's Children 1992. James P. Grant (Executive Director, UNICEF). NY: Oxford U Press, March 1992/100p(8x10")/$7.50pb.

The old world order is visibly dying. This report seeks to contribute to the agenda of the emerging new world order "from the perspective of a worldwide organization which comes into daily contact with some of the greatest failings of the old." These failings were the central issue of the World Summit for Children, held in September 1990 at the UN headquarters [**FS Annual 1992** #10954]. Ten specific propositions are advanced: 1) the promise of the World Summit for Children should be kept: a new world order should bring an end to malnutrition, preventable disease, and illiteracy among so many millions of the world's children; 2) the principle of "first call for children" (protection of the young should have first call on society's resources) should become an accepted ethic of the new world order; 3) doing what can now be done to protect the health and save the lives of millions of children will help—not hinder—efforts to slow population growth; 4) "the growing consensus around the importance of market economic policies should be accompanied by a corresponding consensus on the responsibility of governments to guarantee basic investments in people"; 5) increases in international aid should be based on meeting minimum human needs; 6) international action on debt, aid, and trade should allow people to earn a decent living (the poor world is now transferring $50 billion a year to the rich nations; protectionism in the rich world costs the poor world a further $50 billion a year in lost exports); 7) demilitarization should be linked to significant increases in international aid ("the amount now spent on the world's military exceeds the combined annual incomes of the poorest half of humanity;" the goals of the World Summit for Children could be met by reallocating 1% of military spending in the rich world); 8) the chains of Africa's debt should be struck off (Africa today pays only about one-third of the interest due on its debts—yet this absorbs a quarter of all its export earnings); 9) "a new world order should oppose the apartheid of gender as vigorously as the apartheid of race"; 10) responsible planning of births is one of the most effective and least expensive ways of improving the quality of life on earth. Concludes with a reiteration of the *World Summit's* Year 2000 goals for children (p61) and nine tables of comparative data. [**NOTE**: Fresh frontiers in progressive advocacy; note especially the emphasis in proposition #4 on "basic investments."]

(child welfare in the new world order)

C. IMPROVING GOVERNANCE AND LEARNING

1. Globally Shared Values

200

Request for Help with Preparation of a Club of Rome Report on "Governance for the 21st Century," Yehezkel Dror (Prof of Political Science, Hebrew U of Jerusalem), *Technological Forecasting and Social Change*, 40:2, Sept 1991, 209-212.

An open solicitation for ideas and suggestions for a draft report to the Club of Rome on 21st century situations, specifications that governance must meet in values and visions, alternative macrostructures of governance, governance restructuring principles, new modes of citizen enlightenment, and new university programs and training patterns. Some tentative thoughts on the CoR report, "as an incitement and preliminary frame for shared thinking:" 1) governance lags behind a rapidly changing world: many core elements of governments are relatively stable in the face of radical transformations in knowledge, values, and situations; 2) if the speed of government innovation is not accelerated, the gap between incremental improvements in government and rapid transformations in its environments will grow into an abyss; 3) yet governance must play a pivotal role, and the quality of governance becomes more crucial to the future of humanity; 4) all societies must transform themselves in important ways to meet global imperatives and prevent decline; 5) the fundamental *problematique* is that deficits in governance quality will carry even greater risks of high costs in the 21st century; 6) strenuous efforts to upgrade governance are essential, but this is a very difficult task; tinkering with institutions can bring unanticipated and undesirable consequences; 7) promising ideas on significantly upgrading governance are scarce; most proposals are too incremental or too utopian [**NOTE: The Capacity to Govern: Report to the Club of Rome** will be published in five languages in 1995.]

(**Club of Rome governance report: call for ideas**)

201

International Relations in a Changing Global System: Toward a Theory of the World Polity. Seyom Brown (Prof of Politics, Brandeis U). Boulder CO: Westview Press, Oct 1992/190p/$44.00;$16.95pb.

The world polity is the global pattern of structures and processes for creating and resolving conflicts and for making and implementing rules. A theory of the world polity, as distinct from a theory of international relations, is needed to deal with the central predicament of the human species: failure to develop systems of governance to keep pace with humanity's expanding power to alter the natural world. A normative framework starts with assumptions about world interests, or what is good for the world as a whole: survival of the human species, reduction in killing and brutal treatment, provision of basic conditions for healthy subsistence of the world's peoples, protecting individual citizen rights, preserving cultural diversity, and protecting the environment. These imperatives imply four categories of needed policies and institutions: keeping conflict from escalating, preventing threats to the environment, providing minimum health subsistence, and fostering inter-country and trans-country accountability. Modifying international political behavior to seek these ends would be a major step toward world community. This will require active and skillful leadership of the morally committed. (**policy to address world interests**)

202

Post-Modernism: The Search for Universal Laws, Vaclav Havel (President, Czech Republic), *Vital Speeches of the Day,* 60:20, 1 Aug 1994. (Excerpts entitled ***The New Measure of Man*** in *NY Times* Op-Ed, 8 July 1994, A27.)

The modern age has ended, and many things indicate that we are going through a transitional period, when something is on the way out and something else is painfully being born. The distinguishing features of transitional periods are a mixing and blending of cultures and a plurality of intellectual and spiritual worlds. These are periods when all consistent value systems collapse, when cultures distant in time and space are discovered. This state of mind, today called post-modernism, is related to the crisis of science as the basis of the modern conception of the world. The relationship to the world that modern science fostered and shaped appears to have exhausted its potential. It fails to connect with the most intrinsic nature of reality and with natural human experience. It produces a state of schizophrenia: man as observer is becoming completely alienated from himself as a being. Experts can explain anything in the objective world, yet we understand our own lives less and less. In the post-modern world, everything is possible and almost nothing is certain. We stand helpless before global challenges because our civilization has essentially globalized only the surface of our lives. Individual cultures increasingly lumped together by contemporary civilization are realizing with new urgency their own inner autonomy. Cultural conflicts are increasing and are more dangerous today than at any time in history. "The central political task of the final years of this century, then, is the creation of a new model of co-existence among the various cultures, peoples, races and religious spheres within a single interconnected civilization." It is clearly necessary to invent organizational structures appropriate to the multicultural age. But such efforts will fail if they do not grow out of something deeper, out of generally held values. Human rights must be an integral part of any meaningful world order. Yet it must be anchored in a different place, a science that can transcend its own limits. Two examples are the "anthropic cosmological principle" that we are not just an accidental anomaly but are connected to the evolution of the universe, and the "Gaia hypothesis" that Earth's surface forms a single system and that we are parts of a greater whole. Both ideas provide an awareness encoded in all religions. The only real hope of people today is probably a renewal of our certainty that we are rooted in the Earth and the cosmos. [ALSO SEE: ***The End of the Modern Era*** by Vaclav Havel (*New York Times*, 1 March 1992, E15).] (**universal values needed**)

203

Spiritual Politics: Changing the World from the Inside Out. Corinne McLaughlin and Gordon Davidson (Sirius Community, Shutesbury MA). Foreword by His Holiness The Dalai Lama. NY: Ballantine Books, Aug 1994/475p/$12.95pb.

Authors of **Builders of the Dawn: Community Lifestyles in a Changing World** (Stillpoint, 1985; **FS Annual 1986** #7662) apply their understanding of the Ageless Wisdom tradition (also called the Perennial Philosophy or the Sacred Science) to world events. The Ageless Wisdom is the golden thread connecting the hidden, mystical teachings within the major religious traditions. It provides a broad context, enabling a view of interconnections in the evolutionary process. ("New Age" teachings are seen as popularizations of the Ageless Wisdom, sometimes watered down or distorted.) Joining the spiritual and material dimensions of life, politics is the art of governance that synthesizes opposing views into a higher level of understanding and addresses the greatest good for the greatest number. Chapters discuss the Ageless Wisdom through history, the planetary web of life, the symbolism and significance of world events, whole-systems thinking as the new transformational politics, politics as if people mattered (the psychological dimension includes self-esteem, cooperation, community, empowerment, releasing enemy images), the mental causes of world events (linear and polarized thinking, secularization of public life, negative media images), the emotional causes of world events, the cosmic causes of world events, the soul and spiritual destiny of nations, the new planetary economics, planetary stewardship, and inner and outer work for planetary evolution. Concludes that "it's time to wake up from the slumber of materialism...the fate of the world is in our hands—or, more accurately, in our minds and hearts." The nations of planet Earth will be healed and made whole only through a unitive spirit that synthesizes the best in all opposing positions and finds win/win solutions to problems. [**NOTE**: A likely Bible for those who follow the Ageless Wisdom and an interesting alternative worldview for others. Hardcore social scientists will see it as beyond our galaxy. Yet there are similarities here to the urgings of Vaclav Havel (above).]

(**planetary evolution and spiritual politics**)

204

Global Responsibility: In Search of a New World Ethic. Hans Küng (Director, Institute for Ecumenical Research, U of Tübingen, Germany). NY: Crossroad Publishing Co, June 1991/158/$18.95; $12.95pb (first published in Munich in 1990).

The three parts (and basic themes) of the book have striking titles: **1) No Survival Without a World Ethic**: on the end of the great modern ideologies (criticism of the achievements of the West, demystification of the ideology of progress), the rising world constellation of postmodernity (transition to an ethically responsible society, a technology that serves humanity, reconciliation of freedom and justice, a post-capitalist and post-socialist economy, a post-patriarchal society), "planetary responsibility" as the slogan of the future, the need for a coalition of believers and non-believers, postmodern requirements (freedom and justice, equality and plurality, solidarity with the environment, peace and not just coexistence, and ecumenism and not just tolerance); **2) No World Peace Without Religious Peace**: an ecumenical way between fanaticism for truth and forgetfulness of truth, human dignity as a basic criterion (all religions should agree on a basic norm of authentic humanity—what is good for human beings helps them to be truly human), a combination of steadfastness and readiness for dialogue ("capacity for dialogue is capacity for peace"); **3) No Religious Peace Without Religious Dialogue**: an ecumenical theology for peace between Christians, Jews, and Muslims; imperatives for inter-religious dialogue. Concludes that religions must engage in constructive pro-existence and cooperation, and a closely interwoven network of inter-religious information. (**world ethic needed for survival**)

205

Morals Equals Manners. Ruth Nanda Anshen. Mt. Kisco NY: Moyer Bell Ltd (Colonial Hill), Mar 1992/134p/$14.95.

The founder and editor of several philosophy of culture book series (e.g., Convergence, Perspectives in Humanism, World Perspectives) asserts that re-examining the meaning of moral philosophy and manners (or conduct) promotes Einstein's principle of unified field theory and Whitehead's unitary structure of all reality. Morals equals manners constitutes rational foresight and moral imperative. It is an attempt to point the way in which we can think of ourselves as members of a single world society on the basis of a single moral system, while retaining cultural pluralism and individuality. The paramount moral issue of our time is the need for a world community now taking shape in the form of a Cultural Magna Carta. We have no choice but to turn to the idea of a Cultural Magna Carta which respects the autonomy of cultural diversity of customs, while recognizing the values shared by all peoples. We live in an era in which such cultural cooperation becomes imperative. (**Cultural Magna Carta proposed**)

206

Reinventing the Future: Global Goals for the 21st Century. Rushworth M. Kidder (*The Christian Science Monitor*). Cambridge MA: MIT Press, Nov 1989/194p/$17.95.

Book-length version of a Special Report in *The Christian Science Monitor* (25 July 1988; **FS Annual 1990** #9585), based on an April 1988 Wingspread conference bringing together an international group of 35 people from 12 nations to consider reasonable goals for humanity and how to meet them. The four goals concerned: **1) Closing the North-South Gap**: redirect development strategies away from exclusive reliance on economic factors, target development efforts on fulfilling noneconomic goals; **2) Improving East-West Relations**: return to a world without nuclear weapons insofar as achievable, encourage confidence-building measures that reduce tensions, restrain the conventional arms trade among nations, increase economic cooperation; **3) Halting Environmental Degradation**: create national plans for sustainable land use, establish a planetary trust for conservation of living resources, establish an international system of environmental accounts and a system of global rents for conservation of living natural resources, increase worldwide prices of fossil fuels to levels consistent with their costs; **4) Finding Ethical Ways to Balance Rights with Responsibilities**: increase awareness of moral dimensions of behavior, support codes of ethics for international business, inculcate a reverence for the future, increase awareness of the holistic nature of global problems, establish a child's bill of rights, promote community service to inculcate a sense of caring, develop a global syllabus of issues that affect everyone, channel human energies into constructive reforms. Four mechanisms for action are listed: use existing institutions (governments, NGOs, the news media, foundations), invent new institutions, involve individuals through volunteer efforts, and change individual attitudes to generate the political will to address problems. [**NOTE**: An excellent introduction to global problems and necessary actions, with a succinct set of fundamental goals. The attention to ethics as one of the four goals is unique among the three dozen or so agendas identified in **FS Annual 1990**, pp179-183).] (**four global goals**)

207

Shared Values for a Troubled World: Conversations with Men and Women of Conscience. Rushworth M. Kidder (President, Institute for Global Ethics, Camden ME). Foreword by Harlan Cleveland. San Francisco: Jossey-Bass Publishers, April 1994/332p/$22.00. (Brief version in *The Futurist*, July-Aug 1994, 8-13.)

Ethics is rapidly becoming a global survival issue as important as the population crisis, environment, the nuclear threat, the North-South gap, and the need to reform education. The three central trends of our global tomorrow are worldshrink, technobulge, and the need for consensus building based on shared values. Kidder presents interviews with 24 global-minded people, including Vietnam survivor Le Ly Hayslip, Australian historian Jill Ker Conway, the late Kenneth Boulding, Newton Minow, John W. Gardner, Derek Bok, Jeane Kirkpatrick, Oscar Arias, and UNESCO Director-General Federico Mayor. From them, he distills eight universal values for humanity: 1) *love* (including compassion, solidarity, mutual assistance); 2) *truthfulness* (or honesty; being able to trust people); 3) *fairness* (or justice, fair play, even-handedness, treating others as we wish to be treated); 4) *freedom* (or liberty, including a sense of individuality and the right to express ideas freely); 5) *unity* (or cooperation and community, as counterbalance to freedom; expresses the individual's role in a larger collective); 6) *tolerance* (listening to different points of view; embracing diversity); 7) *responsibility* (caring for others and for future generations); 8) *respect for life* (responsible use of force, distaste for killing). These eight core values are the "highest rung on the visionary ladder." They give us the way to build downward to the level of goals, plans and tactics: where things really happen and the world really changes. One cannot fully embrace this code of values without being forced, sooner or later, to come to grips with the major issues of our time. [**NOTE**: A constructive start on the important theme of shared values; don't be put off by the lightly journalistic interviews. For contrast, see Samuel P. Huntington's dour view of *The Coming Clash of Civilizations* (#059). Are cultural divisions stronger than universal human values? Neither Kidder nor Huntington compares the two.]   (**eight universal values**)

208
The Inner Limits of Mankind: Heretical Reflections on Today's Values, Culture and Politics. Ervin Laszlo (Rector, Vienna Academy for the Study of the Future). Foreword by Alexander King (President, Club of Rome). London: Oneworld Publications, March 1989/146p/$7.95pb. (Order in US from Meyer Stone, 2014 Yost Ave, Bloomington IN 47403.)

Author of the Club of Rome report on **Goals for Mankind** (Dutton, 1977) states that the truly crucial limits confronting mankind are not outer but inner: the bounds of human will and understanding that obstruct our evolution towards a better future. We suffer from a serious case of culture lag. On the personal level, inner limits are constituted by "hardening of the categories" of an age now behind us—the unrecognized obsolescence of modernism. On the cultural level, inner limits reside in the atrophy of positive images and visions of the future of human society. On the political level, inner limits manifest themselves in the failure of the majority of the world's governments to implement needed cooperative policies. A few basic ground rules are needed to transcend the inner limits. The truly universal values of universal brotherhood, love for one's neighbor, and the golden rule of treating others as we wish to be treated are common to all cultures. The ground rules of sustainability, development, and equity rest on the universal need for life, progress, and justice. We should replace antiquated notions such as coexistence with more adequate concepts such as "interexistence." And only those long-range policies that bring positive-sum results should be implemented. If the historical process continues to unfold without major catastrophes, it will bring a globally integrated social, cultural, and technological system. But present tendencies to centralization and homogenization would transform into decentralization with coordination, and mutual solidarity with respect for differences.
   (**ground rules to overcome culture lag**)

209
Why Future Generations Now? Edited by Katsuhiko Yazaki (President, FGAF). Future Generations Alliance Foundation (10 W 56th St, NYC 10019; 212/582-1147 or 1-1-3-2900 Umeda, Kitaku, Osaka 530; 06/344-6121), May 1994/372p/$20.00pb. [English language edition (159p); Japanese language edition (213p).]

Sakae Shimizu (Chairman, Kyoto Forum) surveys "the desperate crisis caused by our highly developed civilization; our generation has been living as if we are the last generation," and proposes the concept of caring for "future generations" as key to every future decision. Businessman **Katsuhiko Yazaki** warns of destruction of our external world and our internal world, and calls for five actions for the sake of future generations: Beyond Egoism, Beyond Economism, Beyond Now-ism, Beyond Nationalism, Beyond Scientism (not letting sci/tech dictate our lives). Korean futurist **Kim Tae-Chang** (President, Institute for the Integrated Study of Future Generations, Osaka) writes that all problems come from the excessive imbalance of modern civilization, and that we must pass the legacy from past generations on to future generations (to do so, he proposes Global Governance, a new theory of value for the global age, environmental education to enhance past/present/future solidarity, and hoped-for new leadership of 21st century Asia). **Wendell Bell** (Prof of Sociology, Yale U) explains why caring about future generations can benefit the present generation and why we ought to do so in any case. **Emmanuel Agius** (U of Malta; editor, *Future Generations Journal*) discusses conserving our common heritage for future generations and principles of intergenerational responsibility. **Allen Tough** (U of Toronto) lists seven spheres where future generations will benefit from our actions today (peace/security, sustainable environment, studying potential catastrophes, improved governance, valuing knowledge, healthy children, and widespread learning opportunity). **Rick A. Slaughter** (U of Melbourne) offers six reasons why we should care about future generations, and seven actions to take (including the disciplined study of futures and a pledge to future generations).   (**future generations as key value**)

210
The Global Commons: Policy for the Planet. Harlan Cleveland (Prof Emeritus, U of Minnesota). Aspen CO: The Aspen Institute & Lanham MD: University Press of America, Oct 1990/118p/$29.50;$13.75pb.

Summation of the 40th Anniversary Symposium of The Aspen Institute, expanding on an earlier concept paper prepared by Cleveland on **The Global Commons (FS Annual 1990 #9609)**. This emerging concept includes important parts of the human environment: the physical environment (the atmosphere, outer space, the oceans, Antarctica), biological and cultural diversity, and the information commons (managing the global flow of information). Sixty propositions about the Global Commons as a new policy frontier are proposed, e.g.: 1) the Commons environments belong to no one—or to everyone at once; 2) "in our time, there is a new class of problems, requiring unprecedented kinds of solutions; they are global: people everywhere have to widen the scale of what they think about"; 3) the governance of the Global Commons is to the social sciences what "global change" is to the natural sciences—the next frontier; 4) costs and benefits of actions to protect and develop the atmospheric commons will have to be shared in a manner widely agreed to be "fair"; 5) the environmental destruction that leads the poor to deepen their own poverty is the same process which leads to consumption by the rich that pollutes the environment; 6) abating global warming may come to be regarded not as costly but as very profitable; 7) the essence of global behavioral change is the pervasive spread of knowledge, which has produced a worldwide demand for choice, participation, and democracy; 8) the idea of information as a commons could be good news for fairness, requiring the highest priority given to universal education and to empowering the powerless; 9) we are beyond the point of needing more research before acting; we need to act on what we know; 10) the world is inching toward a new consensus: "the environment is fast moving to the top of the world's agenda; beyond 'human rights' there is human solidarity, a fairly new idea that transcends national boundaries and may turn out to be the glue that holds us all together"; 11) biological diversity is the essence of our common heritage; equally relevant is the diversity of human culture. [NOTE: Some leading edge concepts, especially the inchoate bundling of "the brainwork commons" together with the "physical and biological commons."]

("Global Commons" as emerging concept)

211
Ten Keys to World Peace, Harlan Cleveland (President, World Academy of Art and Science), *The Futurist,* 28:4, July-Aug 1994, 15-21.

Two tries at world order have been made in this century. The aim of "the third try" cannot be "world order," but to ensure peaceful change in a world made safe for diversity. Ten guidelines for managing peace in a pluralistic world: 1) "no nation, region, race, or creed is going to be in general charge;" 2) nations and their citizens can and will pool their collective learnings in win-win systems; 3) for much of what needs to be done, people can agree on next steps; 4) some common norms are already widely accepted (territorial integrity, nonuse of nuclear/chemical/biological weapons, helping refugees, no colonial rule or official racial discrimination, equality of women, human rights); 5) most of the world's people, and even their governments, might agree on some even more far-reaching norms (insulating local conflicts to prevent their spread, a third World War as impermissible, economic growth with fairness, children should not be hungry); 6) a review of what works best in the new world disorder forces belated recognition of the crucial role of major NGOs; 7) some global issues require actions by millions of individuals and families; 8) when governments have to work together to make something happen, they increasingly decide to act by consensus; 9) almost nothing in world affairs must involve everyone; rather, what's needed for solving each problem is a community of the concerned; 10) in matters affecting the globe, those who act have an obligation to explain what they are doing and why. Concludes with comments about the emerging "club of democracies." [ALSO SEE: **World Peace and the Human Family** by Roy Weatherford (London & New York: Doubleday Aug 1993/172p).]

(**managing peace in a pluralistic world**)

2. Expanding and Reshaping the U.N. Role

212
Empowering the United Nations, Boutros Boutros-Ghali (Secretary General, UN), *Foreign Affairs,* 71:5, Winter 1992-93, 89-102.

"A new chapter in the history of the UN has begun. With newfound appeal the world organization is being utilized with greater frequency and growing urgency." The new era has brought new credibility to the UN, along with rising expectations. The UN machinery, which had often been rendered inoperative by the dynamics of the Cold War, is suddenly at the center of many problems. The end of the Cold War has led to a dramatic expansion of UN peacekeeping services (in the first half of 1992, there was a fourfold increase in costs). This points to the need for immediately available cash, personnel, and equipment. Other comments are made on the continued failure of most member states to meet their financial commitments to the UN, mounting needs for durable economic and social development, the need to rethink the question of sovereignty ("a major intellectual requirement of our time"), new possibilities for contributions from the burgeoning number of regional associations and the huge network of NGOs (e.g., in "post-conflict peace-building"), and the need for UN change in the post-Cold War era. "Hope has been crucial; achievement is now required. Beyond declarations, beyond position-taking, the time is here to look at ideas as plans for action. Beyond restructuring, the culture of the UN must undergo a transformation."

(**needed UN reform**)

213
The United Nations in a Turbulent World. James N. Rosenau (Director, Institute of Transnational Studies, USC). International Peace Academy (NYC), Occasional Paper Series. Boulder CO: Lynne Rienner Publishers, Fall 1992/87p/$8.95pb.

For more than three centuries, the overall structure of world politics has been founded on an anarchic system of sovereign nation-states that did not have to answer to any higher authority. This state-centric world is no longer predominant. A complex multi-centric world of diverse and relatively autonomous actors has emerged. The various transformations at work in world politics are enlarging, and will continue to enlarge, the UN's centrality in the emergent global order. As its roles expand, the opportunities for the UN to serve as an agent of change seem bound to multiply. What then can be done to maximize the UN's chances of functioning as an agent of positive rather than negative change? Six recommendations are proposed: 1) reconsider the sovereignty principle so that it is subject to more than one interpretation; 2) enhance UN authority by establishing a permanent UN mission in the capital of every UN member, which makes services available to individuals and organizations in the multi-centric world, as well as to host governments (services would include information about peacekeeping activities and the work of various technical agencies); 3) consider addition of a people's assembly to the UN, in which representatives would be directly elected (but such a legislature might be counterproductive); 4) create a global "Peace Corps" service of volunteers to cope with UN system overload; 5) consider new procedures for selecting future Secretary Generals; 6) enlarge the bully pulpit by creating, say, five new Deputy Secretaries General (or UN Ambassadors-at-Large) who would visit national capitals and engage chiefs of state and other key elites in dialogue. [ALSO SEE: Rosenau's **Turbulence in World Politics** (#046 in this Guide) for the author's elaboration of the key theme of transition from a state-centric world of some 200 actors to a multi-centric world of hundreds of thousands of essential actors.]

(**needed UN reform**)

*214
Renewing the United Nations System. Erskine Childers (Ireland) with Brian Urquhart (Ford Foundation). *Development Dialogue* 1994:1/213p. (Available from Dag Hammarskjöld Foundation, S753 10 Uppsala, Sweden; or Ford Foundation, 320 E 43rd St, NYC 10017.)

The fourth in a series of studies on the UN System by Urquhart and Childers, sponsored by the Hammarskjöld and Ford Foundations. The major constitutional transformation of disparate elements into an integrated UN is not attainable now. This study addresses "less radical alternatives," mostly the "irreducible minimum needed to enable the system to face the enormous challenges which now confront it." Proposed changes include: 1) a common seat for the UN System, bringing together the scattered headquarters of the Specialized Agencies; 2) a new UN System Consultative Board to provide a mechanism for monitoring the coherence and efficacy of the UN system; 3) a comprehensive forward program and budget for the UN system; 4) several new Deputy Secretary-Generals, including a Deputy Secretary-General for International Economic Cooperation and Sustainable Development; 5) new instruments for multilateral economic management; 6) only one UN System office in any developing country, each headed by a UN Coordinator; 7) a single UN Development Authority consolidating all present UN development funds; 8) an independent Ombuds-Panel on the Human Rights Performance of the UN System; 9) a single Governing council for Humanitarian Assistance; 10) an independent commission to strengthen a seriously debilitated international civil service; 11) a UN Parliamentary Assembly to enable citizens of member-countries to have their own representatives in a specific UN organ. [ALSO SEE: the three other reports in this series, on issues of UN leadership (*Development Dialogue* 1990: 1-2), reorganizing the Secretariat, and humanitarian emergency machinery (both in *Development Dialogue* 1991: 1-2).]

(UN structural reforms)

215
A Successor Vision: The United Nations of Tomorrow. Edited by Peter J. Fromuth. Lanham MD: United Nations Association of the USA and University Press of America, 1988/385p/$41.25;$17.50pb.

Report of the UN Management and Decision-Making Project, a two-year research program funded by the Ford Foundation to strengthen the effectiveness of the UN and its immediate affiliated organs. The UN has rendered many services of great value, but there is now deep skepticism about its capacity to respond usefully to most global problems. The world has changed since drafting of the UN Charter in 1945: the number of independent countries has increased almost threefold, economic activity is globalizing, the nature of conflict is shifting away from the "aggressor-victim" model, global environmental risks are emerging, and there is now a semipermanent presence of massive numbers of stateless, displaced persons. A "new vision" includes the following proposals: 1) developing a staff level capacity to monitor data on "global watch issues" and to give prominent attention to the most urgent problems; 2) establishing a small Ministerial Board in affiliation with ECOSOC for the conduct of global watch consultations; 3) a more systematic approach to consensus-building, where common interests are identified and converted into cooperative action; 4) a two-step approach (establishing a UN Advisory Commission, and then a UN Commission) to a UN system that can develop integrated responses to global issues; 5) creating a single Development Assistance Board to replace the separate executive boards of UNDP, UNFPA, WFP, and UNICEF; 6) setting up multilateral arms reduction inspection teams to enhance peace and security. **(UN structural changes needed)**

216
United Nations: A Working Paper for Restructuring. Harold Stassen. Minneapolis MN: Lerner Publications. (800/328-4929), July 1994/125p/$14.95pb.

Former Governor of Minnesota, and one of the eight US delegates to the 1945 San Francisco Conference where the original UN Charter was conceived, proposes a UN restructuring for its 50th year in the form of detailed revisions and additions to the original Charter. He does not propose a world government, but "an improved center of cooperation between sovereign governments." This includes such ideas as: 1) a highly-trained and well-equipped United Nations Legion consisting of not more than 250,000 volunteers, to serve as a police and peace force; 2) a super peacemaking corps including a World Panel of Mediators, a World Board of Arbitration, and a World Court of Equity; 3) a Research Institute on People and Governance to suggest revisions of national, regional, and international organizations; 4) proportionate voting power in the UN General Assembly; 5) a new method of regular financial support, such as an 0.5% duty on all international trade of goods and raw materials; 6) extension of the Security Council from 15 to 21 members, with Japan and Germany as permanent members; 7) a Universe Environmental Institute to hold annual scientific conferences; 8) an annual Worldwide Conference of Religions, to find nonviolent and just solutions for future interrelationships of the peoples of the world. Also the Preamble and the purposes of the UN in Chapter 1, Article 1 should be expanded to include environmental concerns. **(UN Charter revisions proposed)**

217
Rethinking International Cooperation. Harlan Cleveland (Prof and former Dean, Humphrey Institute) and Lincoln P. Bloomfield (Prof of Political Science, MIT). Minneapolis MN: U of Minnesota, Hubert H. Humphrey Institute of Public Affairs (301 19th Ave S.), May 1988/36p/free.

Suppose that in the midst of a real war, we were asked to recommend a postwar system of international cooperation—as aides to Roosevelt, Churchill, and Stalin undertook as WWII drew to a close. Today we can no longer afford world war to stimulate rethinking the international system: rather, we must learn how to carry out 'post-war planning' without having the war first. We must acknowledge the centripetal pull of community and socio-cultural roots, a reality dismissed by many world order enthusiasts. At the same time, a new scientific revolution is creating both new needs and new possibilities for international action. We must also consider flaws in the six founding assumptions of the UN, as concerns the power of world community, the ability of the major powers to halt aggression, the ability to create familiar legislative institutions at the global level, the unimportance of economic equity issues, nation-states as the only important actors, and the inevitability of progress to supranational government. However, there are some norms of international behavior that have been widely accepted: territorial integrity, the inviolability of diplomatic missions, the non-use and non-proliferation of nuclear weapons, international responsibility for helping refugees, immunity of civilian aircraft and ships, and decolonization. Some lines of action: 1) in a complex, dangerous, and interdependent world, updated rules of the road and norms are needed, aimed at limiting potential calamities; 2) bring main non-governmental groups into the international planning and decision-making process; 3) design ways to isolate and insulate local conflicts around the world from external intervention; 4) to resolve conflicts, make sure that what is happening is widely known, and utilize teams of mediators; 5) develop a body of achievable norms relating to the global commons, to fence off these fragile environments from degradation on whatever pretext; 6) to overcome chronic funding crises, develop income streams by taxing transnational transactions.

(**improving international cooperation**)

218

The Gnat Is Older Than Man: Global Environment and Human Agenda. Christopher D. Stone (Prof of Law, USC). Princeton NJ: Princeton U Press, April 1993/341p/$21.95.

The earth faces many perils, immediate and remote, well-defined and vague. How do we best prepare for them? What sacrifices are merited? What legal and diplomatic structure can best handle global environmental problems? Chapters consider the condition of the earth from the legal perspective, transboundary pollution, managing the global commons, the pros and cons of treaties, the economist's prescriptions of taxes and tradable permits, prevention vs. cure, forms of calamity insurance, and moral dimensions. Two proposals are made: 1) a system of guardians who would be legal representatives for the natural environment (the success of such a regime would depend on significant changes in the substantive law that the guardian would be empowered to invoke); 2) a Global Commons Trust Fund, with revenues from ocean use (a tax of 0.5% of the fish catch would raise $250 million; the same rate on offshore oil and gas would add $375 million), a CO_2 tax of ten cents a ton (raising $2.2 billion per year), selling the rights to park satellites in the geostationary orbit, fees on minerals from the seabed, etc. There will of course be questions on how to allocate the fund: to national governments or the UN, based on population or need, and how to measure need. [**NOTE**: The reference to gnats in the title is obscure and poorly developed. It was suggested by the papers of Stone's journalist father, the late I. F. Stone. Also see proposals for an Environmental Security Trust Fund in Al Gore's **Earth in the Balance** (#161).]

(**Global Commons Trust Fund proposed**)

219

Reforming the Post-Cold-War UN, Rep. Lee H. Hamilton (D-Ind.), *The Christian Science Monitor*, 1 Dec 1992, p19.

The UN is experiencing the best of times and the worst of times. It is now very close to attaining the ideals of its charter; yet it has never been more overburdened and underfunded. The end of the Cold War has vastly expanded UN responsibilities: it has launched 13 peacekeeping operations in the last five years, as many as in the past 40 years. But resources have not kept pace, and the UN must eliminate redundant, obsolete, and questionable programs. The US can help by: 1) building consensus in support of reform; 2) supporting an expansion of the Security Council to enhance legitimacy and to persuade wealthy countries to assume greater UN burdens; 3) helping the UN respond better to crises by enabling member states to provide military units on short notice; 4) paying our UN dues on time and in full; 5) pushing for revision of UN dues assessments so that Japan, Germany, and the Persian Gulf states pay a larger share; 6) exploring new sources of funding such as a "peace endowment" created by public and private donations and taxes on airline travel and arms sales.

(**needed UN reform**)

*220

International Public Finance: A New Perspective on Global Relations. Ruben P. Mendez (UN Development Programme). NY: Oxford U Press, May 1992/339p/$45.00; $24.95pb.

Establishing a system of international public finance is a new and "potentially controversial" idea whose time has come. Poverty and disease have engulfed entire nations, crop failures and famines have become chronic, human well-being in LDCs continues to stagnate and regress, disparities in the wealth of nations have reached an all-time high, and environmental degradation has reached global dimensions. At the same time, the economies of the world have reached an unprecedented degree of interdependence. The problems cited are all too immense, too complex, and too costly to be solved by individual nations. They require concerted action and concerted resources. Existing international institutions are inadequate to solving these problems. International private finance suffers from the same kind of market failures as laissez-faire does nationally, and the limited public sector that exists internationally is oligarchic. The flow of public funds for development and welfare is almost completely voluntary, politically motivated, and patchwork in nature. It is sorely unequal to the magnitude of the task.

A new institutional framework is needed to mobilize and allocate resources as governments do in nation-states. Such a framework should be universal in coverage, and aim for the benefit of all countries and peoples. Such a system will open up new vistas for examining international problems and new avenues for approaching them. Elements of a possible system of international public finance might include: 1) **International Taxation**: on international trade, specific traded commodities such as oil and other minerals, surpluses in balances of trade, consumption, the North-South "brain drain," marine polluters, military expenditures, arms transfers, possession of weapons (all previously proposed at UN fora); 2) **The Global Commons**: charges for mining ocean beds, fishing on the high seas, navigation and overflight, use of Antarctic resources, use of the moon and other celestial bodies, "parking fees" for geostationary satellites, allocation of the radio section of the electromagnetic section; 3) **Macro-economic Measures**: special drawing rights, revenues from IMF gold sales, a UN lottery; 4) **Disarmament**: a means of reducing negative externalities (the end of the Cold War has placed it within our reach). In sum, this book is "a starting point for a new discipline of international public finance." [**NOTE**: A timely notion indeed, and absolutely certain to be controversial, especially in the US.] (**global public finance needed**)

221

The United Nations: Structure and Leadership for a New Era. Report of the 22nd UN Issues Conference. Muscatine IA: The Stanley Foundation, 1991/24p/free.

Report of a February 1991 Stanley Foundation conference, noting that the end of the Cold War and a worldwide rise in political pragmatism have created an opportunity for long-overdue reform of the UN. The 22 participants urged the following action: 1) reorganizing the Secretariat with 4 to 6 under-secretaries-general (instead of the current 25); 2) sharply reducing the annual General Assembly agenda of more than 150 items (many of these are trivial or merely holdovers from the distant past); 3) changing the composition of the Security Council to give more say to regional powers such as India and Brazil (the five permanent members stem from WWII). Participants were divided as to whether more coordination of the UN's 15 specialized agencies is possible or desirable; most agreed that efforts are duplicated.

(**UN structural reform**)

222

The UN System and NGOs: New Relationships for a New Era? The Stanley Foundation. Muscatine IA: The Stanley Foundation, 1994/30p/free.

Report of the 25th UN Issues Conference, held at Harriman NY in Feb 1994. The emerging relationship between nongovernmental organizations and the UN reflects some essential changes that have occurred in the world as to how people are organized and how they promote their agendas. Four factors have broadened the NGOs' scope over issues and policy formulation within the UN system: the diminishing importance of the state as the central site of political activity, the growth in social movements concerned with human rights and the environment, the new problems and opportunities arising from the demise of the Cold War, and higher expectations and demands on the UN system without a corresponding increase in resources. The 19 conference participants all agreed that NGOs must be accounted for within the UN's decision-making processes. A hearings process at the UN, similar to that of national legislatures, could provide valuable information. NGOs could also provide intelligence to various UN agencies. Creative leadership from the UN, the NGOs and governments will be necessary to foster long-term collaboration. Chairman **Richard H. Stanley** concludes by questioning the possibility or practicality of credentialing or regulating the diverse lot of NGOs. Rather, those NGOs that make credible and useful contributions will be heard. (**NGOs in the UN system**)

223

Collective Security and the United Nations: An Old Promise in a New Era. 26th UN of the Next Decade Conference. Muscatine IA: The Stanley Foundation, 1991/36p/free.

Report of a conference held in Ireland in June 1991, noting that with the end of the Cold War, international cooperation is now possible. The term "collective security" is a very narrow concept which traces its roots to Woodrow Wilson. The type of system envisioned by Wilson rests on assumptions of nondiscrimination (that corrective action will be taken regardless of who the aggressor and victim may be) and certainty (that the system will respond automatically and reliably). The UN "collective security" system is discriminatory and far from certain; in fact, it is actually a continuation of the victorious WWII alliance. A viable security system with both cooperative and collective measures would seriously address the roots of insecurity, reduce military threats, organize preventive diplomacy and crisis prevention efforts, and develop a workable enforcement system. Security can also be enhanced by radical reductions in arms levels, perhaps through an arms transfer registry, a levy on international arms sales, and/or making aid to LDCs conditional on their limited arms expenditures. (**promoting collective security**)

224

Changing Concepts of Sovereignty: Can the United Nations Keep Pace? Muscatine, Iowa: The Stanley Foundation, Fall 1992/36p/free.

Report of the 27th UN of the Next Decade Conference, convened at Mackinac Island in July 1992. Over the years, sovereignty became the cornerstone of the modern nation-state system. But, especially since WWII, nations have ceded limited portions of their sovereignty through treaties and the creation of regional economic and security groupings. Today's challenge to sovereignty comes not from nations agreeing to cede it, but from a fundamental erosion of the power of the state to control its affairs. This erosion is caused by information technologies, integration of the global economy, unmanageable issues, and emergence and ascendance of new nonstate actors. Sovereignty is about power, and "the simple fact is that in today's world power is much more dispersed." Moreover, the currency of military power has declined relative to other currencies such as economic strength and technological prowess. Nation-states are not likely to disappear, but they will have to learn to wield their more limited powers in a more ambiguous world, where individuals will have multiple loyalties that are often transnational. As the central organ in current international governance, the UN must continue to adapt to issues of sovereignty in order to be effective. The 25 Conference participants agreed on the need for greater representation of new actors on the world scene. The UN does not grant sovereignty, but does license it by granting membership, and thus may be able to develop criteria which would lead to "revocation" of the license. Several participants stressed the need to create a global "civil society" and to pursue a global agenda of interlinked issues beyond the competence of any one nation to address. (**eroding sovereignty and UN reform**)

225

The UN Role in Intervention: Where Do We Go From Here? Muscatine IA: The Stanley Foundation (216 Sycamore St), June 1993/31p/free. (319/264-1500)

Report of the 28th United Nations of the Next Decade Conference, convened in Salzburg in June 1993. The 19 participants agreed on three fundamental points: 1) that the UN should prepare to play a larger role in dealing with conflicts around the world; 2) that the greatest threats of the future will arise around "survival issues" (poverty, environment, population pressures, migration, human rights); 3) that the world is in the midst of massive change, with globalization altering human linkages and interests. Most participants anticipate that the UN is in for a period of "muddling through" (one participant worried about "too much muddling and not enough getting through"). Most also advocated enhancing UN ability to intervene in conflicts, which will require military planning and moving beyond the ad hoc basis of making military forces available to the UN. This could be done by making arrangements for national troops to be on call to the UN, or by a small standing force that could respond quickly ("an international foreign legion"). Some participants argued that it is time to abandon the concept of collective security and move to a new cooperative security system that gives priority to peaceful conflict prevention. Key elements of such regional systems: avoiding an arms race, rejecting unilateral use of force, seeking mediation of disputes, and using collective force when necessary.

(**UN peacekeeping enhancement**)

226

Human Rights for the 21st Century: Foundations for Responsible Hope. A U.S.—Post-Soviet Dialogue. Edited by Peter Juviler (Co-Director, Columbia U Center for the Study of Human Rights) and Bertram Gross (Distinguished Prof Emeritus, CUNY-Hunter College), with Vladimir Kartashkin (Lumumba U, Moscow) and Elena Lukasheva (Russian Academy of Sciences). Armonk NY: M.E. Sharpe, Oct 1993/288p/$59.95;$19.95pb.

A three-year dialogue constituting the first extensive, multinational attempt to consider the future of human rights in the post-Soviet world. The editors admit that there are huge obstacles; nevertheless, "we look to the year 2000 as the possible dawn of a human rights era...a 21st century whose opening years might become historic turning points in humankind's halting progress toward genuine civilization." One major obstacle is the paradox that, in our present "information age," most people in the world are little informed or misinformed about human rights, their relevance to our needs, their violation, and their fulfillment. Essays are in three parts: **1) The Ex-USSR: Endings and Beginnings**: actors in the drama speak out, nationality rights, rights before October 1917, the need for a common humanitarian space, postcommunist new thinking on human rights; **2) The USA: Progress and Regress**: *Bertram Gross* on the paradox of both triumphs and tragedies, a Russian view of US principles and practice (commenting on social inequality, discrimination, homelessness, women's problems), recurring tests of US civil liberties, double standards in US foreign policy and human rights; **3) Toward the 21st Century**: *Vladimir Kartashkin* on a common global home that rests securely on the rule of international law ("it is time to expand the competence and increase the efficiency of the UN in the sphere of human rights"), *Bertram Gross* and *Vladimir Kartashkin* on goals for a stronger UN (a general conference of UN members in 1995 for reviewing the Charter, appointing the first UN High Commissioner for Human Rights and creating the International Criminal Court, completing the first draft of a global bill of rights and duties in 1998 to observe the 50th anniversary of the Universal Declaration of Human Rights, UN proclamation of the first decade of the new century as "The Human Rights Decade"), *Charles Henry* on human rights education for a new world order, *Riane Eisler* on changing roles of women and men and the partnership model of human rights, *Bertram Gross* on a healthier US, *Henry Shue* on the family of basic rights, and *Peter Juviler* on rethinking rights without communism as a threat. [ALSO SEE: **FS Annual 1995** #13129 for a "U.S./Post-Soviet Dialogue," on transforming work.]

(Human Rights Decade ahead?)

227

Saving Failed States, Gerald B. Helman (former US ambassador to UN-Geneva) and Steven R. Ratner (Council on Foreign Relations), *Foreign Policy*, No. 89, Winter 1992-93, 3-20.

Examples such as Haiti, Yugoslavia, Somalia, Sudan, Liberia, and Cambodia suggest a disturbing new phenomenon: the failed nation-state, utterly incapable of sustaining itself as a member of the international community. As these states descend into violence and anarchy, they imperil their own citizens and threaten their neighbors though refugee flows and random warfare. The current collapse has its roots in the vast proliferation of nation-states since WWII. The "self-determination of peoples," a right enshrined in the UN charter, was given more attention than long-term survivability. The idea that states could fail offended the notions of decolonization and self-determination. Conventional remedies to help people in political and economic distress have met with scant success. In that the traditional view of sovereignty has decayed, it is time to consider an expanded effort by the UN toward nation-saving responsibilities. Three models for UN guardianship are possible: 1) "governance assistance" for states that still have some type of minimal government structure—where a weak state has not yet failed; 2) a more intrusive conservatorship for those states that have failed, where the state delegates certain government functions to the UN; 3) direct UN trusteeship, where states relinquish control over their affairs for a defined period. **(UN guardianship of failed states)**

228

The Future Role of the United Nations in an Interdependent World. Edited by John P. Renninger (UNITAR). Dordrecht & Boston: Martinus Nijhoff, Dec 1989/ 283p/$78.00.

The UN Institute for Training and Research was established to enhance the effectiveness of the UN—a mandate that has never been more relevant than at the present time. These papers from a UNITAR International Roundtable held in Moscow in September 1988 discuss the changing global environment, political and military aspects of international security, world economic problems, sustainable development, and North-South relations. Some major conclusions: 1) the UN had been paralyzed by the Cold War, but rapprochement between the US and USSR provides an opportunity to perform more effectively some of the functions for which the UN was established; 2) the UN role in international security, especially peace-making and peace-keeping, should be enhanced (participation of national contingents in UN forces should be as wide as possible); 3) the UN should assume a global watch responsibility, developing "a type of early warning system for economic, social, environmental, and other global concerns"; 4) the world community is "in great need of a holistic and integrated view of world economic and social problems and possible solutions to them," to be provided by an organ in which the heads of the UN specialized agencies are members; 5) the UN should convene annual summit meetings to be attended by the major economic powers with appropriate representation of other countries; 6) the UN system needs intellectual inputs from the outside, to stimulate and invigorate debates taking place in various UN fora. **(new roles for the UN)**

229

Waiting for the Millennium: The United Nations and the Future of World Order. J. Martin Rochester (Assoc Prof of Political Sci., U of Missouri-St. Louis). Columbia SC: U of South Carolina Press, June 1993/347p/$39.95.

The history of the UN system can be seen as the steady erosion of the initial euphoria in the post-WWII period, with periods of "decline" and "crisis" punctuated by short-term revival and bursts of renewed hope. If it was premature to pronounce the death of the UN in the 1980s, as many had done previously, it is also premature to be euphoric about the UN's future in the 1990s; both "bad realism" and "bad idealism" are to be resisted. In a spirit of "realistic idealism," Rochester discusses the logic of global institution building, the litany of sermons about the global crisis that has desensitized many to the existence of crisis, the present international system (characterized by growing diffusion and ambiguity of power, growing fluidity of alignments, a broadening concept of national security, more intricate patterns of interdependence, the growing role of nonstate actors), the weaknesses of the UN and problems of reform, and such prescriptions as improving competence of UN personnel, a smaller number of super-departments in the UN Secretariat (each to be headed by a Deputy Secretary-General), adopting a Global Risk Assessment Program or Bureau of Global Watch to identify and prioritize problems, and possible Charter reform. [**NOTE**: Cautious thinking, notable for comments about international relations scholars who have tended to steer clear of the UN in recent times "lest they be branded guilty of...utopian futurism and risk pariah status in the

IR fraternity...Excessive use of the terms 'earth' and 'planet' can damage one's credibility." *Avoiding* use of these terms, however, should also be grounds to question credibility.] **(UN reform)**

230

The United Nations and a Just World Order. Edited by Richard A. Falk (Princeton U), Samuel S. Kim (Princeton U) and Saul H. Mendlovitz (Rutgers U School of Law; Director, World Order Models Project). Studies on a Just World Order, No. 3. Boulder CO: Westview Press, Sept 1991/589p/$71.50;$24.95pb.

An anthology of 41 seminal articles and documents in three parts: **1) Changes and Continuities**: what we have learned about peacebuilding, lawmaking and world order, developments in UN decision-making, prospects for global governance, peace and development; **2) The UN and World Order Values**: international peace and security, the new international economic order and the basic needs approach (by Johan Galtung), social justice, and ecological balance; **3) The UN and the Future**: the future of the UN system (by Marc Nerfin), the UN of Tomorrow (by the UN Association of the USA), the case for a World Authority that would still allow nation-states to be maintained, and a proposed Movement For A Just World Peace by Saul Mendlovitz (long-run targets for 2012 include a global tax scheme, complete disarmament with an alternative security system, decision-making authority given to an ecological regime, and a regional and global human rights regime). **(UN and world order values)**

231

One World or None: Prescription for Survival. Errol E. Harris (Prof of Philosophy Emeritus, Northwestern U). Atlantic Highlands NJ: Humanities Press, June 1993/203p/$35.00;$15.00.

The Earth's environment is rapidly being disrupted with potentially disastrous effects on human and other life. Prompt remedial action is imperative, but is not being taken. No expedients can be effective unless they are global in scope; action only by national governments is not sufficient. International agreements to act in concert are of little use unless their observance can be guaranteed. It is thus essential to establish immediately a form of world authority that can legislate globally and enforce world law on individuals without resort to warfare. Chapters discuss the state of the planet (borrowing heavily from **State of the World 1992**), the lack of attention to change, the problem of sovereign nations, power politics, the benefits of an international civil society, countering objections to the idea of world government, the anatomy of a world government (five continental divisions are proposed, broken into not more than 1,000 electoral districts that conform somewhat to present national boundaries), and campaigning for ratification of the Constitution for the Federation of the Earth. A 60-page appendix presents the draft of the Constitution, first ratified at the World Constituent Assembly at Innsbruck in 1977, and most recently amended at the fourth session of the Assembly in 1991. Articles discuss the World Parliament, the World Executive, the Integrative Complex for planning, the World Judiciary, the World Ombudsmus, and an 18-point Bill of Rights for the Citizens of Earth. [**NOTE**: A valuable updating of a perennial idea whose time may yet come. Further information available from the World Constitution and Parliament Association (1480 Hoyt Street, Suite 31, Lakewood, CO 80215), which seeks a "complete paradigm alternative" to replace the UN, which "cannot be changed into a global agency adequate to maintain peace and meet the needs of humanity."]

(Constitution for World Federation)

232

World Union on the Horizon: The Case for Supernational Federation. James A. Yunker (Prof of Economics, Western Illinois U). Lanham MD: University Press of America, April 1993/332p/$56.50;$27.50pb.

"Establishment of a properly designed supernational federation at the present point in world history would substantially improve the probability of a generally favorable evolution of human civilization into the future." A Federal Union of Democratic Nations is proposed that is sufficiently flexible to permit its inauguration in a world dominated by nationalism, yet sufficiently active and substantial to form a viable focus for long-term processes of human unification. In terms of authority and power, it would fall somewhere in-between the UN of today (largely an ineffectual assemblage of speechmakers) and the typical large nation-state. The Union would have legislative, executive, and judicial branches, exercising powers of taxation and armed with military forces. The three major impediments to world government are: 1) ideological conflict, which can be overcome by "democratic market socialism"; 2) nationalism, which can be dealt with by appropriate political design (the single most important right of nation-state members would be that of free secession from the Union, backed up with the right to maintain independent military forces); 3) the economic gap, which can be overcome by a worldwide development program. A World Economic Equalization Program is proposed, involving large-scale transfers of physical and human capital. A simple computer simulation of the program suggests that, at the relatively modest cost of 3-4% of GNP in the richer nations, living standards in the poorest regions could rise to 80-90% of those in the richest regions within 35 years. Concludes that the presence of a supranational state will especially improve prospects for effective action in the interrelated areas of population control and environmental preservation.

(Federal Union of Democratic Nations proposed)

233

Ending War in Our Lifetime: A Concrete, Realistic Plan. Hugh McTavish. Dixon KY: West Fork Press (800/517-7377), Jan 1994/342p/$24.95;$17.95pb.

We can and will soon create permanent world peace. It will be done by creating a Federation of Nations (FON) to keep the peace between its member nations. The only way this can be done is for all member nations to surrender control of their militaries to the FON. It is essential that representatives to FON are democratically elected, and that FON guarantee in all member nations the principle of freedom of speech. Each national member of FON will supply a quota of soldiers and pay for them; remaining expenses will be covered by a tax directly proportional to a nation's Gross National Consumption. Nations will retain the power to regulate their economies and print money, and the FON will not fund projects for economic development (indeed, international trade should be restricted, because it increases the likelihood of war). Because the FON would protect member nations from unrestrained competition, societies would be free to reduce their populations. The parable of the tribes means that, for the past 10,000 years, societies have always competed against each other; fusing our militaries with other nations is not a surrender to the enemy, but a rational step to improve our lives. An appendix provides a proposed constitution for the FON (sees no chance that the FON could evolve from the UN). [**NOTE**: Idealistic, bombastic, and verbose—but perhaps of some interest to a few readers. The book is

234
Planning in the UN City. Ha-Sang Yoo (NYC). NY: Vantage Press, Oct 1987/243p/$16.95.

A US citizen born and raised in South Korea describes major shortcomings of the present United Nations location (a noisy and polluted area, haphazard scattering of missions, inadequate space, etc.) and proposes locating UN headquarters in a neutral nation, perhaps a unified East and West Germany to symbolize objectives of world peace. The World Capital Zone and UN City would include 150 national towns constructed in a harmonious way. The UN could be financially supported by a quasi-independent international corporation that operates hotels and transport services. Chapters give details on UN City design, peace building architecture, peace space, the traffic system, parks and recreational facilities, and other UN Cities in the world to spread the peaceful mood. A companion volume, **Administering the UN City** (Vantage, 1987/277p/$16.95), describes the UN City charter, the relationship between the UN and UN City, the UN Corporation and revenue raising (the UN Air Line, the UN Bank, the UN Mass Media), and the relationship between UN City and the host nation. [**NOTE**: A naive utopia with various charts, figures, diagrams and drawings—but despite awkwardness and idealistic verbiage, the basic idea is intriguing: why not move the UN? The national towns idea, incidentally, is somewhat like the World Showcase area at Walt Disney's Epcot Center.]

(**UN City proposed**)

3. Culture Lag and UNESCO's Potential Role

235
Vancouver Declaration. Final Report of UNESCO Symposium on Science and Culture for the 21st Century: Agenda for Survival. Ottawa K1P 5V8: Canadian Commission for UNESCO (99 Metcalfe St), July 1990/314p.

The Declaration, from a September 1989 symposium in Vancouver, states that "Survival of the planet has become of central and immediate concern. The present situation requires urgent measures in all sectors—scientific, cultural, economic, and political, and a greater sensitization of all mankind." Our species has become by far the largest factor for change on the planet. The consequences are human population growth, global pollution, an accelerating destruction of the habitat of life, and expenditure of resources on war and preparing for war. The origin of our predicament lies fundamentally in certain developments in science: especially the classical, mechanical picture of the universe. The present situation requires new visions rooted in a variety of cultures: the perception of an organic macrocosm that recaptures the rhythms of life, overcoming the fragmentation of the body-spirit-mind unity, and a radical transformation of models of development. Science and technology are indispensable, but can only succeed through an integration of science and culture that leads to a sense of purpose, and an integrative approach designed to overcome the fragmentation that has led to a breakdown in cultural communication. "Time is short—every delay in establishing a world eco-cultural peace will only increase the cost of survival."

The 17 signatories to the declaration include Mahdi Elmandjra, Carl-Goran Hedén (President, World Academy of Arts and Sciences), Alexander King (President, Club of Rome), Eleonora Masini (President, WFSF), Digby McLaren (President, Royal Society of Canada), and Soedjatmoko (former Rector, UNU). The bulk of the volume is devoted to working papers and presentations on the role of man in the universe, production-investment-control processes in the environment, creativeness and survival, reconciling the diversity of interests with freedom and human rights, ethics and survival, predicting the evolution and cultural dimensions of change, science and survival, fusion of science and culture as key to the 21st century, and social innovations for survival.

(**integrative science for survival**)

236
Global Mind Change: The Promise of the Last Years of the Twentieth Century. Willis Harman (President, Institute of Noetic Sciences, Sausolito CA). Indianapolis IN: Knowledge Systems, Inc. (7777 W. Morris St), March 1988/185p/$16.95.

Former engineering professor at Stanford and futures researcher at SRI International states that, throughout history, the most fundamental changes in societies have come not from dictates of governments and the results of war, but through vast numbers of people changing their mainds—sometimes only a little bit. Every society's knowledge system is parochial—even modern science. The knowledge system of our society is based on positivism and reductionism, while ignoring altruism, courage, virtue, and eternal values. "It is impossible to create a well-working society on a knowledge base which is fundamentally inadequate, seriously incomplete, and mistaken in basic assumptions." Indeed, we appear to be going through a profound change in our dominant metaphysic, from one that studies only the measurable world and views the basic stuff of the universe as matter-energy, to one that views mind or consciousness to be primary. This may seem as outrageous as the heliocentric universe did in early 17th century Europe; it can be seen as "the second Copernican revolution," in that no such fundamental change has occurred in Western thought for four centuries. The value emphases of the trans-modern world will probably include at least the following: man in harmony with man (a rebalancing of the masculine and the feminine, and a great leveling of rich and poor societies), individual self-realization, decentralization and an appreciation of cultural diversity (an ecology of cultures), and the global management of global issues (care and use of oceans and atmosphere, sharing resources, and control of chemicals and weapons). This shift at a fundamental level of belief implies basic change in our institutions, along with redefinitions of work, global development, global security, and beliefs in the feasibility of peace. If the basic assumptions underlying modern society are shifting, society in only a few generations will be as different from today's modern industrial society as today differs from the Middle Ages—and in ways that we can only vaguely intuit. [**NOTE**: Harman has no suggestions as to how to speed up this transformation. Indeed, much of his argument is familiar, e.g. Harman announced "The New Copernican Revolution" 19 years ago (*Stanford Today*, Winter 1969). Nevertheless, this "impossible future" (see Basil McDermott, **On the Future of the Impossible**, *Alternatives: Social Transformation and Human Governance*, 13:1, Jan 1988, 103-116, **FS Annual 1988-89** #8825) may be underway—although not quite as Harman envisions it—and only now beginning to quicken its pace. Even if less than Copernican in its dimensions, could there be any more important vision of the future to consider?]

(**a second Copernican revolution?**)

237
Cosmopolis: The Hidden Agenda of Modernity. Stephen Toulmin (Prof of Humanities, Northwestern U). NY: The Free Press, Jan 1990/228p/$22.95.

In the 17th century, a vision of society arose that captivated the western mind for the next 300 years. It was a vision of Cosmopolis, a society as rationally ordered. The vision fueled extraordinary advances in all fields of human endeavor while perpetuating a hidden agenda: the delusion that human nature and society could be fitted into precise and managable rational categories. The modern era of Descartes and Newton became synonymous with the pursuit of strict rationality. But the idolization of a narrow rationality distracted people from the concrete and practical demands of human life and nature. Under the weight of the passions and predicaments of the 20th century, these wishful intellectual structures have collapsed. In the transition to Post-Modernity, we have a choice between two attitudes toward the future: we can face the future and ask about the "futuribles" open to us, or back into it with no such horizons or ideas. But "far from extrapolating confidently into the social and cultural future, we are now stranded and uncertain of our location." The project of Modernity has lost momentum, and we need to fashion a successor program. But, with eyes lowered, we are backing into a new millennium, with little serious attention to the questions of where we shall be. We can neither cling to Modernity in its historic form, nor reject it totally. The task is to reform our inherited modernity by humanizing it. "The key problem is no longer to ensure that our social and national systems are *stable*; rather, it is to ensure that intellectual and social procedures are more *adaptive*." All the changes of mind that were characteristic of the 17th century's turn from humanism to rationalism are being reversed: the Modern focus on the written, the general, the universal, and the timeless is being broadened to include the oral, the particular, the local, and the timely. The social and political functions that need serving after 2000 call for more subnational and transnational institutions, and the ideas of ecosystems and adaptability. [**NOTE**: An academically reputable version of futurist Willis Harman's **Global Mind Change** (above).]

(**transition to Post-Modernity**)

238
New World, New Mind: Moving Toward Conscious Evolution. Robert Ornstein (President, Institute for the Study of Human Knowledge) and Paul Ehrlich (Prof of Biological Sciences, Stanford U). NY: Doubleday, Jan 1989/302p/$18.95 (Simon and Schuster Touchstone edition, April 1990/$9.95pb).

The human mental system is failing to comprehend the increasingly changing and dangerous modern world. Events will continue to be out of control until people realize how selectively the environment impresses the human mind, and how our comprehension is determined by our biological and cultural history. Our nervous system and our world are mismatched; we are out of joint with our times, and are losing control of our future. The mismatch interferes with the relationships of human beings to each other and with their environments. Human beings have to adapt to the environments in which they live. The only means of resolving the problem is through conscious change. Biological evolution is much too slow to help, and undirected cultural evolution is still too sluggish. We must take evolution into our own hands and create a new evolutionary process based on a different kind of education and training to help us understand long-term threats. For example, we should be teaching probability in our elementary mathematics (everyone makes probabilistic decisions daily) instead of algebra (one of the least-used kinds of mathematics).

The old mind is being challenged by many scattered efforts. Can we bring these efforts together to produce a large-scale program for a rapid change of mind? A "curriculum about humanity" is proposed to counter the "hacked-up knowledge [that] makes it impossible for most people to decode their world." A basic education should center not on memorizing Trivial Pursuit-like details, but on understanding ourselves, our society, our environment, and our possibilities. Unfortunately, there is a chicken-or-egg problem: the key to changing the curriculum is changing the minds of adults, and the key to new-minded adults seems to be training them early. So both must be attempted at once. Because the rate of change is increasing, adapting to change and the notion of "fleeting truths" must be the center of any new kind of teaching. [ALSO SEE: **To Govern Evolution** by Walter Truett Anderson (#022 in this Guide), not cited by the authors.]

(**new mind needed for a new world**)

239
Higher Education Cannot Escape History: Issues for the Twenty-First Century. Clark Kerr (President Emeritus, UC). Frontiers in Education Series. Albany NY: State U of NY Press, Jan 1994/248p/$59.50;$19.95pb.

"Higher education cannot escape history as it moves from serving royalty and the upper classes, the ancient professions and the church, to serving all persons and all institutions in the more industrialized societies of modern times and in societies based more on new knowledge and higher skills." Although it follows its own internal logic of development, especially in response to its faculties, higher education has never been fully autonomous, and much of its history has been written by confrontations of internal vs. external pressures.

These essays from the past two decades discuss such topics as the increasing influence of the nation-state over higher education, the internationalization of learning, programs to foster a more adequate global perspective [**FS Annual 1987** #8632], heritage vs. change, rising controversies over "equality," a "convergence model" of universal access and advancement of merit, the academic ethic and the professoriate, the decline of academic citizenship (observance of ethics, willingness to participate in shared governance effectively), four orientations to purposes of higher education (status quo preservationists, evolutionary expansionists who welcome new forms, concentrationists who would select one true mission, and transformationists who would use higher education to change society), and the purposes of US higher education.

Of particular interest is a 1992 essay introducing José Ortega y Gasset's **Mission of the University** (1930; Transaction Books, 1992). Kerr agrees with Ortega's emphasis on "general culture" as the great theme of the day: the system of ideas concerning the world and man which belong to our times. He then makes his own list of "the expected great ideas and great issues of the 21st century so that students might better be able to cope with the challenges of the new age" (p174). They include issues of war/peace/conflict resolution, the roles of religion and nationality, gender/race/class, pathologies of industrial civilization, implications of the information revolution, the population explosion and the future of the environment, prospects for Third World nations, new mentalities and new cultures, problems of transition away from communism, competition in the global economy, comparative cultures, and decision-making processes. Such a curriculum centered on general culture would give students a broad learning experience, "helping them to think horizontally as well as vertically." [**NOTE**: This could also be described as an exemplary curriculum for futures studies or world futures.]

("**general culture" curriculum needed**)

*240
Preparing for the Twenty-First Century. Paul Kennedy (Prof of History, Yale U). NY: Random House, March 1993/428p/$25.00.

Author of **The Rise and Fall of the Great Powers** (Random House, 1987; **FS Annual 1988-89** #8862) shifts his focus to consider humanity's encounter with technology, economic change, and population growth. "The greatest test for human society as it confronts the 21st century is how to use the power of technology to meet the demands thrown up by the power of population; that is, how to find effective global solutions in order to free the poorer three-quarters of humankind from the growing Malthusian trap of malnutrition, starvation, resource depletion, unrest, enforced migration, and armed conflict—developments that will also endanger the richer nations, if less directly." Chapters in **Part 1** discuss general trends: the demographic explosion, the communications revolution and the rise of multinational corporations (global transmission of information may not necessarily lead to universal enthusiasm for the Western way of life), world agriculture and the biotechnology revolution (biotech could very well worsen the indebtedness and trading position of 7 poor countries), robotics and automation (longer-term implications threaten to exacerbate the global dilemma by eliminating many jobs), dangers to our natural environment, the declining usefulness of the nation-state (but no adequate substitute has emerged to replace it). In sum, the population explosion in the poor nations will lead to increased environmental damage and social stress, while globalization and new technologies in the rich nations may undermine traditional methods and locations of agriculture, manufacturing, and business in general.

Chapters in **Part 2** consider the preparedness of the world's regions and nations: **1) Japan**: probably the country least likely to be hurt by overpopulation, mass migration, environmental disasters, and globalized production; Japan has a purposeful and utilitarian education system, and is engaged in the most enormous industrial retooling for growth that the world has ever seen (but it faces considerable dangers such as nuclear proliferation in Asia and a surge in Chinese power); **2) India and China**: both nations are in a race against time to keep their population growth from eroding gains in agriculture and manufacturing; gains in the standard of living threaten the local environment and the earth's atmosphere; **3) The Developing World**: the developed economies appear to have all the trump cards in their hands and their advantages are growing as technology erodes the value of labor and materials (the chief assets of LDCs); a small but growing number of countries is moving away from "have-not" status, but many more remain behind; **4) The Erstwhile USSR and its Crumbled Empire**: the region's many problems could have serious impacts elsewhere, but the nations of Eastern and Central Europe do have lots of talented and ambitious people, and "at least they are out of jail"; **5) Europe**: the EC nations appear relatively comfortable, but face major challenges in creating a thriving unified body which will assume a responsible world role; **6) The US**: it may not be a "loser" from global change, but it could be less than a clear "winner"; the US will probably continue to muddle through (as Britain did a century ago when faced with a similar erosion of power), with the long-term implication of steady and relative decline.

Concludes by emphasizing three key elements in any general effort to prepare for the 21st century: enhancing the role of education, improving the status of women, and intelligent political leadership. "If my analysis is roughly correct, the forces for change facing the world could be so far-reaching, complex, and interactive that they call for nothing less than the reeducation of humankind." [**NOTE**: Outstanding survey of global trends and sobering regional prospects. Amply deserves its Spring 1993 best-seller status.] (**population/technology impacts**)

241
Is Humanity Suicidal? Edward O. Wilson (Prof of Science, Harvard U), *The New York Times Magazine*, 30 May 1993, 24-29.

From the great diversity of large animals, *Homo sapiens* has gained intelligent control of Earth. Unlike any creature that lived before, we have become a geophysical force. The human species has doubled to 5.5 billion in the past 50 years, and is scheduled to double again in the next 50 years. But our species retains hereditary traits that add greatly to our destructive impact. We are tribal and aggressively territorial. In our search for food, we have reduced animal life in rivers, lakes, and now, increasingly, the open ocean. Everywhere we pollute the air and water, lower water tables, and extinguish species. With people everywhere seeking a better quality of life, the search for resources is expanding even faster than population. It is accelerated further by a parallel rise in environment-devouring technology.

Opinions on the human prospect fall loosely into two schools. *Exemptionalism* holds that, since humankind is transcendent in intelligence and spirit, our species has been released from the iron laws of ecology that bind other species, and that civilized human beings will somehow find a solution. The opposing idea of reality is *environmentalism*, which sees humanity as a biological species tightly dependent on the natural world. At the heart of this worldview is the conviction that human physical and spiritual health depends on sustaining the planet in a relatively unaltered state. Wilson argues that we are smart enough and have time enough to avoid an environmental catastrophe. But a redirection of much of science and technology will be required, as well as a reconsideration of our self-image as a species. There are reasons to believe that we have entered what will someday be called the Century of the Environment. The human hand is now upon the physical homeostat, with actions having been taken to restore the ozone layer and a good prospect of slowing global warming. But the human hand is not upon the biological homeostat. "Humanity is now destroying most of the habitats where evolution can occur." Mass extinctions are being reported with increasing frequency in every part of the world, and the reports are probably only a very small percentage of the actual number. Perhaps within 50 to 100 years, more science and entrepreneurship will be devoted to stabilizing the global environment. (**Century of the Environment under way**)

242
Science for the Post-Normal Age, Silvio O. Funtowicz and Jerome R. Ravetz (both at The Research Methods Consultancy, London), *Futures*, 25:7, Sept 1993, 739-755.

In every age, science is shaped around its leading problems, and it evolves with them. After centuries of triumph and optimism, science is now called on to remedy the pathologies of the global industrial system. Science was previously understood as steadily advancing in the certainty of our knowledge and control of the natural world; it is now seen as coping with many uncertainties in risk and environment issues. The reductionist, analytical worldview is being replaced by a systemic, synthetic, and humanistic approach. The old dichotomies of facts and values, and of knowledge and ignorance, are being transcended. Natural systems are now recognized as dynamic and complex. The science appropriate to this new condition will be based on assumptions of unpredictability, incomplete control, and a plurality of legitimate perspectives. Evaluation of scientific inputs to decision-making will require an extended peer community—an extension of legitimacy to new participants in policy dialogues. This democratization of science is not a matter of benevolence; rather, it is the most effective means for avoiding disasters that result from stifling of criticism. Post-normal science is also a response to the current tendencies of postmodernity, which reflects the loss of hegemony of a single worldview. **(post-normal science emerging)**

243

One Society, One Wissenschaft: A 21st Century Vision, Howard Newby (Chairman, Economic and Social Research Council, Swindon UK), *Science and Public Policy*, 19:1, Feb 1992, 7-14.

The 27th Annual Lecture of the International Science Policy Foundation, noting that the "linear model" of science translating into technology which provides the impetus for social and economic progress is incomplete. It creates a vocabulary that is a major obstacle to the crossfertilization of the social sciences and the natural sciences. An "interactive model" is needed that takes into account the relationship between science, technology, and society. Social science should be an integral activity in understanding the process where science and technology leads to economic and social well-being. There are signs that the tide is beginning to turn in the age-old debate in the natural sciences between reductionism and holism. Many branches of the natural sciences have come to appreciate that at least part of the world may best be characterized by complex outcomes and non-linear relationships. There is a growing acceptance that analysis of the whole is qualitatively much more complex than multiple analyses of the parts. Chaos theory marks one of modern science's first attempts to recognize the importance of the complex world of outcomes, as distinct from underlying laws. If the natural world is inherently chaotic, then the natural sciences, the social sciences, and the humanities share a common cause in domesticating the world just enough so that we can live with it. We should thus welcome the re-emergence of one *Wissenschaft*, the unity of knowledge.

(transition to broader interactive model)

244

Schools for the Twenty-First Century, David Orr (Prof of Education, Oberlin College), *Resurgence*, No 160, Sept-Oct 1993, 16-19. (Extracts from an Oct 1992 Schumacher Lecture; full text from Schumacher Society, Box 76, RD3, Gt. Barrington MA 01230.)

Most people in industrialized societies believe that their educational systems need radical reform. Although divided about how to go about it, there is wide agreement on the need to make society more competitive in the global economy. But there are better reasons to rethink education related to issues of human survival. The generation now being educated will have to do what we have been unable or unwilling to do: stabilize world population, reduce greenhouse gases, protect biological diversity, conserve soils, use energy and materials with great efficiency, etc. For the most part, however, we are still educating the young as if there were no planetary emergency. "Resolution of the great ecological challenges of the next century will require us to reconsider the substance, process, and purposes of education at all levels." Necessary tasks include: 1) developing more comprehensive and ecologically solvent standards for truth—a broader science and a more inclusive rationality; 2) challenging the hubris in the hidden curriculum that economic growth is good and all knowledge is equally valuable; 3) addressing the flaw in the modern curriculum that teaches a great deal about individualism and rights, but little about citizenship and responsibilities; 4) questioning the widespread assumption that our future is one of constantly evolving technology and that this is desirable; 5) encouraging ecological education, which requires the re-integration of experience into education, a new curriculum organized around the "ecological design arts," spreading ecological intelligence throughout the curriculum, thinking how we might reconnect things, and ecological management of institutions. [NOTE: This long-term futures perspective is notably absent from other educational critiques. ALSO SEE: Orr's book on **Ecological Literacy** (SUNY Press, 1992; **FS Annual 1993** #12006), **Education, Cultural Myths, and the Ecological Crisis** by C.A. Bowers (SUNY Press, 1993; **FS Annual 1994** #12613), and **Critical Essays on Education, Modernity, and the Recovery of the Ecological Imperative** by C.A. Bowers (NY: Teachers College Press, June 1993/220p/$45.00;$18.95pb).]

(ecological education for long-term survival)

245

Peace & World Security Studies: A Curriculum Guide (Sixth Edition). Edited by Michael T. Klare (Prof of Peace and World Security Studies, Hampshire College, Amherst MA). Boulder CO: Lynne Rienner Publishers, May 1994/425p/$22.00pb.

Formerly titled **Peace and World Order Studies**, the new title reflects expansion of the field to encompass a broader range of threats to human well-being and survival. *Part 1* provides five essays on new directions in peace studies, discussing the post-Cold War era, new approaches to international peacemaking, a Third World view of global peace and security, a feminist perspective, and the nexus between peace studies and international security studies. *Part 2* provides thoughtful essays and 2-4 representative course syllabi for each of 14 areas: introductory courses in peace studies, war and peace in the post-Cold War era, the new nuclear agenda, North-South relations, conflict resolution, international law and the UN, psychology and peace, the economics of peace and security, development and global poverty, the environment and population growth, human rights, racial and ethnic conflict, feminist perspectives on militarism and violence, and nonviolent movements.

(peace curriculum guide)

246

Global Politics in the Human Interest. 2nd Edition. Mel Gurtov (Dir of Intl Studies, Portland State U). Boulder CO: Lynne Rienner Pubs, July 1991/271p/$16.95pb.

First published in 1988 (**FS Annual 1988-89** #8827), this textbook seeks to redefine national and global security in ways that promote the "human interest," defined as satisfaction of the basic material and nonmaterial needs of the great majority of the planet's people. Underlying the analysis is a set of Global Humanist values, stressing peace, social and economic justice, political justice, ecological balance, and humane governance. These values carry a set of positive assumptions about the nature of humankind, and optimism about prospects for humane change.

Global Humanism is prompted by both idealism and a hardheaded concern about structural violence within and between societies. It seeks to go beyond left and right, and has an explicitly normative approach, in contrast to Realism and Corporate Globalism, which claim to be a value-free framework for understanding the world system.

Chapters discuss the state of the planet, interdependence, Realism and Corporate Globalism contrasted with Global Humanism, human rights and underdevelopment in the Third World (encompassing 75% of world population), the military crisis of the two First World superpowers (with special attention to the nuclear danger), and the quest for security in the "Second World" of advanced economies (East and West Europe, Japan, Canada, Australia, and New Zealand). Concludes with an agenda for transforming world politics in the human interest, which includes: 1) setting the conditions for food self-reliance (perhaps the single most important objective in world politics today); 2) environmental protection as part of a program of humane economic and social development; 3) developing incentives for states to avoid war and move to a common security system; 4) addressing unemployment by redirecting investment into agriculture and work cooperatives; 5) education for a global citizenry.

(**world politics and Global Humanist values**)

247
International Futures: Choices in the Creation of a New World Order. Barry B. Hughes (Prof of International Relations, U of Denver). Boulder CO: Westview Press, Aug 1993/205p/$49.95 (includes software disk).

A textbook on potential global developments, combined with a computer simulation model called International Futures (IFs) that simulates population, food, energy, environmental, economic, and political developments from 1990 to 2035 in 10 geographic regions of the world. Chapters discuss action in the face of uncertainty, values and the future (material progress vs. sustainability, economic growth vs. equality, individual security vs. collective security), global change (demography, energy, environment, technology, economy), using a model to investigate change, pursuing security and peace, pursuing economic well-being and equality, modernism vs. ecoholism, and preferred futures (IFs allows selection of up to ten "goal variables"). [**NOTE**: Does not advocate any specific vision, but seeks to help the student develop one. Hughes is also the author of **World Futures** (Johns Hopkins, 1985; **FS Annual 1985** #6465) and **Continuity and Change in World Politics** (Prentice-Hall, 2nd edition, Aug 1993), which he recommends as a companion volume to **IF**.]

(**International Futures computer model**)

248
Global Order: Values and Power in International Politics. Third Edition. Lynn H. Miller (Prof of Political Science, Temple U). Boulder CO: Westview Press, April 1994/269p/$55.00;$17.95pb.

An update of the 1990 second edition (**FS Annual 1991** #10297), with chapters discussing optimistic and pessimistic visions of human capability, changing social values, the growth of the Westphalian system, the 20th century challenge to the Westphalian order of nation-states, realism vs. idealism in international politics, statist vs. world order perspectives, minimizing the resort to violence, peacemaking for the 21st century, the search for economic well-being (curbing population growth, transnational corporations, fulfilling basic needs), development of international human rights standards, intervention in the name of human rights, the closing of the world frontier (humanity's impact on a shrinking planet, the end of limitless abundance, the changing Law of the Sea), and better times in a globally integrated civilization (true security, economic justice, human dignity). [**NOTE**: The topics covered in this textbook appear to have changed little, if at all, from the first edition of 1990, which also topped out at 269 pages.] (**global order textbook**)

249
World Politics: Trend and Transformation (Fourth Edition). Charles W. Kegley Jr (U of South Carolina; President, International Studies Assn) and Eugene R. Wittkopf (Louisiana State U). NY: St. Martin's Press, 1993/614p/$35.95pb.

Since 1989, the world has witnessed dramatic and virtually unimaginable changes. The end of the Cold War is propelling a transformation of world politics whose scope and dimensions continue to unfold daily. Today, the world stands on the threshold of a new era; yet, despite all that is radically different, there is much that remains the same. Chapters in this textbook are in four parts: **1) Change and Transformation**: image and reality, realist and idealist world views, a systems theory of international politics, neoliberal institutionalism (complex interdependence as a world view), theories of change (long-cycle theory, world system theory, dependency theory or the pattern of dominance); **2) Relations Among Global Actors**: foreign policy decision-making, the role of leaders in making world history, great power rivalry in the 20th century, the North-South conflict over global inequality, nonstate actors (the UN, EC, NGOs, multinational corporations); **3) Low Politics** (matters of material well-being): the world political economy, free trade and protectionism, the international monetary regime, North-South relations, demographic trends, population projections, food security, managing the global commons, emigration patterns, the political economy of oil; **4) High Politics** (war/peace issues): trends in military capabilities, war and other modes of violence, paths to peace.

A concluding chapter poses 12 questions about the future; how they are answered will significantly shape world politics for decades to come: Are nation-states obsolete? Is interdependence a cure or curse? What is the "national interest?" Are technological innovations a blessing or burden? Of what value is military power? Is war obsolete? Has the quest for empire ended? (If so, why prepare for military defense?) What price military pre-eminence? Is the world preparing for the wrong war? Is human well-being better off in a world of perpetual growth or a steady-state economy? Are we witnessing the "end of history" as far as the struggle between despotism and democracy is concerned? Will geoeconomics or ecopolitics replace geopolitics? Is a new world order unfolding?

(**world political trends textbook**)

*250
Scholarship Reconsidered: Priorities of the Professoriate (Special Report). Ernest L. Boyer (President, Carnegie Foundation). Princeton NJ: The Carnegie Foundation for the Advancement of Teaching, Dec 1990/147p/$8.00pb (dist. by Princeton U Press).

On campuses across the US, there is a recognition that the faculty reward system does not match the full range of academic functions, and that professors are often caught between competing obligations. Too often, students are the losers because teaching is not well rewarded. Moreover, the disciplines have become increasingly divided, the curriculum is fragmented, and the educational experience of students frequently lacks coherence. A new vision of scholarship is required that clarifies campus missions and relates the work of the academy more directly to the realities of contemporary life. The work of the professoriate should be seen as four separate, yet overlapping functions: **1) The Scholarship of Discovery**: research that contributes to the stock of human knowledge and the intellectual climate of an institution; **2) The Scholarship of Integration**: making connections across the disciplines and placing the specialties in larger context (such work is increasingly important, as traditional disciplinary categories prove confining); **3) The Scholarship of Application**: service activities tied directly to one's field of knowledge and relating it to real life (such service is serious and demanding work, requiring the rigor traditionally associated with research activities); **4) The Scholarship of Teaching**: the work of the professor becomes consequential only as it is understood by others (teaching at its best means not only transmitting knowledge, but transforming and extending it). A diverse national network of colleges and universities is needed, in which the full range of human talent is celebrated and rewarded; each institution should take pride in its own distinctive mission, and seek to complement rather than imitate the others. [**NOTE**: An important redefinition that could help promote the necessarily integrative study of world futures. The report politely avoids the harsh criticism (**FS Annual 1991** #10820/10824) that much of what poses as "research," often forced by perverse institutional reward systems, is trivial and/or useless by any reasonable standard.]

(**four types of scholarship**)

ADDENDUM

*250-A

Uncommon Opportunities: An Agenda for Peace and Equitable Development. Report of the International Commission on Peace and Food (M.S. Swaminathan, Chairman; Madras, India). London and Atlantic Highlands NJ: Zed Books, Oct 1994/210p/$55.00;$19.95pb.

"The astonishing events of the past few years...make this a time of uncommon opportunities for accelerated progress on issues of concern to all humankind." The ICPF, largely supported by grants from UNDP and UNESCO, seeks to build on the work of earlier independent commissions chaired by Willy Brandt, Gro Harlem Bruntland, and Julius Nyerere. In an opening "Message From the UN Secretary General," **Boutros Boutros-Ghali** points to the broad range of topics examined here, demonstrating the interrelated nature of the challenges of peace and development. "Reflecting on development is...the most important intellectual challenge of the coming years." It seems clear that macro-economic growth can no longer be deemed sufficient for development purposes: for economic and social development to take place, it is important to promote expansion of employment opportunities, improvement of educational and health networks, support for the role of women in development, pursuit of equality between the sexes, and democratization—"a hitherto ignored dimension of the development challenge." In the Foreword, **Federico Mayor** (Director General, UNESCO) points to the "overriding challenge of nurturing a worldwide culture of peace," and the many unsettling ideas of the Commission that "should be encouraged since imagination and daring are precisely what we need at the present time." The Commission held five plenary meetings in the 1989-1993 period, and this report is based on the findings of six working groups studying a wide gamut of issues in the emerging global context.

The report concludes that we have all the resources necessary to arrive at "a system that guarantees the right of each individual to human security in its widest meaning—peace, food, employment, and education for all." A global community of democratic nations is the greatest safeguard against war and famine, and the climate of freedom which democracy generates is highly conducive to rapid economic development. The new international political climate has also created the possibility of a massive redirection of resources from defense to development. A "new intellectual perspective" is needed to entertain the possibility of completely abolishing war as an instrument of national policy, to carry the movement of democratization to its logical conclusion (making a representative form of government the minimum requirement for participation in the UN), to create a new cooperative security paradigm, to recognize employment as "a fundamental human right that must be guaranteed by all," to accelerate agricultural development, and to recognize that humankind is the master of its own destiny.

The central thrust of the Commission's proposals is summarized in 15 strategies: 1) *restructuring the UN* to make it more representative and democratically functioning; 2) replacing the state-centered competitive security framework with a *cooperative security system* that unconditionally guarantees the security of member nations by means of a standing world army; 3) drawing up a detailed plan for a *50% reduction in global defense* spending by the year 2000, with resources re-deployed to combat poverty and environmental degradation; 4) placing a proposal before the Security Council for a *universal ban on possession of nuclear weapons* by any nation; 5) coordinating strategies for *full employment* as a human right in all countries, by removing tax disincentives for job creation, ending the bias toward capital-intensive technology, raising minimal education and training standards, improving labor market information, etc.; "as long as we continue to believe that society is truly helpless to manage job growth, there will be strong resistance to the full employment goal...full employment can be achieved by any country that has the will and determination to achieve it"; 6) promoting commercial agriculture and agro-industries can *create one billion jobs* in developing countries in the next decade; 7) adopting a *global employment program* at the 1995 UN Summit, focusing on elimination of protectionist trade policies, debt rescheduling, and accelerated technology dissemination; 8) create an *international development force* under the UN consisting of demobilized military personnel and young professionals, to promote people-centered, sustainable development initiatives; 9) establish *model district programs* in many countries to improve use of natural, technological, human, institutional, and financial resources in a sustainable manner; 10) *eliminate crop losses* in the former USSR by acquiring foreign production and storage technology supported with massive public education; 11) build up new social institutions to support *education in entrepreneurial and management skills*|; 12) *launch a worldwide program to improve the quantity and quality of education* in all nations; 13) negotiate an international *agreement to alleviate debt* for the 60 poorest countries; 14) continue the *shift in thinking about development* not just as material achievements but as a social process by which human beings develop their capacities and release their energies for higher achievement; 15) give highest priority to *controlling and reversing the proliferation of small arms* in all countries; agreements should severely restrict production and sales.

[**NOTE**: A remarkably integrative and inspiring report that ties together many key concerns (full employment, disarmament, development, sustainability) into a bold and original package. It truly deserves to be in a category by itself, and ought to be a lodestar for thinking, debate, and action for many years. This is what good futures thinking ought to be about, articulating "what is imminently possible, not what is immediately inevitable."]

(global full employment possible)

PUBLISHER/TITLE INDEX

Ablex Publishing Corp., 355 Chestnut Street, Norwood NJ 07648
- *The Technology Gamble* (Hamelink, 1988) #108

Anchor/Doubleday, 1540 Broadway, New York NY 10036
- *The Gaia Atlas of First Peoples* (Burger, 1990) #190
- *New World, New Mind* (Ornstein/Ehrlich, 1989) #238

Atlantic Monthly Press, 19 Union Square West, 11th Floor, New York NY 10003
- *The Life Era* (Chaisson, 1987) #031

Ballantine Books, (div. of Random House), 201 East 50th Street, New York NY 10022
- *Spiritual Politics* (McLaughlin/Davidson, 1994) #203

Bantam Books, 666 Fifth Avenue, New York NY 10019
- *Powershift* (Toffler, 1990) #051

BasicBooks, 10 East 53rd Street, New York NY 10022
- *A Framework for Survival* (Cahill, ed., 1993) #145

Blackwell Publishers/Blackwell Business, 238 Main Street, Cambridge MA 02142
- *Global Formation* (Chase-Dunn, 1989) #131
- *The Race to the Intelligent State* (Connors, 1993) #097
- *Managing in the Information Society* (Masuda, 1990) #100
- *Service Industries in the World Economy* (Daniels, 1993) #122

Beacon Press, 25 Beacon Street, Boston MA 02108
- *State of the Peoples* (Miller, 1993) #189

Brookings Institution, 1775 Massachusetts Ave NW, Washington DC 20036
- *Global Engagement* (Nolan, ed., 1994) #087
- *Protecting the Dispossessed* (Deng, 1993) #142

Business One Irwin, c/o Richard D. Irwin, 1818 Ridge Road, Homewood IL 60430
- *The Secret Empire* (Lowe, 1992) #114

Cambridge University Press, 40 West 20th Street, New York NY 10011
- *Governance Without Government* (Rosenau/Czempiel, eds., 1992) #045

Canadian Commission for UNESCO, 99 Metcalf St., Ottawa, Ontario K1P 5V8 Canada
- *Vancouver Declaration* (1990) #235

Carnegie Foundation for the Advancement of Teaching, 5 Ivy Lane, Princeton NJ 08540
- *Scholarship Reconsidered* (Boyar, 1990) #250

Celestial Arts, c/o Ten Speed Press, PO Box 7327, Berkeley CA 94707
- *The Creative Imperative* (Johnston, 1986) #028

Chatham House Publishers, Box 1, Chatham NJ 07928
- *The Real World Order* (Singer/Wildavsky, 1993) #066

Chelsea Green Publishing, PO Box 428, White River Junction VT 05001
- *Beyond the Limits* (Meadows et al., 1992) #162

Conway Data Incorporated, 40 Technology Park, Atlanta GA 30313
- *A Glimpse of the Future* (Conway, 1992) #012

Cornell University Press, 124 Roberts Place, Ithaca NY 14850
- *The Global Restructuring of Agro-Food Systems* (McMichael, ed., 1994) #123

Council on Foreign Relations Press, 58 East 68th Street, New York NY 10021
- *Enforcing Restraint* (Damrosch, ed., 1993) #073
- *A Framework for Survival* (Cahill, ed., 1993) #145
- *Managing the World Economy* (Cowhey/Aronson, eds., 1993) #113
- *Nation Against State* (Gottlieb, 1993) #056

Crossroad/Continuum, 370 Lexington Ave, New York NY 10017
- *Global Responsibility* (Kung, 1991) #204

Crown Publishers, (div. of Random House), 201 East 50th Street, New York NY 10022
- *Savages and Civilization* (Weatherford, 1994) #058

EarthPress, 4882 Kellog Circle, Boulder CO 80303
- *Agenda 21* (Sitarz, ed., 1993) #158

Wm. B. Eerdmans Publishing Co., 255 Jefferson Ave SE, Grand Rapids MI 45903
- *The Technological Bluff* (Ellul, 1990) #109
- *What I Believe* (Ellul, 1989) #036

Edward Elgar c/o **Ashgate Publishing Co.** Old Post Road, Brookfield VT 05036
- *The End of Sovereignty?* (Camilleri/Falk, 1992) #047

Ford Foundation, 320 E 43rd Street, New York NY 10017
- *Renewing the United Nations System* (Childers/Urquhart, 1994) #214

Foreign Affairs, 58 East 68th Street, New York NY 10021
- "Empowering the United Nations" (Boutros-Ghali, Winter 1992) #212
- "The Clash of Civilizations" (Huntington, Summer 1993) #059
- "The Plutonium Genie" (Perkovich, Summer 1993) #079
- "The Rise of the Nonprofit Sector" (Salamon, July-Aug 1994) #062
- "Trade Lessons from the World Economy" (Drucker, Jan-Feb 1994) #112

The Foundation for a Conscious Evolution, PO Box 1941, Sonoma CA 95476
- *The Revelation* (Hubbard, 1993) #030

The Free Press, c/o Simon and Schuster, 1230 Ave of the Americas, New York NY 10020
- *Cosmopolis* (Toulmin, 1990) #237
- *The End of History and the Last Man* (Fukuyama, 1992) #038
- *The Transformation of War* (van Crevald, 1991) #070

Future Generations Alliance Foundation, 10 West 56th Street, New York NY 10019
- *Why Future Generations Now?* (Yazaki, ed., 1994) #209

Futures, Butterworth-Heinemann Ltd., Linacre House, Jordan Hill, Oxford OX2 8DP UK
- "After Insularity" (Goldstein/Rapkin, Nov 1991) #044
- "Environmental Problems and Sustainable Futures" (Marien, Oct 1992) #176
- "Global Scenarios" (Godet et al., April 1994) #116
- "Science for the Post-Normal Age" (Funtowicz/Ravetz, 1993) #242
- "Transformations" (Sternberg, Dec 1993) #009
- "WORLD 2000" (Halal, Jan/Feb 1993) #010

Futures Research Quarterly, World Future Society, 7910 Woodmont Ave, Suite 450, Bethesda MD 20814
- "Globalization and the Future of Cities" (Behrman, Spring 1992) #124
- "Invariances and Determinism in Global Forecasting" (Platt, Summer 1993) #024

The Futurist, World Future Society,
7910 Woodmont Ave, Suite 450, Bethesda MD 20814
- "50 Trends Shaping the World" (Cetron/Davies, Sept-Oct 1991) #014
- "The Global Commons" (Cleveland, May-June 1993) #171
- "The Highly Probable Future" (Coates, July-Aug 1994) #011
- "Rethinking International Governance" (Cleveland, May-June 1991) #043
- "Telepower" (Pelton, Sept-Oct 1989) #102
- "Ten Keys to World Peace" (Cleveland, July-Aug 1994) #211
- "Wild Cards" (Rockfellow, Jan-Feb 1994) #018

Gordon and Breach, PO Box 786, Cooper Station, New York NY 10276
- *The New Evolutionary Paradigm* (Laszlo, 1992) #020

Greenwood Press, 88 Post Road West, PO Box 5007, Westport CT 06881
- *The Emerging Worldwide Electronic University* (Rossman, 1992) #103
- *The Next Three Futures* (Wagar, 1991) #041

The Guilford Press, 72 Spring Street, New York NY 10012
- *Global Shift, 2nd edition* (Dicken, 1992) #111

Harcourt Brace Jovanovitch, 1250 6th Ave, San Diego CA 92101
- *To Govern Evolution* (Anderson, 1987) #022

HarperBusiness, 10 East 53rd Street, New York NY 10022
- *Fast Forward* (Carlson/Goldman, 1994) #015
- *Post-Capitalist Society* (Drucker, 1993) #049

HarperSanFrancisco, Icehouse 1-401, 151 Union Street, San Francisco CA 94111
- *The Universe Story* (Swimme/Berry, 1992) #026

Harper & Row (now HarperCollins) 10 East 53rd Street, New York NY 10022
- *Reality Isn't What It Used to Be* (Anderson, 1990) #007

Harvard University Press, 79 Garden Street, Cambridge MA 02138
- *AIDS in the World* (Global AIDS Policy Coalition Mann, 1992) #147
- *Population Policies Reconsidered* (Sen et al., eds., 1994) #137

Houghton Mifflin, 215 Park Ave South, New York NY 10003
- *Earth in the Balance* (Gore, 1992) #161
- *The Overview Effect* (White, 1987) #033

Hubert H. Humphrey Institute of Public Affairs, U. of Minnesota, 301 19th Ave S, Minneapolis MN 55455
- *The Future of "Development"* (Cleveland/Lubis, 1989) #183
- *Rethinking International Cooperation* (Cleveland/Bloomfield, 1988) #217

Humanities Press, 165 First Ave, Atlantic Highlands NJ 07716
- *One World or None* (Harris, 1993) #231

IUCN--The World Conservation Union, Rue Mauverney 28, CH-1196, Gland, Switzerland
- *Caring for the Earth* (Munro/Holdgate, eds., 1991) #160

Indiana University Press, Tenth & Morton Streets, Bloomington IN 47401
- *Women Transforming Politics* (Bystydzienski, ed., 1992) #195

Institute for Research on Public Policy, PO Box 3670 South, Halifax, Nova Scotia B3J 3K6 Canada
- *Governing in an Information Society* (Rosell et al., 1992) #099

International Development Research Centre, PO Box 8500, Ottawa, Ontario K1G 3H9 Canada
- *For Earth's Sake* (Soto, et al., 1992) #185

Island Press, 1718 Connecticut Ave NW, Suite 300, Washington DC 20009
- *Freedom for the Seas in the 21st Century* (Van Dyke, et al., eds., 1993) #153
- *Global Marine Biological Diversity* (Norse, 1993) #152
- *Our Country, The Planet* (Ramphal, 1992) #159

Johns Hopkins University Press, 701 West 40th, Suite 275, Baltimore MD 21211
- *The Global Resurgence of Democracy* (Diamond/Plattner, 1993) #067
- *International Peacekeeping* (Diehl, 1993) #090

Jossey-Bass Publishers, 350 Sansome Street, San Francisco CA 94104
- *Birth of a New World* (Cleveland, 1993) #042
- *The Nonprofit Sector in the Global Community* (McCarthy, et al., 1992) #063
- *Shared Values for a Troubled World* (Kidder, 1994) #207

Knowledge Systems Inc., 7777 West Morris Street, Indianapolis IN 46231
- *Global Mind Change* (Harman, 1988) #236
- *Sacred Eyes* (Keck, 1992) #027

Lerner Publications Co., 241 First Ave N, Minneapolis MN 55401
- *United Nations: A Working Paper for Restructuring* (Stassen, 1994) #216

Little, Brown & Co., 34 Beacon Street, Boston MA 02108
- *The Waning of Humaneness* (Lorenz, 1987) #035
- *War and Anti-War* (Toffler/Toffler, 1993) #071

MIT Press, 55 Hayward Street, Cambridge MA 02142
- *Beyond Natural Selection* (Wesson, 1991) #023
- *Critical Condition* (Chivian, et al., 1993) #146
- *Global Networks* (Harasim, ed., 1993) #101
- *The Human Impact on the Natural Environment*, 4th edition (Goudie, 1994) #151
- *Preventing a Biological Arms Race* (Wright, ed., 1990) #081
- *Reinventing the Future* (Kidder, 1989) #206
- *Technology 2001* (Leebaert, ed., 1991) #105
- *Water* (Clarke, 1993) #154

Millennium Institute, (formerly Institute for 21st Century Studies) 1161 N. Kent Street, Suite 610, Arlington VA 22209
- *Global 2000 Revisited* (Barney, 1993) #163

William Morrow, 105 Madison Ave, New York NY 10016
- *Awakening Earth* (Elgin, 1993) #025
- *G-Forces* (Feather, 1989) #016
- *Global Paradox* (Naisbitt, 1994) #050
- *Megatrends 2000* (Naisbitt/Aburdene, 1990) #017

Moyer Bell Ltd., Colonial Hill, RFD 1, Mount Kisco NY 10549
- *Morals Equals Manners* (Anshen, 1992) #205

New Amsterdam Books, 171 Madison Ave, New York NY 10036
- *International Society* (Luard, 1990) #048

New York University Press, New York University, 70 Washington Square South, New York NY 10012
- *A World Fit for People* (Kirdar/Silk, eds., 1993) #004

Martinus Nijhoff
- *The Future of the United Nations in an Interdependent World* (Renninger, ed., 1989) #228

W. W. Norton, 500 Fifth Ave, New York NY 10010
- *The Global Economy* (Brock/Hormats, eds., 1990) #117
- *Life After Television* (Gilder, 1992) #104
- *Saving the Planet* (Brown, et al., 1991) #166

- *State of the World 1993* (Brown, et al., 1993) #169
- *State of the World 1994* (Brown, et al., 1994) #168
- *Ultimate Security* (Myers, 1993) #172
- *Vital Signs 1994* (Brown, et al., 1994) #167

Oneworld Publications, County Route 9, PO Box 357, Chatham NY 12037
- *The Inner Limits of Mankind* (Laszlo, 1989) #208

OECD Publications, Organization for Economic Cooperation & Development, 2001 L Street NW, Washington DC 20036
- *Long-Term Prospects for the World Economy* (OECD, 1992) #118

Oxford University Press, 200 Madison Ave, New York NY 10016
- *Beyond Charity* (Loescher, 1993) #141
- *Beyond Interdependence* (MacNeill, et al., 1991) #170
- *Emerging Viruses* (Morse, ed., 1993) #148
- *Human Development Report 1994* (UNDP, 1994) #178
- *Human Development Report 1993* (UNDP, 1993) #179
- *Human Development Report 1992* (UNDP, 1992) #180
- *International Public Finance* (Mendez, 1992) #220
- *Pandaemonium* (Moynihan, 1993) #053
- *State of the World's Children 1994* (Grant/UNICEF, 1994) #198
- *State of the World's Children 1992* (Grant/UNICEF, 1992) #199
- *World Resources 1992-93* (World Resources Institute, 1992) #150

Pantheon Books, (div. of Random House), 201 East 50th Street, New York NY 10022
- *The First Global Revolution* (King/Schneider, 1991) #005

Penn State University Press, 820 N. University Drive, Suite C, Barbara Bldg, University Park PA 16802
- *The New Global Economy in the Information Age* (Carnoy, et al., 1993) #110

Persea Books, 60 Madison Ave, New York NY 10010
- *Tempest, Flute, and Oz* (Turner, 1991) #029

Plenum Publishing Corp., 233 Spring Street, New York NY 10013
- *Laser Weapons* (Anderberg/Wolbarsht, 1992) #074

Pluto Press, c/o Westview, 5500 Central Ave, Boulder CO 80301
- *Low Intensity Democracy* (Gills, et al., 1993) #069

Population Crisis Committee, 1120 19th Street NW, Washington DC 20036
- *World Access to Birth Control* (Camp, ed., 1992) #136

Population Reference Bureau, 777 14th Street NW, Suite 800, Washington DC 20005
- *1994 World Population Data Sheet* (Haub/Yanagishita, 1994) #135

Princeton University Press, 41 William Street, Princeton NJ 08540
- *The Gnat is Older Than Man* (Stone, 1993) #218
- *Grasping the Democratic Peace* (Russett, 1993) #065
- *Turbulence in World Politics* (Rosenau, 1990) #046

Putnam, 200 Madison Ave, New York NY 10016
- *The Choice* (Laszlo, 1994) #021

Random House, 201 East 50th Street, New York NY 10022
- *Preparing for the 21st Century* (Kennedy, 1993) #240

Lynne Rienner Publishers, 1800 30th Street, Suite 314, Boulder CO 80301
- *Bringing Women In* (Kardam, 1991) #194
- *Collective Security in a Changing World* (Weiss, ed., 1993) #088
- *Global Politics in the Human Interest*, 2nd edition (Gurtov, 1991) #246
- *Global Transformation and the Third World* (Slater et al., 1993) #188
- *Peace and World Security Studies* (Klare, ed., 1994) #245
- *The Wave of the Future* (Staley, 1992) #091

Routledge, 29 West 35th Street, New York NY 10001
- *A New World Order* (Ekins, 1992) #187
- *Global Ecology* (Smil, 1993) #174
- *How Nuclear Weapons Spread* (Barnaby, 1993) #080
- *Saving Our Planet* (Tolba, 1992) #165
- *The United Nations in a Turbulent World* (Rosenau, 1992) #213
- *The World Environment 1972-1992* (Tolba/El-Kholy, 1992) #149

St. Martin's Press, 175 Fifth Ave, New York NY 10010
- *Crystal Globe* (Cetron/Davies, 1991) #013
- *World Politics* (Kegley/Wittkopf, 1993) #249

Charles Scribner's Sons, c/o Macmillan, 866 Third Ave, New York NY 10022
- *Out of Control* (Brzezinski, 1993) #052

Shambhala Publications, Horticultural Hall, 300 Massachusetts Ave, Boston MA 02115
- *Evolution* (Laszlo, 1987) #019

M. E. Sharpe, 80 Business Park Drive, Armonk NY 10504
- *How Credit-Money Shapes the Economy* (Guttman, 1994) #133
- *Human Rights for the 21st Century* (Juviler/Gross, eds., 1993) #226
- *Programmed Capitalism* (Estabrooks, 1988) #098

Simon & Schuster, 1230 Ave of the Americas, New York NY 10020
- *The Death of Money* (Kurtzman, 1993) #121
- *The Great Reckoning*, revised edition (Davidson/Rees-Mogg, 1993) #120
- *Metaman* (Stock, 1993) #032
- *The Population Explosion* (Ehrlich/Ehrlich, 1990) #138

The Stanley Foundation, 216 Sycamore Street, Muscatine IA 52761
- *Preventing Weapons Proliferation* (Spector/Foran, 1993) #084
- *The United Nations* (22nd UN Issues Conference, 1991) #221
- *The UN System and NGOs* (25th UN Issues Conference, 1994) #222
- *Collective Security and the United Nations* (26th UN of the Next Decade Conference, 1991) #223
- *Changing Concepts of Sovereignty* (27th UN of the Next Decade Conference, 1992) #224
- *The UN Role in Intervention* (28th UN of the Next Decade Conference, 1993) #225

State University of New York Press, State University Plaza, Albany NY 12246-0001
- *Higher Education Cannot Escape History* (Kerr, 1994) #239

Times Books, c/o Random House, 201 East 50th Street, New York NY 10022
- *Millennium* (Attali, 1991) #127

The Trilateral Commission, 345 East 46th Street, New York NY 10017
- *International Migration Challenges in a New Era* (Meissner et al., eds., 1993) #144
- *Keeping the Peace in a Post-Cold War Era* (Roper, et al., 1993) #089

Union of Concerned Scientists, 26 Church Street, Cambridge MA 02138
- *World Scientists' Warning to Society* (Kendall, 1992) #164

United Nations Population Fund,
220 East 42nd Street, New York NY 10017
- *Population, Resources and the Environment* (Myers, 1991) #139

United Nations Publications, 2 UN Plaza, Room DC2-853, New York NY 10017
- *An Agenda for Development* (Boutros-Ghali, 1994) #177
- *Change: Threat or Opportunity for Human Progress?* (Kirdar, ed., 1992) #003
- *Debt and the Environment* (Miller, 1991) #184
- *Global Outlook 2000* (United Nations, 1990) #001
- *The Global Partnership for Environment and Development* (UN Conference on Environment and Development, 1992) #157
- *Report on the World Social Situation 1993* (UN Dept. of Economic and Social Development, 1993) #002
- *World Economic Survey 1993* (UN Dept. of Econ. and Social Info. and Policy Analysis, 1993) #119
- *World Investment Report 1991* (UN Centre on Transnational Corporations, 1991) #132
- *The World's Women 1970-1990* (UN, 1991) #191

United Nations University Press, Toho Seimai Bldg, 15-1 Shibuya 2-Chome, Shibuya-ku, Tokyo 150, Japan; distributed in U.S. by UNIPUB 4611-F Assembly Drive, Lanham MD 20706-4391.
- *Cities in the 21st Century* (Sept 1991) #143
- *Women, Households and Change* (Masini/Stratigos, eds., 1991) #192

United States Institute of Peace Press, 1550 M Street NW, Washington DC 20005
- *Minorities at Risk* (Gurr, 1993) #055

University of Arizona Press, 1230 N Park, No. 102, Tucson AZ 85719
- *World Travel and Tourism Review, vol. 1* (Hawkins/Ritchie, eds., 1991) #125

University of California Press, 2120 Berkeley Way, Berkeley CA 94720
- *The New Cold War?* (Juergensmeyer, 1993) #060

University of Chicago Press, 5801 South Ellis Ave, Chicago IL 60637
- *A Short History of the Future* (Wagar, 1989) #039
- *A Short History of the Future*, 2nd edition (Wagar, 1992) #040

University of Oklahoma Press, 1005 Asp Ave, Norman OK 73019
- *The Third Wave* (Huntington, 1991) #064

University of South Carolina Press, 1716 College Street, Columbia SC 29208
- *International Business and Governments* (Behrman/Grosse, 1990) #115
- *Waiting for the Millennium* (Rochester, 1993) #229

University Press of America, 4720 Boston Way, Lanham MD 20706
- *A Successor Vision* (Fromuth, 1988) #215
- *The Global Commons* (Cleveland, 1990) #210
- *World Union on the Horizon* (Yunker, 1993) #232

Unwin Hyman, 8 Winchester Place, Winchester MA 01890
- *The Management of International Tourism* (Witt et al., 1991) #126

Vantage Press, 516 West 34th Street, New York NY 10001
- *Planning the UN City* (Yoo, 1987) #234

Wadsworth Publishing Co., 10 Davis Drive, Belmont CA 94002
- *Global Communications and International Relations* (Frederick, 1993) #095

Walker and Company, Walker Publishing, 720 Fifth Ave, New York NY 10019
- *The SETI Factor* (White, 1990) #034

West Fork Press, Dixon KY 42409
- *Ending War in Our Lifetime* (McTavish, 1994) #233

Westview Press, 5500 Central Ave, Boulder CO 80301
- *Biological Weapons* (Roberts, ed., 1993) #082
- *Democracy and Democratization* (Sorenson, 1993) #068
- *Global Gender Issues* (Peterson/Runyan, eds., 1993) #196
- *Global Order, 3rd edition* (Miller, 1994) #248
- *The International Missile Bazaar* (Potter/Jencks, 1994) #083
- *International Relations in a Changing Global System* (Brown, 1992) #201
- *An Introduction to the World-System Perspective* (Shannon, 1989) #130
- *Mass Communications and American Empire,* 2nd edition (Schiller, 1992) #107
- *The Military in New Times* (Burk, ed., 1994) #075
- *Non-Offensive Defence for the Twenty-First Century* (Moller/Wiberg, 1994) #086
- *Revolutions in Knowledge* (Zalk/Gordon-Kelter, eds., 1992) #197
- *Security Without War* (Shuman/Harvey, 1993) #085
- *Strengthening Nuclear Nonproliferation* (Bailey, 1993) #078
- *The United Nations and a Just World Order* (Falk et al., eds., 1991) #230

Word Publishing, c/o Capital Cities/ABC Inc, 5221 N O'Connor Blvd, Suite 1000, Irving TX 75039
- *The New World Order* (Robertson, 1991) #061

World Priorities Inc., PO Box 25140, Washington DC 20007
- *World Military and Social Expenditures* (Sivard, 1993) #076

World Resources Institute, 1709 New York Ave NW, Washington DC 20006
- *Compact for the New World* (New World Dialogue, 1991) #182
- *World Resources 1992-93* (WRI, 1992) #150

Worldwatch Institute, 1776 Massachusetts Ave NW, Washington DC 20036
- *Critical Juncture* (Renner, 1993) #092
- *Saving the Planet* (Brown, et al., 1991) #166
- *State of the World 1993* (Brown, et al., 1993) #169
- *State of the World 1994* (Brown, et al., 1994) #168
- *Vital Signs 1994* (Brown, et al., 1994) #167

Yale University Press, 92A Yale Station, New Haven CT 06520
- *World Forests for the Future* (Ramakrishna/Woodwell, eds., 1993) #155

Zed Books, c/o Humanities Press, 171 First Ave, Atlantic Highlands NJ 07716
- *Earth Politics* (von Weizsäcker, 1994) #173
- *Global Ecology* (Sachs, ed., 1993) #175
- *In the Wake of Affluent Society* (Latouche, 1993) #186
- *Making Women Matter*, 2nd edition (Pietila/Vickers, 1994) #193
- *The State of the World's Mountains* (Stone, ed., 1992) #156

SUBJECT INDEX

Ageless Wisdom 203
Agenda for Peace and Equitable Development 250-A
Agenda 21:
　abridgement 158
　summary 157
agro-food systems, globalization 123
AIDS in the world 147
anti-eye low energy laser weapons 074
associational revolution and global governance 062

biodiversity in oceans 152
biological arms race ahead? 081/082
birth control, access increasing 136
birth experience and planetary crisis 030
broader population policy needed 137

Century of the Environment under way 241
children, UNICEF annual report 198/199
cities and globalization 124
civilizations as basis of future conflict 059
club of democracies in formation 042
Club of Rome governance report 200
collective intervention, growing legal support 073
collective security 088, 092, 223
Commission on Developing Countries and Global Change 185
Commission on Peace and Food 250-A
computer-mediated global society emerging 098
computer model of international futures 247
computers and international communications 101
computing in 2001 105
conscious evolution 021/025, 030, 238
Constitution for World Federation 231
constructivism as postmodern worldview 007
cooperation replacing single-country hegemony 044
"cooperative security" as key principle 087
corporate alliances 113
corporate culture, transnational 107
corporations, transnational 111, 114/115
cosmos unfolding 026
cultural diversity 042
Cultural Magna Carta proposed 205
cultural reexamination and restraint, need for 052

debt and environmental crises intertwined 184
decline, global alternatives to? 037
democracy, liberal, triumph of? 038
democratization, third reverse wave ahead 064
depression ahead? 120
developing countries, new approaches to 177/185
development myths 186
displaced people and refugees 142

ecological education for long-term survival 244
Ecozoic era, transition to 026
education, broadening needed 031, 239, 244, 250
electric economy, volatility of 121
electronic university, global 103
environment:
　as "national security" 172
　problems, overviews 149/151, 176
　trends, impacts and responses 149
environmental concern, new era of 169
environmental refugees, 150 million in 2050? 140
Epoch III maturation, transformation to 027
eroding sovereignty and UN reform 224
ethic for sustainable living 160
ethics for planet 031, 159, 204, 206/207
ethnic conflicts 053/057
ethnicity as key force in world politics 053
ethnopolitical conflict increasing 055
evolution:
　conscious 021/025, 030, 238
　grand synthesis 019
　need to govern 022
　new paradigm 020
　of culture 028
　retrograde? 035
　theory reconsidered 023
　to a sustainable society 025
evolutionary future, action for 021
evolutionary humanism for a Life Era 031
evolving cultural worldview 029

Federal Union of Democratic Nations proposed 232
feminist critique of social science and world politics 196/197
finance for global governance 220
food insecurity ahead 168
foreign direct investment trends 132
foreign policy for US in Post-Cold War era 085
Fourth World quest for self-determination 190
forests, world 149/150, 155
fragile new democracies as problematic 067/068
fused militaries to bring peace 233
future generations as key value 209

Gaia atlases 190
gender and world politics 196
"general culture" curriculum needed 239
General Evolution Research Group 020
G-Forces, geostrategic view of 016
global arms tax proposed 094
"global brain" emerging 102
global classroom emerging 103
"global commons" as emerging concept 210
Global Commons Trust Fund 153, 218

Global Commons Trusteeship Commission proposed 171
global communication trends 095
Global Compact urged 117
global environmentalism questioned 175
global forecasting, long term 024
global goals 206
global governance 143
global infrastructure in 30 years 012
global jobs deficit growing 129
global labor marker emerging 128
global mafia: the new communism? 072
Global Marshall Plan (Al Gore) 161
Global Mind Change as second Copernican revolution 236
global order textbook 248
global priorities 165
global public finance needed 220
global revolution underway 005
global scenarios for 2000 116
global third sector, rise of 062
global viral epidemic threat 148
global warming to feed on itself? 155
global wild cards 018
globalization:
  of agro-food industry 123
  of economic activity 110/114
  and cities 124
  of services 122
governance without government 045
government and transnational corporations 115
grassroots movements for global change 187
green infoglut underappreciated 176
ground rules to overcome culture lag 208

health and environmental problems 146
health and human rights 145
history compressed 052
HIV infections in 2000 147
Human Development Index 178/180
human evolution and space exploration 033
human impact on the environment 151
Human Rights Decade ahead? 226
humaneness waning? 035
humanitarian assistance 145
humanity as suicidal? 241

indigenous people, rights of 189/190
information-based global economy 110
informatics policy 108
information society as globalism 100
information society impact on governance 099
information society in 2005 097
infotech and world development 096
infotech in the 1990s 105
infotech revolution through 2010 106
international cooperation, how to improve 217
International Futures computer model 247
international society emerging 048
investment, foreign direct, trends 132

just world peace, agenda for 093

knowledge economy 051

labor market globalization 128
"life era" 031
limits to growth, overshoot 162
low-intensity conflict, new era of 070
low-intensity democracy in Third World 069

Mafia, global threat 072
marine biodiversity strategy 152
megacities, UNU symposium 143
meganational firms 114
megatrends 017
"Metaman" as evolving superorganism 032
migration pressures growing 144
military spending, world trends 076
missile proliferation in Third World 083
Modern Age, end of 008, 202
money, world form needed 133
mountain areas endangered 156
myths of development 186

naval peacekeeping and UN 091
networking issues and prospects 101
"new world order" denounced 061
new world order, need to build 163
new world social charter proposed 178
NGOs in the UN system 222
non-offensive defense 086
non-profit organizations worldwide 062/063, 222
North/South differences on the environment 185
nuclear arsenals 073, 080
nuclear proliferation 078/080
nuclear weapon use by terrorists? 080
nuclear winter threat continues 077

ocean governance 152/153
overpopulation disaster 138
overshoot of earth's limits 162
"overview effect" from outer space 033

peace curriculum guide 245
peace in a pluralistic world 211
peacekeeping 089/092
"people-centered world order" advocated 179
perceptual paradigms in conflict 025
Planetary Birth Experience 030
planetary evolution and spiritual politics 203
plutonium regime needed 079
population/environment challenges 139
population growth 134/139
population/technology impacts 240
post-development 186
post-modern military's role in a multi-centric world 075
post-modern world view 007, 237
post-normal science emerging 242
"PPE problem" (poverty/population/environment) to negate child health advances? 198

refugee crisis growing 141/142
refugees, environmental 140
religious nationalism vs. secular nationalism 060
retrograde human evolution? 035
Right Livelihood Awards 187

savagery of urban civilization 058
scholarship for world futures study 250
science for a post-normal age 242
scientists, warning to humanity 164
services, globalization of 122
SETI, program acceleration in late 1992 034
social evolution, need to steer 019
sovereignty principle reconsidered 047
spiritual politics to change world 203
"states+nations" approach to ethnic conflicts 056
sustainability, key indicators on 167
sustainable development defined 150
sustainable future 162
sustainable global economy, how to shape 166
"sustainable progress" goal needed 166
sustainability, key indicators 167

technique as driving force creating unreason 109
technological environment, transition to 036
technology choice, how to improve 108
technology forecasts for 2025 011/012
telecomputer age to replace TV and HDTV 104
textbooks for world futures 246/249
Third Wave war and peace 071
Third World marginalized 188
Third World view of global environment 159
three blocs and the have-nots in 2000 013
three world regimes, 1990-2200 039
transformation, eight underway 009
transition to Post-Modernity 237
travel and tourism 125/126
trend overviews:
　Carlson/Goldman 015
　Cetron 013/014
　Coates 011
　Feather/G-Forces 016
　Halal/World 2000 010
　King/Club of Rome 005/006
　Naisbitt/Megatrends 017
　United Nations 001
tribalism and transnationalism 049
two worlds of post-international politics 046

United Nations:
　Charter revisions proposed 216
　City proposed 234
　cooperative security 085/088
　economic survey 119
　and environmental issues 149
　financing options 220
　guardianship of failed states 227
　and human development 178
　and human rights 226
　humanitarian assistance 145
　and indigenous peoples 189/190
　and intervention 225
　Maritime Agency proposed 091
　and NGOs 222
　peacekeeping enhancement 089, 225
　possible alternatives to 231/233
　reform needed 163, 212/230
　and refugee crisis 141/142
　in turbulent world 213
　and women 193
　and world order values 230
　on world social trends 001/004
UNCED (United Nations Conference on Environmental Development) 157/158
ungendering world politics 196
universal values needed 202, 207
universe story 026
urban civilization, new savagery 058

values, universal 202, 207
Vancouver Declaration (UNESCO) 235
viruses, global threat 148
volatility of electric economy 121

water crisis, global overviews 149/150, 154
weapons proliferation regimes 084
West African chaos as model for future? 054
Western Hemisphere sustainability compact 182
wild cards in global affairs 018
women:
　and development 194
　empowerment strategies 195
　global trends 191
　impact of change upon 192
　UN role in advancing 193
world depression ahead? 120
world economic trends 112/121
world ethic needed for survival 204
world forests 149/150, 155
world future for the next 200 years 039/041
world military spending: slow decline 076
world money 133
world nomads, rich and poor 127
world of 1,000 countries? 050
world order values 093
world political trends textbook 249
world political/economic issues 004
world politics and Global Humanist values 246
world population at 12.6 billion in 2010 134
world population up 25% by 2010 135
"world problematique" and "world resolutique" 005
world resources guide 150
world scientists warn humanity 164
world social charter proposed by UNDP 178
world-system theory 130/131
world tourism trends 125/126

zones of peace and democracy extending 066

AUTHOR INDEX

Anderberg, Bengt 074
Anderson, Walter Truett 007, 022
Anshen, Ruth Nanda 205
Attali, Jacques 127

Bailey, Kathleen C. 078
Barnaby, Frank 080
Barnet, Richard J. 129
Barney, Gerald O. 163
Behrman, Jack N. 115, 124
Berry, Thomas 026
Boutros-Ghali, Boutros 177, 212
Boyer, Ernest L. 250
Brock, William 117
Brown, Lester R. 166/169
Brown, Seyom 201
Brzezinski, Zbigniew 052
Burger, Julian 190
Burk, James 075
Bystydzienski, Jill M. 195

Cahill, Kevin M. 145
Camilleri, Joseph A. 047
Camp, Sharon L. 136
Carlson, Richard 015
Carnegie Foundation for the Advancement of Teaching 250
Carnoy, Martin 110
Cetron, Marvin 013/014
Chaisson, Eric 031
Chase-Dunn, Christopher 131
Childers, Erskine 214
Chivian, Eric 146
Clarke, Robin 154
Cleveland, Harlan 042/043, 171, 183, 210/211, 217
Club of Rome 005/006, 200
Coates, Joseph F. 011
Commission on Developing Countries and Global Change 185
Connors, Michael 097
Conway, McKinley 012
Cowhey, Peter F. 113

Damrosch, Lori Fisler 073
Daniels, P.W. 122
Davidson, Gordon 203
Davidson, James Dale 120
Deng, Francis M. 142
Diamond, Larry 067
Dicken, Peter 111
Diehl, Paul F. 090
Dixon, Hugh McTavish 233
Dror, Yehezkel 200
Drucker, Peter F. 049, 112

Ehrlich, Paul R. 138, 238
Ekins, Paul 187
Elgin, Duane 025
Elliott, Michael 072
Ellul, Jacques 036, 109
Estabrooks, Maurice 098

Falk, Richard A. 230
Feather, Frank 016
Frederick, Howard H. 095
Fromuth, Peter J. 215
Fukuyama, Francis 038
Funtowicz, Silvio O. 242
Future Generations Alliance Foundation 209

Gilder, George 104
Gills, Barry 069
Global AIDS Policy Coalition 147
Godet, Michel 116
Goldstein, Joshua S. 044
Gore, Al 161
Gottlieb, Gidon 056
Goudie, Andrew 151
Grant, James P. 198/199
Gross, Bertram 226
Gurr, Ted Robert 055
Gurtov, Mel 246
Guttman, Robert 133

Halal, William E. 010, 106
Hamelink, Cees J. 108
Hamilton, Rep. Lee H. 219
Harasim, Linda M. 101
Harman, Willis 236
Harris, Errol E. 231
Haub, Carl 135
Havel, Vaclav 202
Hawkins, Donald E. 125
Helman, Gerald B. 227
Hubbard, Barbara Marx 030
Hughes, Barry B. 247
Huntington, Samuel P. 059, 064

Institute for Research on Public Policy 099
International Commission on Peace and Food 250-A
IUCN—The World Conservation Union 160

Johnston, Charles M. 028
Johnston, William B. 128
Juergensmeyer, Mark 060
Juviler, Peter 226

Kaplan, Robert D. 054
Kardam Núket 194

Keck, L. Robert 027
Kegley, Charles W. Jr 249
Kendall, Henry 164
Kennedy, Paul 240
Kerr, Clark 239
Kidder, Rushworth M. 206/207
King, Alexander 005/006
Kirdar, Üner 003/004
Klare, Michael T. 245
Kothari, Rajni 037
Küng, Hans 204
Kurtzman, Joel 121

Laszlo, Ervin 019/021, 208
Latouche, Serge 186
Leebaert, Derek 105
Loescher, Gil 141
Lorenz, Konrad 035
Lowe, Janet 114
Luard, Evan 048
Lutz, Wolfgang 134

MacNeill, Jim 170
Mann, Jonathan M. 147
Marien, Michael 176
Masini, Eleonora 192
Masuda, Yoneji 100
McCarthy, Kathleen D. 063
McLaughlin, Corinne 203
McMichael, Philip 123
Meadows, Donella H. 162
Meissner, Doris M. 144
Mendez, Ruben P. 220
Mendlovitz, Saul H. 093
Millennium Institute 163
Miller, Lynn H. 248
Miller, Marc S. 189
Miller, Morris 184
Møller, Bjørn 086
Morse, Stephen S. 148
Moynihan, Sen. Daniel Patrick 053
Munro, David A. 160
Myers, Norman 139/140, 172

Naisbitt, John 017, 050
Newby, Howard 243
Nolan, Janne E. 087
Norse, Elliott A. 152

Organisation for Economic Co-operation and Development 118
Ornstein, Robert 238
Orr, David 244

Pelton, Joseph N. 102
Perkovich, George 079
Peterson, V. Spike 196
Physicians for Social Responsibility 146
Pietilä, Hilkka 193
Platt, John 024

Population Crisis Committee 136
Population Reference Bureau 135
Potter, William C. 083

Ramakrishna, Kilaparti 155
Ramphal, Shridath 159
Renner, Michael 092
Renninger, John B. 228
Roberts, Brad 082
Robertson, Pat 061
Rochester, J. Martin 229
Rockfellow, John D. 018
Roper, John 089
Rosell, Steven A. 099
Rosenau, James N. 045/046, 213
Rossman, Parker 103
Russett, Bruce 065

Sachs, Wolfgang 175
Sagan, Carl 077
Salamon, Lester M. 062
Schiller, Herbert I. 107
Sen, Gita 137
Shannon, Thomas Richard 130
Shuman, Michael H. 085
Singer, Max 066
Sitarz, Daniel 158
Sivard, Ruth Leger 076
Slater, Robert O. 188
Smil, Vaclav 174
Sørensen, Georg 068
Sommer, Mark 094
Soto, Alvaro 185
Spector, Leonard S. 084
Speth, James Gustave 181
Staley, Robert Stephens II 091
Stanley Foundation 221/225
Stassen, Harold 216
Sternberg, Ernest 009
Stock, Gregory 032
Stone, Christopher D. 218
Stone, Peter B. 156
Swaminathan, M.F. 250-A
Swimme, Brian 026

Tehranian, Majid 096
Toffler, Alvin 051, 071
Tolba, Mostafa K. 149, 165
Toulmin, Stephen 237
Trilateral Commission 089, 144, 170
Turner, Frederick 029

Union of Concerned Scientists 164
UN Centre on Transnational Corporations 132
UN Conference on Environment and Development 157
UN Dept of Economic and Social Information and Political Analysis 119
UN Development Programme 178/180
UN Environmental Programme 149/150, 160, 165
UN General Assembly 001

UN Department of Economic and Social
  Development 002
UN Publications 191
UN Roundtable on Global Change 003/004
UN University 143
UNESCO 235
UNICEF 198/199

van Creveld, Martin 070
Van Dyke, Jon M. 153

Wagar, W. Warren 039/041
Walzer, Michael 057
Weatherford, Jack 058
Weiss, Thomas G. 088
Weizsäcker, Ernst Ulrich von 173
Wesson, Robert 023
White, Frank 033/034
Wilson, Edward O. 241
Wishard, William Van Dusen 008
Witt, Stephen F. 126
World Priorities, Inc. 076
World Resources Institute 150, 182
Worldwatch Institute 092, 166/169
Wright, Susan 081

Yazaki, Katsuhiko 209
Yoo, Ha-Sang 234
Yunker, James A. 232

Zalk, Sue Rosenberg 197

FUTURE SURVEY Will Keep You Updated on World Futures—and Much More!

World Futures and the United Nations is the first in a projected series of *Future Survey* guidebooks focusing on important topics.

Each guide draws on a unique information bank of more than 13,000 abstracts of books, reports, and key articles, prepared by Michael Marien for the monthly *Future Survey* and republished each year in **FS Annual**. Thousands of readers in many areas of professional life—government leaders, business executives, consultants, environmentalists, college professors, and students—have relied on this unique abstract journal published continuously since 1979.

In addition to reporting on world futures and the global economy, *Future Survey* covers defense and disarmament, environment and resources, world regions and nations, energy, food and agriculture, society and government, the US economy, cities and transportation, crime and justice, health and education, communications, science and technology, and methods to shape the future.

A subscription to *Future Survey* will keep you up-to-date on the latest and most important thinking about world futures—and many more related views on the multiple transformations of our time.

---

1) To subscribe to *Future Survey*:

☐ Please begin my subscription to *Future Survey* (includes 12 monthly issues plus **FS Annual**).

☐ **Individual** ($79.00/yr)

☐ **Library/Institution** ($119.00/yr)

Start my subscription with:

☐ Volume 17, No 1 (Jan 1995)
☐ Current Issue
☐ Volume 18, No 1 (Jan 1996)

☐ Please send my overseas subscription by Air Mail. I am adding $25 per year to my subscription payment.

Total Due: $ _____

2) To order **Future Survey Annuals:**

Please send me the following **FS Annuals** at $35 each ($30 each for three or more).

Future Survey Annual 1995 $____
   (available May 1995)
Future Survey Annual 1994 $____
Future Survey Annual 1993 $____
Future Survey Annual 1992 $____
Future Survey Annual 1991 $____
(Ten earlier **Annuals** are also available)

Total Due: $ _____

3) To obtain additional copies of **World Futures and the United Nations**:

☐ Please send _____ additional copies
   (1-4 copies   @ $25.00 each)
   (5-24 copies @ $20.00 each)
   (25-99 copies @ $15.00 each)
   (100+ copies @ $12.50 each)

Total Due: $ _____

4) To reserve the next *Future Survey* Guidebook:

The second guidebook in this series, **Environmental Issues and Sustainable Futures**, will be available in Summer, 1995. Please reserve ____ copies at $25.00 each.

Total Due: $ _____

5) To receive all WFS publications as they appear:

☐ Please enroll me as a Comprehensive Professional WFS Member ($175.00/year).

Total Due: $ _____

Preferred Method of Payment: ☐ Check or money order enclosed (payable to World Future Society).

☐ Please charge my ☐ MasterCard ☐ Visa ☐ American Express account.

Card Number: **Expiration Date:**

Signature: **Name** (please print):

Address:

State or Province: **Zip or Country:**

Return to World Future Society, 7910 Woodmont Avenue, Suite 450, Bethesda, Maryland 20814.
(You may also place your order by phone 301 656-8274 or fax 301/951-0394.)

CURRENT AFFAIRS

WORLD FUTURES AND THE UNITED NATIONS

An Annotated Guide to 250 Recent Publications
by Michael Marien

$25.00

This guidebook will change the way you think about our changing world!

For the first time ever, both professionals and concerned citizens have an overview of recent thinking about momentous global changes now underway. In addition to short-term and long-term surveys by futurists and other generalists, important thinking is identified here on such key concerns as post-Cold War politics, peacemaking, globalizing information, the global economy, population growth, health threats, global environmental problems, development issues, more equitable gender relations, globally shared values, and reforming the United Nations as it marks its 50th Anniversary. Today, the United Nations is more important than ever. Indeed, as this guide clearly shows, the UN is a major but underappreciated contributor to pivotal thinking about global trends and preferable futures.

"An ideal guide to much of the best recent thinking about world futures and the United Nations...an indispensable service."
—Harlan Cleveland, President,
World Academy of Art and Science

"A most insightful survey and analysis of world governance and possible U.N. futures."
— Rashmi Mayur, President,
Global Futures Network, Bombay, India.

"A well-structured, well-selected and reader-friendly guide...ought to make a significant contribution."
—Yehezkel Dror, Professor of Political Science,
Hebrew University of Jerusalem

"Looks very good; the thinking is sharp, the vision is comprehensive, and the writing is lively."
—W. Warren Wagar, Distinguished Professor of History,
State University of New York, Binghamton University

"In a world that is changing daily, we must stay abreast of our exploding knowledge on global development, ideas, and strategies. Marien offers a near-comprehensive guide to the State-of-the-Earth and where it is headed."
—William E. Halal, Professor of Management,
George Washington University;
and Director, WFS "World 2000" Project

"If there were more works of this nature, people would spend less time searching and more time creatively thinking about future global issues."
—Dennis Pirages, Director,
Harrison Program on the Future Global Agenda;
and Professor of Government, University of Maryland

Michael Marien is founder and editor of *Future Survey*, published monthly since 1979 by the World Future Society.